Employment and Work Relations in Context Series

Series Editors

Tony Elger
Centre for Comparative Labour Studies,
Department of Sociology,
University of Warwick

Peter Fairbrother
School of Social Sciences
Cardiff University

The aim of the *Employment and Work Relations in Context Series* is to address questions relating to the evolving patterns and politics of work, employment management and industrial relations. There is a concern to trace out the ways in which wider policy-making, especially by national governments and transnational corporations, impinge upon specific workplaces, occupations, labour markets, localities and regions. This invites attention to developments at an international level, marking out patterns of globalization, state policy and practice in this context, and the impact of these processes on labour. A particular feature of the series is the consideration of forms of worker and citizen organization and mobilization in these circumstances. Thus the studies address major analytical and policy issues through case study and comparative research.

TRADE UNIONS AT THE CROSSROADS

Peter Fairbrother

MANSELL

London and New York

First published in 2000 by
Mansell Publishing, *A Cassell Imprint*
Wellington House, 125 Strand, London WC2R 0BB
370 Lexington Avenue, New York, NY 10017–6550

3 2280 00764 6235

British Library Cataloguing-in-Publication Data
A catalogue record for this book is available from the British Library.

ISBN 0–7201–2202–3

Library of Congress Cataloging-in-Publication Data
Fairbrother, Peter.
    Trade unions at the crossroads / Peter Fairbrother.
        p. cm.—(Employment and work relations in context)
    Includes bibliographical references and index.
    ISBN 0–7201–2202–3
    1. Trade-unions—Great Britain.   2. Industrial relations—Great
Britain.   3. Trade-unions—Great Britain Case studies.
4. Industrial relations—Great Britain Case studies.   I. Title.
II. Series.
    HD6664.F23   1999
    331.88'0941—dc21
                                                            99–28631
                                                            CIP

Typeset by York House Typographic Ltd
Printed and bound in Great Britain by Bookcraft (Bath) Ltd

CONTENTS

For Sydney Stephen Dunn (1916–1998)

FIGURES

TABLES

PREFACE

Over the past few years, the terrain of workplace unionism has changed in stark ways. Corporations have, in the now familiar jargon, 'down-sized'; there has been a fragmentation and reinstitutionalization of the state sector; enterprises and plants have been closed down and in some cases relocated; managerial hierarchies have been reconfigured in various ways; and workers face considerable uncertainty about their futures. Not surprisingly, these developments also raise major questions for trade unions. This book examines the impact of the recent phase of restructuring through a focused and detailed study of local trade unionism, albeit within the framework of unions beyond the workplace.

There has been considerable debate in recent years about the policies and prospects of trade unionism in the United Kingdom. A general pessimism about the future of trade unions has been reflected in both academic debate and the various policy debates that have taken place within trade unions. In contrast, the argument in this book is that unions are at a watershed in their history. While the predominant forms of unionism in the 1980s served to underwrite bureaucratization, incorporation and economism, thus providing evidence for debates about strengths and weaknesses of unions during this period, the foundations were laid for forms of independent and autonomous workplace unionism in the 1990s. After a decade of restructuring in manufacturing, utilities and the state services, there may now be a prospect of union renewal.

One of the distinctive features of the book is that it presents material relating not only to manufacturing but also to the public sector and privatized utilities, often overlooked in debates about unions. In addition, the book develops an argument that trade unionism in these three sectors, far from being irrelevant and marginal, is beginning to renew itself in distinctive and imaginative ways. In the long run this is likely to change the pattern of trade unionism evident in Britain and other capitalist countries.

Unions clearly face uncertain futures. They are grounded in particular histories and traditions, which often fail to equip them to meet the scale of change seen in the past two decades. Union memberships must make choices about how they organize and how they operate. The relations of democratic accountability and control within unions have often been reduced to relatively narrow preoccupations with electoral forms, though an adequate account of union democracy must lead to a consideration of the complex of relations at various levels of union organization and practice. In this respect, the focus on local or workplace levels of unionism is an appropriate way to open up a discussion about the complicated relations between members and their representatives at all levels of unions. Second, union memberships are diverse, with members expressing varied social identities, related to gender, class, ethnicity, region, sector and industry. Over time, these bases of identity can come to have a facticity and salience which inhibits or enables participation and involvement, representation and recognition, within very diverse structures. It is no longer sensible to characterize union memberships in terms of undifferentiated categories, such as male, skilled and employed in manufacture. Even if this was relevant in the past, it is no longer. None the less, discussion, debate and an institutional recognition of identity raises difficult questions for unions as they wrestle with the problems of the moment.

The book reports research carried out in manufacturing, utilities and the state services under two ESRC research grants (R000232006 and H52427504495). The research focuses on twenty-four union groups, distributed equally between the three sectors. These groups cover the following: state services (social services in local government, and social security and inland revenue from the civil service); utilities (water, gas and telecommunications); and manufacturing (heating components, car parts, electronic components and telecommunications). The union groups were divided between manual and non-manual unions, according to their presence in any particular set of workplaces.

Some will be unhappy with the approach to research in this book. It is not an exemplar of the fashion for aggregate databases, which allow researchers to make general statements about the past, present and future, with an air of certainty. Rather, it is an exploration of the social processes that constitute trade unionism in a complex society. It is an attempt to open up debate, to suggest varied ways of looking at the web of social relations around work and employment. In this way, it opens up questions about the organized section of the workforce, and by implication it may throw some light on the difficulties experienced by trade unions, in expressing the concerns of members, extending the boundaries of unionism to include the unorganized and relating trade unionism to the concerns and preoccupations of the community.

Overall, the book raises questions about the place of unions in the polity. At a time when there is scepticism in many quarters about the future of unions, it is important to examine the problems and difficulties facing union memberships. If this type of enquiry is not undertaken then extraordinary claims will be made about what union memberships can or cannot do: either union memberships with a mere change of will or interest will do everything or they are really institutions of a past era soon to be forgotten. Against these views, I argue that unions, as social and political organizations, are borne out of struggle, conflict and uncertainty. This is an ongoing process and on these decisions depends the prospect of some degree of freedom and equality or a rather bleak darkness. Union memberships now face choices about their futures, but the way decisions are made and the outcomes will be neither easy nor straightforward.

ACKNOWLEDGEMENTS

In the course of conducting the research for this book and writing it up I incurred many debts, as I was provided with help, assistance, advice and encouragement. My first debt is to the many trade union members, at all levels of the unions studied, who provided me with unqualified support and assistance during the course of the research. Many spent hours with me discussing, debating and informing me about their unions, the problems they saw facing their unions and the successes that were achieved from time to time. They also confided their worries and anxieties about the future. While I cannot name them for obvious reasons, they have my heartfelt thanks. Second, I would like to thank the managers of many of the enterprises and agencies who willingly met me and shared their concerns about trade unionism. In some cases, particularly in the civil service, managers were unwilling to meet and be interviewed. This was a regrettable development and indicates an unease and insecurity that does not bode well for the future. Third, I thank a range of people who contributed to the research in a variety of ways, helping to collect data, discuss ideas and develop understandings about the way unions are developing and changing: Keith Butler, Frances Jones, Sylvia Juba, Richard Lampard, Jim Lewis, Iain Liddell, Phil Mizen, Elaine Pullen, Geoff Stratford and John Whitefoot. Their help ensured that the research was effective and completed on time. Fourth, there are a number of people with whom I have debated trade unionism over a long period and whose advice and ideas enter into this book in a variety of ways, particularly Huw Beynon, Simon Clarke, Trevor Colling and Bob Fryer. Finally, the manuscript or sections of it were read by a number of people, giving me advice, asking for clarification, suggesting other ways of presenting the arguments. They are Bob Carter, Jud Cornell, Tony Elger, Peter Haynes, Gavin Poynter, Al Rainnie and Jeremy Waddington. Of course, none of these people bears any direct responsibility for the arguments presented in the book, but they did help me think through the difficult questions. They have my thanks. Finally, I would like to acknowledge a special debt I have to Leslie Mannaseh, with whom I have debated the situation and fate of unionism for many years. I have learnt more about the complexity of unionism during these discussions than from the many books written on the subject. I hope this book is testimony to the value of such debate and friendship.

ABBREVIATIONS

ACTSS	Association of Clerical, Technical and Supervisory Staffs (part of the TGWU)
AEEU	Amalgamated Engineering and Electrical Union
AEU	Amalgamated Engineering Union
APEX	Association of Professional, Executive, Clerical and Computer Staff
APT&C	Administration, Professional, Technical and Clerical
AScW	Association of Scientific Workers
ASE	Amalgamated Society of Engineers, Machinists, Smiths, Millwrights and Patternmakers
ASSET	Association of Supervisory Staffs, Executives and Technicians
ASTMS	Association of Scientific, Technical and Managerial Staffs
AT&T	American Telephone and Telegraph
AUEW	Amalgamated Union of Engineering Workers
AUFW	Amalgamated Union of Foundry Workers
BT	British Telecommunications plc
CCT	compulsory competitive tendering
CEU	Constructional Engineering Union
CIPFA	Chartered Institute of Public Finance and Accountancy
COHSE	Confederation of Health Service Employees
CPSA	Civil and Public Services Association
CSCA	Civil Service Clerical Association
CSEU	Confederation of Shipbuilding and Engineering Unions
CWU	Communication Workers Union
DATA	Draughtsmen and Allied Technicians Association
DHSS	Department of Health and Social Security
DMU	district management unit
DSS	Department of Social Security
EETPU	Electrical, Electronic, Telecommunication and Plumbing Union
FDA	Association of First Division Civil Servants
FMI	Financial Management Initiative

GDP	gross domestic product
GMB	formerly General, Municipal, Boilermakers and Allied Trades Union
GSSO	Gas Staffs and Senior Officers
HEO	higher executive officer
HRM	human resource management
IPMS	Institute of Professionals, Managers and Specialists
IRSF	Inland Revenue Staff Federation
JCC	joint consultative committee
JSSC	joint shop stewards committee
LACSAB	Local Authorities Conditions of Service Advisory Board
LJC	local joint committee
MSF	Manufacturing, Science and Finance (formed from a merger between the ASTMS and TASS in 1988)
NALGO	National and Local Government Officers' Association
NCU	National Communication Union
NEC	national executive council
NHS	National Health Service
NJCs	national joint councils
NUCPS	National Union of Civil and Public Servants
NUPE	National Union of Public Employees
PAYE	Pay As You Earn
PCS	Public and Commercial Services Union
POEU	Post Office Engineering Union
PSPRU	Public Services Privatisation Research Unit
PTC	Public Services, Tax and Commerce Union
SCPS	Society of Civil and Public Servants
SCS	Society of Civil Servants
SDCA	Second Division Clerks Association
SEO	senior executive officer
SRB	special review body
STE	Society of Telecom Executives
TASS	Technical, Administrative and Supervisory Section Amalgamated Union of Engineering Workers
TGWU	Transport and General Workers' Union
TQM	total quality management
TUC	Trades Union Congress
UCATT	Union of Construction, Allied Trades and Technicians

UCW	Union of Communication Workers
UNISON	merged union of COHSE, NALGO and NUPE, established 1 January 1994
VAT	Value Added Tax
WIRS	Workplace Industrial Relations Survey
WMCC	West Midlands County Council
WMEB	West Midlands Enterprise Board

PART I
AN INTRODUCTION

1 WORKPLACE UNIONISM

The British trade union movement is in a parlous state. After two decades of extensive economic restructuring, accompanied by major legislative reforms, trade unions face an uncertain future. Throughout the 1980s and into the 1990s, trade union membership has declined massively, and union leaders and their members have lost their former prominence and place in the polity. Taken together, this amounts to a massive reversal of trade union fortunes in the United Kingdom, and raises questions about the future of unions. Increasingly, trade union memberships in Britain and elsewhere face the uncertainties of internationalized economies and states, which pose a further question about the type of future that awaits. The signs are not propitious.

The British model of trade unionism has traditionally exhibited a strong emphasis on workplace organization, particularly in the manufacturing sector, albeit within established and relatively stable forms of union organization beyond the workplace. In the context of British trade unionism, therefore, one important uncertainty about the way trade unions are developing and changing is how the past two decades have impacted on unions at the local level. It is in workplaces and localities that trade union memberships come together and give content to the rather abstract notion of unionism; workers join or withdraw from unions, come together, discuss and vote, elect representatives and delegates to speak on their behalf. It is at workplace and local level, too, that trade union representatives meet local managements and each other, giving form to the notion of collective organization and representation. These are the ligaments of trade unionism and it is here that the weight of the changes of the past two decades is felt and experienced.

This book seeks to explore these concerns and to contribute to debates about the place and prospect of trade unions, in the United Kingdom and elsewhere. It examines the recent history of trade unionism in three economic sectors (the public sector, the privatized utilities and manufacturing), in one region (the Midlands, and principally the West Midlands). Of course, regions vary, in their industrial composition, their histories and ways of living, their languages and cultures, and all of these impact on the form and character of trade unionism (Martin *et al.*, 1996). The point remains, however, that developments in one region give clues and indications about the ways in which unionism in general is changing. By comparing developments in three principal sectors, each located as part of the national economy, it is possible to retain a recognition of the specificity of place alongside the significance of sector.

The argument

The argument presented in this book is that trade unionism in Britain is being reconstituted in order to address the debilitating effects of the economic and political restructuring of the past three decades, and that this reconstitution is being driven by developments at the workplace and local level. This pattern of restructuring has undermined the prevailing post-war arrangements, where union leaders played active roles in the polity, where trade unions were generally regarded as crucial to economic prosperity and where notions of citizenship were developed with trade unions as part of the political industrial estate (Taylor, 1995). From 1979, a series of anti-union governments dismantled these social arrangements. This was made possible by the passage of a series of restrictive trade union laws, the onset of major industrial restructuring, particularly in the former heartlands of British trade unionism, and a consequent decline in trade union membership and resources. The result was that trade unions were forced to try to come to terms with a future in which they no longer enjoyed the economic and political influence they once exercised.

In the light of these developments, a set of arguments emerged during the 1980s over the place and future of trade unions in the United Kingdom (Chadwick, 1983; Brown, 1983; Batstone, 1984; Spencer, 1985, 1989; Millward and Stevens, 1986; Bassett, 1986; Batstone and Gourlay, 1986; MacInnes, 1987; Batstone, 1988). While some argued that unions had entered a stage of irreversible decline, others were more cautious, pointing to the continued presence and, in some cases, apparent stability of trade unions at a local level. None the less, it is undeniable that unions have experienced considerable uncertainty about their future, an uncertainty which became more pressing in the 1990s. It was in these circumstances that trade unions began to examine their methods of organization and recruitment, representation of members and future role (TUC, 1984, 1991, 1994a, b).

The union form of organization is one that is rooted in the complex of labour–capital relations. These relations embrace the direct control of labour within specific labour processes, the managerial regulation of labour through large-scale private and public corporate structures, labour as a commodity within wider labour markets and the political regulation of labour through the state. Unions to some extent must address all of these features, responding to and addressing the processes of restructuring and recomposition that are taking place. As part of this process it is necessary to consider the question of managerialism, since one of the features of these changes is the redefinition of managerial hierarchies and the implicit implication for relations between managements and workforces. In the abstract, this restructuring is part of the process of the recomposition of the labour–capital relation at the point of production and service; it is part of the complex, dynamic and mediated processes of supervision and direction of the sale of workers' labour power in the modern economy (Marx, 1976, pp. 943–1084). One aspect of these relations of subordination and exploitation is the restructuring and recomposition of managerial hierarchies in both the private and public sectors in the 1970s and 1980s. The redefinition of management *qua* management is central to this process, with its associated wage systems, changing forms of work and employment, the articulation of ideologies of management and the changing role of the state. In this process, trade unions are a form of collective worker organization that both questions these relations and, paradoxically, affirms them.

Thus workplace relations provide the fulcrum for the day-to-day experience of much trade unionism. It is on the basis of this form of collective organization in the British context that representatives negotiate on behalf of the membership and their leaders represent it in a variety of forums, including political ones. This is a view of unions as 'intermediary organizations' positioned as collective organizations representing workers to employers and the state (Müller-Jentsch, 1988). It is predicated on an assumption that trade unions are organizational entities which, theoretically at least, are distinct and separate from the state and employers. Of course, union leaderships may enter into alliances with the state or employers or be drawn into cooperative relationships at both employer and state level. It is in this respect that arguments are developed about the autonomy and independence of trade unions as well as the degree to which unions should cooperate with employers or the state in the pursuit of union policy.

The base of trade unionism is at the workplace. It is at this level that the coercive social relations organized as a labour process at the immediate point of production provide the crucial terrain of collective organization and class struggle (Braverman, 1974; Brighton Labour Process Group, 1977; Elger,

1979). The collective character of the labour process, involving both cooperation between workers and coordination of the tasks of labour, provides the
material basis for both collective organization, in the form of trade unions, and
resistance, in the form of trade union activity. But this is also a dynamic
relationship in that the form of trade unionism, the way in which the trade
union organizes and operates and the consciousness of trade unionism
expressed by members, is not only shaped by the labour process, but in turn
moulds and fashions the particular configuration of the labour process. It is
this struggle, between workers and managers, over employment conditions,
the circumstances of work, the individual and collective relations between
managers and workers, that constitutes the detail of the social relations of the
labour process.

While the focus of the study is at the workplace and local level, exploring the
way that trade unions have organized, mobilized and operated in conditions of
economic decline and insecurity of employment, it is also necessary to consider the broader context within which unions as a whole organize and
operate. For most members most of the time, trade unionism begins and ends
at work. It is here, on a day-to-day basis, on individual issues as well as collective
ones, that members begin and learn their trade unionism. It is also at this level
that trade unionism comes to life, in organizing and questioning the detail of
the wage relationship. However, as argued in this study, trade unionism
comprises highly contested sets of relationships, undergoing change and
generating uncertainty during the 1980s and 1990s. Unions as a whole operate
at a number of different levels, locally, regionally and nationally, sometimes
internationally. They deal with managements, with governments and with
governmental and non-governmental agencies. Increasingly in the British
context, unions have looked to the supra-state level of the European Union
(EU), developing links and relationships with other European unions as well as
dealing with EU agencies. The way unions as a whole organize and operate
thus has a bearing on the fate and fortunes of workers as union members at a
local level.

It is argued in this book that trade unions as institutions remain embedded
within the social relations of production. How they organize and operate
depends on the complex of relations at the workplace level and beyond. Trade
unions carry with them their own histories and traditions and must respond to
particular sets of relations in different sectors and regions, according to the
occupational composition of their memberships. Many unions faced declining
memberships as economic and political restructuring proceeded. In some
instances it became difficult for unions to maintain an organized presence at
workplace level. As the balance of power in many workplaces shifted towards

managements, it became difficult for union negotiators to represent their memberships in an ongoing and regular way. The apparent strength of many unions in the 1970s was revealed to be rather hollow and insubstantial at a local level, at the workplace. With restructuring and the shifting relations between labour and capital there can be no one fixed pattern of organization and activity. It is possible that some trade union memberships will simply disappear or wither in the face of the uncertainties of work and employment. Others will reconstitute themselves and begin to organize in the light of these changing circumstances and conditions, perhaps beginning to develop forms of union- ism which parallel those elsewhere. What is clear is that trade unions, as collective organizations rooted in the workplace, will continue to play a critical part in the ongoing process of restructuring the relations between labour and capital.

Expansion and convergence

The analysis rests on two frequently acknowledged features of the post-war period, and particularly of the 1960s and 1970s. The first feature is that the 1960s and 1970s saw a dramatic increase in unionization, reflected in the expansion of union membership as well as the signs of an emergent union consciousness and practice in hitherto quiescent areas, such as the public sector. It was also a period when unions in sectors coming to prominence began to reorganize so as to place their organizations on firmer foundations. This organization enabled more active forms of mobilization, reflected in engaging many memberships in various forms of collective action for the first times in their history. The second feature of this period, less often remarked upon, is that there was an increasing convergence in industrial relations practices and procedures across different occupational groups and sectors. For example, the former Whitley-type arrangements, premised on consultation and cooperation, that had long characterized the public sector began to give way to more formalized negotiating committees (although still designated Whitley Committees). The public sector unions developed strategies and practices in their approaches to bargaining and negotiation which mirrored practices long evident in other sectors, such as manufacturing. It is in this sense that the 1970s became the decade of public sector militancy and activity, as measured by strike action and related forms of collective activity (Fryer *et al.*, 1978; Fairbrother, 1989a; Fielding, 1995; Ackers *et al.*, 1996; Gallie *et al.*, 1996; Martin *et al.*, 1996).

One argument to explain this apparent convergence in the 1960s and 1970s is that the organization and operation of the public sector changed profoundly during this period. Against the background of centralization of public sector structures and the massive expansion of employment in this area, the foundation was laid for the recomposition of the public sector as a major employer. There are a number of aspects to these developments. First, successive governments used incomes policies as key instruments in the management of the economy, with the consequence that the public sector became a focus of attention. In an attempt to increase productivity and maintain a compliant workforce, wage systems were revised, with the introduction of bonus and related arrangements (Kessler, 1994). These initiatives provided part of the impetus for the stimulation of workplace activism, particularly in the manual occupations, in the public sector (and beyond) as workers attempted to address the outcomes of these policies. Second, there was an increased emphasis on the introduction of managerial techniques and procedures associated with the private sector into these areas of employment to achieve increased control over state workforces and to realize the ambitions of economic policy. This was a partial move, in the sense that there was no attempt to recompose hierarchical organization of the public sector. Third, in part as a consequence and in part as one element of the modernizing agenda of the time, the traditional bargaining forums were transformed, so that public sector unions were able to bargain and represent their memberships in more direct ways than in the past. The push for this transformation came in large part from the public sector unions themselves as they sought to relay the bases of their organizations during this period. This recomposition of work and employment reinforced the perception of common experience across economic sectors that stimulated common patterns of unionism. These developments underlined the importance of workers in the public sector combining by joining unions, and also acting in collective ways to secure their concerns.

Another aspect of these developments in unionism from the 1960s onwards was the increased involvement of unions in the polity. Building on assumptions of liberal democracy, as a political forum where a plurality of interests had a positive part to play in elaborating notions of citizenship and rule, the case was developed for formal recognition of unions as important political actors in the state (Dahl, 1961, 1985; Flanders, 1970). Even critics of liberal democracy developed analyses which placed the trade union movement as a key institution in the political compromises and accommodations that characterized much of the post-war development of liberal democratic states (Miliband, 1969, 1982; Hyman, 1989). Trade unions were then, even from within competing perspectives, seen as an integral part of liberal democratic rule in the UK and elsewhere.

These patterns of involvement in the polity were evident in various ways. At the most transparent level, union federations in a number of countries, including the Trades Union Congress (TUC) in the United Kingdom, came to formal agreements with political regimes whereby the 'economic' interests of trade unions were recognized, via legislation, consultation, cooperation and, in some countries, centralized bargaining and agreements (Australia, Sweden, Germany). Such accommodations were very much in evidence in the United Kingdom during the 1960s and especially in the 1970s, from 1974 to 1979, the so-called 'social contract' period. The then Labour government reached an agreement with key sections of the trade union leadership over a range of issues, including wage levels, legislation and policies aimed at recognizing the place of labour in the polity (Panitch, 1975; Crouch, 1979). While this was not an easy time for either the government or the trade union leaderships, it set the precedent for this type of cooperation and union involvement.

A particular form of unionism emerged during the 1960s and 1970s. This was a trade union movement, particularly in the manufacturing and related industries, that rested on an apparently active workplace membership and in which trade unions were organized so as to participate and represent these memberships in the polity, with governments and as a partner to the Labour Party. None the less, the role of unions, politically and economically, was persistently problematical and contested throughout this period. There is ample evidence of the way in which workplace unionism was challenged by managements, particularly in the manufacturing sector, but also more broadly (Lane and Roberts, 1971; Lane, 1974; Nichols and Beynon, 1977; Beynon, 1984). Relations between labour and capital at the point of immediate production remained contested throughout the voluntarist period of industrial relations as well as in the neo-corporatist era of the 1970s. The recognition of unions had to be fought for, and managements remained opposed to collective organization by workers, as an encroachment on their prerogatives to manage, although such opposition was mediated in a range of ways, depending on the political and economic relations of the moment (Thornett, 1987, 1998). Moreover, despite the public appearance from time to time, the partnership with the Labour Party was often contested and 'contentious' within both trade unions and the Labour Party (Coates and Topham, 1986; Minkin, 1991). There was always a tension in these relationships, which flowed over to periods when the Labour Party was in office.

The outcome was a trade unionism which organized and rested on a vulnerable base of workplace unionism and a national leadership which was increasingly detached from this membership, as major figures sought accommodations with governments (Coates, 1989). On the one hand, the 1960s and

1970s were a period when trade union leaderships played a leading role in political affairs. On the other hand, this cooptation encouraged a form of unionism where the emphasis was on leaders and less on the membership at a workplace level. However, it was not that workplace trade union organization was neglected by trade union leaderships; it was that the locus of decision-making and policy formulation centred on national leaderships and not on the membership at a workplace level. In retrospect, such a shift in emphasis, as well as the bitter struggles with such workgroups as the coal miners, resulted in a form of unionism that was vulnerable and ill-equipped to meet the problems that arose from exclusion from policy-making and decisions about economic restructuring. Rather than creating the basis for a thriving and prospering trade union movement, the 'social contract' period marked a prelude to a weak and impoverished trade union movement in the 1980s.

Union decline

It is against this background that arguments about the decline of trade unions in the 1980s and 1990s have been developed. At a general level, it is argued that, in comparison with the 1960s and 1970s, trade unions no longer have a marked presence, with respect to either the economy or the polity (Marsh, 1992; McIlroy, 1995). In the economic arena, unions face more confident managements, implementing policies of restructuring often without explicit reference to unions. No longer are trade union leaderships party to the formulation of policy and programmes which take into account the specific concerns and interests of their memberships. In other words, the power and influence of trade unionism over the past two decades has suffered a decisive set-back.

Three measures of decline are frequently identified in these arguments. First, there has been a major decline in trade union membership, both absolutely and relatively. The decline in trade union membership has been massive over the past two decades. By 1997, union membership had fallen from a high point in 1979 of 13,200,000 to 7,117,000. This massive decline has been accompanied by a drop in the density of union membership from 56 per cent in 1979 to 39 per cent in 1989 and to 30 per cent in 1997 (Waddington, 1992a, p. 290; Cully and Woodland, 1998, p. 353). By any standards this is a major reversal for trade unions, raising questions about the resources available to unions, their organizational strength (both nationally and at workplace level) and their future prospects. These, however, are aggregate figures and it is proper to remember that there are differential patterns to this membership decline, by sector, occupational grades and union. Between 1989 and 1997, the rate of decline for women members was less than for men, less for part-time workers than full-time, less for non-manual than manual, less for workers in workplaces with fewer than 25 employees than for larger ones, and less for workers employed in services rather than production (Cully and Woodland, 1998, pp. 356, 357).

This prompts questions about the ways in which the locus of unionism is changing. It is the case that the view of trade unionism as centred on the manufacturing and 'production' sectors is now outdated. The balance is shifting from manufacturing unionism to white collar and service unionism. While this shift began in the 1960s, the decisive moment was in the 1980s. Alongside this feature, the gender composition of union membership is changing dramatically, away from men and towards women. Thus, the previously well unionized occupations for male workers (plant and machine operatives, transport, communications and craft jobs) are likely to continue to decline, and union membership to fall accordingly.

Second, trade union memberships have appeared more quiescent and far less likely to engage in various forms of collective activity, particularly industrial action such as strikes, than in the past. The relocation of unionism away from the manufacturing centres towards the public sector and the utilities is also reflected in the pattern of strikes and industrial action during this period (on the 1980s, see Fairbrother, 1989a). There was an extensive decline in the incidence of strikes during this period, usually taken as a key indicator of the shifting balance between labour and capital. While, in general, pay remained the most frequent reason for strike action, in the context of the type of restructuring taking place in the public sector, involving job loss, intensification of work and increased managerial forms of control, industrial relations became more contentious and adversarial (for local government, see Laffin, 1989; more generally, Marsh, 1992). Thus, while unions remained a force in the economy, there were signs that the locus of industrial action was shifting from manufacturing to the public sector.

Third, there has been a reconfiguration of industrial relations as a result of work and employment restructuring, as well as a shift in the balance of power between trade unions and employers. During this period, a set of legislative changes tilted the balance towards employers by placing restrictions on union organization and operation, especially in relation to industrial action (Smith and Morton, 1993, 1994). It was also a period when a general pattern of managerial restructuring and recomposition of managerial hierarchies increased the emphasis on devolved bargaining arrangements. In line with these developments, the *de facto* incomes policies of the period, unions had less leverage over the outcomes of national bargaining than previously.

There has recently been considerable debate about the marginalization and, in a limited number of cases, exclusion of trade unions (Smith and Morton, 1993). The conceptualization of exclusion is derived from the work of Gold-thorpe (1984) and others (e.g. Crouch, 1986), who saw the introduction of exclusion policies as a process of denying workers access to the resources of collective power. This notion is developed further by Smith and Morton (1993, p. 97), pointing to the way the British government has pursued exclusion vigorously, for the purpose of empowering the state and other employers to mobilize exclusion policies 'to permit an intensification of the rate of appro-priation of surplus value or surplus labour'. The notion of exclusion implies a restructuring of the labour market to exclude a role for unions, as a con-sequence of their lack of resources to organize and operate collectively. Although there are clearly examples where unions have been excluded, particularly at greenfield sites, by far the most common experience has been something short of exclusion; it has been the marginalization and restriction of unions within workplaces. Unions continue to be recognized for the purpose of bargaining over terms and conditions of work and employment, although the scope of issues is more likely to be restricted and managements have begun to explore alternative ways of relating to their workforces.

Thus, this was a period of extensive managerial restructuring and reorgani-zation, in the private and public sectors, which further tilted the balance against unions as nationally based organizations. The implications of such developments for trade unions are varied. While such developments do not mean the end of trade unionism in these sectors, they do point to a possible need to reposition and redefine the remit of unions. One feature of these developments is the shift in the locus of trade union activity from the national and regional level to the local and workplace level. This shift mirrors the ways in which the balance of industrial relations has shifted as part of economic and political restructuring during the 1980s and into the 1990s. It is at the workplace and local level that the full impact of this restructuring has been experienced.

Unions at a workplace and local level

A number of existing literatures and analyses address issues which relate to an examination of the dilemmas faced by trade unions over the past two decades. These include examinations of management policies and practices (Guest, 1987; Cousins, 1988; Marginson *et al.*, 1988; Martinez Lucio and Weston, 1992; Purcell, 1993; Bacon and Storey, 1996), studies of the institutions of industrial relations (Ferner, 1988) and surveys and case studies of collective bargaining (Spencer, 1985; Millward and Stevens, 1986; Millward *et al.*, 1992; Darlington, 1994). There has, however, been little recent research which focuses directly on the social processes underpinning the relationships between management and unions, particularly at a plant or workplace level. The historically informed research by Friedman (1977) addresses the dynamics of work and employment relations in manufacturing industry and traces out the relationships between collective bargaining and the experience of wage labour. Many of these issues were further examined in the compilation by Terry and Edwards (1988) focusing on engineering in the Midlands region during the post-war period.

Complementing this work there is a rich vein of research on workplace trade unionism in manufacturing during this period, including Beynon's (1984) notable study of the Ford factory at Halewood, where the dynamics of workplace unionism are explored, including the relationship between the workplace leaders and regional officials; and the Batstone *et al.* (1977) study, which explores the bases of steward organization and activity in a major manufacturing plant. It also includes the studies focusing on women workers in manufacturing by Pollert (1981), Cavendish (1982) and Westwood (1984). Complementing the latter theme, Cockburn (1983) explores the way men use their control at work to disadvantage women workers in the print industry. Many of these issues are further explored in the more recent publication by Darlington (1994), who returned to the Halewood Ford factory as well as studying other manufacturing plants in Merseyside.

Throughout the 1980s and into the 1990s there has been considerable debate about management restructuring and local trade unionism, focusing on arguments about management change, flexible work practices, the demobilization of unions and changes in patterns of union organization. There was considerable debate about the patterns of change involving workplace unions (e.g. Brown, 1983; Chadwick, 1983; Spencer, 1985; Bassett, 1986; Millward and Stevens, 1986; Fairbrother, 1987a, 1988; Marsh, 1992; Ackers *et al.*, 1996). Some argued that local unions were in the process of becoming demobilized (e.g. Holloway, 1987); others that unions remain an important and relatively stable influence at the workplace level (e.g. Batstone and Gourlay, 1986; MacInnes, 1987; Marsh, 1992); still others that behind the appearance of stability and continuity there have been important changes in union organization and practice (e.g. Terry, 1989; McIlroy, 1995; Ackers *et al.*, 1996). An important issue in the debate is the precise relationship between management initiatives and strategies and workplace unionism (Batstone *et al.*, 1984; Ferner, 1988; Ackers *et al.*, 1996).

A principal theme running through the wider debate is the identification of continuities and/or change in collective bargaining procedures at a workplace level. Three main arguments are advanced. First, it has been claimed that, in many areas of employment, managements have successfully moved towards the introduction of non-core workforces, team working and informal consultation arrangements, with the result that workplace unions are being by-passed (Brown, 1983; Millward *et al.*, 1992; Hunter *et al.*, 1993). Some research has viewed these developments as part of a move by some managements, particularly in vehicle components manufacture, to introduce 'Japanese' style techniques of production (Turnbull, 1988; Elger and Fairbrother, 1991). A second strand of argument claims that workplace unions are being demobilized. Although the institutional arrangements relating to bargaining are being maintained, the basis for active collective initiatives has been effectively undermined (Holloway, 1987; Terry, 1989; Smith and Morton, 1993, 1994). One important thread of this argument is that while there may be the appearance of institutional stability and continuity, the substance of bargaining has been reduced because unions are no longer in a position to give more than a formal response. The third type of argument advanced is that, despite change and management initiatives, unions remain an important and relatively stable influence at a workplace level (Batstone and Gourlay, 1986; MacInnes, 1987; Marsh, 1992). In developing this latter argument, commentators have pointed to a range of indicators that measure the presence and persistence of unions, number of stewards, types of issues dealt with, contacts with management and facilities (Millward *et al.*, 1992).

These themes have been taken up in the most comprehensive aggregate data analysis on workplace industrial relations during the 1980s and 1990s, carried out under the auspices of the programme of Workplace Industrial Relations Surveys (Daniel and Millward, 1983; Daniel, 1986; Millward and Stevens, 1986; Millward *et al.*, 1992). The earlier Millward and Stevens report provided a distinctive characterization of the trends in workplace trade unionism in Britain, covering such matters as a narrowing of the scope of collective bargaining and an increase in the formalization of procedures. More recent studies, including that by Millward *et al.* (1992), point to a continued decline in the number of establishments with recognized workplace trade unions and a continued restriction of facilities.

This type of research is highly suggestive and provides an appropriate context in which to locate and develop arguments about the patterns and processes of change that may be occurring. However, it only takes the first steps in analysis, noting associations between employment patterns and the incidence of trade unionism. As such, the research gives very little insight into the processes of change that may be occurring. It illuminates the patterning of institutional arrangements, rather than the dynamics of relationships between workers and their employers. While the survey data are necessary and valuable, the implied nature of the data should be noted (Fairbrother, 1987b).

It is equally important to explore these questions by focusing specifically on the social processes underpinning workplace management–union relationships. In an intriguing essay, Jones and Rose (1986) question a frequent assumption in the literature (e.g. Chadwick, 1983), namely that there is a direct relationship between changes in work and employment relationships and collective bargaining practices. The argument, however, tends to blur the different aspects and components of collective bargaining, the reorganization of the institutional arrangements of bargaining, employee representation and collective bargaining relations. It is thus unclear whether the impetus for change is the politics of the workplace (as suggested by Jones and Rose), company policy more generally or the union beyond the plant. Even so, Jones and Rose develop an important case for looking at the politics of workplace unionism in any assessment of the process of union involvement in restructuring work and employment. The problem is that Jones and Rose do not consider the relations between local union organization and the wider union beyond the locality, at a district, regional and national level.

With reference to the public sector unions and those organizing in utilities, Ferner and his colleagues explore the notion of political contingencies, which, they argue, have consequences for the course of action pursued by the management and unions of public utilities (Ferner, 1988; see also Batstone *et al.*, 1984). The strength of this approach is that it directs attention towards management decision-making and raises the question: what is the significance of government policies and management decisions for trade union organization and action? The answers provided by Ferner are predicated on an assumption about the degree of political autonomy between policy-makers and managers of the utilities. It is far from clear that the process identified by Ferner is at work in the public services or the newly privatized sectors. It should also be noted that Ferner's argument focuses on national union organization and management, and is much less concerned with workplace activity.

Unions rebuilding themselves

The arguments about British trade unionism have focused increasingly on the current position of trade unions in the broader economy. Unions have begun to explore strategies for rebuilding themselves and addressing the dramatic seepage of membership during the 1980s. Against this background, major unions, such as the Transport and General Workers Union (TGWU) and the GMB, embarked on focused recruitment campaigns. Organizational rationalization was also seen as an appropriate response and there were a series of mergers involving major unions within the civil service, the public sector more generally and manufacturing, aimed at rebuilding the foundation of unionism in these sectors on a firmer basis (Waddington, 1992b).

As part of this re-examination of trade unionism, the TUC has begun to look to its forms of organization and operation, in particular to reverse the falling membership levels, both within particular trade unions and across the unionized workforce as a whole (Undy *et al.*, 1996). In 1987, it initiated a series of reviews, under the auspices of its Special Review Body (SRB) (TUC, 1988a, b, 1989). One of the main concerns was to address the problem of falling membership, and towards this end financial services were actively promoted to encourage membership recruitment and retention (Waddington and Whitson, 1997). While there was experimentation and encouragement of union initiatives on these issues, the attempts to reverse the membership trends and to open up new areas of recruitment among the relatively non-unionized sectors, such as private services, have at best been only partially successful and at worst a failure. This position is duplicated throughout much of Western Europe (Waddington, 1999).

In the more recent debate (mid-1990s) under the label New Unionism, the TUC drew on international experience and experiments, in Australia, the Netherlands and the United States of America, to promote a re-examination of the way unions organize and operate (TUC, 1997). Equally importantly, unions have increasingly begun to look at ways whereby the organization and activity of the union at a local level could be developed and enhanced, evident in the debates within the constituent unions that formed UNISON in 1993 (Terry, 1996). More generally, a range of national union leaderships has begun to examine the bases of union organization, focusing specifically on the bases of membership recruitment and retention. The difficulty facing unions is to diagnose the nature of the problem facing union memberships at a workplace level.

In these debates about the ways unions are developing or might develop, some commentators have deployed two models of unionism to focus the diagnosis of problems and their solution. First, a service model of unionism has been elaborated, where the argument is that unions should reorganize so as to serve their memberships more effectively and efficiently (Bassett and Cave, 1993). From the point of view of union organization and operation, leaders are there to support and service a relatively passive and atomized membership.

Second, an alternative model has been a view of unionism where the emphasis is on organizing and providing the basis, as Hyman suggests, for a 'living collectivity' (Hyman, 1989, p. 179). In this account the membership is an active participant, contributing to the development of the collective focus and organization of the union. More generally, debates about these distinctions and their complex interrelationship have become the grist of recent debate about trade unions and trade unionism (Hyman, 1994; Fiorito *et al.*, 1995). It is increasingly argued that the presentation of these models as stark contrasts is misleading, and that a more nuanced account is necessary which acknowledges the interrelationship between servicing and organizing in practice (Boxall and Haynes, 1997, pp. 572–3).

Taking note of these observations, the focus in this study is on the bases of membership participation and leadership accountability and responsiveness as critical conditions for collective organization and practice (Fairbrother and Waddington, 1990; McIlroy, 1995, 1997; Terry, 1996). In this respect, the relationship that is explored is between leaders, particularly at a local level, and their members. In principle, there are two sides to the form of unionism implied by this relation, one where the emphasis is on centralized forms of leadership and where unions organize and operate to stimulate and coordinate passive, dispersed and often disaggregated memberships, and one where unions organize and operate on the basis of active membership involvement, participation and decision-making within the wider union framework (Fairbrother, 1996a, pp. 140–3; Heery, 1998a, pp. 362–3). The question is whether there is an integration or a pattern of disengagement between leaders and their members both at a local level and more broadly (Fairbrother, 1994a, pp. 166–9; Foster and Scott, 1998a, pp. 139–40, 146). Central to these concerns is a focus on the emergent relationship between the workplace level and the broader union movement.

Union sclerosis or union renewal

In the light of recent history, unions face major challenges as they come to terms with the changes that are taking place in the economy and the polity. It is of course important to acknowledge the contradictory features of union organization and activity and the way outcomes may involve sclerosis or renewal, both within the workplace and beyond. In circumstances where unions have been challenged and are threatened with demobilization and marginalization they face critical choices. In the British context, with the strong emphasis on collective bargaining and the institutionalization of industrial relations around such negotiations, the workplace level of organization and activity is pivotal for any effective recovery or challenge to these developments. As a corollary to this feature, managerial strategies have increasingly focused on the recomposition of the workplace, with an emphasis on individualized forms of employment relations as well as attempts to narrow union concerns or remove the relevance of unions at a workplace level. How unions respond to these challenges is critical for an understanding of how they might develop and prosper.

The focus on the prospects of union renewal has evoked sharp debate. Union renewal refers to the way unions organize and compose themselves in the circumstances of restructuring and reorganization at the workplace level and beyond so as to lay the foundations for active, engaged and participative forms of unionism in the context of the flux and flow of labour–capital relations (Fairbrother, 1989b, pp. 3–7; 1996a, pp. 111–15). While union renewal at a workplace level is pivotal for sustaining and building membership and for confronting the specifics of managerial policy, it is the case that renewal beyond the workplace is equally important to protect workplace unionism from its own vulnerabilities. Such threats may come from a number of sources: from wider corporate strategies, such as investment and rationalization plans; from the more indirect impact of labour market conditions on employment insecurities and managerial leverage; from state-orchestrated enhancement of employers' prerogatives; and from attempts to play off different sections of workers against each other. Thus, while workplace relations are central to an understanding of the conditions for and processes of renewal, it is also important to take into account the persistent dilemmas of union organization and activity, which are grounded in the experience of work relations but also in the need for unions to marshal solidarities and address political challenges beyond specific workplaces.

The arguments about union renewal are complex. The principal focus to date has been on workplace organization and activity, examining the bases of membership involvement and activity. Arguments in this area have been opened up by Fosh and Fairbrother, both of whom address a complex of issues. Their argument is that the restructuring of work and employment relations, towards decentralized and devolved managerial structures, provides the conditions for a resurgence or a discovery of local trade unionism and a flurry of local activity where there was none previously (Fairbrother, 1990a; Fosh, 1993). This argument is developed by Fosh, who points to 'surges' of membership involvement in workplace trade unionism, related 'to the impact of events or developments that disturb the local union context' (Fosh, 1993, pp. 580–1). Such developments include 'changes taking place in management–union relations, changes in the wider political situation or changes within the union itself'. The impact of such events is, according to Fosh, 'mediated by several factors such as local leadership style, industrial relations atmosphere, past experience of the workplace union and structure of the local union', with most emphasis given to the degree of inclusivity of leadership style. This is further developed to elaborate the features of such approaches, drawing attention to the collectivist and participatory aspects as critical to the process of union renewal, although overlooking political affiliation and involvement (compare with Darlington, 1994; Gall, 1998).

The argument here is that unions are at a watershed in many sectors, where they face new pressures, associated with the extensive restructuring that has taken place over the past two decades. The question is: what are the aspects of union organizations and mobilization that are included in the processes of renewal? In the context of restructuring and the ways in which these processes of change are mediated at a workplace level, there is an initial question of whether a union workgroup is able to *survive* these developments. The patterns of restructuring may be such that established union groups face a narrowing activist base, where memberships are beleaguered and uncertain in the face of change (Fairbrother *et al.*, 1996). In these conditions, a process of renewal may involve *recruiting new generations* of activists, a feature of workplace unionism in general but more urgent in conditions of change where managements are able to exert a leverage over the course and practice of industrial relations. In situations where there has been pressure on unions at a workplace level, from management initiatives and from the neglect or removal of established activists and local leaderships, the *survival* of the union depends on the recruitment of activists to replace and support local leaderships and to provide the organizational means necessary to face these new challenges. Where such replenishment does not take place, the incumbent leaderships may become isolated from members, defensive and beleaguered in outlook, or they may simply shrink in numbers as a process of attrition takes place. Whatever the case, the scope for union representation and activity in such workplaces is limited unless a process of renewal occurs (Colling, 1995; Fairbrother *et al.*, 1996).

A feature of the recent past has been the extensive restructuring of employment relations in the utilities and public sector. It must be noted that the forms of union organization in the public sector, until relatively recently, rested on minimal workplace organization, since the locus of bargaining and representation was at a national rather than a workplace level (Fryer *et al.*, 1974; Drake *et al.*, 1980; Maillie *et al.*, 1989). However, the extensive recomposition and devolution of managerial hierarchies altered the terrain of bargaining relationships in these traditionally centralized areas of employment, thereby *inviting* workplace union activity where little existed before. Such developments have often been accompanied by managerial pressures to alter the bases of workplace unionism, restricting the opportunity of unions to represent workers in key areas of employment, via out-sourcing, contracting out and casualization (Fairbrother *et al.*, 1996; Poynter, 1999). In these circumstances, unions have attempted to *build* or *maintain* some form of workplace unionism in these areas of employment, often under difficult conditions.

Increasingly, a feature of the uncertainty of unions in Britain has been the contraction of union membership within the long-established areas of organization and the relative expansion of employment in areas where there has been little tradition of union organization and activity. It is the case that union membership has been limited in the expanding areas of private service employment, such as retail, tourism and leisure industries, raising the prospect of large swathes of employment with little or no union organization. Equally importantly, in these areas of employment as well as elsewhere there are groups of workers, such as youth, who often appear reticent about joining unions and where unions have begun to introduce focused strategies of recruitment and union development (Heery, 1998a). For unions attempting to address such developments, there is the prospect of *reorienting* existing forms of workplace unionism or *building* some form of workplace union organization to address the new contours of employment. Such developments would mean working with and among these work groups in novel and distinctive ways, developing more accessible and relevant forms of organization and operations for these areas of employment.

Relations between workplace level unionism and the wider union organization are complex and often contradictory. One recent argument that explicitly addresses these relations is by McIlroy (1995), who has developed a series of arguments about the emerging relationships between these levels of union organization and activity. In this respect, he robustly asserts that in the literature on union renewal there has been an over-emphasis on the workplace, ignoring the importance of national coordination and the relations between the workplace and the union beyond (McIlroy, 1995, pp. 138, 163). The basis of the McIlroy argument is that there has been widespread and profound 'debilitation of workplace unionism' during the 1980s. As indicators of this decline he points to the trends in union density, the ending of closed shop arrangements, the reduction in the number of workplace union representatives, the contraction of the 'coverage and scope' of union bargaining and the decline, in aggregate terms at least, of industrial action (McIlroy, 1995, pp.

97–144). His argument is that rather than union renewal there has been a process of 'coercive fragmentation', particularly in the public sector, where increasingly it is difficult for unions to coordinate their activity and deploy, on behalf of work groups, the 'external power unavailable in the enterprise' (McIlroy, 1995, p. 138, see also 1997). In a valuable comment, McIlroy argues for enquiry that recognizes the varied and differing roles of activists, other lay members and full-time officials, noting that there are 'no final, fixed situational fissures' as exemplified by the one-dimensional distinctions between 'bureaucracy' and 'democracy' (McIlroy, 1995, p. 122). Rather, if unions are to change and develop then part of that process is the interrelationship between the workplace and the wider union organization, with engagement on policy and practice within and beyond the workplace. A close examination of these relationships may reveal the way new sorts of *mutual support* between workplace unionism and wider union organization are possible. It may also reveal the limitations of and barriers to such developments.

While McIlroy opens up debate, his is a limited account for two reasons. First, he has an undeveloped account of the complexity and detail of workplace organization and action in trade unions. What must be remembered is that the restructuring that has taken place in manufacturing and the public sector is uneven, diverse and profoundly contradictory. These features point to the necessity of re-examining the argument of union renewal and the need to develop a more adequate way of interpreting the real changes occurring at a workplace level, taking into account the variation of experience and the context in which local or workplace unions organize and operate, and assessing what this might mean for the future of trade unionism. Second, the emphasis in the McIlroy commentary is on the persistent pressures towards the centralization and bureaucratization of the union movement. Rather than develop an argument that challenges the basis of this form of organization and activity, McIlroy (1995, p. 122) implies that the 'fragmentation and weakness' of the workplace can only be countered by 'a cutting edge in radical engagement with the labourist politics of the here and now and organizational articulation with the wider union, as well as with other workplaces'. The result is an affirmation of this form of organization, where there is a democratized bureaucracy and where militant strategies and goals inform centralized practices and procedures (Kelly, 1996).

The focus of the McIlroy analysis overlooks the tensions between pressures for democratization and for bureaucratization (Hyman, 1989, pp. 149–65, 166–87). Bureaucracy, it is argued, comprises three sets of fragile relations: the separation of representation from mobilization; a hierarchy of control and activism; and the detachment of formal procedures of policy formulation and decision-making from members' experiences (Hyman, 1989, pp. 181–2). When presented in this way, it is apparent that the workplace is pivotal not only in sustaining and building membership organization but also in constituting a 'vital counterpoint' to the bureaucratic tendencies so evident in many trade unions. While coordinated activity, addressing broader issues and defending workplace unions from their own vulnerabilities is critical, it is also the case that the solidarities implied by trade unionism evolve from worker organization, experience, debate and engagement. It is this commitment which provides the basis for the resilience and effectiveness of workplace unionism, the well-spring of an active unionism in the workplace and in the wider union organization. Thus, while the focus of the arguments about union renewal have been on the workplace, the analysis should not be restricted and confined to this level of organization and activity. It suggests that there should be a consideration of the particularity of union form, the conditions and circumstances for the development and articulation of one form compared to another (see Hyman, 1996).

The implication of the analysis is that there are contending pressures towards union sclerosis *and* union renewal both within and beyond the workplace. Not only are there pressures towards union renewal but union stagnation remains a possibility, at a workplace level and in relation to the wider union organization. The basis of union organization and activity is the complex of work and employment relations, in which members are located and on the basis of which workers combine and act together. The configuration of these relations, the mode and pattern of state intervention, the institutionalization of work and employment relations mean that workers construct their unionism in particular ways and limit others. It also implies that workers will come together as members and develop their trade unionism on the basis of varied combinations of understanding, involving local and national union traditions and forms of organization, politics and various experiences as workers in occupations and carrying out differing jobs. The continual recomposition of these relations presents opportunities for collective reorganization; equally, the established and routine ways of organizing and operating as union members may become relatively fixed and immutable as workers wrestle with the uncertainties of the future.

The book

The focus of this book is on the local level of union organization and activity, on the assumption that this is pivotal for an understanding of the position and prospects for trade unionism. This view is based on the premise that for most union members the *reality* of unionism is at the workplace. It is in terms of the routines and disruptions of work and employment that members experience their trade unionism. This may involve the pursuit of individual concerns and grievances, or it may mean collective activity around pay and other conditions of work and employment. Workplace activity may also entail responding to national union decisions, attending meetings or conferences with delegates from other workplaces and working with full-time and lay officials. One important and difficult complication is that many workforces are scattered, by office and workplace, making the connection between union branch (as the base unit of organization) and the member an attenuated one. None the less, it still remains the case that it is at the workplace that unionism comes to life for most members.

Of course, it is necessary to locate the workplace level of organization and activity within the wider framework of the social relations of production. In the recent period, workplace relationships have been influenced by state and employers' policies intended to achieve the twin objectives of restructuring and union demobilization. Legislation has curtailed individuals' rights against employers and limited union activities, thereby having the effect of expanding employer rights in relation to trade unions. Furthermore, the effectiveness of collective activity has been restricted by legislation which, in practice, outlaws secondary industrial action. Employers have introduced policies to demobilize workplace unionism by individualizing the workplace through such measures as merit pay, individual contracts and workplace or company-based profit-sharing schemes. In addition, casualization, part-time working and the proliferation of site shift-working arrangements within public and private sector service industries indicate fragmentation and differentiation among workgroups.

The research reported in this book was designed to address the proposition that management restructuring has recast the conditions for workplace trade unionism in the public services, utilities and manufacturing, and that this has resulted in a process of union renewal. A major restructuring and reorganization of management structures and work practices is in process, with important implications and consequences for workplace trade unions. This is a package of policies, especially in the public sector, which constitute a unified approach to management practice and have the objective of creating a more controlled and malleable workforce than has existed hitherto. Nevertheless, the realization of these policies is very complicated, leading to variations in managerial practice. There are very different patterns of change taking place, involving unions in different ways and resulting in conflicting interests and concerns at different levels of management.

Two broad, and often contradictory, processes of development were evident during the 1980s. First, there was a continuity and reaffirmation of workplace-based unionism in many industrial sectors, particularly in manufacturing. Second, there was a move towards decentralization and devolution of union organization, especially in the public services. In order to highlight these uneven tendencies three themes are developed in the book: organizational instability at the workplace; the limits of bureaucratization at the workplace; and the pressures towards the reaffirmation of workplace union autonomy.

The subject of the book is local unionism in the West Midlands. The book begins with a brief history of the West Midlands (Chapter 2), where the research was carried out. This area is one of the traditional heartlands of trade unionism in the United Kingdom. It underwent a major deindustrialization during the 1980s, transforming the region in decisive ways. This account is complemented by a brief history of the unions studied, locating them as particular types of unions which have responded to the problems of the 1980s and 1990s in distinct ways, according to the modes of organization and histories, the occupational groups which make up their membership, the industrial sectors in which they are located and, of course, the specificities of the region and locality.

The core section of the book presents the recent histories of these unions in their localities. The chapters in this section are presented in three succeeding blocks: Part II on manufacturing, Part III on privatized utilities and Part IV covering the public sector. The idea behind this division is that these are the distinctive features and developments in each major sector. For this reason it was important to distinguish between the three sectors and present the arguments initially in relation to the specific circumstances of each sector. Within each part, there is an 'introduction' presenting the major issues and themes that emerge in each sector. This introduction is then followed by a number of chapters presenting the detail of the research on the unions studied. Finally, each part is concluded with a general section, titled 'Unions at work', which summarizes and draws the themes of each part together, identifying themes and examining the debates about union renewal.

Part II (Manufacturing) presents the research on unions in four factories in four chapters. These factories were engaged respectively in the production of electronic equipment, telecommunications equipment, car parts and heating equipment. There is nothing particularly special about these factories. They all had reasonably long histories in the region, the workforces had been organized into trade unions for much of the post-war period and they had experienced the vicissitudes and fortunes of this period.

Part III addresses unionism in the privatized utility sector, focusing on telecommunications, gas and water in three successive chapters. Given the scattered nature of the workforces in these industries, the focus is on union branches rather than workplace unions. Scattered employment in these industries, coupled with the disruptions and uncertainties associated with privatization, placed particular pressures on the unions, which are explored in some detail.

Part IV presents the material on the public sector, focusing on restructuring in the public services. Three chapters present the material, covering inland revenue, social security and local government services. In view of the extensive restructuring that has taken place in the public sector, the unions organizing in this sector have responded and developed their unionism in notable ways.

Following these core chapters, the argument about local unionism in the 1990s is drawn together in Part V. The ways in which these experiences result in difficult and different issues for unions are examined. This draws attention to the changes taking place as unions reconsider their forms of organization and attempt to meet the challenges of this period. In this chapter the thesis of union renewal is explored, pointing to the very different trajectories becoming evident in the public services, utilities and manufacturing. Finally, the overall implications of the study are presented, with a consideration of what these developments might signify for workers in a political world where the previous certainties of social democracy no longer apply.

2 THE SHIFTING CONTOURS OF UNIONISM

During the 1980s, trade unions throughout the UK faced an uncertain future. There were at least three aspects to these developments. First, at the immediate point of production labour processes were recomposed, laying the foundation for flexible work and employment relations. Such developments occurred within the broader pattern of restructuring that was taking place in different industrial sectors as well as the state sector. Second, there was a regional aspect to these developments, involving a major deindustrialization in the traditional heartlands of British trade unionism. The West Midlands exemplified these developments in marked ways. Third, a succession of governments had little interest in consulting with trade union leaderships about economic policies; on the contrary, they were concerned to legislate a restrictive terrain for trade unions. Taken together, these developments provided the occasion for many unions to review and reconsider the way they organized and operated.

Forms of union organization

The research reported in this book is based on a study of ten unions, among the largest and most active in the United Kingdom. The unions were:

Manufacturing

- AEU: Amalgamated Engineering Union (subsequently part of Amalgamated Engineering and Electrical Union, AEEU).
- GMB: formerly General, Municipal, Boilermakers and Allied Trades Union.
- MSF: Manufacturing, Science and Finance.
- TGWU: Transport and General Workers' Union.

Utilities

- NCU: National Communications Union (subsequently part of Communication Workers Union, CWU).
- NALGO: National and Local Government Officers' Association (subsequently part of UNISON).
- GMB.

Public sector

- CPSA: Civil and Public Services Association (subsequently part of Public and Commercial Services Union, PCS, established 1998).
- NUCPS: National Union of Civil and Public Services (subsequently part of the Public Services, Tax and Commerce Union, PTC, which in turn merged with the CPSA to form the PCS).
- IRSF: Inland Revenue Staff Federation (subsequently part of PTC).
- NALGO.
- NUPE: National Union of Public Employees (subsequently part of UNISON).

As with unions elsewhere, these unions had experienced at first hand the pressure and uncertainties of the 1980s, at both local and national levels. They responded to the economic restructuring in various ways, in some cases with mergers, in others with internal reviews of organization and operation, while in others there was little obvious response.

In abstract terms, unions are distinguished, each from the other, in terms of a set of distinctions relating to the way in which workers combine together. At a general level, unions are institutionalized expressions of the essential inequality of the capital relation, with specific reference to the individual's immediate relation to capital at the point of production. Formally, union collective organization is an expression of three sets of tensions: between an emphasis on decentralized or centralized ways of organizing and operating; between egalitarian or hierarchical structures and relations; and between participative or remote forms of involvement and activity. These features of collective organization and practice evolve in the course of constructing and developing unionism again and again. The forms of organization and methods of operation are not immutable, and it is thus possible for workers to organize and reorganize themselves and their organizations in the course of struggle at the point of production.

This analytic framework is derived from Drake *et al.* (1980). It is used to distinguish between two forms of unionism: centralized and layered (organized according to the principle of leadership predominance) or devolved and participative (organized according to the principle of membership participation).

The principle of leadership predominance

A union organized according to the principle of leadership predominance emphasizes the need for a shrewd and calculating leadership, providing a steady downward flow of communication and information to the membership. These leaders owe their position to their expertise and knowledge and not necessarily to their popularity and rapport with the membership. Such unions often begin to resemble external agencies providing services at a cost (subscriptions) to their clients (members). This is a form of organization and operation where the structures of representation and accountability are centralized, not only at the national level but at all levels of representation. Union members in such unions do not share any responsibility for the active genesis and pursuit of the union's objectives, nor would they necessarily see any virtue in such involvement.

The members of such unions are expected to evaluate the union's achievements and, if dissatisfied with the service provided, either resign or find some mechanism through which to effect change: for example, by organizing an electoral challenge to the incumbent leadership. A membership that rebelled would attempt to change the personnel or improve the methods of communications so as to secure a better service. Once new leaders are installed or a reformed system is in operation the union membership would expect to return to a state of relative quiescence. In other words, this is a form of unionism based on relations between leaders and members that are maintained, even with a change of leadership (unless, of course, the form of union organization itself is questioned and altered).

In this form of unionism, leaders may want to introduce changes or policies which they suspect may not meet favour with the membership (such as embracing political causes). In such instances, these leaders are likely to resort to subterfuge or hope that the bulk of members would not care as long as routine union matters and concerns are dealt with. Otherwise, these leaders will be compelled to use the union's extensive system of communication and information provision to persuade a quiescent membership that the proposed course of action is correct. Voting by members would not be to exercise control but to voice either consent or opposition to the proposals of leaders.

This is a centralized form of unionism where the process of representation is separated from that of mobilization. Representatives operate in externalized ways, calling for a mobilization of the membership where and when appropriate. It is a form of unionism where the processes of accountability and control are relatively attenuated, not relying on sustained active membership participation. Members are consulted when necessary, with membership involvement often confined to ratification and endorsement of decisions taken elsewhere.

The principle of membership participation

A union organized on the principle of membership participation is one where the leadership and members place emphasis on the active involvement of members in the genesis and development of union policy, in the execution and administration of bargaining and negotiation, in the development of organization and the control of officials. While the degree of involvement may be variable in practice, it is a form of unionism which places a value on this activity. The purpose of communication and the provision of information and resourcing in the union aims to supplement and stimulate membership participation.

The relations between leaders and members are two-way, embracing a continuous dialogue between members, representatives and officials throughout the union. Dissatisfaction with union policies or the activities of representatives are expressed by active participation in the democratic structures of the union. On occasion this can be contentious and bitter, as different viewpoints are expressed and representatives called to account, within a framework of accountability and participation.

The role of elections in such a union is not to choose the most appropriate person to whom the union can safely be entrusted for a period, but to place in office those who appear most likely to accept the responsibilities of election through a system of continuous accountability. For their part, representatives and officials are obliged to debate union policy, strategy and tactics through the same system of collective organization and representation. It is in this way that the principle of participation provides opportunities for the legitimate exercise of leadership.

This principle integrates the procedures of representation with the processes of union mobilization. Representatives are accountable to the membership and full-time officials service the membership, giving specialist support where required; at the same time, this form of union organization and operation is marked by participatory relations at all levels of the union, where members articulate and express their experiences. There is an integration between members, as active participants in union affairs, and representatives and full-time officials speaking and acting on behalf of the membership. This is a mutually reciprocal relationship, which provides the basis for this type of unionism.

The unions

Most unions have developed over long periods of time, often in a piecemeal fashion, according to the ways members are located at workplaces, the traditions of organization, the ideologies of unionism and the exigencies of recognition and bargaining, often in hostile circumstances. Thus, in practice, unions combine elements of both principles in their structures and methods of operation (see comments by Boxall and Haynes, 1997, pp. 572–3). The mix of leadership predominance and membership participation has been shaped by membership preferences, the organization of management, the system of collective bargaining, relations with other unions, the customs and traditions of trade unionism and especially the policies which unions seek to pursue. In a review of each union covered by the study, these features of trade union organization and operation will be considered.

Amalgamated Engineering and Electrical Union (AEEU)

The AEU (and its forerunners), one of the two unions that formed the AEEU in 1992, was a long-established union, and had its roots in the nineteenth century as one of the founders of British trade unionism. For many decades it was the second largest union in the United Kingdom, largely recruiting male skilled workers. However, with the decline in union membership in the 1980s, it slipped to the fourth ranking position, becoming the third largest union again following a merger with the Electrical, Electronic, Telecommunication and Plumbing Union (EETPU) in 1992 (with a combined membership in 1993 of 884,463, of whom 63,355 were women – 7 per cent) (TUC Annual Report, 1993). The union organizes on the basis of sections – engineers, foundry workers, construction workers and electrical workers – reflecting the occupations and industries it covers.

The union has its origins in the early nineteenth-century trade protection societies. These societies were often short-lived and the leaders were subject to police harassment and persecution. In 1851, the Amalgamated Society of Engineers, Machinists, Smiths, Millwrights and Patternmakers (ASE) was established through a merger of fewer than half the members of a number of societies, covering engineers, smiths, millwrights and moulders. Some societies failed to take part in the merged union, such as the boilermakers. By the 1860s the union was relatively well established, although it faced problems following legal rulings relating to union funds. Increasingly, the leadership advocated the importance of political lobbying to secure legal recognition and union rights. The AEU was established in 1920 with the merger of ten unions, with no further major amalgamations until 1967, when it merged with the Amalgamated Union of Foundry Workers (AUFW), and then 1970/1, when it merged with the Draughtsmen and Allied Technicians Association (DATA, subsequently renamed Technical, Administrative and Supervisory Section), the Constructional Engineering Union (CEU) and the Steel Smelters' Union to form the Amalgamated Union of Engineering Workers (AUEW).

During the 1970s and into the 1980s, the AUEW had a troubled history. Broadly, the union leadership was divided into an increasingly right-wing dominated grouping, based on the manual worker components of the union (engineering, construction and foundry sections) and a left-wing (Communist) leadership, whose primary base was the Technical, Administrative and Supervisory Section (TASS). On 25 January 1984, in an attempt to reach a political settlement within the union, the four component sections voted in favour of replacing the four sections with a much looser two-section amalgamation: the engineering, construction and foundry sections formed one section and TASS the other. In May 1986, the manual section reverted to its earlier title, the Amalgamated Engineering Union. The TASS subsequently withdrew from the AEU and merged with another non-manual engineering-based union, the Association of Scientific, Technical and Managerial Staffs (ASTMS), in 1988 to form Manufacturing, Science and Finance (MSF).

The membership of the union covered almost the entire ambit of manufacturing across both the public and private sectors. This coverage included members in aircraft and shipbuilding, engineering and other industries, as well as the public utilities. None the less, despite this broad industrial coverage, for much of its history the union was an exclusivist organization, in both membership and policy. One feature of the developments in the 1920s and subsequently was that the union began to move away from its more exclusive craft worker base, and increasingly became a general union for the engineering industry, indicated by the decline of skilled workers as a proportion of all members, from 75 per cent in 1920 to 50 per cent in 1960 (Undy *et al.*, 1981, p. 70). However, it was not until 1926 that union rules were relaxed so that unskilled workers could join and it was not until 1943 that women were admitted to membership. Not surprisingly, the policy focus of the union has often stressed the interests and concerns of the male skilled membership of the union, to the detriment of other sections of the workforce.

Organizationally, the union has had a mixed history. Since the founding of the ASE there has been a composite form of organization, with localized autonomy, based on district committees, but centralized financial control. While there were subsequent revisions of rules relating to organization, the union remained a centralized federation at a national level. Hostility between key sections of the membership and the leadership became marked at critical points of the union history, such as with the emergent shop stewards movement of the early part of the twentieth century, and during the First and Second World Wars. In response to these pressures, a series of reforms was initiated by the leadership, which qualified the traditional exclusivity of the union, and introduced a combination of direct and indirect membership elections for key district, divisional and national officials. The outcome was a form of populist leadership, with comprehensive formal democratic accountability at different levels of the union (see Fletcher, 1973; Frow and Frow, 1982).

The other side of these organizational arrangements is that the membership was organized via shop steward forms of representation in plants and workplaces. Such arrangements provided the potential for relatively independent forms of representation, particularly with the collapse in the 1970s of industry-wide federations, such as the Confederation of Shipbuilding and Engineering Unions (CSEU). However, this potential was limited by the hold of the union's electoral history. Via a series of committee structures, factory and workplace representatives were tied into the wider union, geographically and functionally. The result was a complicated pattern of representation, where participation in national structures was promoted through a series of electoral arrangements based on geographically based branches, rather than workplace-centred branches. Although there have been recent moves to change these arrangements, and secure more direct forms of workplace representation, the hold of history remained.

Thus, for much of its history the union has been characterized by a strong democratic and participative tradition, at least for a wide layer of relatively skilled male and often politicized activists. This was evident in a number of ways, via the activity of the powerful local union organizations within the union, based especially on visible and elected district secretaries and committees as well as the increasingly prominent work-based steward organization. However, there was also considerable evidence throughout the union's history of tensions between these levels of union organization and activity and the central leaderships in the union. The Executive Council was composed of full-time officials (including the president and secretary) elected for three- to five-year periods and representing branch constituencies; in 1972 the rules were changed to allow postal ballots of the membership. In contrast, the National Committee comprised an annually elected lay membership, via a sequence of delegated elections, based in branches and proceeding to the district committees, and then the divisional committees (or their equivalents). There were tensions not only between the central leadership and activist local (district/workplace) levels but also within these different layers of representation and organization.

Further complicating the patterns of leadership and accountability within the union were the political factions that increasingly dominated the union. There were powerful factions of activists within the union, supported by a wide range of potential power bases in workplaces, districts, divisions and committee structures. By the 1960s a combination of ideological divisions within the activist membership and a 'highly competitive electoral system' provided the opportunity for an unofficial but influential two-party system of government (Undy *et al.*, 1981, p. 105). The leadership was largely dominated by the right (moderates), apart from a brief period in the 1960s and early 1970s, when the left-led (progressives) factions made major gains (Undy *et al.*, 1981, pp. 105–16). The shifting combinations and alliances involved in these electoral struggles were the grist of politics for much of the union's recent history.

By the 1980s and 1990s, the union was established as one of the leading right-wing unions in the United Kingdom, pursuing relatively conservative political policies. After the merger with EETPU in 1992, the new union consolidated itself as the major right-wing bloc in engineering and related industries, indicated in the 1980s by its active participation in attempts to secure single union agreements. This initiative was seen as a counter to managerial policies aimed at marginalizing and excluding unions, especially in greenfield sites but also elsewhere (Garahan and Stewart, 1992). None the less, workplace-based steward forms of representation remained prominent, especially in major conurbations such as the West Midlands.

Overall, this is a complex and complicated union which has long been an influential and dominant player in British history. It displays many of the tensions and difficulties that underpin political organization and struggle within unions. On the one hand, the history of the union reveals tensions between powerful local organizations and central leaderships. On the other, these divisions are cross-cut by the often debilitating and reactive struggles that took place between powerful organized political factions that dominated politics of the union for much of its recent history. The outcome is a union which is highly democratic and quite participative, but also one where there has been a strong element of exclusivity and reaction, providing the base for divisive and debilitating politics within the union.

Civil and Public Services Association (CPSA)

The largest trade union in the civil service, until amalgamations in the 1990s, was the CPSA (with a membership in 1993 of 124,504, of whom 87,818 were women – 71 per cent) (TUC Annual Report, 1993). It was founded in 1903, when the Assistant Clerks' Association was formed. While it had a slow beginning, the expansion of government services in the First World War resulted in an expansion of union membership, from 4,000 members in 1920 to 16,500 in 1922 and 20,012 in 1924 (Humphreys, 1958, p. 231). This growth took place by individual recruitment and a series of amalgamations in the immediate post-war period, resulting in the founding of the Civil Service Clerical Association (CSCA) in 1922. One feature of this early expansion was the increased recruitment of women members, particularly as a result of amalgamations with the all-women Writing Assistants Association (1920), Civil Service Typists Association (1921) and Association of Women Clerks and Secretaries (1921). After 1923, direct recruitment prevailed, from the widening areas of clerical employment in the civil service as well as from women's or ex-service associations.

Gradually, the CSCA became the major clerical union in the civil service. The 1930s were difficult for the association, which was embroiled in recruitment competition with the Ministry of Labour Staff Association, the Court Officers' Association and the IRSF. In 1939, these unions came to a partial accommodation, with the establishment of the Civil Service Alliance, covering typing and clerical grades, and comprising the CSCA, Ministry of Labour Staff Association and IRSF. In 1969, the CSCA changed its name to CPSA, following the transfer of the Post Office from the civil service a year earlier. The CPSA eventually incorporated the Ministry of Labour Staff Association in 1973, followed by the Court Officers' Association in 1974, thereby resolving one of the outstanding divisions among clerical and related workers.

The initial impetus for unionization came from dealing with grade grievances and concerns, primarily by petitions or memoranda to senior civil servants and the government. This required leaders skilled in drafting such documents and presenting the case to senior civil servants. These were leaders who knew 'the rules of the game' and how to use the regulations and procedures to the advantage of the membership. As members of staff sides of the Whitley Committees, the leaders of the CPSA and its forerunners (and

those of other civil service unions) became skilled advocates of their memberships' concerns. In addition, these leaders became skilled at lobbying and
campaigning for improvements and changes in civil service conditions. The
role of the membership was generally confined to attending meetings, delegating responsibility to leaders and giving 'responsible' support to the initiatives
of national leaders.

Humphreys (1958) argues that the clerical service unions, initially organized
in response to the deterioration of wages and conditions in the late nineteenth
century, became advocates of reform of the civil service, which resulted in the
Whitley arrangements immediately after the First World War. She claims that
in the lead-up to government agreement to these procedures, civil servants
expressed a degree of militancy, with the threat of strikes, which was not seen
subsequently, when the unions settled into a pattern of relative stability, with
an expanding membership and leaders skilled in presenting cases on behalf of
their members.

This was a style of unionism that persisted well into the 1970s. The focus of
activity was on the preparation and presentation of the case, on behalf of either
individual members or the collective membership, often seeking support from
MPs and raising issues in parliamentary forums, and occasionally using the
media to publicize problems and grievances. From time to time, the members
were called on to protest, to attend protest meetings, to lobby and support
campaigns, often responding with a remarkable degree of enthusiasm. This
form of unionism did not rely on the day-to-day participation and organization
of the office (or workplace) membership; it was a style of unionism built
around active and committed national leaders.

The union had a long political history, going back to the early 1920s.
W. J. Brown, then General Secretary of the CSCA, was a populist socialist who
persuaded the union to support his political aspirations, first in the Labour
Party and subsequently as an independent Member of Parliament. In 1920, the
Clerical Officers' Association (a predecessor union) voted to affiliate to both
the TUC and the Labour Party. The union also decided to promote its own
candidates for parliamentary election, agreeing to the candidature of Brown in
the 1922 and 1924 general elections. However, following the General Strike,
the Trades Dispute Act of 1927 prevented civil service unions from affiliating to
the TUC or the Labour Party. The CSCA nevertheless agreed to support the
political aspirations of Brown, who was eventually elected as MP for Wolverhampton West in 1929. This began a divisive period, over the allegiances of
Brown, who broke with the Labour Party in 1931, initially in association with
Oswald Mosley. Brown clashed frequently with the national executive committee, finally resigning from the union in 1948. After the Second World War,

when legal restrictions were removed, the union voted in favour of TUC affiliation but rejected affiliation to the Labour Party.

The union also had a long history of organizing women workers. Union organization by women civil servants arose from grievances within specific all-women grades, such as the women clerks grade, writing assistants grade and typist grades, initially outside the CSCA and other male-based unions. Following the reorganization of the civil service in 1920, and the ending of sex-based grades, women were recruited by the formerly all-male clerical and executive unions, particularly the CSCA, which, along with other civil service unions, deliberately recruited women members into the association, and absorbed women-only unions, particularly in the period 1920–2.

The CSCA was a centralized union, long dominated by male negotiators and advocates, and with a membership which was responsive rather than actively involved in policy formation and industrial activity. It was, as Humphreys (1958, p. 227) suggests, a 'special sort' of trade unionism, 'strong and active, yet in harmony with the traditional political neutrality of the Civil Service in a democratic state'. It was only in the 1970s, and particularly the 1980s, that this form of organization was questioned, as the union became more frequently involved in active forms of industrial action.

As early as the 1960s, the union's membership began to consider more active forms of industrial action in pursuit of pay and related claims. In 1961, in the context of a pay pause initiated by the government, the then CSCA announced a ban on overtime and a work-to-rule in opposition to this decision (Kelly, 1980, p. 106). A day before the proposed action, the government ended the pay pause and implemented agreed pay awards. While the proposed action did not take place, this was a decisive moment for the union, since it was the first time in the union's history that such action had been decided upon. Following this event, sections of the union membership and their leaders advocated the adoption of a union strike policy, which was eventually agreed at the 1968 annual conference (Kelly, 1980, p. 107). CSCA members in the Post Office Corporation (established on 1 October 1969 and formerly part of the civil service) went on strike over the operative settlement dates for pay and related agreements, involving a few hundred members in strikes and up to 10,500 members in mass walk-outs (Kelly, 1980, p. 108). The first strike within the non-industrial civil service occurred in 1973, when members of the then CPSA and the Society of Civil Servants (SCS) initially staged walk-outs, rallies and protest meetings over the government's failure to implement due pay awards. These events were followed by a national one-day strike, principally involving the CPSA, although some members of the SCS and the Customs and Excise Federations also participated (Kelly, 1980, pp. 109–10).

The 1970s was a decade when civil service unions, including the CPSA, faced governments advocating policies which threatened the traditional job security of the civil service and traditional pay arrangements and procedures. During this decade, the union membership was involved in a range of industrial action, including overtime bans, demonstrations and lobbies. In 1979, the CPSA and the Society of Civil and Public Servants (SCPS) participated in a joint one-day stoppage in February, selective strike action and sympathy strike action against dismissals, particularly in Scotland. A second one-day strike was held on 2 April 1979, leading to further rounds of negotiations and a settlement on 11 April, followed by a resumption of normal working on 2 May 1979 (Kelly, 1980, pp. 114–17). This level of activity continued into the 1980s, after the election of a Conservative government in 1979, culminating in the five-and-a-half-month pay dispute in 1981, involving this union and all the other non-industrial civil service unions. Subsequent to these events, there was a decline in national action, although sections of the membership in some departments, such as social security and employment, continued to pursue pay claims and related matters during the 1980s.

The union leadership was politically divided from the late 1960s onwards, between supporters of Militant Tendency (a Trotskyist faction then within the Labour Party) and moderate (or conservative) union members, vigorously opposed to Militant Tendency. These divisions were reflected in dramatic swings between the two factions on the NEC, dissension among full-time officials and partisan decisions by senior union officers, especially over appointments. More recently, there were signs of a rapprochement between left Labour Party supporters (non-Trotskyists) and the moderates, which resulted in a period of political stability in the union. With the legally encouraged move to postal balloting in the union, the left, and particularly Militant Tendency, have found it difficult to maintain their presence in national elections. In the 1989 elections Militant Tendency was left with only one member on the executive (Maksymiw, 1990, p. 104). Even so, the union conference was often dominated by the left groupings, with the result that there was frequently a disjunction between conference decisions and the leadership responsible for implementing these decisions. Regroupings among left candidates for senior office in the union resulted in some gains for left candidates. In January 1998, the union merged with the PTC, covering the major administrative grades in the civil service to form the PCS, although it is unlikely that this development will end the history of electoral struggle.

The CPSA membership was principally female (72 per cent of its 116,681 members in 1996), although, as in many unions in Britain, the senior leadership of the union was disproportionately male, resulting in a gendered division within the union, whereby the interests of the predominantly low-grade female membership were represented by male leaders at both branch and national levels. In addition, the political divisions within the union were debilitating, with the union frequently riven by struggle between the two leadership groupings, neither of which was in a position to provide continuous leadership. None the less, the national leadership of the conservative faction was often dominated by women, providing a stark contrast with the male dominance of the left groupings.

During the 1990s a limited process of union reorganization began, following the massive restructuring of the civil service during the 1980s and 1990s. The restructuring involved a reorganization of the civil service, with the advent of agencies and privatization. Accompanying these developments, the managerial style hardened in ways that the union membership found difficult to address. Consultation between management and union representatives was less common; the scope of national collective bargaining became very limited; and union memberships found themselves increasingly by-passed. While the political struggles between different political groupings continued, the national leadership began to encourage a more devolved form of organization based on regional offices, and successfully advocated merger with the other large civil service union, the PTC.

General, Municipal, Boilermakers and Allied Trades Union (GMB)

The GMB has long been the third largest union in the United Kingdom, with members across almost every sector of the economy (with a total in 1993 of 830,743, of whom 306,190 were women – 37 per cent) (TUC Annual Report, 1993). It has had an uneven history, in part reflecting an erratic and for many years remote and relatively authoritarian regional and national leadership. In recent years, it has undertaken a number of reviews of organization and operation, aspiring to become one of the leading general unions in the country. As one indication of this aspiration, the union has been at the forefront in developing a positive approach towards the European Union.

The origins of the union lie in the late nineteenth century, and the growth of general unionism. The forerunner of the modern union is generally seen as the National Union of General Workers, founded in 1989, with Will Thorne as the General Secretary. Thorne was a prominent member of the Social Democratic Federation and an active socialist. Although the union was inclusive in its approach, recruiting unskilled and semi-skilled workers, usually low-paid, the nucleus of the early membership was the relatively skilled and well-paid gas stokers whose industrial successes stimulated others to join the union. As a result, the union has long had a large membership in the gas industry.

The early inclusiveness of the union was reflected in the merger with the National Federation of Women Workers in 1921. This merger was accompanied by the promise of a separate women's section and a national women's officer. The Federation leaders were of the view that the future for a separate women's union was limited, and that their future lay with the larger well established and male-led unions, provided there were guarantees that recognized the specificity of their interests, at least organizationally (Maksymiw, 1990, p. 143).

During the 1930s, the union had lost its earlier impetus, partly owing to the long-term incumbency of the original leadership of the union, as well as a cumbersome and outdated organizational structure. While reforms were introduced, including a changed district structure, the union lost members to NUPE, which was successful in recruiting manual council workers (under the control of local authorities) and manual hospital employees. In addition, the TGWU, which recruited actively in the manufacturing sectors, also began to recruit in traditional GMB areas (Clegg, 1964).

After the Second World War, the union suffered from its relatively centralized and authoritarian leadership, which took the form of regional fiefdoms (Maksymiw, 1990, pp. 143–6). The union was divided into a series of geographical regions, whose regional secretaries had considerable authority and influence within the union. These secretaries were second only to the general secretary, and dominated the executive, effectively controlling and running the union (Maksymiw, 1990, pp. 146–7). In effect, the union was characterized by very limited membership involvement: local and regional officials controlled and organized the day-to-day activity of the union, undermining the development of local lay leadership structures.

One important feature of the union organization was the slow development of workplace forms of representation. Initially, the executive was opposed to the shop steward form of organization evident in other unions, such as the TGWU. Shop stewards were formally circumscribed by rule, and during the 1950s and 1960s there was a series of notable disputes involving shop stewards and leaders of unofficial action in factories and related workplaces (Beynon, 1984). These tensions came to a head in a famous strike in 1970 at the Pilkingtons glass manufacturing firm in St Helens (Lane and Roberts, 1971). An unofficial strike closed the factory for seven weeks, and the subsequent unsuccessful attempt by the local strike committee to set up an alternative union was an indicator of much bitterness and cynicism about the GMB. The union was seen to fail its membership, and its continued hostility to both unofficial action and local organization became a handicap.

Following these events, the union began the process of reviewing its regional and workplace organization. This process of reorganization continued throughout the 1970s and into the 1980s, resulting in a more responsive and outward-looking union. One example of the changed focus of the union is that during the 1980s, partly for instrumental reasons, positive discrimination policies were introduced to give greater prominence to women members, by 1996 over half the membership. In 1988, the conference agreed that ten seats on the central executive council should be reserved for women. However, as with many unions these developments have not always been accompanied by the infrastructural support necessary for the involvement of women members in the activity of the union.

While the general structure of the union has not changed in any notable ways, the GMB now appears more accommodating to active workplace union committees. There has been a limited attempt to restrict the remit of the regional officers and to promote workplace union activity. In part, this occurred in the context of the move away from industry-level bargaining towards negotiations at plant level. As with other centralized unions, regional officials were no longer in a position to exercise dominance within the union. This development has allowed workplace union representatives to play a more active role in the union over the past few years, and to qualify the union as a regional officer-led union.

Inland Revenue Staff Federation (IRSF)

The IRSF was the main union in the Inland Revenue, dating back to the end of the nineteenth century (with a membership in 1993 of 59,044, of whom 37,019 were women – 63 per cent) (TUC Annual Report, 1993). By the late 1970s the union was the largest and most significant department-based union in the civil service. Although there had been a number of department-based unions, such as the Ministry of Labour Staff Association (1912–73), by the 1970s most of these had merged with other civil service unions, leaving the IRSF as the notable exception. Its membership consisted of the majority of revenue assistants and revenue officers in the department, or their equivalents in the past. In 1996, the IRSF merged with the then NUCPS to form the PTC.

The history of the union goes back to the late nineteenth century, with the establishment of the Association of Tax Clerks in 1892. Until 1900, tax clerks were not recognized as civil servants, being under the local control of surveyors of taxes; their pay was low, they had no pensions and overtime was compulsory. As income tax was extended, particularly after 1842, the work of local offices increased. With the stabilization of their employment, tax clerks began to petition for civil service status and privileges during the 1880s. They established a permanent committee in 1891, although it was temporarily disbanded as a result of the victimization of three leading clerks. The Association of Tax Clerks was founded at a general meeting in January 1892 in London. Initially the Association was relatively inactive, confining its concerns to securing parliamentary assistance to deal with problems faced by tax clerks. In 1900, the Association obtained recognition from the Board of Inland Revenue, which agreed to an increase in pay and a stabilization of their employment, although the clerks were still not recognized as civil servants. By 1914, following lobbying and pressure from Members of Parliament, tax clerks were included as part of the civil service established staff, and received salaries commensurate with those in the general civil service (Humphreys, 1958, pp. 38–9).

In 1922, the organization of the union was placed on a more regular footing, with the appointment of a general secretary and the establishment of an office. The name of the association was also changed to the Association of Officers of Taxes (Humphreys, 1958, p. 104). The decision was taken at this time to build the union as a single-department organization, thereby going against the trend elsewhere among the larger civil service unions to organize on a cross-departmental basis. In 1923 the Association of Women Tax Clerks merged with the Association of Officers of Taxes, followed by the entry of members from the Association of Temporary Male Tax Clerks in 1926. A federation with the National Association of Assessors and Collectors of Taxes was agreed in 1935, leading to the establishment of the Inland Revenue Staff Federation in 1936. In the following year the Valuation Office Clerical Association joined the Federation and in 1938 the three members of the Federation amalgamated to form a single union, also known as the Inland Revenue Staff Federation (Humphreys, 1958, pp. 140–2).

While the IRSF never affiliated to the Labour Party, the Association of Tax Clerks affiliated to the TUC in 1911, the first civil service clerical union to do so. Apart from the period 1927–45, with the imposition of Section V of the Trade Disputes and Trade Unions Act of 1927, which forbade affiliation by the civil service unions to outside bodies, such as the TUC and the Labour Party, the union and its successor, the IRSF, maintained its TUC affiliation. It has always had a commitment to developing as a department-based and department-focused union, although throughout its history it played an active role in inter-union associations, particularly those linking the various civil service clerical unions. However, the IRSF leadership also attempted to pursue policies which cut across the grain of cooperation with other trade unions, although it was supportive of the civil service confederation, the Council of Civil Service Unions (Humphreys, 1958, pp. 142–4; Maksymiw, 1990, p. 164).

The IRSF was a centrally organized union, with three constituent sections, taxes, collection and valuation. At the base of the union were the branches, composed of IRSF members from each tax district, collection office and valuation office. While the conference was the sovereign body, the national executive was responsible for the day-to-day activity of the union between conferences. As with most unions, the national executive was supported by a set of full-time officers, the principal ones being the general secretary, deputy general secretary, three assistant general secretaries, an education, training and campaign officer, a general treasurer and two regional officers. This union has had a majority of women members since the early to mid-1960s, but was and remained a male-led union.

For many decades, the IRSF was an active but moderate union, committed to petitioning, lobbying and playing an active part in the Whitley arrangements in the Inland Revenue. As with the two main civil service unions (CPSA and the then SCPS), the IRSF was an active participant in the five-and-a-half-month civil service pay dispute in 1981, with some tax branches heavily involved in the action. In the mid-1980s, there were partly successful attempts to revive the office organization as the principal means of meeting the implications of increasingly devolved management structures. By the end of the 1980s, there were major internal divisions among the leadership about the best way to respond to government initiatives and proposals, particularly over pay.

Part of the background to division over union policy was the relatively long history of conflict and dispute between the national leadership and the branch leaderships of the larger branches. For nearly fifteen years a number of left-led branches had been critical of the rather conservative and accommodating stance taken by the national leadership, particularly the full-time appointed staff. In 1988 the national leadership proposed a programme of union reform, to increase the number of policy-making members on the national executive and to introduce membership ballots and a regional structure within the union. The conference rejected these proposals, except for that relating to a regional structure, with the first officer appointed to the Birmingham office in 1988 and a second in the Liverpool office (Maksymiw, 1990, pp. 163–4).

By the 1990s, the union was an anomaly within the civil service, as a department-based union. With the advent of privatization and the externalization of functions of the civil service, it became more and more difficult to justify its continued existence as an independent union. Not only was there the prospect of a rapidly contracting membership base, particularly with the computerization of taxation records and procedures, but the boundaries between civil service employment and elsewhere were no longer fixed and the union faced the prospect of organizing a more diversified and multi-employer membership.

However, the union was an anomaly in a second respect. While it was a centralized union, with the principle policy decisions decided at a national level, it was also a union where national leaders were early to recognize the importance of active and participative membership at the office or local level. Although there is no necessary contradiction between these two aspects of organization, the distinctive feature of the IRSF was the willingness of the national leadership to encourage locally based activity, particularly in the context of an increasingly devolved management within the department. The problem for these leaders was that such encouragement of local leaders and an active membership did not always result in a compliant membership.

Manufacturing, Science and Finance (MSF)

MSF was formed in January 1988, following a merger between two very different unions, ASTMS and TASS (with a membership in 1993 of 552,000, of whom 143,520 were women – 26 per cent) (TUC Annual Report, 1993). The ASTMS had a tradition of organization where the branches had considerable financial and political independence, whereas the TASS branches were tightly circumscribed, the union organizing on the basis of full-time officer leadership and control (Carter, 1991). While the merger brought together two unions organizing overlapping and contiguous memberships, in occupational and class terms, the merging of the different structures and opposed methods of operating and organizing was difficult (Carter, 1991, 1997).

The ASTMS was itself born out of an earlier merger in 1968, between the Association of Supervisory Staffs, Executives and Technicians (ASSET) and the Association of Scientific Workers (AScW). This first merger brought together a largely supervisory union (ASSET) in the engineering industry and a union which recruited technicians and related staff in the engineering industry and scientific workers in education (AScW). From this time and into the 1970s the union membership expanded rapidly, extending into areas of limited union-ization or non-unionism. The result was that the union covered an increasingly diverse membership in engineering, finance, health and education, civil aviation and a range of processing and manufacturing industries.

ASTMS, led by Clive Jenkins, a rather charismatic but idiosyncratic leader, occupied a prominent position as a left Labour union, despite a politically conservative membership. Organizationally, the union was characterized by a significant degree of branch and workplace autonomy. It was marked by a 'high degree of formal democracy', indicated by the circulation of detailed minutes and reports, as well as open political debate within the union, at all levels, although the actual involvement of the membership in this process was always very limited (Carter, 1997, p. 12; see also Carter, 1986). According to Carter (1997, p. 12), the result was an isolated and introverted autonomy: 'The very structure of the union encouraged the isolation of workplace groups and structured a lack of interest in wider union affairs.' It was a union where there was a duality between the pursuit of day-to-day issues in the workplace, via workplace groups, and branches which were often organized on a geographical basis covering a number of workplaces. These forms of organization were supported by a professional staff of full-time officials in the regions.

TASS was a very different union. It was very centralized, led by a cohesive group of officials who were members of or clearly identified with the Communist Party of Great Britain and its supporters. The union had its origins in the engineering and shipbuilding industries in the 1920s, and while its membership growth was slow, it benefited from the general expansion of engineering in the years after the Second World War. In 1970 it entered into an amalgamation with the then AEUW. As already noted, this merger was not a success, partly because of the particular organizing traditions in TASS, including the appointment of politically acceptable officials, and increasingly because of the political divergence between the left-led TASS and the right-wing leadership of the AUEW.

The appointed full-time leadership controlled the union, determining the way it developed and the policies it pursued. There was little time for, or consideration of, dissenting views. Tight control over the branches and local activity was critical for this form of leadership, with the full-time officers employed on a ratio of 1:2,500 members in 1986, thereby allowing for considerable direct involvement and activity in branch and local affairs (Carter, 1991, p. 44). In addition, the forms of representation in TASS were indirect, in the sense that delegates to the annual conference were elected at district conferences attended by 165 representatives (out of a membership of 260,000). These 165 delegates in turn elected most of the union's other representatives (Carter, 1991, p. 44). In view of the dominance of the broad left political bloc, there was little opportunity for dissent, debate or contestation over policy and practice.

In the mid-1980s, the two unions entered into merger discussions and subsequently joined together to form MSF in 1988. The conditions for the merger were fourfold. First, relations between the two unions in the engineering industry were generally amicable, especially in the changed climate of the 1980s, which had ended the jurisdictional disputes of an earlier period. The two unions faced the threat of declining memberships as a result of restructuring and deindustrialization. Second, there had been a decline in the prominence of the engineering membership within ASTMS, following the expansion of the union into the insurance sector. One outcome was that the engineering sections within the union were more favourably disposed towards a merger with the largely engineering-based TASS, as a way of recovering some of their former pre-eminence within the union. Third, there was a growing disaffection with the leadership style of the union, including the rightward shift in the politics of the then general secretary, Clive Jenkins. It was thought by engineer leaders that a merger with TASS would lead to a political realignment within the union, and restore the unionism of the earlier years. Fourth, the limits of membership increase by the two independent unions, by further mergers or direct recruitment, appeared to have been reached. In the climate of the 1980s, and faced with limited membership expansion, the unions faced financial difficulties (Carter, 1991, pp. 43–4).

In the event, the merger was fraught. There was an initial struggle at the national level between the well organized and disciplined TASS officials and national representatives and the more diverse political leadership of ASTMS (Carter, 1991). However, an ASTMS model more or less prevailed, combining two features of branch organization. First, ASTMS activists were able to retain control over branches, keeping full-time officials at a distance. The three-year period of branch integration allowed the experienced ASTMS activists to consolidate their positions in the merged branches. Second, branch autonomy and sovereignty was retained *vis-à-vis* the centre, focused on independent regional and branch funding. This general trend was confirmed in 1991, with the election of Roger Lyons (from ASTMS) to replace Ken Gill, the then incumbent general secretary (from TASS).

Problems continued, with a declining membership, financial problems, a shifting balance between the different sections of the membership and continued sectarian struggle within the union between two political blocs, loosely based on the former unions. More interestingly, the union has begun to debate different models of unionism in an attempt to come to terms with the changing political conditions of trade unionism. On the one hand, there is an argument for a service union, where the emphasis is on members as individuals and the union as an organization which services individual concerns. The background to this is that the union was well served in the past by a group of professional officers and lay leaders, servicing a passive membership. On the other hand, the union has officially adopted an organizing model of unionism, where the assumption is that the union will not survive unless it reorganizes on the basis of a 'strong network of trained and motivated shop stewards' (Carter, 1997, p. 15). In this perception of the union, workplace organization should be strengthened, with local representatives dealing with day-to-day issues, while full-time officers take on more strategic goals and concerns.

Thus, a union which was born out of a merger between two unions organized on the basis of very different traditions and practices has ended up affirming the importance of workplace organization and sovereignty. Throughout the 1990s, there was a struggle over these different conceptions of unionism, which for much of the time left unions in the traditional engineering areas very much isolated. In the West Midlands, as elsewhere, these union groups faced the harsh realities of union decline and de-industrialization. It is against this background that these wider debates within the union had an urgency, which clearly was not always acknowledged by the national leadership.

National Communications Union (NCU) (subsequently Communication Workers Union, CWU)

The NCU (subsequently the CWU) was composed of two separate groups of members, an engineering group, principally composed of men, and a clerical group, with an overwhelming majority of women members (with a combined membership in 1993 of 126,376, of whom 26,094 were women – 21 per cent) (TUC Annual Report, 1993). These two groups of workers were employed in different sections of the British Telecom workforce, and historically represented by two unions. In 1985, the Post Office Engineering Union (POEU), covering operatives, merged with the Post Office and Telecoms Group of the CPSA, representing clerical and related staff, to form the NCU. Subsequently, in 1995, the NCU merged with the Union of Communication Workers (UCW), covering the hourly paid grades in the Post Office, to form the CWU, although this most recent merger did not have a tangible effect on the way the previous NCU membership organized and operated.

The unions that made up the NCU had their origins in Post Office in the early part of the twentieth century. Initially, the Post Office was responsible only for postal services, under the control of the state, until the inclusion of the telegraph services as part of the Post Office in 1869. This was followed by the incorporation of the telephone system in 1912. Subsequently, there was a phenomenal expansion of postal and telephonic communications, with significant growth in the range of services offered. The Post Office remained a civil service department until the Post Office Act in 1969, which made it a public corporation. This was followed in 1981 by the Telecommunications Act, which made the telecommunications business a separate public corporation (for a brief history, see Batstone *et al.*, 1984, Chapters 2 and 3). In 1984, the telecommunications corporation, British Telecom, was privatized and subsequently reorganized (Ferner and Terry, 1997). Throughout the latter period of major changes in ownership and the increasing commercialization of these enterprises, the unions maintained their broad areas of traditional representation and organization.

The institutional division of the NCU, between clerical staff and operatives, was reflected in branch organization, with separate branches for each set of members. In the 1990s there were moves to create merged branches in many areas of the country, although in the Birmingham area of the West Midlands attempts to merge some of the engineering branches with the clerical branch were unsuccessful. Indeed, attempts to merge the old engineering branches, distinguished by out-of-date functional divisions, such as internal staff ('indoor' workers) and external staff (line maintenance workers and others who worked outdoors), were also unsuccessful until late 1996. Then, two of the three engineering branches (the internal branch and a branch representing 'other' grades) effected a merger (on changes in the composition of the POEU membership, see Bealey, 1976).

The origins of the two sections of the union are to be found in moves by civil servants and related municipal and public sector workers to organize in the first part of the twentieth century. As in many other sections of civil service staff at the time, these workers were caught up in the diverse and often bitter struggles to establish unionism in these areas of employment. With the establishment of the POEU in 1919, the unionized division of the workforce along gender lines was institutionalized until the merger in 1985, although even then this division was more or less maintained because of the separate branch organization for each set of members. During the 1980s, steps were taken to develop a single integrated structure with one rule book. However, until the early 1990s each group had its own network of branches, rule books and support staff. In addition, there was a group executive for each section, although there was also a single national executive council for the whole union membership.

In the context of the reorganization and changes in British Telecom, the NCU continued to organize and operate as a highly centralized union, at a district level as well as within divisions and nationally. During the 1980s there were moves within British Telecom to introduce elements of decentralization in bargaining arrangements and to assert elements of managerial control over work-related issues and the introduction of new technologies. These developments created problems for the NCU and the other recognized unions, the Society of Telecom Executives (STE, representing managerial grades) and the Union of Communication Workers (UCW, representing postal staff). These three unions and the two segments of the NCU usually negotiated separately with the corporation, although there were a number of items subject to joint negotiations, such as disciplinary procedures and superannuation (Ferner and Terry, 1997, p. 114). None the less, the relationships both within and between these unions were not easy, and there was a long tradition of union rivalry and conflict. This was most evident during a major strike in 1987, when the STE and the UCW settled first and thus left the NCU both isolated and exposed to a rather aggressive corporate stance.

The 1980s and 1990s created difficulties for the NCU, especially in the way it organized and operated as a union. As the corporation went through a process of managerial devolution and recentralization, the union attempted to follow the managerial reconfiguration that was taking place. During the 1980s district managers were given more authority to negotiate and bargain at this level. In many respects this dovetailed with the pattern of organization in the NCU, whereby local branch leaderships, representing geographically based memberships, started to develop and open up local bargaining arrangements. This provided an impetus within the union to recognize the newly acquired authority of these leaderships. None the less, the formal centralized union structure was maintained, and these local leaderships bargained within this framework.

With the recentralization of managerial structures in the 1990s, and the divisionalization of the corporation, the centralized basis of the union was reaffirmed. For a time, it had appeared that there would be a progressive weakening of the national leadership as district and branch leaders asserted their independence within the prevailing union structures. However, with the reassertion of national authority, reinforced by a complex of divisional and bargaining relationships, the local leaderships, in the West Midlands and elsewhere, found themselves somewhat isolated and fragmented as they dealt with local difficulties and divisional issues (see Ferner and Terry, 1997, p. 118).

National Union of Civil and Public Servants (NUCPS)

The NUCPS was the second largest trade union in the civil service (with a membership in 1993 of 111,831, of whom 39,935 were women – 36 per cent) (TUC Annual Report, 1993). Its origins went back to the nineteenth century, when the Second Division Clerks Association (SDCA) was established in 1890, covering the lowest permanent clerical staff in the civil service (Humphreys, 1958, pp. 42, 149–50). With reorganization of the civil service in 1920 into four grades (writing assistant class, clerical class, executive class and administrative class), the SDCA was faced with a dilemma over representation. Since most of the second division clerks were assigned to the executive class, the SDCA transferred its representation to this grade and renamed itself the Association of Executive Officers of the Civil Service. In 1921 it merged with the Association of Staff Clerks and Other Civil Servants, a department grade assigned to higher executive posts. A third organization, the Society of Civil Servants, established in 1918, represented intermediate clerks, who were assigned to the general executive class. In 1922 it affiliated with the National Federation of Postal and Telegraph Clerks (a break-away from the Union of Post Office Workers). In 1930 this union merged with the Association of Executive Officers to form the Society of Civil Servants (SCS).

The union continued to expand and broaden its representational base, in particular with the acquisition of the Association of First Grade Officers of the Ministry of Labour in 1972 and the Customs and Excise Federation in 1975. The union was renamed the Society of Civil and Public Servants (SCPS) in 1976, reflecting its increasingly diverse composition, in particular with the expansion of its representation to include what were termed 'fringe bodies', workers in the associated areas of central government employment, such as the Civil Aviation Authority. The union renamed itself NUCPS in 1988, following a merger with the Civil Service Union, which further extended the representational base of the union, to include members from messenger and telephonist grades, as well as others. In 1996, the NUCPS merged with the IRSF to form the PTC, which in turn subsequently merged with the CPSA in 1998 to form the PCS.

The SCPS and its predecessor benefited from the enormous expansion of civil servants in the middle level grades. Between 1950 and 1979, the union increased its membership from 36,000 to 105,560, a 239 per cent increase. This growth was in part from successful recruitment of new entrants and in part from amalgamation and merger with other civil service unions, such as the Customs and Excise Group and the Association of Officers of the Ministry of Labour in 1975. By 1978, the union density was 85 per cent and, despite government policies discouraging union membership during the 1980s, the union was able to maintain union membership at this level.

The NUCPS approach to bargaining and negotiations was similar to that of the CPSA. It was a form of unionism characterized by leaders, skilled and experienced in lobbying governments and representing members in day-to-day union activity, and where members were neither expected to nor did play an active part in union affairs. This style of unionism persisted into the 1970s. The barriers to promotion from lower grades into the middle range of grades were lessened, with the result that there was an influx of younger and more activist members into grades covered by predecessor unions to the NUCPS. During this decade the national leadership of the union was reinforced with the election of left-wing national leaders, mainly either members of the Communist Party or on the left of the Labour Party. This was a leadership that was prepared to adopt a more robust response to government policies, particularly on wages and incomes policies. As part of this approach these leaders were willing to campaign among the relatively quiescent membership to encourage support for industrial action. One outcome of these policies was that the union affiliated to the TUC in 1978. In the late 1980s, with the implementation of the Conservative legislation on trade unions and the virtual collapse of the Communist Party of Great Britain, a moderate labour leadership began to predominate, especially among the lay leadership, and the previous leadership either found new political clothes or was marginalized.

An impetus towards a more activist-focused unionism was the threat to job security and to the national pay agreements covering the civil service. On 10 January 1973, in protest against government pay policy, union members participated in national protest meetings for the first time in the union's history. This was followed by limited participation in the 27 February 1973 strike (Kelly, 1980, p. 110). In 1979, in protest against pay policies, SCPS members, together with the CPSA, embarked on consultative meetings, protest meetings over suspensions, selective and lightning strikes. Strike pay levies were organized and strike pay was distributed to members involved in selective strikes. The union was an active participant in two national stoppages, further protests and the five-and-a-half-month pay dispute in 1981. Following the defeat of the unions in 1981, the national leaders were reluctant to consider industrial action in support of further national campaigns, although department-based members, especially in the social security areas, were prepared on occasion to stop work and implement other forms of non-strike industrial action in opposition to increased work intensification and deteriorating conditions of employment.

One outcome of the pay campaigns in the late 1970s was an extensive debate within the union about industrial action, bargaining arrangements and forms of union organization. In 1979, the union leaders commissioned a study of the organization and operation of the union, with a view to considering the establishment of workplace forms of representation and a comprehensive regional structure (Drake et al., 1982). However, the leadership of the union remained unconvinced of the desirability of this form of organization and persuaded a special conference to agree only to qualified reorganization (Society of Civil and Public Servants, 1983). There was a fear among the national left-wing leaders, in particular, that a comprehensive reorganization at branch level by the recognition of workplace-based stewards and related resourcing at branch and regional levels would lead to an unacceptable degree of autonomy at these organizational and representational levels. As a result, the union remained relatively centralized in both form and organization, despite the partial acknowledgement of the importance of active and involved local and branch levels of representation and delegacy.

Despite the left political leadership from the mid-1970s to the late 1980s and a public commitment to address the unequal involvement of women in leadership positions, women members remained disproportionately under-represented among the senior union leadership, with only one of the seven principal officers being a woman in the 1980s and none in the 1990s. In 1996, the proportion of women members in the union was 48 per cent, with male membership at 77,438 and female membership at 71,973. In these circum-stances, there was a series of attempts to improve the participation of women in national union affairs. The national executive committee implemented a series of policies aimed at increasing the formal participation of women members in the union at a national level. Key to this was a policy of targets for the proportion of women elected to the NEC, which resulted in a substantial increase of women members on the executive, reaching 50 per cent of the executive grade members by the 1990s. However, there was no equivalent policy for recruitment to full-time officer posts.

The union continued to operate in a relatively centralized form, having taken limited steps to develop more devolved forms of organization. There was a continuing reluctance to commit resources to both branch and regional level, although the terrain of unionism in the civil service had shifted in ways that placed an increased premium on this level of activity. Over the past decade there was a process of fragmentation (through the establishment of agencies) and privatization of the civil service. These developments placed a premium on developing locally based activity, reflected in the initiation in 1997 of an organizing campaign, 'A Voice in Every Workplace'. The aim was to develop an organizational presence in all offices and workplaces. This initiative, plus the merger with the CPSA in 1998, provided the opportunity for a more active reconsideration of local and workplace organization within the union, although only limited steps were taken in this direction.

Transport and General Workers' Union (TGWU)

The TGWU was, until the establishment of UNISON, the largest union in the United Kingdom (with a membership in 1993 of 1,036,586, of whom 189,615 were women – 18 per cent) (TUC Annual Report, 1993). It was founded in 1922, following the merger of a number of unions representing dock workers and a range of transport workers. Subsequently, via further mergers and amalgamations as well as individual membership recruitment across a range of unions, it became one of the most influential unions in the United Kingdom, both industrially and politically. It is a general union covering workers in a wide range of industries, production workers in most manufacturing industries, civil air and road transport, dock workers, passenger buses and public services. In some sectors, it takes on the features of an industrial union, particularly oil refining, flour milling and docks. It also has a membership among clerical and administrative staff in some of these industries, particularly in manufacturing (Maksymiw, 1990, p. 329).

At the time of its founding, under Ernest Bevin, the union was organized as a series of trade groups, such as dockers and road transport workers, which was complemented by a geographical form of organization on an area basis. Constitutionally this was an attempt to balance the virtues of sectionalism, acknowledging that trade groups should have the autonomy to deal with their own affairs, with unity via forums which grouped all members on an area basis, at least on issues such as finances, strike action and general union policy. The national executive thus represented both the national trade groups and the geographical areas that comprised the union, a form of organization that has been maintained.

The union expanded its membership and coverage dramatically, with a series of amalgamations, in almost every year until the 1940s. One of the most important amalgamations was with the Workers' Union in 1929, which brought in over 100,000 workers, from engineering and elsewhere (Hyman, 1971). The union throughout this time was led by Ernest Bevin, who, along with Frank Cousins subsequently, was an influential player within the Labour Party. Both achieved Cabinet Office in Labour governments. It was thus an expanding union, industrially influential and politically important.

The prevailing pattern of organization established in the 1920s provided opportunities for centralized leadership dominance as well as for the emergence of devolved forms of leadership (McIlroy, 1995, pp. 164–5). On the one hand, until the 1970s this was a union dominated by general secretaries able to exercise considerable power within the union. The basis of this exercise of power lay in the ways successive general secretaries were able to use their tenure, a large and diverse conference meeting every two years and their influence over the appointment of full-time officials. Via their links with the regional and trade group secretaries, these officials dominated the union and ensured orderly processes of succession. However, on the other hand, this was a union which from the early 1960s promoted a steward form of organization, particularly in the manufacturing sector, which provided a counter to the dominance of full-time officials. In the 1960s, first Frank Cousins and then Jack Jones, as general secretaries, used their position to encourage the extension of workplace-based organization. This initiative involved the formal recognition of a steward form of organization in workplaces and factories, via the establishment of district committees and the appointment of district officials, in part at the expense of the traditional authority of the trade group form of organization.

The thrust of reforms in the 1960s was to entrench the steward form of organization within the TGWU. There was an encouragement of workplace organization, and the development of the types of steward committees, particularly in the larger manufacturing workplaces, that would make this possible, especially across the West Midlands, a centre for these developments. According to Maksymiw (1990, p. 334) this took five forms:

1. A shift from national (industry-wide) to plant and factory bargaining.
2. An extension of the scope and range of local and workplace bargaining.
3. An increase of lay representation on company, regional and national negotiating bodies.
4. The introduction and extension of reference-back procedures to the membership.
5. The development and encouragement of district forms of representation to overcome trade group fragmentation.

Such developments were contested, particularly by sections of the incumbent full-time officials, but these initiatives were in line with the changes taking place in manufacturing industry. The result was that the TGWU acquired a reputation in the late 1960s and early 1970s as a steward-based trade union. Throughout the 1970s, there was an extension of lay elected leaders on union committees, increasingly exercising control in relation to appointed officials. In short, there were shifting relations between full-time officials and convenors/stewards, which made for a complex pattern of leadership, representation and participation in this union (Beynon, 1984).

Eventually, in the late 1970s and early 1980s, the consequence of these changes was a weakening of the dominance of the general secretary. Increasingly, the national executive members, as elected rather than appointed officials, began to assert themselves and thereby qualified the power of the general secretaries. Even so, with the election of William Morris as general secretary in 1991, the first Afro-Caribbean leader of a major British trade union, there was a renewed focus on the role of the general secretary. Morris has been a leading sceptic of the rightward drift in the Labour Party and its rebirth as New Labour, and his re-election in 1996, against a New Labour-supported candidate, reaffirmed the position of the TGWU as an independent and critical trade union in British politics.

During the 1980s the union suffered a major decline in membership, falling from 2,076,466 in 1979 to 1,218,241 in 1990, a fall of 41.3 per cent. By 1996, the membership stood at 906,910. This prompted the union to re-examine how it recruits and represents members. In the late 1980s it embarked on a series of well publicized recruitment campaigns in an attempt to reverse the decline in its membership. In 1986, it initiated its *Link-Up* recruitment campaign, in an attempt to recruit low-paid, temporary and part-time workers. While this particular campaign was not as successful as had been hoped, these initiatives were a stimulus to much debate about the conditions under which workers join trade unions and the ways in which unions retain members (Whitson and Waddington, 1994). The union also began to look at the way it organized and provided services to members. This period of review involved commissioning a report to examine the way the union was organized and operated, resulting in the streamlining of union services and the closure of a number of the smaller union offices in the regions, but nothing more fundamental.

The TGWU was for many years a pacesetter within the trade union movement. For much of its history, its general secretaries were dominant figures within the union as well as major players in the wider labour movement. The union was very closely associated with the emergence in the 1960s of a devolved union organization and structure. None the less, the tension between trade group centralization and steward autonomy remained. The result is a union where lay representation and involvement remains important but where the union has come under considerable pressure to reorganize on the basis of a professionalized and managerialist officialdom in the 1980s and 1990s (Heery and Kelly, 1994).

UNISON

The major union event of the 1990s was the merger in 1993 of three large public sector based unions – Confederation of Health Service Employees (COHSE), NALGO and NUPE – to form the largest union in the United Kingdom, UNISON (with a combined membership in 1993 of 1,486,984, of whom 954,848 were women – 64 per cent) (TUC Annual Report, 1993). This was a merger between two unions viewed as relatively centralized in their organization and operation – COHSE and, especially, NUPE – and a decentralized union, NALGO (Undy *et al.*, 1981, p. 80; Terry, 1996). In order to highlight these features of union organization and their implications for the merged union, the history of NALGO and NUPE will be briefly reviewed. (This is not to downplay the importance of COHSE in this merger, but this union and its membership lie outside this study; for an excellent history of COHSE, see Carpenter, 1988.)

National and Local Government Officers' Association (NALGO)

For much of its history from the 1960s to the 1990s, NALGO was the largest non-manual union in the United Kingdom and a major union in the TUC. It began as a union for administrative, technical, clerical and professional workers in local authorities, but expanded its representation to include staff in the utilities, such as gas, electricity and water, as well as the health service and higher education. In the 1970s and particularly the 1980s it developed into a union whose lay leadership, both local and national, played an influential part in the organization and operation of the union. In this respect, it was known as a lay-led union, unlike its immediate counterpart, NUPE.

The membership of NALGO was diverse and varied, reflecting the non-manual grades in the areas of employment covered by the union. This membership ranged from low-paid clerical workers, typists, telephonists and technicians to relatively high-paid accountants, lawyers, architects and town planners. The majority of its membership was employed in local government, which often created the impression that it was a town hall union. During the 1960s and 1970s, and into the 1980s, it expanded its membership dramatically. From 1970 to 1979, overall membership increased by 71 per cent and female membership by 112 per cent (TUC Annual Reports). There was, however, a decline in membership during the 1980s, a modest 4 per cent from 1980 to 1989 (with female membership increasing by 1 per cent), though membership fell in 1990 and rose again in 1992.

The union has a long history. Founded in 1905, as the National Association of Local Government Officers, it had its origins in the founding of the Liverpool Officers' Guild in 1896 (Spoor, 1967). It began life as a staff association, eschewing the links and associations of trade unionism. As the first full-time general secretary wrote in the association journal in 1911, 'anything savouring of trade unionism is nausea to the local government officer and his association' (Maksymiw, 1990, p. 193). It was both a staff association and a largely male union, composed of town hall staff who were often anti-union in outlook and sentiment.

During and after the First World War the union reorganized and began to develop itself as a more conventional union, although pursuing its objectives in a moderate and cooperative way. In 1920 the association registered as a union, and with the publication of the Whitley Committee Report in 1917–18, the union began to pursue the objective of a National Whitley Council for Local Government, achieved in 1943. However, it was not until 1946 that the first national salary scales for local government officers in England and Wales were achieved. It was also in the immediate aftermath of the Second World War that NALGO broadened its remit to include members employed in the utilities and the health service, when these services were removed from municipal authorities and established as statutory bodies by the Labour government. With this development, NALGO reorganized on a qualified trade group basis, locating membership in employer-based branches, with district and national service conditions committees. These two developments – the Whitley form of negotiation and organization on the basis of service conditions – laid the foundations for the modern NALGO. The union changed its name in 1952 from the National Association of Local Government Officers to the National and Local Government Officers' Association, to reflect the more diverse membership it then represented.

The union was organized on the basis of a branch structure. These branches, some 1,400 in the early 1990s, were based on a set of principles which combined geography and employer. As a result, branches were distinguished by service conditions and the branches in the different service groups often bore little relationship to each other, thus making the possibility of coordinated action across service groups unlikely, especially on local issues. Branches elected one delegate to one of twelve district councils. These councils organized separate service conditions committees for each service group, and elected from within their membership a national executive council. Over time the NEC came to dominate policy formulation and a small group of senior members effectively controlled the NEC. As noted by one commentator, the NEC was 'dominated by the most senior, long-standing members, and fails to provide a representative cross-section of the membership as a whole' (Taylor, 1978, p. 242). This form of domination, coupled with the emergence of an activist membership, led to acrimonious debates at the annual conference, when local leaders attempted to make the NEC accountable and the dominant sections of the NEC attempted to dampen down the enthusiasm and activity of these activists.

The collective bargaining arrangements in local government and the statutory bodies (latterly the privatized utilities and the restructured health service) were highly centralized, which further complicated the prevailing pattern of organization. There were local and regional Whitley structures in each service group, which fed into one of several national joint councils. These committees were multi-union and became the focus of much of the activity by lay and full-time leaderships and officialdom in the union until well into the 1980s. During the late 1970s there was a move to lay down a steward form of representation, although in practice this was a hesitant and uneven development. In the 1980s, there was a shift in the locus of decision-making away from the committees to more devolved levels of the managerial hierarchies. The impact within the union was mixed, although there was a further impetus towards local organization and activity in local government, and the beginnings of more general active steward forms of organization and representation. While these developments in local government still took place within the long-standing centralized and formalized bargaining arrangements for the industry, a more activist membership was evident, particularly in such areas as social services and housing. Elsewhere, and particularly in the privatized utilities, there was a reorganization of the formerly centralized bargaining arrangements, with the introduction by managements of changed arrangements, combining aspects of managerial devolution on some issues and a reassertion of centralized policy-making on other issues.

It is within this context that the NALGO membership entered into the negotiations to create UNISON. NALGO in a variety of ways was a lay-led union, with important restrictions on the role and activity of full-time officials, particularly in relation to branches. However, for much of its history these restrictions were relatively inconsequential, since the membership was largely compliant and in agreement with the conservative stances taken by the general secretaries and the NEC. In the 1960s and 1970s this began to change and, with the emergence of an activist membership, prepared to question long-standing practices, the political composition of the NEC began to shift towards the left. In 1961 it added a strike clause to its constitution, and in 1970 the union authorized its first official strike, involving eighteen members in the Leeds local government branch. In 1964 the union finally affiliated to the TUC, after twelve conference debates on the subject and six membership ballots. The membership increasingly showed a willingness to pursue concerns at a local level, via strikes and related forms of industrial action (Undy et al., 1981, p. 228). These developments were also given a further impetus with the development of an embryonic steward system in the branches, often prepared to express a commitment to an activist form of unionism. By the 1970s, it had become a leading public sector union, with an increasingly activist workplace base.

During the negotiations to establish UNISON, the then NALGO leadership, supported by the membership, argued for a union that acknowledged 'branch autonomy and finance' and 'lay control at all levels' (Terry, 1996, p. 94). Upon being asked to clarify the meaning of these two items, particularly in relation to the role of full-time officials, the NALGO negotiating team stated: 'autonomy in the ability of the branches to have and hold their own funds and spend them as they chose' (Terry, 1996, p. 94). This point was elaborated further, with the claim that members wanted a union where the lay officials continued to exercise power at a district level, without constraint from full-time officials. Throughout the negotiations, the NALGO negotiators defended the position that branches should be autonomous and that lay members should prevail at all levels of the union. This was a rather romanticized version of the practice within NALGO, since full-time officers often played decisive roles in the formulation of policy and the pursuit of union objectives, particularly in negotiations. Nevertheless, the union negotiators argued their case strongly and with some effect (Terry, 1996).

National Union of Public Employees (NUPE)

In many areas, and especially local government, NUPE was the counterpart union to NALGO, organizing and representing manual workers. This union was the fifth largest in the United Kingdom for much of the post-war period; it had long been a member of the TUC and an affiliate of the Labour Party. In the 1960s and particularly the 1970s it expanded its membership base at a phenomenal rate, as well as embarking on a series of major industrial disputes, which placed it at the forefront of union militancy and activism in this period.

NUPE had its origins in 1888 with the establishment of the London County Council Employees' Protection Society. From this start, branches were founded elsewhere and in 1894 the organization adopted the name Municipal Employees' Association. In 1908, following personal clashes among the leadership, the union split, with one section retaining the title of Municipal Employees' Association and eventually becoming a founding union of the GMB in 1923, and the other adopting the title of National Union of Corporation Workers, and becoming NUPE in 1928.

Initially the union was largely confined to London, and it survived because of 'close political links with the various Councils' (Maksymiw, 1990, p. 268). However, with the reorganization of local government in 1929 and the transfer of responsibility for trunk roads, higher education and aspects of health to the county councils, NUPE began to recruit unorganized rural road workers. The leadership was energetic and committed to extending NUPE membership throughout the country, and the 1930s was a period of substantial growth, often at the expense of the GMB. Recruitment was largely on the basis of grievances and membership problems, rather than pay bargaining, since there was little local bargaining over pay during this period.

The leadership of NUPE in the 1930s, under Bryn Roberts, actively but unsuccessfully campaigned for national negotiating arrangements in the public sector as well as industrial unionism. These calls were repeatedly rejected by the TUC, and thus did not become part of the broader campaigns pursued by the TUC. During the Second World War NUPE benefited from the establishment of the National Whitley Council for road workers and then the Local Authority Whitley Council for non-trading services. Subsequently, in 1948, the Whitley arrangements in the National Health Service were reorganized, resulting in a centrally determined system for wages and conditions. Not only was NUPE able to present these developments as accomplishments by the union, it was also able to utilize them to further its appeal within the public services as an active and involved trade union.

The union benefited directly from the enormous expansion of public services in the 1960s and 1970s, becoming large and activist. In the late 1960s, following the introduction of incentive payment schemes into local government, the union began to review the way it organized and operated. Until this time it had been very reliant on an active and involved full-time staff. In part, this was a carry-over from the recruitment campaigns in the 1930s, when the bearers of the union's traditions were the full-time officials, who 'got on their bikes' and recruited road workers and others throughout the country. Following the introduction of incentive payment schemes, the union took the decision to establish a workplace steward structure, promoting local representation and bargaining. This was followed by a commissioned study in 1974 into the conditions for and development of an integrated workplace steward system.

The 1974 study, led by Bob Fryer (perhaps the most influential and effective academic researcher on and with public sector unions from the early 1970s onwards), resulted in an influential report entitled *Organisation and Change in the National Union of Public Employees* (Fryer *et al.*, 1974). What was notable about the report was the recommendation to integrate the membership more effectively into the union, via stewards, and with a more accountable leadership, through committees and related activity. None the less, the report was silent on the place and position of the influential full-time area officers and they remained largely in place, with their traditional authority broadly maintained. For this reason, it can be claimed that NUPE, despite these innovative reforms, which continued into the 1980s, remained a full-time officer-led union.

By the end of the 1970s, the benefits of the reforms were clearly evident, with NUPE developing into the most active and politically enlightened union in the public sector during this period. Not only did the union members pursue their objectives in an active manner, but the union leaders, at local and national levels, were major participants in attempts to redefine the boundaries of unionism in a set of campaigns which went well beyond the instrumental economism often associated with pay campaigns to question patterns of work organization and the objectives of public service. In addition, the union was very active in re-examining the basis of representation within the union, and in particular the representation of women members, almost two-thirds of the membership.

These developments and initiatives came to a head in 1979, in the so-called 'winter of discontent'. Over a three-month period, the four major unions in the public sector – NUPE, COHSE, GMB, TGWU – pursued a diverse and divided strike campaign in favour of a series of claims that would benefit the low paid. It resulted in the unions rejecting the TUC policy of cooperation with the then Labour government and its pay policies (Dorfman, 1983). While there was dispute among the participating unions about how best to prosecute the campaign, NUPE took the lead and devolved responsibility for the strike to local level committees. In the events following the campaign, the NUPE membership were persuaded to settle for modest increases in their wages, following a commission enquiry into these claims. The union leadership, and in particular the full-time cadre, took steps to reassert control of the disgruntled membership. The result was a reaffirmation of the importance of centralized forms of organization and activity, as well as the importance of recognizing the demands of electoralism and the negative consequences for the Labour Party of direct opposition and criticism from union affiliates.

By the later stages of the 1980s, the union stance could be described in the following terms:

> Convinced that the only way to stop the changes [introduced and encouraged by the Thatcher government] was to ensure the election of a Labour government, closely associated with the Labour Party and hence aware of the debates concerning electoral disadvantage to Labour of public service strike action, NUPE and COHSE increasingly came to advance the concept of a well-disciplined, politically sensitive and well co-ordinated approach to public sector unionism. (Terry, 1996, p. 93)

This recognition, Terry argues, explains the well disciplined and relatively effective strikes by NUPE members in the mid-1980s, particularly the ambulance workers' dispute. The important point to note, however, is that the NUPE leadership increasingly turned their back on worker activism and the autonomy generally associated with such developments. It was against this background that NUPE entered into negotiations about the formation of UNISON in the early 1990s.

The approach of the NUPE leadership to the negotiations was relatively straightforward, advocating a form of unionism that recognized the principles of responsible and representative unionism. This took the form of advocacy of integration of branches into the overall union structure, with a substantive leadership role for full-time officials at all levels, as well as explicit recognition, in rule, of interest groups by the branch structure. These groups included low-paid part-time women members, but also other groups, such as black members, gays/lesbians and members with disabilities. This included a view of unionism where the emphasis was on the importance of 'planning, co-ordination and predictability in policy-making' (Terry, 1996, p. 100). In many respects, the experiences of the 1980s had underwritten a particular view of unionism for the 1990s which was reflected in the NUPE advocacy for a leadership-led union.

UNISON

The establishment of UNISON involved an attempt to establish a distinct form of unionism, with a new approach to union government, rather than one that combined elements of all three participating unions (see Terry, 1996). However, at a formal level, it would appear that the outcome was a negotiated compromise, whereby the concerns of the three unions were incorporated in different ways. Underpinning this approach to unionism was the principle of representativeness (known as proportionality). This principle was predicated on the proposition that union memberships are differentiated and that the formal and actual recognition of key aspects of this differentiation is central to the future of the union. This was complemented by an equally important principle, that of participative and relatively autonomous branch forms of organization, supported by full-time officials but not controlled by such officials. The outcome was a tension within the union. On the one hand, there was an implicit recognition that the restructuring of the 1980s and 1990s placed a premium on local organization and activity. In practice, the new union retained much of an idealization of the principles informing the NALGO membership during the 1980s and 1990s. On the other hand, there was a view that the only effective way to deal with the impact of restructuring was via relatively centralized forms of organization and activity. In this respect, there was an attempt among the head office staff to affirm the full-time office traditions associated with NUPE.

The ongoing problem for the union is how to realize these aspirations in practice. Two developments have taken place which put the union at the crossroads of the future of unionism. First, the ongoing restructuring in the public sector and the privatized utilities is such that the recomposition of managerial hierarchies is continuing, but in sharply differentiated ways. Second, union members increasingly find themselves in situations where they have to address this diversity, in the way they organize, as branches and as service groups, discovering in the process that the bedrock of a sustainable form of unionism is a participative and involved branch form of organization (Fairbrother *et al.*, 1996). Thus the debates about the form and place of local and workplace unionism continue.

Summary

The unions covered by the study were organized in a variety of ways in the three sectors. They had developed distinctive approaches and ways of representing their memberships, rooted in the complex arrangements and relations defined by work and employment, the particular traditions of trade unionism that emerged in each sector, politics of union organization and activity, the circumstances of bargaining and the varied forms of organization and representation in these trade unions. None the less, there was not an infinite pattern of variation from one trade union to another. The unions in the public sector had emerged out of highly centralized traditions, while the unions in the engineering sectors had developed relatively well established localized forms of representation. Thus, within sectors, there was a tendency for unions to organize in broadly similar ways, despite different formal arrangements and the varied politics espoused by leadership groupings.

In order to explore the ways in which these forms of unionism were worked out in practice, twenty-four union groups in one region, the West Midlands, were studied from 1990 to 1996 (see Appendix). These unions were distributed over the three sectors: public services, privatized utilities and manufacturing. At a general level, a broadly based restructuring of work and employment relations was taking place. More specifically, there were important differences of experience, in part rooted in the particular developments in each sector, and in part as a result of the recomposition and reorganization occurring both within and between these unions during the period. These were not isolated or idiosyncratic developments, and unions in this region, and the United Kingdom more broadly, were faced with a set of choices about how they might develop and reconstitute themselves as collective organizations. These choices are examined in the sectoral case studies.

3 THE WEST MIDLANDS: PLACE AND TIME

The geographical focus of the study is the West Midlands. It was within the West Midlands that the union branches in this study organized and operated, although the branch boundaries in some unions were not coterminous with the region, particularly for unions which organized in the utilities. This region experienced some of the harshest aspects of the deindustrialization of British manufacturing that began in the 1970s and came to the fore in the 1980s. This was a tough time for workers in the region as many faced job loss, a dramatic restructuring of work and employment relations, and the end of many of the certainties of the 1950s and 1960s. During the 1980s, the region lost its political identity, with the abolition in 1986 of the county council, which had attempted to provide some overall coordination and focus for economic activity and related infrastructural support in the region. By the 1990s, there were few reminders left of the region as an administrative and political entity.

The West Midlands region

One of the neglected areas in the study of trade unionism is its geography. At a general level, accounts of trade unions have tended to overlook the specific features of change and development at a regional level and the way this might impact on the organization and activity of trade unions. None the less, by implication, many studies of trade unions have had a regional focus because of the actual context and location of the unions studied (Cohen and Fosh, 1988; Darlington, 1994; Williams, 1996, 1997). More generally, it has been common for trade union analysts to examine the ways in which trade unions may be located within different labour markets and political contexts, developing an account in relation to these features. The implicit suggestion is that there are likely to be variations in the impact and consequences of change at a regional level for the place and position of trade unions in these localities.

In a recent study, Martin *et al.* (1996) focused explicitly on the question of regionalism and trade union change and development, addressing the patterns of union decline during the 1980s and 1990s. The authors situated their analysis with reference to the observation that industrial relations systems (and by implication patterns of trade unionism) have been studied at two levels, the national level and the workplace, tracing out developments at each level and the interrelationships between them. As they note, this focus overlooks the importance of the geography of unions, and specifically the importance of taking 'regional and local spheres' of the capital–labour relation into account (Martin *et al.*, 1996, p. 14).

Taking up this aspect of analysis, the overall focus of this study is the West Midlands region, a key region in the economic restructuring that took place during the 1980s. The region is, as its name suggests, located in the centre of the country, as indicated in Figure 3.1.

The region has been a major manufacturing centre, with a long tradition of active trade unionism. The region comprises the counties of Hereford and Worcester, Warwickshire, Staffordshire, Shropshire and the former West Midlands County Council (WMCC), before its abolition in 1986. The WMCC comprised the metropolitan district council areas of Birmingham, Solihull, Dudley, Sandwell, Wolverhampton, Walsall and Coventry. These administrative and political units are represented in Figure 3.2. Although the principal focus of the study is on employers and trade unions mainly based in the Coventry and Birmingham areas, it should be noted that a number of unions go beyond these boundaries, and in one case beyond the West Midlands region itself.

The West Midlands region covers an area of 13,013 square kilometres (5.4 per cent of Great Britain). In 1996, it had a population of 5,316,600 (9.3 per cent of the GB population). The total employment population (employees in employment) was 2,104,000 (9.5 per cent of the GB employment population). Of this population, 26.9 per cent were manufacturing employees and 68.1 per cent were services employees. In the 1990s there had been an increase in the number of people in employment, by 9.7 per cent between 1992 and 1997 (GB average 7.4 per cent). While the increase in male and female employees during this period was broadly similar (6.8 and 5.9 per cent respectively) total part-time female employment expanded most rapidly (15.6 per cent), representing 45.6 per cent of total female employment in the region in 1997. The unemployment rate for the region was 6.3 per cent, a decline since 1992, when it was around 11 per cent (Central Intelligence Office, 1998).

The West Midlands is a manufacturing region in a number of senses. First, it

Figure 3.1 The West Midlands region of the United Kingdom

Figure 3.2 The West Midlands region by administrative division

has long been a manufacturing dependent region, with the highest proportion of people employed in this sector in Great Britain. Second, it is a region where more gross domestic product (GDP) has been attributable to manufacturing than to any other sector. Third, while the service sector accounted for 68.1 per cent of the region's employment in 1997 (an increasing proportion during the 1990s), it was largely dependent upon and linked into the manufacturing sector. When these features are coupled with the fact that the labour market was highly self-contained, in that the majority of people in the West Midlands both lived and worked in the region, the significance of manufacturing for the region is evident (Government Statistical Service, 1997, p. 323).

Nevertheless, it is important to note the internal variations within the region. There were a number of local authority districts within the region where the incidence of manufacturing industry and the dependence on manufacturing were much less marked than the aggregate figures indicate. In the more rural and dispersed areas, the concentration of employment in manufacturing directly was as low as 10 per cent. In an area such as Shropshire, to the west of the region, agriculture was a base industry for its economy. In 1996, 24 per cent of all Value Added Tax (VAT) registered businesses in Shropshire were in agriculture, compared with 0.6 per cent in the West Midlands county and 9.6 per cent in the region as a whole. However, agriculture was an area of economic activity that accounted for a very small level of employment in the region as a whole, 1.1 per cent in 1996 (Central Intelligence Office, 1998, p. 21).

The region has two large cities located within it, Birmingham and Coventry, as well as a range of other relatively large conurbations. These cities have been the focus for the industrial development in the region, and were originally the sites of industrialization (Wood, 1976). In the 1990s, Birmingham was the largest municipal authority in Britain, with a population of over one million. In the 1960s the city population expanded and the city effectively incorporated a number of satellite towns as satellite conurbations. To the north-west of Birmingham is the 'Black Country', an area of well over a million people containing towns such as Wolverhampton, Walsall, West Bromwich and Dudley. To the south-east is Coventry. It is a smaller city of just over 300,000 people, with an engineering base to its economy.

A metal manufacturing region

It has been argued that the West Midlands as a region has a long-term coherence to it, which arose from the continuity of development during the nineteenth and into the twentieth century (Wood, 1976). In this respect, it is a region where metal-forming and engineering predominated during the nineteenth century, based on the changes and developments that came with the Industrial Revolution. Centred on Birmingham and the Black Country, the West Midlands became a major iron manufacturer in the first part of the nineteenth century. Towards the middle of the century, less specialized iron production was increasingly located in the Black Country, while the production of more highly finished goods was located in Birmingham. This pattern of production was the foundation of the economic restructuring and relocation that took place in the ensuing decades.

In the mid-1860s the region's metal-based industries faced a number of problems, which had the effect of stimulating a comprehensive reorganization and refocusing of metal goods production and related production activity. This restructuring laid the conditions for the relative prosperity of the region in the twentieth century. Four developments are seen as decisive by Wood (1976, p. 31). First, the accessibility and economic availability of raw materials (such as coal and iron ore) ended and it became more difficult and costly to obtain them. Second, with technological development in steel production some products, such as wrought iron, were no longer economically attractive and the firms involved in such production began to decline in importance. Third, the location of the region in the centre of the country and away from sea port facilities became a handicap in securing raw materials and transporting finished goods. Finally, this was the period of the development of the large-scale mechanized factory, and firms in the area were slow to adapt to this coming feature of metal production and manufacture.

During the nineteenth century, the focus of industrial production shifted in two ways, laying the foundation for the patterns of the twentieth century. There was a transformation of the metal processing and assembly industries in the region (Wood, 1976, pp. 31–3). Broadly, firms adapted by developing large-scale finishing plants and a range of small specialist suppliers, usually small firms dependent on the larger firms. The foundation for integrated engineering and metal goods production thus became a feature of the region. These changes were accompanied by the establishment of firms based on precision engineering and the associated skills for this type of production. It was against this background that the automobile industry developed in the West Midlands region. Many of the founding firms of this industry developed out of earlier firms involved in engineering, bicycle production and carriage-making. While relatively few of the progenitor firms survived after the First World War, the manufacturers of accessories and parts remained and continued to adapt to meet the requirements of the developing automobile industry.

Of the two main cities in the region, Birmingham was one of the main industrial centres of Britain in the nineteenth century. Long characterized by a metal-based economy, the major areas of employment have continued to be in engineering, and vehicle and vehicle component production. In the first half of the twentieth century, the structure of industry became more concentrated and externally owned, with small firms dependent on large firms. New industries were also founded during the early twentieth century, including rubber tyre production and food and drink production.

The second city, Coventry, developed out of a different industrial tradition, based on the ribbon and watch-making trades. At the end of the nineteenth century the foundation for the prosperous vehicle industries was laid, first with the move towards bicycle production, followed by motor car manufacture. As with Birmingham, the stamp of light and medium-sized engineering has continued to characterize the Coventry labour market. In addition, new industries were located in the city, in particular artificial fibre production. During the inter-war period, Coventry became a centre for the production of books and automobiles, attracting large-scale engineering firms, particularly in machine tool production. After the Second World War, Coventry, and the nearby towns of Bedworth, Kenilworth, Leamington Spa, Rugby and Warwick, was the fastest growing part of the region, focused on vehicle production and ancillaries in engineering and metal goods production.

During the twentieth century the manufacturing base in the region changed, with the adaptation of existing industries and the development of new related specialisms, particularly in engineering and metal industry production. In the 1950s the prosperity of the region reached its zenith (Wood, 1976, p. 50). This was a period of expansion in jobs for male manufacturing employees and female non-manufacturing employees. Most notably, male employment in the region in this decade expanded at a rate that was 50 per cent above the national average (Wood, 1976, p. 51). The region was also the site of considerable inward migration up until the mid- to late 1960s, and a population growth above the national average rate (Wood, 1976, pp. 42, 46). These patterns reflected the expansion in employment opportunities in the region, particularly in the post-war period. As a corollary, unemployment in the region was low during this period, the result of the ongoing labour market shortage in the region.

The region was also the site of growing public service sector employment, as part of the development of welfare services and provision during the 1950s and especially in the 1960s. There was an expansion of education and health facilities, as well as an extension and formalization of social and personal service provision. These were areas of increasing female employment, often on a part-time basis. This aspect of the regional employment structure was part of a more general pattern of development throughout Britain in this period.

Decline and change

The West Midlands had a troubled history during the 1980s, the roots of which lay much further back in time. It was long known as a centre of manufacturing, particularly engineering and assembly work related to the automobile industry, but manufacturing employment in the region had been in decline since the 1960s, with the metal industries in a state of collapse and retrenchment since the mid-1970s. Compared with the national economy, manufacturing in this region has performed badly. The rate of unemployment has continued to rise from the mid-1970s onwards, and the local economy failed to diversify until the early 1990s.

As an indication of the scale of the downturn, one estimate suggests that the West Midlands lost over 300,000 manufacturing jobs during the 1980s (Department of Employment, 1995, p. 7). A combination of factors contributed to this decline, including the recession of the early 1980s, the continued push by employers to raise productivity levels and the subcontracting of service-type activities in the manufacturing sector to the service sector. A further decline in manufacturing employment occurred following the recession of 1990–2, with 70,000 jobs disappearing between 1991 and 1993 (Department of Employment, 1995, p. 7). Within the region, the brunt of this decline was borne by the core areas of Birmingham, the Black Country and Coventry. These were the areas most dependent on manufacturing, and the persistence of relatively high unemployment levels here was part of the ongoing restructuring of the manufacturing sector (Department of Employment, 1995, p. 8).

Throughout the 1980s and 1990s, the central core of the region consistently had high levels of unemployment, with rates in excess of the regional average, and well above the national average. In these areas, metal goods industries predominated, and in particular vehicles, automotive components and general engineering. These industries were concentrated in the metropolitan area, and accounted for 17 per cent of all employment in the region. Even so, these industries were not exclusively located in this core area, and automotive components and other like products were produced in many centres in the region, including towns outside the metropolitan area. In short, the core area had traditionally been, and remained, strongly dependent upon manufacturing industry, but there was also a spread of these industries throughout the region (Department of Employment, 1995, p. 8).

The patterns of decline and stagnation were experienced in particularly acute ways in Birmingham. By the early 1980s the unemployment rate for the city was nearly 20 per cent, with some of the inner city areas, with their large Afro-Caribbean and Asian communities, reaching 50 per cent (Martin and Pearce, 1992, p. 500). Nearly 60 per cent of the jobs in 1971 had been in manufacturing, whereas by 1981 this had fallen to around 30 per cent. One of the fears relating to this decline and deprivation in the city was that the apparent social cohesion of Birmingham would collapse, with a prospect of increased social division and intensifying violence and desperation. In the 1980s, it was a city with some of the worst urban problems in Europe (Martin and Pearce, 1992, p. 500).

Similar patterns were evident in Coventry, the second largest city in the region. There were, however, two additional features to Coventry which accentuated the economic decline that took place in the 1970s and 1980s. First, this was a labour market characterized by a high but removed concentration of ownership. Of the largest fifteen manufacturing enterprises in the city in the early 1980s, only one head office was based in Coventry, with a further three in the West Midlands. Second, in all but three cases, less than half the employment of these companies was located in the city. These two features meant that Coventry as an economic area was not likely to be centre-stage in the investment and disinvestment decisions made by the major manufacturing companies with bases in the city. It was a vulnerable local economy. However, despite major job losses over fifteen years and extensive restructuring, engineering and vehicle assembly remained central to the Coventry labour market and local economy. Over 40 per cent of the city population had current or recent work experience in the engineering sector. The other major area of employment in the city was public services (central and local government), with women holding a third of the full-time jobs in this sector.

According to one study of the West Midlands economy, the decline in economic activity and prosperity during the 1970s and into the 1980s was 'characterized by a fall in investment, productivity, output and employment' (Flynn and Taylor, 1986, p. 874). As noted above, the local economy of the region was highly integrated and interdependent. It was centred on the metal-using industries, with the vehicle industry at the centre of a web of dependent supplier and accessory firms. However, investment in manufacturing and productivity was at a low level throughout the post-war period. Flynn and Taylor (1986) note that the level of investment was poor throughout this period, as a result of investment decisions rather than the industrial structure of the local economy. This pattern of investment had a knock-on effect on productivity, which was also consistently lower than in other UK regions. By

1981 the net output per manufacturing employee in the region was 13 per cent below the national average. The outcome was a massive decline in employment levels in the manufacturing sector. However, the paradox of this collapse in manufacturing was that overall employment levels in the region remained stable, with an expansion in service sector employment between 1971 and 1978. This shift in the balance between manufacturing and service employment continued into the 1990s.

By the mid-1980s there was some evidence to suggest that some of the more long-term trends towards deindustrialization had begun to weaken and, in certain areas, were being reversed (Department of Employment, 1995). The change in the economic base of the region is indicated by changing employment patterns during the 1980s. In 1978, manufacturing accounted for some 45 per cent of employment in the region, but by 1991 this had declined to 30.4 per cent. This should, however, be placed in the broader perspective of changing patterns of manufacturing employment in the United Kingdom as a whole. Overall, by 1991, manufacturing accounted for only 21.2 per cent of total employment and the West Midlands region still had the highest proportion of manufacturing employment in the United Kingdom (Department of Employment, 1995, p. 7).

In the mid-1990s, there were signs that the West Midlands had begun to lead the way out of the latest phase of the recession. According to the Department of Employment (1995), the first reason is that West Midlands manufacturing industry has an ability to produce export goods. The second, and more important, reason is that the restructuring of manufacturing in the region involved a shift away from 'commodity type metal-based products' to 'higher value added products which are less price competitive and better able to sustain growth', such as motor vehicle and automotive component industries (Department of Employment, 1995, p. 10). The evidence suggests that these industries led the recovery in the West Midlands, assisted by significant inflows of inward investment into the region, accompanied by the location of assembly plants by companies such as Toyota and Honda. These developments stimulated demand for the products of West Midlands based component suppliers, illustrated by the forty major West Midlands firms already supplying components to the new Toyota plant. These trends were further underwritten by the high levels of dependency between manufacturing and service industries in the region, as well as between manufacturing industries themselves. As a result of such linkages and interrelationships with others, an upturn in one industry could have important knock-on effects. Conversely, it also meant that the effects of economic down-turns were felt more sharply in regions such as the West Midlands (Department of Employment, 1995, p. 10).

The decline in employment in the manufacturing sector was offset by the increasing expansion of service employment in the region, particularly from the mid-1980s onwards. One key feature of this form of employment was the expansion of service provision to the manufacturing sector, in the form of catering, cleaning and other ancillary services for this sector. It became relatively common for manufacturing enterprises to contract out ranges of services that were seen as distinct from the core business of enterprises as they attempted to reposition and establish themselves within their markets. In addition, there was also an expansion of other private services, involving retail services, financial services, personal services and tourism, and in particular business tourism (on this last point, see Martin and Pearce, 1992, pp. 500–1).

Alongside these developments, the region was a beneficiary of the state restructuring that was taking place nationally. In particular, the region made a net gain in the civil service restructuring that took place from the early 1980s onwards (Marshall *et al.*, 1997). Between 1979 and 1995, the West Midlands experienced regional growth in civil service employment, with the West Midlands county civil service employment increasing by 6 per cent during the period. Of the remaining areas of the region, Shropshire increased its civil service employment by 42 per cent (1,326 person equivalents), whereas in the other authorities there was a decline in civil service employment over the same period. Numerically, the increase in West Midlands county and Shropshire (2,237 person equivalents) was partly offset by the decline elsewhere in the region (813 person equivalents). This pattern suggests the consolidation of civil service work in the region, as smaller rural officers were closed and integrated into larger offices (Marshall *et al.*, 1997, p. 612). Overall, the paradox was that in the context of declining national civil service employment and major manufacturing decline, the region gained civil service employment.

The politics of economic and social regeneration

One mark of the regeneration of the region was the increased activity of local authorities in developing policies to address the deindustrialization that had taken place. During the early 1980s all the local authorities in the region extended the scope and scale of their activities concerned with local development (Spencer *et al.*, 1986, pp. 131–63). There was an unevenness in this process, particularly between Birmingham and the others, reflecting the differential resource bases available to local bodies.

Alongside this feature of regional organization, there was a lack of political coherence and focus within the West Midlands and across the Midlands as a whole. They were very fragmented areas politically, reflected in varied local authorities, covering semi-rural areas such as Warwickshire and the large metropolitan conurbations of Birmingham and Coventry in the West Midlands, and Nottingham and Leicester in the East Midlands. There were attempts to establish a political coherence within the West Midlands, although not across the Midlands as a whole. With the creation of the West Midlands County Council in 1974 an administrative and semi-political unit (although without elected representation) was established. This unit provided the foundation for a broader political unit which could have served to focus union and political activity in the area. However, the WMCC was disbanded by the Thatcher government in 1986, and the area returned to the fragmented and isolated political arrangements which had long characterized it.

Spencer and colleagues (1986) argued that the abolition of the WMCC removed an agency which had the potential to organize and coordinate a planned regeneration and development of the region. The WMCC had limited revenue raising powers and the capacity to devote those resources for the benefit of the region, working in tandem with the local authorities covered by it. In addition, it provided a focus and basis for lobbying central government for additional resources and policies for the benefit of the region. With the removal of the WMCC, the local authorities all became members of the West Midlands Enterprise Board (WMEB). This body was established in 1982 by the WMCC, as a limited company, with a majority of directors who were local councillors. The purpose of the board was to provide financial assistance to the manufacturing sector. In 1985 district councils were enabled to nominate members to the board and, in conjunction with a merchant bank, steps were taken to develop additional sources of finance for investment and support. While the WMEB had limited success as a support agency, it never acquired the political voice of the WMCC.

A further development of significance in the West Midlands was the emergence of Birmingham as a so-called European city (Martin and Pearce, 1992). In the 1980s Birmingham City Council began the process of breaking with its relatively parochial past by developing an international perspective focused on Europe as part of a comprehensive and effective economic development strategy for the city and associated areas. These initiatives focused on the European Commission. Birmingham and parts of the surrounding region were designated by the Department of Trade and Industry in 1984 as an Assisted Area. This nomination enabled the local authority to secure a range of funding allocations from the European Community (subsequently the

European Union). By the early 1990s the city was acknowledged as one of the most proficient in the UK in obtaining European funding and developing an appropriate economic development strategy (Martin and Pearce, 1992, p. 500). In addition, the city began to develop a political voice, not only within the UK but also in Europe. The most tangible evidence of this shift came with the active involvement of the city in the Eurocities network, based on leading European 'second cities'. Taken together, these developments indicated a significant shift in the political and economic location of the city and by extension the region.

Unions in the West Midlands

Each of the unions included in the study had a substantial membership in the West Midlands region. As noted, manufacturing experienced a major reversal in the 1970s and particularly the 1980s, although such employment had been declining since the 1960s and in the metal industries since the mid-1970s. At the same time, there were signs that the patterns of employment in manufacturing were beginning to shift, following the rationalization and reorganization of many establishments. In an area with a long tradition of active local and workplace unionism, particularly in vehicle manufacture, these changes had major effects on local trade unionism, prompting arguments about the neutralization and demobilization of trade unions, and the need for a 'new realism' (Chadwick, 1983; Bassett, 1986). Alongside these trends, public sector employment has, over the past decade, become more prominent, and not just in numerical terms. Significantly, the public sector, specifically public services and utilities, has long been an area of employment in which successive governments have had a direct concern. In particular, new management and corporate forms of organization have been introduced, with important implications for the patterns of workplace unionism in the area (Fairbrother, 1988).

Of note, the West Midlands is an area where there has been a long tradition of active workplace trade unionism, particularly in vehicle manufacture. In the 1960s, this tradition of unionism was regarded as typifying and exemplifying, in a vigorous form, British industrial relations (Terry and Edwards, 1988). More specifically, Terry (1988a) notes the relatively recent history of the engineering industry, and its associated unionism, in the region. The expansion of motor vehicles and aircraft manufacture took place in the 1930s, involving company restructuring and expansion, the professionalization of management and in some cases a more tolerant view of unionism by management (Grainger, 1988;

Jefferys, 1988). This, coupled with the wartime requirements for employers to recognize agreed terms and conditions of employment and the tacit recognition of steward forms of representation, resulted in the development of plant-level organization and bargaining, evident in the West Midlands engineering industry.

However, this was a very uneven form of union organization, and the success of workers in establishing collective organization depended on a combination of factors, including managerial strategies, occupational heterogeneity, available union resources and worker leverage. By the end of the war, as noted by Terry and Edwards (1988), union organization in the Midlands engineering industry was more developed than before the war, but was still marked by considerable unevenness and patchiness. The available evidence suggests that the crucial dimension for the development of unionism in the decade following the war was the presence of workplace activists, prepared to organize, often in clandestine ways, and often in the face of managerial hostility (Terry and Edwards, 1988; see also Terry 1988b). One consequence was a variation in the ways unions organized and operated, ranging from the forms of direct democracy characteristic of some of the craft unions to centralized forms of organization with limited membership involvement and participation. Towards the end of the 1960s and with the reforms of the early 1970s, associated with the formalization of industrial relations procedures and practices, there was evidence of a greater degree of uniformity of plant-based organization in manufacturing, around steward structures, and centralized convenor and steward authority (Terry and Edwards, 1988, p. 223). These, however, remained contested arrangements, partly depending on managerial strategies and initiatives, as well as the deepening crisis in the manufacturing sector in the region during the 1970s and into the 1980s.

At the same time, although public sector unionism, for example in local government, was beginning to expand and develop a more active form of union representation, in this period it was very much secondary to the political prominence and economic importance of the manufacturing sector. However, with economic and employment restructuring during the 1970s and 1980s, the balance between the public sector and manufacturing shifted. During this period, the public sector accounted for an increasing proportion of employment in the region and, in line with developments elsewhere, public sector unions have come to play an active and increasingly important role. The expansion of public sector unionism in the region was part of a more widespread pattern of development involving increased employment in the public sector in the 1960s and 1970s, followed by the extensive restructuring of the 1980s and 1990s.

What is unclear from these observations is whether public sector unionism in the West Midlands developed distinctive regional characteristics, as was the case in the manufacturing sector, or whether this was a relatively uniform form of unionism irrespective of region. Although the evidence is not available, it is reasonable to suppose that public sector unionism was marked by the socio-political relationships of the region and in this respect had a distinctive regional face. Although the boundaries vary, the organization and composition of public sector unions were grounded in the communities that made up the region. Members of public sector unions were by and large from and part of the community, by family connection and education. In these respects, this was a workforce that had a regional identity, by city or town if not by region. In addition, public sector union memberships were generally grouped by locality, in branches, and in a number of cases by area forms of organization. Such organization reinforced a sense of local identity, underwritten by the local inter-union structures, such as trades councils. It should also be noted that unionism in the area was dominated by the manufacturing sector, with the result that this was a template for unionism in the region, including in the public sector. However, it was also the case that the public sector unions were nationally organized and focused, thereby tempering the region-specific features of unionism. In some areas of public sector employment, it was the case that the middle-level and senior grades in the civil service as well as in the utilities were required to be job mobile as a condition for promotion. Thus, it is likely that while there was a local basis to union identity in the public sector, it was also the case that until the 1980s this was offset by the centralized forms of union organization in this sector and the mobility of some grades.

The other dimension of unionism in the region concerned the supra-union political organizations, whether in the form of the TUC or the local trades councils. The West Midlands TUC theoretically provided a focus for unions in the region. However, it was located in Birmingham and, since most of the office bearers also came from Birmingham, there was a tendency to affirm the regional union movement as a Birmingham-based movement. Further, individual union groups tended to reflect the political fragmentation of the region, and focus their activity on the cities or towns in which they were located. Further complications were added in 1990 when the TUC educational service, which initially covered the West Midlands with parallel arrangements in the East Midlands, was merged to cover the whole of the Midlands area. Despite the regional brief of the TUC, the consequence was that diverse local arrangements did not necessarily facilitate union cooperation and activity on a regional basis.

Attention must also be given to the trades councils, located in the main conurbations, which theoretically provided the basis for union unity and coordination. In 1996, the Birmingham Trades Council was one of two trades councils in Britain with a full-time officer, and could have provided the basis for concerted and developing organization in the area. The reality, however, was very different. These councils were voluntary bodies and relied on the willingness and individual commitment of individual trade unionists to sustain and carry these bodies. The overall pattern was very uneven, with many of the larger unions connecting with their trades councils in tenuous ways. Usually trade unions sent delegates who had an interest, often in terms of political affiliations to the Labour Party, and, in the past, the Communist Party or one of the smaller political groups that were active in the trade unions. The result was that these councils were prone to become forums for the politics of political illusion, with participation in council activity as a substitute for active involvement within unions. There was seldom any sustained and accountable relationship between the delegates to the trades councils and the union memberships, although delegates may have been diligent in providing written or verbal reports to the appropriate union committees. This was most clearly seen in Birmingham, where the council has long been dominated by a small left-wing and parochial clique, hostile to those who did not agree with its politics, and focused almost entirely on Birmingham as if it was the centre of the British trade union movement and working class. This combination of parochialism and the tenuousness of the links with union affiliates further weakened the potential effectiveness of these bodies.

West Midlands unions in a national context

The patterns of unionism in the West Midlands were part of a more general process of change within the country as a whole. The conclusion drawn by Martin and colleagues (1996) is that the West Midlands occupied a pivotal place within the national patterns of change and development in Britain. They saw the West Midlands as an area where the patterns of unionism lay between the increasingly thin and precarious unionism of the South and East and the more resilient unionism of the North and West. It is in these respects that it is possible to examine the West Midlands as a critical region in the context of the broader pattern of change in British unionism.

The place of unions in the West Midlands takes on a particular hue within the patterning of unionism in the country as a whole. It has long been the case that the focus and concentration of British unionism has been in the North and West, where unions were founded, in line with the organization and geography of industrial development in the nineteenth century. During the 1920s and 1930s the advent of mass production industries was associated with an expansion of unionism into the emergent labour industries in the South East and the Midlands. The result was a reduction in the regional differences in union membership and density, although the traditional areas retained an importance as enduring sites of trade unionism (Martin *et al.*, 1996, pp. 41–7).

The main period of expansion of unionism in the West Midlands, reflected in membership levels and density, took place in the early post-war period. While it has been argued that there was a more general dispersal of unionism across the country from the 1950s onwards, Martin and his colleagues (1996) caution against this as an adequate picture of unionism in Britain. They argue that while there was a spread of unionism to the Midlands and the South, union density remained high in the North and West. In other words, it is necessary to disaggregate the spread of unionism by membership patterns and form, region by region. The unionism in these areas was marked by distinctive patterns in managerial approaches and work patterns, as well as 'historically constructed and locally embedded socio-political traditions' (Martin *et al.*, 1996, p. 50).

The significance of these observations is that in the 1980s and 1990s, with the decline of unions, the regional distinctions between the North and West, on the one side, and the South and East, on the other, were reinforced with a sharper decline in the South and East. The only exception was the West Midlands, which stood out as a distinctive traditional union region. Here the collapse of union membership was disproportionately large when compared with other traditional union areas. There was a shift in bargaining from multi-employer bargaining to employer and, less so, plant bargaining, with a sharp decline in collective bargaining coverage, measured by union membership density and recognition. One implication is that the particular form of the restructuring that took place in the region, the socio-politics of the area, the patterning of unionism, resulted in a unionism that was more vulnerable to change than the more institutionally embedded forms of trade unionism in the North and West.

Summary

The West Midlands region is an area with a long tradition of unionism, in particular areas within the region. In this respect the region is one of the traditional sites of unionism in Britain. However, it is an area which has gone through major periods of economic and industrial restructuring, with a major impact on the form and the embeddedness of unionism in the region. It was a unionism that was clearly locked into the politics of the region, although the political base for union and labour politics was of more recent origin than elsewhere. The result was a vulnerable form of unionism, in particular in the metal manufacturing sector.

However, as with other areas of the country, the West Midlands was the site of an expanding and developing public sector. While this may not have been reflected in large numbers, when compared with manufacturing employment in the region, it was none the less an area of employment that expanded during the 1960s and 1970s. Moreover, in the 1980s, it was a site of political attention, as governments initiated policies of extensive restructuring and organization in this sector, including the privatization of utilities. In these respects, public sector unionism in the region faced particular sets of challenges. Yet these were not regionally specific initiatives, although the history of this unionism in the area, the socio-political embeddedness of this area of union representation and the community basis for public sector unionism influenced both the way unionism was defined and its place within the region.

Thus the West Midlands region was a trade union heartland that suffered a major retreat of engineering trade unionism during the 1970s and 1980s. The prevailing traditions of unionism gave way to a narrowing of the scope and structure of collective bargaining. It is in this context that the unions in the area sought to maintain a presence, reconsider their mode of organization and operation, and address the difficulties and uncertainties resulting from the ongoing restructuring of work and employment relations in the region. This restructuring during the 1980s and 1990s allows an appropriate contrast to be drawn with the 1980s boom in the South and the decline and reconstruction that has taken place in the North. It is thus a particularly appropriate region in which to examine the contours of unionism over the past decade.

PART II
MANUFACTURING

INTRODUCTION

In Britain, throughout the 1980s and into the 1990s, there was extensive change and reorganization in the private sector, setting the scene for an increasingly defensive form of trade unionism. In manufacturing, management took steps to decentralize budgetary control and devolve the management of the labour process to establishment level. Moves were taken to establish more flexible workforces through changes to numbers employed, forms of work organization and pay policies (Pollert, 1991). A feature of this process of change was the uneven and somewhat piecemeal changes in relations between workers and management, signified through increased managerial control of work organization, increased range of work tasks and an intensification of work (Elger, 1991).

This extensive restructuring of the manufacturing sector was starkly evident in the West Midlands. Here it involved plant contraction and closure, extensive job loss, reorganization of work and employment, the contracting-out of ancillary services and a changed bargaining agenda (Tailby and Whitson, 1989; Pollert, 1991). At a more general level, these developments were part of the economic crisis faced by the manufacturing sector, reinforced by government policies which had the effect of initiating a process of deindustrialization (Glyn, 1992; see also Coates, 1999). Commentators pointed to the increased internationalization of manufacturing, corporate restructuring, managerial strategies (including human resource management) and the recomposition of work organization (Crouch, 1993).

The internationalization of manufacture

Capitalist economies have developed over the past twenty years, particularly in relation to the globalization of the economy. The implication of this type of analysis is that productive units influence one another, and divisions at one site are affected by changes at others (Dicken, 1992). Such developments have prompted debates about the place of the state in these processes. One argument suggests that globalization involves the 'hollowing out' or reduction of state powers and structures. The argument, briefly, is that finance, production and markets have become pre-eminent and no longer confined by political space (Ohmae, 1990, 1995; Dicken, 1992). Deregulation and diminishing intervention by the state is part of the subordination of the state to transnationals. These organizations are increasingly setting the terms of political debate. This view leads into an argument that economic globalization has resulted in the emergence of supranational and transnational state structures. Some argue that this is likely to lead to the replacement of traditional nation states. The argument is that transnational political structures emerge to mediate and facilitate capital formations (Ohmae, 1990, 1995). Such views are challenged by accounts which continue to argue that the state plays a critical role in capitalist accumulation and regulation of capital, labour, trade and coordination (Hirst and Thompson, 1996).

The increased competitiveness and internationalization of production and trade was expressed in two ways in the manufacturing sector. First, there were moves by the medium and large manufacturing corporations to broaden their base of operations beyond the United Kingdom in substantive ways. Such developments were part of a broader set of developments involving the increased prominence of multinational manufacturers operating across national borders. Accompanying this process was the pattern of deindustrialization that occurred in the advanced capitalist societies, indicated by the declining proportion of employees located in manufacturing employment. Second, there was increased foreign ownership of manufacturing enterprises in the UK during this period. This penetration of the UK manufacturing sector involved US, Japanese, Korean and European firms, particularly German companies. In these various ways the terrain of manufacturing was recast.

The restructuring of the West Midlands manufacturing sector, identified in Chapter 3, was part of a much broader patterning of change in the politics of production in advanced capitalist states, from the mid-1960s onwards. At a general level the expansion that took place in the early post-war period, often associated with the maturation of Fordist modes of production (Piore and Sabel, 1984), faced increasingly contradictory politics in the accumulation of capital, with consequent implications for productivity and profit levels. It was within this broader context of capital development that manufacturing enterprises faced deepening problems in the 1980s.

There have been extensive debates about the collapse of Fordist modes of production and the hesitant shift to forms of flexible specialization (Hirst and Zeitlin, 1989). The argument is that the prevailing Fordist mode of production, based on mass production techniques and procedures, involving the production of standardized goods for mass consumption, was coming to an end and being replaced by more discriminating and differentiated goods, produced on a quality basis and by skilled workforces. However, this type of argument was conceptually undermined by accounts which focus on the UK manufacturing sector, in terms of the complex interplay between international forces (trade relations, international competitive structures, financial relationships) and domestic forces (government policies, the impact of trade unions, national financial pressures). Some commentators argued that the result was an economy characterized by 'low wages, low productivity, low skills and low investment' (Nolan and Walsh, 1995, p. 76; see also Tailby and Whitson, 1989, pp. 5–7).

Within the broad purview of such developments, the manufacturing sector has been extensively reorganized, as a consequence of competition between producers, combined with antagonism between labour and capital. The driving force of accumulation impels capital to find new ways to develop productive relations, imposed on industrial capital by the pressures of competition. This involves seeking out new markets, lengthening the working day, forcing down wages, intensifying labour and transforming methods of production. These may involve labour-saving machinery, Taylorist hierarchical control methods, increased division of labour, deskilling and fragmentation of tasks, and the separation of manual and intellectual labour.

Management and work relations

One aspect of the restructuring that has taken place in the manufacturing sector over the past decade and a half has been the articulation of managerial practices and approaches based on developing employee commitment and identification with company aims (Pollert, 1996). These initiatives have been part of a package of measures, ranging from a comprehensive reorganization of plants, with new layouts, distinctive work procedures and methods, usually within a human resource management (HRM) framework, to much less comprehensive and more hesitant proposals for change, often referring to HRM policies in little more than a rhetorical sense. In some cases, the restructuring that took place under the rubric of HRM was extensive and comprehensive; elsewhere it was much more hesitant and often had the appearance of an *ad hoc* set of policies, introduced over relatively long time scales, with references to HRM much less prominent (Elger and Fairbrother, 1991).

The restructuring of manufacturing corporations during this period raises important questions about the recomposition of work organization and work practices (Elger, 1990). One shift in manufacturing enterprises involved the increased qualification of the multidivisional firm. During the 1980s, there were moves in many enterprises, as part of the more general restructuring that was taking place, to externalize non-core activities. While there was an unevenness in the implementation of these policies, few medium and large manufacturing firms were untouched by the development (Pollert, 1991). As part of this development, managerial strategies increasingly emphasized the question of control, focusing on the workplace or the local business unit. Accompanying this, work routines and procedures were reorganized in a number of cases, sometimes dramatically with the introduction of cellular forms of working, while elsewhere changes were fairly limited, confined to stock control measures and a slow but cumulative introduction of flexible work practices. None the less, most enterprises have moved towards the introduction of more open communication systems, with team briefings and related measures.

At a workplace level, such reorganization was cast in terms of direct and immediate relations between local managements and their workforces. In many cases this resulted in forms of working based on notions about the individualization of the employment relation, such as multitasking, team working and consultation about work routines (Atkinson, 1985). While there was debate about the extent to which these developments evoked positive responses about the increased satisfaction that comes from variety and discretion over the organization of the working day, it was also the case that such initiatives raised questions relating to career progression, the recognition and preservation of skills and job security.

There is evidence that the shift of such responsibility to an establishment level is relatively widespread (Edwards, 1987). It has often been accompanied by establishment-level bargaining on pay and conditions, although it may also be the case that local managements were restricted in their authority insofar as pay limits were still likely to be set by decisions at a headquarters level. Increasingly, the larger manufacturing companies have begun to pursue policies to develop company-specific approaches to flexible work and employment relations, practices to secure worker endorsement of these changes and the decentralization of operations within enterprises, via business units and the like (Edwards, 1987, pp. 195–200). The trend towards localized and company-based bargaining was thus reinforced during the 1980s.

One aspect of these developments which has evoked comment is that for workers there is now a vulnerability in employment relations that organized and unorganized labour have found difficult to address (Elger and Smith, 1994). It is in this context that it can be argued that the introduction of managerial techniques, often associated with debates about international transplants and patterns of emulation, provides renewed opportunities for managerial control in new circumstances and with techniques modelled on practices elsewhere (Elger and Smith, 1998). Faced with such developments, commentary ranges from a celebration of the importance of globalization, on the one hand, to a focus on its invidious effect on workers and the uncertainty and unevenness of their response and resistance, on the other (Elger and Smith, 1994; Ohmae, 1995).

The impact of these developments for trade unionism has been widely debated, giving rise to arguments about union decline in the 1980s (Batstone and Gourlay, 1986; MacInnes, 1987; Gallie *et al.*, 1996). While there were two broad assessments, irreversible decline and continuity, it was certainly the case that unions in the manufacturing sector experienced considerable uncertainty and change, which became even more pressing in the 1990s (Ackers *et al.*, 1996). The predominant form of unionism in these enterprises had long been centralized and hierarchical, built around the shop steward form of representation (Terry, 1989; Millward *et al.*, 1992). In the past, these unions were often locked into district and industry structures, where wage levels were set and then implemented enterprise by enterprise, giving rise to locally based forms of unionism within broader organizational and representative structures. Such unions had built themselves on the basis of traditional forms of representation, based on the section (often defined in terms of skill) or the assumption that workers were employed at set tasks with regular contact with other workers.

The outcome was unions centred on male, manual and full-time workforces, which for a long time were able to represent their memberships relatively effectively, but which in the 1980s and 1990s faced a declining membership, usually employed on contracting worksites with more assertive managements. In these circumstances, such unions found themselves in vulnerable positions, with employers able to set the terms of the relationship with unions in ways that were unimaginable in the recent past. However, where work organization has been altered, involving team working and related practices, the impact on workplace unions is ambiguous. On the one hand, managements have initiated programmes of reorganization that attempt to win wider support for company ambitions and approaches. On the other hand, workers are still locked into alienating and exploitative work relations. In these circumstances unions continued to have a presence, paradoxically opened up by the tensions and unevenness of these managerial strategies and their implementation (Elger and Fairbrother, 1991; Pollert, 1996).

The study

Throughout the post-war period, manufacturing was central to the prosperity of the West Midlands, and it remains so. This sector underwent nearly two decades of reorganization and restructuring, with devastating effects on employment prospects in the region. The organization of the labour process is a crucial terrain of class struggle because the capitalist labour process consists of coercive social relations (Brighton Labour Process Group, 1977). The manufacturing labour process involves the cooperation of workers and the coordination of work; the collective character of the labour process organizes labour collectively. This is a political arrangement, since the central dynamic of the relations of production is exploitation and the generation of surplus value.

For those within the sector this has been a time of acute uncertainty and insecurity. As the restructuring of manufacturing has continued, so has unemployment as a persistent problem for the young and a prospect for others. As part of the almost continuous process of restructuring, the social relations of production in manufacturing enterprises were recast, with moves towards a form of managerialism based on 'social partnership' with local union leaders and increasingly individualized work and employment relations. The outcome was a diverse and uneven process of change, with the recomposition of management hierarchies and workers facing uncertainty and innovation.

To explore these issues, four manufacturing establishments are studied in detail. The first, based in a small town south of Coventry, produced auto components, and is labelled *Car Parts*. The second case was the main site for the production of telecommunications equipment, located in Coventry and designated *Telecommunications Factory*. The third case, based in Birmingham, was a branch plant producing electronic car parts and is designated *Electronics Factory*. The last establishment, also based in the small town south of Coventry, was responsible for the production of heating units and is referred to as *Heating Factory*.

4 ECONOMISTIC DEFENSIVENESS

In the period of relative prosperity of the West Midlands in the 1960s and into the 1970s, many factory union groups established themselves and achieved recognition, particularly outside the main conurbations of the region. These union groups developed models of unionism which imitated the prevailing forms of organization and representation in the main areas of employment in the region, such as automobiles and related areas of manufacture (Terry and Edwards, 1988). Central to these union developments was the promotion of steward-based representative structures and joint shop steward committees which addressed and occasionally transcended the multi-unionism in many of the factories in the region.

As noted, in practice there were variations in the ways these union groups organized and operated. While the formalization of industrial relations during the 1970s in the manufacturing sector resulted in an increased uniformity of organization, based on steward representative structures, it was also the case that the form of organization could range from relatively open and partici- pative to more centralized and leader dominated (Terry and Edwards, 1988; Hyman, 1989, pp. 149–87). The important point to note is that such variation is rooted in the complex relations between union organization, management policies and the patterns of work and employment relations of the member- ship.

In the context of restructuring, previous patterns of union organization and activity may be affirmed or threatened. One of the most common features of the restructuring of manufacturing corporations during the 1980s and 1990s was an ongoing recomposition of work organization and practices. Corporations implemented these policies in a range of ways, from the very comprehensive to the much more cosmetic. However, by and large, two developments took place in most of the medium and larger enterprises, involving the externalization of non-core activities and a reorganization of work routines and procedures

(Millward *et al.*, 1992). Alongside these developments, there were moves in many firms towards the introduction of localized and company-based bargaining. It is in relation to these occurrences that union factory groups sought to maintain their presence during the difficult period of manufacturing restructuring and reorganization that took place in the region.

The uncertainty experienced by unions in the light of these developments could result in contrasting responses and initiatives by workplace trade union groups. In some cases this resulted in a reinforcement and affirmation of the centralized and hierarchical forms of workplace unionism, built around the shop steward form of representation. Such unionism was associated with a conservative strategy of defensive unionism, based on developed forms of sectional representation. In other cases, local leaderships attempted to develop responses which stressed the importance of promoting more broadly based patterns of representation and the extension of the scope of workplace unionism. These two sides of unionism were evident in a large engineering factory, designated *Car Parts*, where the main shopfloor union leadership pursued policies of defensive economism and the staff union a more participative, although vulnerable, form of unionism.

The factory and the unions

Car Parts factory was engaged in the production of car components, brakes, clutches and related electrical car goods. The factory had been acquired in 1986 by a British-based multinational with subsidiaries in Europe and elsewhere. In practice, the factory was organized and operated as an independent unit, responsible for its own finances. It was located in a relatively small town, of nearly 60,000 persons, a short distance south of Coventry. The factory was a large and prominent employer, the largest manufacturing plant in the town.

In 1986 the factory workforce comprised just over 4,000 shopfloor workers and over 900 staff. With acquisition of the factory by a new parent company in that year, the new owners began a process of reorganization which reduced the workforce by nearly half in the following five years. This reduction of staff created a climate of uncertainty about the future, as the decline in shopfloor and staff numbers took place via voluntary redundancies and natural wastage. These developments prompted expressions of concern about the future of the factory among its workforce and the town's political leaders. By the period 1991 to 1993, there were on average 2,300 shopfloor workers and 600 staff.

The majority of the workforce were male, with women employed in support and ancillary occupations, such as clerical work, canteen work and light assembly, although these demarcations were qualified during the 1980s and into the 1990s. In the past, a relatively large number of women had been employed on the shopfloor, nearly 800 in the 1970s and early 1980s, but this had declined to 150 in 1991. While there was no clear reason for this reduction, the convenor of the shopfloor unions attributed it to the impact of equal pay legislation in the 1970s, although this seemed like wishful thinking on his part. The factory was both gendered and sexist, with frequent crude sexist comments in informal conversation among the male workers.

At *Car Parts* factory, 15 per cent of the workforce were of either Afro-Caribbean or Asian ancestry. There was a relatively long-standing pattern of job segregation along ethnic lines at the factory, with the workers of Afro-Caribbean and Asian ancestry working in the labouring, unskilled and skilled jobs in disproportionate numbers. While most of the more obvious practices associated with racial discrimination, on the part of the company as well as among the workforce, had ended, racist comments by the workforce were common and there was some evidence of persistent institutionalized discrimination at the factory.

Four unions were recognized at the factory, the AEU and the EETPU for the shopfloor and MSF and ACTSS for the staff. The AEU was the dominant union on the shopfloor, with over 95 per cent of the union membership, and the EETPU had no negotiating rights with the AEU representing this membership. In effect, the shopfloor union was the AEU, and was led by a convenor who retired in 1994, having held the position for twenty-four years. MSF was the dominant union among the staff, with 260 members, and ACTSS was relatively small, with under 100 members among the clerical and administrative workers. The convenor of MSF also convened the joint staff committee and had held office for over fifteen years in 1993, when he also retired. These, then, were well established union groupings with long-standing leaderships.

The two unions organized and operated in very different ways. The AEU was a centralized and leader-dominated union. The convenor was the main union leader in the factory, as convenor of the joint shop steward committee, comprising nearly ninety AEU stewards and one EEPTU steward. Altogether, he represented 2,330 union members in 1991, which had fallen slightly to around 2,100 by 1993. As indicated, the AEU was a centralized union organization, which pursued a conservative, largely economistic, agenda of union policies. In contrast, the MSF membership was much smaller, covering a little over 220 members in 1991, although with the transfer of the ACTSS membership of 160 to MSF in 1992 there was an increase in the overall membership of the union. MSF was a more openly organized union than the AEU, relying on a participative representative structure, with the result that while the senior steward was the lead representative for MSF, he was accountable and respons-ive to the area representatives and the membership more generally. The result was two very different forms and styles of unionism in the factory.

Restructuring and reorganization

During the 1980s and into the 1990s, production relations at the factory were recast. A key development occurred in 1986 when the company senior man-agement announced changes to production and related managerial structures. The managerial aim was to 'rationalize' production, creating a slimmed down, multi-skilled workforce. However, this was a relatively slow process and was accompanied by considerable scepticism and worry among the workforce in the late 1980s about the prospects for the future at the factory. In effect, the workforce faced persistent rumours about redundancies, work and employment reorganization, and investment to modernize and update the technology of the factory, with associated implications for the remaining workforce. This was a period when there was talk of creating a flexible workforce and a more responsive and person-focused management under the rubric of human resource management.

The management hierarchy at the factory was organized in a conventional multi-level way, and included plant management, production managers, superintendents and first-line supervisors. 'Foremen', as first-line supervision, were usually promoted from the shopfloor and, while they received some training, which in the 1990s emphasized team building and human resource management, their approach to supervision often had more in common with Victorian school teachers than with modern theories of management. For most shopfloor workers, management began and ended with the 'foremen'. Like 'foremen', superintendents approached their jobs in varied ways, some attempting to develop cooperative relations with their workforces, while others seemingly preferred more authoritarian approaches.

The shopfloor workers at the factory covered the full range of manual engineering work, and were graded as skilled (toolmakers), semi-skilled (piece-rate workers) and others (material handlers). A semi-skilled grade had also been created, covering day workers, maintenance engineers, builders and electricians. All these workers were organized in sections based on functional clusters of work activity, with each section working to a first-line supervisor and including a range of skills. The pay scales were worked out in relation to the piece-work rates, which covered the bulk of workers at the factory.

These patterns of relations had been operative at the factory from the 1950s to the end of the 1980s. The most significant development in the late 1980s was that the corporate and factory management began to divisionalize the factory production areas along functional lines. The aim appeared to be to lay the foundations for the eventual fragmentation and hiving-off of areas of production activity, under relatively independent managerial structures. In this process, areas of cognate activity were brought together in the same geographical areas and the management structures recomposed to reflect the newly integrated production areas. These newly established divisions, four in all, were organized as profit centres, and managements were given the responsibility to organize on this basis. This development was also accompanied by a delayering of the formerly multi-layered managerial structures, and there was a decentralization of managerial responsibility for production and the associated workforce in each area.

These broad changes were accompanied by a twin strategy of reducing the workforce in each division and developing a more multi-skilled and productive workforce. From 1986 to the early 1990s there were substantial reductions in the numbers employed as manufacturing operatives, clerical workers, engineering staff and general administrators. These reductions were achieved by voluntary redundancies and natural wastage. At the same time, a programme was instituted, aimed at creating a multi-skilled workforce, blurring the demarcations between direct and indirect workers. Even so, sections of the workforce remained largely outside this process of change, particularly the toolroom workers, who remained politically dominant within the main shopfloor union, and were thus able to protect themselves from the full force of the restructuring that was taking place.

In 1992, a four-year programme was introduced to establish cell-working across most of the production areas. This initiative was associated with the introduction of new technological processes and procedures, and dedicated and specialized training of sections of the workforce. During the 1990s, the production procedures in the factory were more fully automated, reducing the reliance on skilled craft workers that had long characterized production at the factory. As part of these developments, there was some reduction in the numbers employed in these areas of activity. There was a new managerial emphasis and reference to forms of total quality management (TQM), reflected in team briefings, the introduction of computerized managerial systems and stock control and a more visible and seemingly responsive management. In addition, uniform rates of pay were negotiated for these production areas, and a process of harmonizing conditions between staff and shopfloor workers began. This latter development was extended to all employees in 1993, ending the varied arrangements for sick pay and hours worked.

Overall, this was a factory that had undergone a comprehensive reorganization and recomposition of management hierarchies and associated production, and production-related, activities and arrangements. In the main, these developments were focused on the shopfloor workforce, although staff workers were also involved in the reorganizations that took place. The factory workforce was reduced by nearly a half over a five-year period. What was remarkable about these changes was that while they evoked concern and worry among the workforce, the main shopfloor union leaders cooperated with the management in achieving an ordered and orderly reduction of the workforce.

Organization and representation

The two main unions at the factory, the AEU and MSF, exemplified a stark contrast between centralized and participative forms of organization and representation. On the one hand, as noted, the AEU was a highly centralized union organization, under the sway of an influential and dominant convenor. This was a form of organization that was reflected in the successive layers of representation within the union, from the section representative to the factory-wide union structures (Hyman, 1989, pp. 147–65). On the other hand, MSF was a small staff union organized in a relatively open and participatory way. While it also was a union group that was led by an experienced and influential senior representative, within both the factory and the wider union (as a member of the union's national executive committee), there was a positive transparency in the relations between representatives and the members in this union that was absent in the AEU. This contrast between the two union groups made for difficult relations between them that went beyond the obvious class differences between the union memberships.

As indicated, the main union, the AEU, was organized under the auspices of a shop steward committee, composed of ninety stewards from various sections and shifts in the factory. Stewards represented constituencies that were defined by area of work as well as shift arrangements and agreed annually by the convenor and management representatives. Where there were fewer than thirty members in an area, one steward representative was agreed, and if there were more than thirty members, two stewards. A central stewards' committee, consisting of the convenor, chairperson, secretary and four senior stewards, was responsible for factory-wide negotiations and overseeing individual steward activity. This committee was exclusively male, although it was ethnically mixed, with workers of Asian ancestry often elected as stewards. There was, however, an informal barrier to election to senior leadership positions, with the central committee composed of white males.

At this factory, the sections elected their stewards on an annual basis. In turn, the senior leadership of seven, including the convenor, chairperson and secretary, was elected from and by the steward committee every two years, although this was an annual election until 1990. The election procedure allowed for the persistent dominance of a small clique of leaders. As the steward role was confined to sectional and often individualized forms of representation, it was very difficult for stewards to gain a broader perspective on union affairs, let alone organize as a group to challenge an incumbent leadership. Indeed, the senior leadership had developed the practice of publicly belittling dissenters, critical stewards and members of oppositional political groups. This made it very difficult for such individuals to develop any type of base within the steward committee. It also made it unlikely that any disgruntled senior stewards would lead a challenge to the convenor. Of equal note, there was some evidence to suggest that it was possible that management connived in neutralizing any such opponents to these stable arrangements.

The result was a centralized union organization, operating relatively independently of the wider union, with union activity focused on the convenor and central stewards. They played a decisive part in determining issues and in making agreements with management. The convenor saw himself as central to the continued presence of the union in the factory, and he took a 'hands-on' approach in all negotiations and representations to management. It was noted:

> The convenor reiterated his view that he was central to the union and negotiating structures. He worked with the central stewards and together they formed a cohesive group. The stewards more generally had the role of raising issues in the first instance, but all difficulties and grievances that go through procedure are handled personally by the convenor. This clearly makes him seem indispensable to the union and current arrangements. (Field notes, 1991)

Among the senior steward group there was an affirmation of these arrangements, especially in 1992 and 1993, when rumours began to circulate that sections of the corporate management were of the view that they would be well rid of the union.

The prominence of the convenor within the union membership in the factory was further reinforced by his activity within the union district and regional structures. He was a member of the district committee of the union, which in turn, because of his presence, had become an obstacle to complaints about the character of union organization within the factory; in fact, there was a benign acceptance on the committee that the convenor 'ran' the union in the factory. At the same time, while other senior stewards occasionally indicated concern about the dominance of the convenor, they clearly did not feel able to mount an effective challenge to long-established routines. As a result, these centralized practices were maintained, despite some unease and complaint.

The staff unions organized and operated in a very different way. As with the AEU, MSF had a high union density, 95 per cent of the eligible workforce. The form of representation in the union was one that combined grade and function, with twelve area representatives elected annually by the area membership. The chair and secretary of the union membership were both elected annually by the whole membership at the annual general meeting. The majority of the membership (approximately 180) were male, although the proportion of women employed in MSF areas was increasing, reflecting the changes taking place in the factory as it repositioned itself to compete within both domestic and international markets. In 1991, the MSF membership was still represented in two sections, reflecting the constituent unions that made up MSF, although the senior steward for ASTMS effectively acted as the senior steward for both sections of the membership.

In stark contrast with the AEU, MSF organized and operated in a markedly participatory way. The area representatives played an active part in taking up issues on behalf of their memberships, drawing the senior leadership into negotiations and other activity only when they made no headway or managers were presumptive in their dismissal of the claim being made. These representatives were encouraged to attend union training courses in the area, and together with the senior leadership developed an outward-looking union consciousness. The result was that the area representatives worked closely with their constituent members, developing an active and involved type of unionism.

None the less, it is important to note that there were severe constraints on the degree to which this form of unionism actually prevailed in the factory. Compared with the AEU, MSF was a small union, with few representatives. One consequence was that the factory management paid little attention to MSF and other staff unions, reinforced by the fact that the personnel manager was a former AEU central steward and the camaraderie among these stewards at the time, in the early 1980s, continued on into the 1990s. The mode and form of staff work, as part of a hierarchical engineering labour process, also affirmed individualistic outlooks among the staff, which the union leadership attempted to counteract, especially as job insecurity and uncertainty became more evident. On occasion, this meant that the MSF members rejected the attempts by their leaders to promote collective responses to the changes taking place in the factory.

Industrial relations at the factory

Industrial relations at the factory were organized around piece-work bargaining within the departments. This was complemented by centralized pay negotiations and employment policies, involving the central leaderships of the union groups at the factory and the personnel department. While there were no regular structures for negotiations at the factory, there was provision for joint staff bargaining conferences and works conferences, on an *ad hoc* basis, 'when necessary', although a routine had developed around the annual wage round.

The stability of the union groupings at the factory was reflected in a routinization of negotiations and bargaining. For almost twenty years, the core focus of shopfloor union negotiations had been on the extensive piece-work negotiations, which took place section by section. These localized negotiations involved workplace stewards and their managerial counterparts. While they could occasionally be very divisive and sometimes involved more than one section, they were part of the routine of industrial relations at the factory. Such bargaining was complemented by centralized negotiations on health and safety, pensions policies, restructuring and reorganization of production relations and long-term corporate policy. In these various activities, there was little cooperation between shopfloor and staff unions, apart from pensions policy, where they worked closely together.

For much of the recent history of the factory, negotiations, terms and conditions of employment and production organization were centrally organized. The lead in factory-wide negotiations was taken by members of the personnel department, composed of a personnel manager and industrial relations officer, a training officer and support staff. The personnel manager and industrial relations officer worked closely with the senior union officers on site, and particularly the long-standing AEU convenor. Their stated preference was to work within an established and formalized framework of relations, in cooperation with the central leaderships of each union. These were relationships that had been 'sanctified' by time, since there was a familiarity between these lead personnel, based on not only their length of time in office but also the practice of internal recruitment to the personnel department.

There was a sense in which negotiating arrangements at the factory were predicated on a clear distinction and mutual recognition of the spheres of responsibility between management and the manual union. While management representatives spoke of mutual respect between the senior shopfloor union leadership and members of the personnel department, noting the long-standing arrangements and 'friendship' between the two, the shopfloor convenor identified the secondary and subordinate place of the unions at the factory:

> The convenor seemed to hold the view that there was a clear area of management responsibility and that it was not for the unions to query this. Management could decide a redundancy and it was up to the unions to negotiate the best deal. To query the proposal or the stated reasons for the redundancy would take them into areas that were not really the responsibility of the union. This was clearly illustrated when he spoke of the [company] practice of acquiring factories, slimming down staff levels and then selling off property this released. This was not something for the union to challenge, although they may not be happy about it. (Field notes, 1991)

These views were expressed in the context of the relatively stable and routinized relations between the shopfloor union leadership and the personnel department.

In the 1990s these long-established relationships were potentially threatened, as the corporation authorized and encouraged the divisionalization of the factory's production areas. This move towards 'self-sufficiency' of production and the associated managerial and work organization procedures created the conditions for a break-up of the uniform terms and conditions of employment at the factory. This prospect was noted by the MSF senior representative in the following terms:

> The divisionalisation of the site into various companies, the clutch company, the brake company, and bringing in top managers who only look at that company, and . . . massive decentralisation, so that each of these are stand alone companies, even to the point that the wages system is now looked at being decentralised. That has now created pressures where certainly one of the managers who has been brought in from outside sees the Personnel [Department] as a problem and wants . . . freedom [from it]. (Senior representative, 1991)

However, while this was part of the climate of industrial relations during this period, the personnel department remained a centrally organized and located department within the managerial structure and pay negotiations. Apart from a brief period in 1992, it retained a factory-wide remit and coverage at least until the mid-1990s, and any devolution of bargaining arrangements centred on giving first-line supervisors increased responsibility to deal with individual grievances. None the less, there was speculation in the 1990s among the union leaderships that this arrangement would be increasingly difficult to maintain, and this eventually encouraged a rather robust defence of the personnel department by the two sets of union leaderships at the factory.

Centralized economistic bargaining

The two main unions approached negotiations and bargaining in different ways, the AEU leaders affirming their commitment to centralized and relatively unaccountable representation, and the MSF leaders seeking to maintain their commitment to more open forms of representation, often developing a non-sectional factory-wide perspective on corporate policy. The difficulty for the MSF leadership was that changes in the management approach to bargaining during the 1990s, as well as an increase in the proportion of women members in the union, who had yet to identify consciously with the union or develop the confidence to act as unionists, meant that it was increasingly difficult for leaders to rely on past arrangements and policies.

The AEU

The senior stewards of the AEU had long had a commitment to centralized bargaining and representation. It was common for the senior stewards to decide policy without explicit or direct reference to the section stewards or the membership in general. The basis of this approach was the way in which the convenor and senior stewards constituted a cohesive and 'expert' group, skilled in representing and speaking on behalf of the membership. By the early 1990s, all had been in position for at least five years and, in the face of considerable turnover among the section stewards (at least 20 per cent during the 1980s), these leaders were able to ensure their continued prominence within the union.

The senior steward group presented themselves to the steward body as responsible and experienced leaders who could be relied upon to take decisions on behalf of the membership as a whole. This approach was illustrated by the annual wage claims, where it was usual for the senior stewards, and particularly the convenor, to exclude the section stewards and members from the formulation and pursuit of the wage claim. On one occasion, the stewards were simply asked to agree the claim at one of the fortnightly meetings, without any consultation or discussion with members. In the words of the stewards, 'the central stewards said they wanted to "get the ball rolling". There was no time for consultation' (Field notes, 1989). This non-involvement was compounded by the convenor's decision that no questions from the membership would be allowed at the members' meeting to consider the company offer. When queried, the convenor was reported to have said, 'It is impractical to have questions because there is always the possibility that all members present will have queries about the offer which would mean that the meeting would never end' (Field notes, 1989). Subsequently, the convenor presented the offer and asked for a decision without debate. One of the reasons for this was that some of the stewards were opposed to the offer, which did not recognize the relative disadvantage of the majority of workers in the factory, the piece-work workers. Given the restrictions on discussion by the stewards and members, there was no way to raise some of the disadvantages of the company offer without challenging the convenor and the central stewards. In the event, twenty-six stewards voted against acceptance, all from the group adversely affected by the offer (Field notes, 1989). For the stewards, these arrangements and the attitude of the convenor meant that they tended to confine their activity to their own section. As one said, 'You do your own thing on your section.' If the stewards tried to raise issues with the convenor, 'you end up banging your head against a wall' (Field notes, 1989).

While the stewards had a role in raising issues in the first instance, their activity was largely restricted to this level. The convenor and, to a lesser extent, other senior stewards tended to take up all cases when they moved into procedural stages beyond the section or where the case had implications that went beyond the section. This was resented by the stewards, who frequently complained that issues were not handled fairly and fully. They complained, for example, that they were expected to brief the convenor on the way to negotiations with management, rather than in a considered manner well before negotiations. Although the convenor had a reputation among the stewards as an effective negotiator, this seeming lack of attention to detail confirmed the centralized and remote nature of union leadership at the factory.

Taking up individual grievances and problems on behalf of members had over the years become the touchstone of steward activity for the stewards at *Car Parts*. On one occasion a steward went to represent a 'lad' who had been caught using someone else's stamp, although he had been told that this was a sackable offence. During the hearing the 'foreman', in the steward's words, 'ranted'. Initially, the worker was given three days' suspension and a final warning, but when the steward appealed it was reduced to a half-day suspension and a final warning. When the steward returned to the shopfloor the 'foreman' kept on at him about the case, suggesting that he should have kept out of it. The steward went and saw the 'foreman's' own steward and told him to tell the 'foreman' to 'leave these matters in personnel and not to bring them on to the shopfloor' (Field notes, 1989). At no point in this incident did the steward receive advice or support from the central stewards; nor did he feel under any obligation to report the incident. These stewards tended to operate on their own, often without reference to other stewards or the convenor and the central stewards. The convenor and the central stewards acted to discourage reference to them by the stewards and often acted in a semi-secret way, attempting to settle disputes directly with management, without involving the stewards.

Even where a union committee is based on one union, there are features of work and employment relations that could constitute the basis for division within the union and thus a challenge to the entrenched leadership. For example, at *Car Parts* there was some evidence to suggest that there was a major division between unskilled and skilled workers, with the union leadership dominated by skilled workers. This was reflected in ongoing disquiet about the way wage settlements were structured to disadvantage a particular grade of unskilled worker, the majority in the plant. The difficulty was that there was little opportunity to focus this discontent, except once a year at the time of the settlement.

Thus, the AEU in this factory organized in a highly centralized way, with the stewards maintaining a tradition of sectional activism, but the central leadership became increasingly removed from the day-to-day experience of the membership. In 1992, the consequences of this approach became apparent when the company adopted a more aggressive approach to pay bargaining and presented the union with a limited pay offer of 4 per cent for the first year and the inflation level for the second year. The AEU negotiators organized a ballot on strike action to seek an improved offer, but only 9 per cent of the members voting were in favour of strike action, and consequently the AEU negotiators settled on the company's terms.

MSF

During the 1990s, the MSF union pursued a defensive policy of maintaining its organizational integrity. There were two aspects to this approach. First, the leadership defended the continued presence of the personnel department as the management group responsible for company-wide negotiations at the factory. As the senior representative commented:

> We have found ourselves in a position where as unions . . . it has been in our best interest to defend the Personnel Department . . . [despite spending] all our time at loggerheads . . . because of divisionalisation, and the stresses and strains that they wanted to wrest these powers away and . . . have three separate negotiations on this site. The opportunity of leap-frogging would exist but all other opportunities for the management would also exist. (Field notes, 1991)

The MSF leadership continued to advocate single-site negotiations and bargaining arrangements. In elaborating this policy the union leadership rejected managerial reforms that might jeopardize the organizational basis of the union as a factory-wide one.

The second aspect to the leadership position in this period was to take a leading role in addressing items that involved the whole workforce, staff and shopfloor. In this respect, the union took steps to utilize the facility offered by the joint staff committee, attended by MSF as the largest union and ACTSS (until 1992). MSF was the lead union on this committee, and sought to use it to address company-wide issues. The clearest example of this approach was that the MSF senior negotiator played a leading role in the campaign to develop union pensions policies on site and via the combine committee, covering this factory and two others. This was a notable development at the beginning of the 1990s, when employees were being encouraged to switch to private pension arrangements.

During the first half of the 1990s, the major preoccupation of the membership was job security, as the company introduced a series of small but significant voluntary redundancy schemes. In a sense, the company management was still bound by a defeat in 1981, when it proposed a compulsory redundancy package and, after a ten-day strike involving the then ASTMS membership, withdrew this proposal. However, with increasing uncertainty among the membership, evidenced by a reluctance by members to act as area representatives, the senior union leadership increasingly pursued a defensive policy of maintaining the union organization intact, rather than confronting the management via collective action. Such a policy placed a premium on the senior leadership in negotiations and bargaining forums.

The difficulties faced by the membership in maintaining the union presence in the factory were compounded by a management move to by-pass the union in its relations with the staff workforce. As part of an increased effort to establish direct communication with the workforce, the management introduced six-month 'state of the nation' briefings. These briefings were used by management to reinforce corporate policy; in turn, MSF, in particular, used the occasion as an opportunity to affirm the union approach of addressing issues on a site-wide basis:

> We have got all the top managers lined up before us and that is very good propaganda ground to . . . defend the situation and make them understand that if something happens in the clutch division then the bloke in brakes had better understand that it could affect him. We are site organised, we are site negotiating and nothing is going to happen at a lower common denominator than that. (Senior representative, 1991)

However, there was a sting in this tale, for the senior union leaders. The difficulty they faced with the 'state of the nation' briefings was that MSF members (and others) began to rely on the information and announcements presented by management and came to assume that there were no 'alternatives' to the policies which were previewed at these briefings. For this reason too, it became increasingly important for the MSF leadership to research prospective developments by the company and to present a vocal and informed presence at these meetings, as representatives of the unions on site.

In the early 1990s the company began an attempt to marginalize MSF and work directly with AEU, although this approach was challenged by MSF in 1992. The year began with a set of proposals by the company management to down-size the workforce and to fragment the production operations across two new overarching separate divisions on the one site, with one division physically located in a new dedicated area. Specifically, this involved a set of management initiatives to freeze pay, move staff across the site without protection of pay levels and implement a limited compulsory redundancy package. In response to these proposals, the MSF members were more assertive than their counterparts on the shopfloor, and despite AEU reluctance, managed to achieve single table bargaining in the new site division. This followed a more solidaristic and active opposition to company proposals than had been evident for some time, including effective bargaining between the unions and with management by the lead MSF negotiators. As part of this development, the personnel department lost its pre-eminence for a brief moment as the joint AEU–MSF negotiating team dealt directly with the site line management, thereby breaking with the tradition of informal relations that had previously underpinned the pre-eminence of the AEU.

Further changes took place in 1993, complicating the pattern of relations between the MSF and management. After the opening of the new division, the management began to act in relatively arbitrary ways, without any reference to established agreements and procedures. In view of this development, confirming earlier assessments by the MSF leadership, the union leaders turned back to the personnel department, forging an alliance to re-establish a degree of uniformity of procedure across the two divisions. This switch back, however, did not diminish activity by the MSF leadership, who continued to represent their members in a relatively active way, taking up issues of direct concern to the increasing proportion of women members in the union (30 per cent overall but 50 per cent in the commercial support area), a proportion that was reflected in the leadership of the union, with four of the twelve representatives women (two more than the previous year). The difficulty for the union as a whole was that developing the involvement of newly recruited members was a slow process, and often fraught with uncertainty and tentativeness.

Assessment

Over a long period of time, building on the traditions of unionism which characterized unions in the manufacturing sector in the West Midlands, the AEU had established itself as the largest and the pre-eminent union in the factory (Terry and Edwards, 1988). The composition of the shopfloor union membership was largely male and white. In the case of women, their interests and concerns were subordinated in the context of sectionally focused concerns defined in terms of the dominant male ethos. The highly centralized male leadership in the AEU effectively defined the union agenda for all members, and women were not part of this agenda. In contrast, members from minority ethnic groups played an active part in the main union, as members and as representatives. However, such involvement did not mean that racist practices were non-existent, and there was evidence of informal discrimination and racist comment among the workforce, which flowed over into the steward committee from time to time.

In the face of the dominance of the AEU, the small and much less prominent MSF attempted to develop an alternative form of unionism, where the emphasis was on participation and involvement. Admittedly, this was made much easier by the numbers involved, but they also faced a relatively authoritarian management and, unlike the AEU, attempted to create a space where their interests were recognized. The success of this approach became evident in the 1990s, when the union committee was recomposed with more women members and the concerns faced by the growing female membership in the union began to be articulated and pursued. In this respect, MSF continued to pursue its distinctive approach in the factory.

Overall, the pattern of unionism at *Car Parts* was one of defensive economism. There was a long history of cooperative relations between the senior union leaders and personnel. In this factory, the management was concerned to maintain the long-standing bargaining relationships in the plant. Management had taken steps to decentralize budgetary control and devolve the management of the labour process to establishment level. Moves had been made to establish more flexible workforces through changes to numbers employed and to forms of work organization, as well as pay policies. What is noteworthy is that many of these changes were achieved via collective bargaining. This ranged from the physical reconstruction of workplaces, accompanied by moves to reorganize work procedures and related arrangements, to more mundane and incremental change. In the face of change and uncertainty the unions, particularly the major union, the AEU, reaffirmed a centralized form of factory leadership, based on a steward form of representation. In this way, the leaders were able to establish a cooperative relationship with management, where the routine of membership representation was maintained throughout the 1980s and 1990s.

There were two important features to this process, which underwrote the defensive strategy. The first was that the convenor and his immediate allies maintained a parochial form of unionism, focused on the factory and involving limited connection with other steward committees in the same company at other sites. While the leaders attended the combine committee meetings, their role was to affirm the pre-eminence of a form of unionism that was based on each factory as a relatively discrete and isolated unit. Accompanying this approach, the *Car Parts* leadership maintained 'good' relations with the district officials, who in turn 'left the leadership alone'. The officials came into the factory when required, but there was no evidence of any more active presence and engagement with the local leadership. The second aspect to this form of unionism was the relationship between the central leaders and the personnel department. As indicated, the personnel department was staffed by former shopfloor stewards and a cooperative if not cosy relationship had been constructed between the union and the department. As a result, there was an open door policy for the central leadership, and particularly the long-serving convenor. The union was briefed on company policy and the facilities were there for the union leadership to have an input into the implementation of policy, although not the formulation.

The outcome was a 'corrosive' form of unionism, in that the union representational structure was a facade. The central leadership led from the front, with very little active involvement in policy formulation by the section stewards. From time to time this exclusion resulted in rebellion from groups of stewards, although they were never able to challenge the continued dominance of the central leadership of the union in an effective and ongoing way. The politics of the leadership was moderate Labour and there was an emphasis on the desirability of this type of politics in the context of restructuring. Dissident stewards were occasionally cast as 'troublemakers' or 'Trots', and in this way isolated from the broad body of stewards in the factory. It was a centralized union structure, which remained in place for over twenty years.

A consequence of this pattern of unionism was that the union leadership was relatively effective in ensuring a gradual pattern of reorganization as well as a reduction of the workforce. In addition, the union leadership remained active in defending members at a section level, maintaining the base of active unionism in the factory. While this form of unionism did not allow for any serious engagement with managerial control and initiative at a factory level, since the leadership was relatively compliant, it did permit a continued defence of job controls at a section level (Belanger and Evans, 1988). The result was that this was a form of union representation which ensured the survival of the union on the basis of a defensive form of representation. However, there was no attempt to build or reorient the union in any way. Instead, the union continued to organize and operate as a parochial and defensive body in a factory where the management accepted this form of unionism as the most appropriate way to maintain control.

In contrast, the staff union attempted to build and reorient its approach to union representation in imaginative ways. At a general level, the union faced a difficulty in mapping out a distinctive form of unionism in two ways. First, the AEU set the terms for union organization and representation in the plant, because of its dominance and the close relationship that had been established with the staff in the personnel department. As a small union, comprised of supervisory staff as well as technical workers, MSF was seen as fairly marginal by the personnel staff. In addition, the AEU leadership made much of the division of labour within the plant, casting the supervisory staff as 'management' and thus not to be trusted as trade unionists. Second, the MSF leaders, and particularly the convenor, were often pushed into a position by both the AEU and the personnel department where they were defined as the union and thus were not dealt with as representatives of a broader collective organization. The personnel department encouraged senior union meetings and working parties to deal with issues and problems and in this respect the MSF leaders were often encouraged to participate as relatively independent representatives rather than delegates of their membership. The organization and approach by the AEU simply affirmed this form of representation in the factory.

The bargaining and representational relationships were rooted in sectional forms of work and employment organization. This sectionalism allowed the possibility of union survival while reinforcing divisions within and between unions. This took a number of different forms depending on the lines of division and distinction, as well as the consciousness and forms of group identity associated with sectionally based and organized memberships (see Kelly, 1988, pp. 145–6). There were divisions between the functionally organized sections of the AEU as well as between the senior leaders and the section stewards. In addition, there were divisions between the two unions, based in the division of labour in the plant, and the way this was experienced in forms of work organization and supervision. These fragmented relations were further developed in the context of industrial relations practices and procedures and managerial organization and approaches. It was in these respects that the survival of the unions in this plant rested on a competitive sectionalism (where members were functionally divided, represented by stewards who restricted their concerns to their section or workgroup). This form of representation constituted the organizational basis for a centralized form of union leadership, which was the predominant form of unionism in this factory.

5 BARGAINED ACCOMMODATION AND A CHARADE

In the arguments and debates about trade unionism, authors have pointed to the distinctiveness of non-manual unionism. While union organization of non-manual workers has a relatively long history, it was not until the 1950s and 1960s that trade union membership among these sections of the workforce increased in notable ways (Bain, 1970). Clearly, these developments reflected the changing composition of the workforce as well as an increased willingness by non-manual workers not only to join trade unions but to engage in active forms of trade unionism, especially notable in the public sector (Fairbrother, 1989a). In addition, during the 1980s, unions representing non-manual workers, including an increasing proportion of women workers, developed a higher profile, within both unions and the TUC, as well as more generally (Taylor, 1995, pp. 56–87).

Non-manual workers in the manufacturing sector faced difficulties in establishing themselves as trade unionists. These workers were often located in compromising positions as supervisory staff, as well as numerically less significant than the manual workforce. Commentators have argued that the class position of non-manual workers, particularly in manufacturing, is such that they occupy ambiguous or contradictory class positions (Hyman and Price, 1983, pp. 98–144; Carter, 1995). One of the difficulties was that there were internal separations within manufacturing plants, often with limited links between shopfloor unions and staff unions. Complications in work procedures and the different work situations of staff workers, technical and supervisory, and their associated identities, reinforced the class differences between staff and shopfloor workers in manufacturing (Smith, 1987, pp. 193–226).

In Chapter 4 the situation described was one where the non-manual union was very much in the minority. In the current chapter the focus is on a factory where the majority union was a non-manual one (MSF), and where both manual and non-manual unions faced a comprehensive and extensive reduction in the workforce over a short time period, creating a situation of acute vulnerability for trade union memberships. In these circumstances, there was no pressing imperative on the part of management to challenge union leaderships explicitly, but a process of attrition was allowed to take place, thereby demobilizing and marginalizing the unions in practice. There was a shift in bargaining strength towards management, which meant that the company was in a position to pursue formalized and routine negotiations at the cost of a continued and effective union presence.

The organizational problems for unions in a situation of attrition are acute, especially if the impact of job loss is on those areas where the union has been well represented. For leaders the problems develop a circular aspect as they face a stubborn and unhelpful management and the activist base of the unions contracts. The pressures on union leaders in these situations tended to confirm the vulnerability of union organization. Such trends and patterns were evident at *Telecommunications Factory*, where the majority union was MSF, representing the technical and supervisory staff at the factory. By the mid-1990s, the union no longer organized in an effective way in the factory.

The factory and the unions

Telecommunications Factory was one of three interrelated sites in Coventry. This factory had a long history, going back to the 1930s, and developed into one of the principal employers in the city in the 1950s and 1960s. For much of its history, the factory was engaged in the production of telecommunications equipment. It was, and remained, a relatively large employer in the city, although the 1991 workforce of 3,900 employees had shrunk to a little over 2,000 by 1993, with further reductions during the mid-1990s.

The factory was owned and operated by a large multinational conglomerate, which had entered into a series of partnership and related arrangements with other international firms during the 1970s and 1980s. These initiatives and developments prompted speculation about the future of the corporation and the fate of workforces in its different locations. During the 1980s, in an attempt to reposition the factories in the city in the light of changing international markets, some of the older production sites were closed down and the three remaining sites were organized as a small headquarters unit, a medium-sized high-technology production unit (1,200 employees in 1991) and the larger *Telecommunications Factory*, where large-scale production took place, and where a sizeable research and development section was located. In the mid-1980s, a number of changes were introduced which had a bearing on management–employee relations.

By the 1990s, the two remaining production sites seemed relatively secure. There had been large-scale investment in the smaller site and it exemplified a high-technology approach to the production of telecommunications equipment. This aspect of production development was less evident at *Telecommunications Factory*, although in particular areas there had been extensive investment and reorganization of production, laying the foundation for automated and high-technology production. These two sites organized relatively independently of each other, each with its own managerial structure, and some autonomy over terms and conditions of work and employment. None the less, a regional managerial structure remained in place and personnel activities were coordinated at this level. During this period, a gradual decentralization of managerial responsibility was begun, although, unlike in other similar enterprises in the electronics and telecommunications industry, this was limited and seemingly tentative. As part of this reorganization, the corporate structure in the city was organized on a regional basis (covering the three sites in the city), with senior managerial staff located at the headquarters site.

There were six recognized unions at the factory in 1991: MSF (1,300 members), the Association of Professional, Executive, Clerical and Computer Staff (APEX, 300 members), the Association of Clerical, Technical and Supervisory Staffs (ACTSS membership figures not available, but 'very few'), the AEU (750 members), the TGWU (700) and EETPU (fewer than twenty). The largest union at the factory, MSF, and the others faced a very difficult time in the early 1990s, with successive waves of redundancies resulting in the depletion of union activists and increasing pressures on facility time and representation. By 1990, the two principal unions, MSF and the AEU, maintained a presence on site, based on long-standing leaders who pursued a policy of bargained accommodation as a defensive strategy in circumstances of acute vulnerability. By 1994, however, the AEU leadership was more or less inactive, playing no part in the restructuring process. Similarly, MSF had lost its long-established leadership and the representative structure of the union was more or less inoperative and ineffectual.

A history of attrition

The basic organizational structure of *Telecommunications Factory* had remained more or less the same for at least twenty years. Production activity was divided between a number of interconnected business units located on the one site, reorganizing and introducing new product lines as market requirements changed, or as new products were developed. Since the early 1970s, the factory had been organized into a number of business organizations, each comprising separate managerial structures, production organization, and research and technical development sections. One distinctive feature of the factory was that the majority of employees on site were non-manual, many with engineering and related technical backgrounds appropriate to this industry. It is against this background, after a number of years of speculation, that the regional management began a major redundancy programme during the 1990s.

By 1991, the distribution of the workforce in Coventry was 3,900 employees at *Telecommunications Factory*, 1,200 at the second production factory and 300 in the headquarters office. Within *Telecommunications Factory*, the workforce was broken down as follows: 2,000 non-manual workers, 400 clerical and administrative workers and 1,500 manual workers. Women comprised a third of the workforce. They were a majority of the clerical and administrative workers and the major proportion of the whole of the non-manual workforce. All the part-time workers, 200 in total, were women. Most of the workforce, and nearly all the technical and engineering employees, worked day shifts. The night shift was relatively small, comprised mainly of manual workers, a small number of whom worked part-time. There were very few temporary workers and the only contract workers, at this stage, were employed on specialist technical projects. One innovation to these employment relations, introduced in 1991, was the employment of 52 high-grade computer operators as home workers.

During the 1980s there had been several redundancy programmes, all relatively small-scale. The unions were party to these reductions, seeking to minimize them where possible and negotiating redundancy packages on behalf of their members. In 1988, the unions negotiated what they thought to be a satisfactory redundancy agreement, setting procedures and the terms of the redundancy package. The aim, from the union perspective, was to ensure that all redundancies were voluntary. Beginning in 1990, in anticipation of proposed reductions in staff levels, the company announced new terms for redundancy packages offering higher levels of payment for longer service. In October 1991, as the recession began to unfold, the company announced a reduction in the terms on offer in the redundancy package, effectively reneging on the 1988 agreement. The consequence of the new offer was that the higher paid staff would receive a lesser offer than was the case previously, in a few cases involving a reduction of more than £15,000. However, to offset the impact of this offer, the company offered the retention of higher pay-outs provided those taking redundancy waived their period of redundancy notice.

This change in company policy occurred in anticipation of further large-scale redundancy programmes at the factory. Shortly afterwards, one of the businesses set up at *Telecommunications Factory* failed and was wound up, with the announcement that 600 employees would be made redundant between 1990 and 1991 (400 staff and 200 manual employees). Both the redundancy announcement and the revocation of the redundancy agreement were opposed by the unions at the factory, and particularly by the MSF leadership, which represented the bulk of the non-manual staff. This resulted in a three-day stoppage and a settlement where the former redundancy agreement was neither formally recognized nor rejected by the company. Instead, the company agreed to recognize the agreement on a *de facto* basis, with the requirement that the union leaderships should negotiate individual terms and conditions of redundancy for each programme that was in the offing.

In 1992, a further large-scale compulsory redundancy was announced, amounting to 1,300 employees across all areas. The regional corporate management justified this redundancy in terms of the recession and the business context in which the company was operating, both in the United Kingdom and elsewhere in the world. The numbers employed at *Telecommunications Factory* fell to around 2,300, with proportionate decreases at the other production factory. The part-time staff all but disappeared and by the end of 1993 there were only twenty part-time employees. Overall, the redundancy programme was aimed at non-manual staff in particular, who left the factory in disproportionate numbers during this period.

Throughout this period there was no regular pay increase, with the last negotiated pay increase of 6 per cent taking place in 1991. Shift working was reduced, so that most employees were employed on day shifts and overtime work all but disappeared. However, the management was concerned to maintain output and to develop further potentially lucrative areas of work, and increased subcontracting to enable output levels to be maintained. The approach of the company was to reduce the workforce of the factory to a high-skilled core, making up the difference via contract work. In 1993, a smaller redundancy of 200 employees consolidated this trend even further.

Organization and representation

During the 1990s, the two main unions at the factory experienced severe organizational and representational difficulties, mainly brought about by the impact of the extensive restructuring taking place at the factory during the 1980s and 1990s. In the case of MSF an additional set of problems came with the difficulties created by the difficult merger between ASTMS and TASS which created MSF.

MSF

The main union, MSF, had a long and relatively active history at the factory, having built up an effective organization in the late 1970s and early 1980s. At that time the union membership was organized into two unions, the ASTMS and TASS. The ASTMS organized the engineering staff at the factory, comprising three-quarters of the staff, while TASS organized the technicians and draught office workers. Of the two unions the TASS membership was the more effectively and tightly organized group at a workplace level, while the ASTMS had a more uneven representation across the different sections of workers it represented. None the less, the ASTMS was the more prominent of the two unions, not only because of its size but also because of its involvement in the combine committee covering the factory and in the wider trade union movement in the area (compare with Smith, 1987).

In 1988, the ASTMS and TASS merged to form MSF. The two unions were very different and at a workplace level it was not an easy merger, with a long lead-in time to branch integration. By 1990, the two memberships of TASS and the ASTMS at *Telecommunications Factory* were still organized in two separate branches, although in 1990 the two local leaderships agreed to move to a single structure and dissolve the two separate organizations in the factory. The former senior representative of the TASS group became the new chair of the MSF branch, while the senior representative of the ASTMS became the secretary. At the time, both had full facility time, which was a problem since, in the words of the MSF secretary: 'clearly the company wouldn't have been happy with two people on full facility time' (1990). In the event, the new chair of the branch moved to a position within the company as safety officer, and resigned from active union involvement. From January 1991 the former ASTMS secretary remained as the new branch secretary on full facility time.

The major difficulty facing the new union was to establish an operational representative structure across the factory. In a rather benign comment, the MSF secretary observed that the new union was 'evolving at the moment', largely on the basis of the previous ASTMS structure, in which certain senior representatives for workplaces and grades formed the branch committee. There was a senior site representative for each site and senior grade representatives for the development engineers, testing and commissioning engineers, other engineers and other technical grades. In 1990 and 1991 there was some difficulty in filling all these senior positions, thus weakening the negotiating committee (comprised of the senior representatives, the chair and the secretary) as well as representation across the factory union membership. One area of work, network systems, remained formally under-represented, since no one was willing to take on the job of senior representative, although a former TASS member joined the negotiating committee but would not accept formal recognition as senior representative. This unevenness in representation dated from the early 1990s and, as the difficulties facing the union deepened, became a pattern for other areas covered by the union.

In 1990 the union had 'sixty-odd' representatives, in the words of the secretary 'nominally at least', with some more enthusiastic and committed than others, and some being 'pressed men and women'. The secretary said that it was sometimes difficult to persuade many more than twenty to attend the monthly representatives' meetings. Formally, the industrial relations arrangements were such that if individuals or groups had a problem they were expected to 'chase it up in the first instance through their local representative with the local management and then it proceeds through domestic and works conference' (Branch secretary, 1990). As the company was not affiliated to the Engineering Employers' Federation or a similar body, a works conference with a full-time official was the final stage in the procedure. In practice, many problems were raised directly with senior representatives or, in their absence, with the union secretary. As time went by, even the senior representatives became reluctant to take up issues with a seemingly 'hostile' and tough management, and this fell to the increasingly isolated union secretary.

Prior to the merger, the senior representatives of the ASTMS had met as a policy-making and planning committee on a regular basis. Following the merger, there was an attempt, led by the secretary, to continue this practice in the new union, but it met with only limited success, as indicated by attendance at the negotiation meetings involving the senior representatives of the union. Throughout the 1990s, it increasingly became the case that the senior representatives would only attend meetings of direct interest to them and their immediate membership. This practice was initially legitimated by the fact that some negotiations related only to particular grades or areas of work in the factory, and in these circumstances senior representatives from other areas increasingly excused themselves from the meetings. This practice was illustrated with reference to a meeting in 1991 involving testing and commissioning engineers and dealing with a problem in this area of work. The meeting was attended only by the senior representative from the area where most of those engineers worked. Between 1990 and 1993 this practice became more and more pronounced, and most planning and preparatory meetings

involving the senior representatives were sparsely attended, thereby compromising the unity of the senior representative committee and structure.
Increasingly, the different sections of the union group within the factory began
to act autonomously from each other, although there was still continued
reference to the union secretary.

The MSF membership was also organized as a branch of the union, covering
all members at the three company sites. These meetings were regarded by the
membership as unimportant and were attended by as few as six members.
These branch meetings were viewed by the branch secretary as a necessary
inconvenience and a duplication of the far more important representatives'
meeting. As secretary he was expected to report to both meetings and, as he
commented, his reports were: 'designed to kill two birds with one stone. I've
prepared this month's report today because we have a branch meeting after
work today. The report goes to the branch and the representatives' meeting
which is usually a week and a day later' (1990). In this way the secretary acted
in an expedient and economical way so as to deal with what most members
thought was an unnecessary waste of time, having two meetings on the same
subjects. The problem for the union leadership was that the branch meeting
was necessary to comply with the constitutional requirements of the union.
Thus this union group, like many at the time, was burdened by a so-called
'democratic' right which could not be exercised in any effective way.

So as to deal with the problems raised by poor attendance at the membership meetings, the branch leadership encouraged all workplace
representatives to hold meetings in their sections with their memberships to
discuss what should be raised at negotiations, how to respond to managerial
initiatives or what should go into next year's pay claim. Where members did
not have a representative, then either the secretary or another senior representative, from elsewhere in the factory, would call a members' meeting. From
time to time, mass meetings of members were held, either for a section or for
the workforce as a whole, depending on the issues. Attendance at these
meetings was varied, and not surprisingly was better when they were held with
permission from company management and were therefore on the 'clock'.
When it was necessary to take members off the 'clock' the meeting attendance,
in the words of the secretary, could be 'extremely poor'.

The AEU

The main shopfloor union was the AEU, which covered the majority of the
shopfloor workforce, representing semi-skilled and skilled workers in the

factory. The few unskilled workers and a minority of the semi-skilled workers were members of the TGWU. Altogether the AEU membership comprised 750 members (650 of whom were women) distributed over the two production sites, 98 per cent of the eligible workforce. These union groups were effectively organized by site, with a convenor at each of the two production sites.

The union was organized on the basis of workplace stewards, seventeen in all (thirteen of whom were women) at the main site and each representing a shopfloor section. In one case, where there was extensive labour mobility in the course of work, the ninety workers were represented by six stewards, to keep track of the workforce and to provide appropriate representation. The steward committee did not cover all sections in the factory, principally because union members were increasingly reluctant to come forward as stewards. As the convenor noted, 'We have trouble getting stewards because of hassles from management, so we have to co-opt members. ... Years ago there used to be competition for these steward posts but this has now ended. People do not want to be branded' (1991). In part, in recognition of the way in which the union had been pushed into a defence of a narrowly defined union position, these stewards and their senior representatives restricted their activities to fairly limited and conventional issues, such as individual grievances and piece-work bargaining.

The stewards were organized and based as section stewards, involved principally in negotiations over piece-work rates and problems. Basically, the stewards attempted to deal with issues as they came up. If they were unable to settle the difficulty the convenor would become involved. As the convenor noted, 'The stewards are present at the timing of jobs and they talk to members. If there is a breakdown they talk to the manager of the area and if there is a problem I am called in. I am mainly involved in sorting out a compromise' (1991). Increasingly the piece-work negotiations defined the remit of manual shop steward activity in the factory.

The stewards at the main site met every three weeks, although the attendance was somewhat uneven. At this meeting the convenor had the practice of reporting developments that had taken place during the intervening period, and any negotiations he had had with the company. During the period from 1990 to 1994, the leaders of this union, like the leadership of the main union (MSF), faced difficulties in encouraging activists within the union, as the factory management became more assertive and the redundancy programmes took effect. The convenor noted that by the end of the 1980s many of the stewards were reluctant to take up issues raised by members, presumably because of worries about their own position and the general stress associated with job insecurity. In effect, the union became a shadow union within the factory, with the leaders playing a limited part in factory-wide activity and principally concerned to secure the best terms available for those taking a redundancy package and otherwise representing members on individual cases.

Summary

The union memberships at the factory found themselves under increased pressure from management during the first half of the nineties. As the restructuring proceeded, accompanied by major redundancies, the management pursued a policy of seeking cooperation with the union leaderships or, where this was not forthcoming, a policy of exclusion and isolation. In the case of the AEU, the leadership worked more and more closely with the personnel manager to try to exercise some control over the redundancies that were taking place. In contrast, the MSF secretary was isolated to the extent that he eventually accepted a redundancy package in 1994 and left the company. By this time all but one of the other senior representatives in MSF were acting in name only.

The fragmentation of industrial relations practice

The formal arrangements for industrial relations at the factory involved the personnel department and the six recognized unions. Via regular negotiations, through a joint staff consultative council covering staff unions, and a manual equivalent, as well as a regular sequence of meetings, the unions and management negotiated the terms and conditions of work and employment. Union representatives, particularly from MSF and the AEU, the two main unions at the factory, also raised individual grievances and concerns with the operational management and members of the personnel department.

The problem with these arrangements for the union leaders was that the company management in the region began to pursue a set of policies which had the effect of marginalizing the unions. The basis for this policy was that the bargaining agenda promoted by the company management was increasingly defined as inter-site or site specific; specific issues were dealt with on a site-by-site basis, while other items, such as wage agreements, were negotiated at a regional level. The increasingly rigid way in which bargaining items were defined created complications for the senior union leaderships, who had a site responsibility at *Telecommunications Factory* as well as inter-site responsibilities. As the company restructured production at the two sites, via its extensive redundancy programme, management began to oppose cross-site representation, and to restrict the facility time arrangements for the senior union representatives, on the grounds that as numbers were reduced the range of industrial relations issues dealt with by the senior union representatives also declined.

The encouragement of the move towards site-by-site bargaining was in part to give substance to the establishment of each site as a discrete profit centre, as well as in recognition of the sub-divisions within each site. Accompanying these developments, the company introduced site-specific bargaining arrangements with each union, although the union leaders were resistant to this development. From a management point of view, the aim was to separate out and contain the unions at each site, and to distance one union from the other. The personnel manager summed up what he saw as the positive outcomes of this approach:

> Now the trade unions have a better realisation of the need for the business to be successful. This was not always recognised. Once, years ago, the unions nearly destroyed the company. Now there is a clear understanding of the problems and more so by the manual areas. Maybe it's because of personalities in the unions. The manual unions have had a harder time than the staff. Now there is a changed outlook – both full-time as well as local leaders know the problems the business faces. (1991)

So the management approach was to isolate each site and encourage differentiated union responses. The problem as far as the management was concerned was that the main union, MSF, did not recognize and acknowledge the gravity of the problems faced by the company. Such recognition was seen to be manifested in compliance with and acquiescence to company policy.

In the first part of the 1990s, the MSF leadership continued to resist the thrust of corporate policy, at least rhetorically. However, the rejection of cross-site representation became a key problem for the union leaders, particularly those from MSF. As the branch secretary noted:

> The company has said it will only recognise separate senior representation for the two sites in Coventry. There is a pretty grotesque inequality of numbers in our membership between the two sites [where the membership numbers at the second site were small and dependent on the leaders from the main site]. Formally we have pursued that through procedure and failed to agree but I haven't yet directly challenged them by going to the other site and inviting them to sack me. (1993)

While the question of cross-representation remained ongoing, the union leadership was increasingly pressed by the management to abandon claims for such representation.

One of the ways in which the MSF leadership attempted to resist regional management policy and maintain a policy of resistance was to look beyond the immediate locality, to the experiences of other plants within the company. The senior union leaderships at the factory were members of a combine committee covering the corporation plants throughout Britain, although the active combine membership came from the three main company sites in Britain, including the Coventry sites. This committee had been set up in 1987, and was led by MSF leaders from the different sites covered by the company, with the MSF secretary at *Telecommunications Factory* the incumbent of the one formal position on the committee, that of organizing secretary. Meetings of the combine were held twice a year, and they rotated between the three main sites covered by the committee. In the early 1990s, the combine attempted to address the problem of redundancies across the corporation as a whole and to speak on behalf of the company union membership. However, the company introduced its corporate proposals in such a way that there appeared to be different timetables and sets of arrangements for each site, with the result that the union leaderships were unable to organize a common and concerted approach to the corporate proposals. The combine committee leadership found it difficult to agree a common position and forge a united and agreed set of policies.

Apart from these concerns, much of the activity of the senior union leaderships involved individual grievances and concerns. In the case of the manual unions, where piece-work payment systems still applied, there was an ongoing series of negotiations about problems with these payments, involving both the senior manual union leadership and the section stewards. Similarly, the non-manual union representatives were involved in individual representations, particularly over discipline cases and related grievances, rather than pay issues. While both the manual and non-manual unions had organized themselves to deal with these problems, in the 1990s they were all somewhat overwhelmed and preoccupied by redundancy problems.

Bargaining: compromise and charade

Overall, the company management set the terms and conditions of bargaining and negotiations in the factory. As a precondition, the company management during the 1980s had increasingly centralized, weakening the previous divisional structure and reinforcing the works management and central personnel department. The result was that by the first half of the 1990s the management was in a position to initiate a comprehensive reorganization of the factory, which centred on capital investment, recomposition of the work-force and large-scale redundancies. The unions were placed on the defensive in bargaining, negotiation and the representation of their memberships.

The managerial approach was to marginalize union activity and involvement in the factory and to limit the scope of negotiations. A twin strategy was pursued, removing the basis of piece-work bargaining job by job and replacing it with group productivity bonus schemes, thus reducing the opportunity or 'necessity' for union representation, and dividing the unions from each other, particularly along the manual/non-manual divide. Towards this end, the manual union leaderships were effectively drawn into collaborative relationships focusing on redundancies and how to achieve acceptable terms for their memberships. With the introduction in 1992 of performance-related pay arrangements, in the form of group productivity bonuses, the management took the view that there was less necessity for union representation on pay questions, since they were the responsibility of individual employees, and that unions should restrict their concern to the negotiation of orderly redundancy arrangements and procedures. For the managerial staff, the main 'problem' with the unions came from a troublesome non-manual union leadership; the shopfloor union leadership, in their view, was much more 'reasonable' and 'helpful'.

The initial impact of this managerial approach was most obvious with the shopfloor unions. As the convenor of the largest shopfloor union, the AEU, commented, 'There is no trust whatsoever. There is not trust at all. There has been so much since the early 1980s – cut-backs, redundancies. Members say stuff it, there is no fight, let us go' (1991). Similar sentiments were expressed by other shopfloor union leaders in subsequent years.

The scale and drawn-out nature of this restructuring placed the shopfloor unions in an increasingly defensive position. Work was reorganized, with the introduction of modular or cellular forms of working and group payment schemes, and the redundancy programme continued, escalating for shopfloor workers. The impact of this process of change fell disproportionately on the manual workers, consisting as it did of increased capitalization of the production process and the recomposition of the workforce, via contracting-out, the employment of temporary staff and successive redundancy programmes.

The outcome was a pattern of demoralised compromise bargaining. The shopfloor union leaderships dealt with individual and personal grievances as they came up, but broader strategic bargaining and union representation fell away. While some stewards remained involved in piece-work bargaining, in general these arrangements were replaced with group productivity bonus arrangements, removing the basis for steward representation and organization. It became increasingly difficult for the steward committee to establish a common approach to managerial initiatives, because of different approaches and arrangements in different sections. As these developments proceeded, the union leaderships adopted rather defensive stances and attempted to maintain standards and pursue anomalies or errors in wage calculations and arrangements, as well as authorizing an orderly retreat in terms and conditions of employment. This was illustrated by their encouragment of members in one section to agree to a 10 per cent wage cut in 1993 to avert redundancy. On more general issues, such as proposals to introduce seven-day working for the mainly female workforce at one of the sites in 1992, the two convenors attempted to negotiate a satisfactory set of arrangements, particularly where most of the workers were reluctant to move to a seven-day working arrangement. These negotiations, however, took place in an atmosphere of demoralization about the present and profound uncertainty about the future.

The problem for the shopfloor union leaderships was that they were increasingly isolated from the broader trade union movement in the area and found themselves in defensive situations within the factory, with a membership that was reluctant to pursue immediate work and employment interests actively. By the mid-1980s the unions in the plant no longer played any active role in the Confederation of Shipbuilding and Engineering Unions (CSEU). Further, the shopfloor unions had withdrawn from the combine committee in the early 1990s, following disagreements with the non-manual unions on site about the best way to approach the management in the face of redundancy proposals, with the non-manual unions arguing for a more active response to such proposals. One consequence of this non-involvement in the combine committee was that these union leaderships were relatively isolated from their counterpart memberships in other factories covered by the company. Paradoxically, this isolation was furthered with the establishment of factory branches for the AEU membership, which replaced geographical branches in 1992. In these circumstances, and with increasing pressure from management within the factory to comply with managerial decisions, the union leaderships had restricted capacity to defend and represent their memberships in active ways.

As with the manual unions, the main problem faced by the non-manual union leaderships during the first half of the 1990s was how to cope with the successive redundancy programmes introduced by the company. Representations and negotiations over redundancies dominated the bargaining agenda, which was very much set by the management. Increasingly, the senior union leadership was under pressure as the management sought to renegotiate the facility agreement (on the basis of the falling membership of these unions) and reduce the time available to these leaders to maintain a union presence in the factories. By astute and obstructionist bargaining with management over these issues, the union leaders managed to retain their facility time arrangements, until the leading MSF representative accepted redundancy in 1993.

Initially, the union leaderships sought to oppose the redundancy programme, and were successful in taking the lead in a series of one-day strikes in July and August 1991. However, when the company failed to make concessions, and the members did not support the call from the lead negotiators to oppose the company pay offer in November 1991, the leaders abandoned any further attempt to oppose the redundancy packages. Instead, they sought to bargain up the terms of these proposals via negotiations through the company negotiating committee and the joint staff unions consultative committee.

This was a period in which formal bargaining on company-wide issues became something of a charade, and when the lead MSF representative acquired a reputation among management of being wilfully obstructive of the restructuring programme of the company and 'unhelpful' in his approach to company policy. The problem was that the membership became increasingly divided about how to deal with the management, with a minority prepared to oppose these developments and the remainder more cautious. Reflecting on this situation and the fact that the redundancies tended to fall disproportionately on the high union membership areas, the MSF lead representative commented on MSF member–management relations:

> Tremendously variable. Many members, particularly those who work in an office sort of environment, don't perhaps see things in a straightforward us and them way. The traditional management versus workers approach is a bit more common amongst testing and commissioning engineering workers who work in something far closer to a factory environment, although they have considerable pride in their jobs. But, it is very much a mixed bag. (1991)

What the MSF representative did not say was that the engineering workers had often been promoted into their jobs from the shopfloor and had previously been members of the shopfloor unions, whereas the office workers had often joined MSF as their first ever union. In part, these engineering workers carried their sense of a trade union consciousness over into the staff grades, and for many years were the bedrock for MSF (and the ASTMS) within the factory.

The problem for MSF was that over-reliance on the promotees rather than the direct entrants laid the foundation for the eventual collapse of the union.

As the redundancies proceeded in the 1990s, these promotees were increasingly likely to leave the company. The consequence for the union was devastating. As the branch secretary commented:

> The last year has made obvious something that has been a problem in the past. There have been very heavy redundancies in areas where we had high membership density and this has accelerated in the last year. Probably our overall density now among people who could be eligible for membership is around 25 per cent. The collapse in density has really been quite sudden and has come about because there has been a key imbalance towards redundancies in areas which have been involved in manufacture and their associated white-collar functions like draughtsmen, contract engineers, test engineers. The move towards software has meant that these areas where we were strong have suffered tremendously. (1993)

The branch secretary then went on to illustrate the scale of the collapse by referring to his own area of employment, contract engineering, where the 160 contract engineers in place in 1991 had been reduced to sixteen by 1993. Perhaps not surprisingly, the branch secretary accepted a redundancy package at the end of 1993.

It was against this background that the focus of non-manual union leaders' activity became increasingly narrowly focused. They ended up defining the remit of their concerns as representing individual members over grievances and problems that occurred in the course of work in the factory. These representatives, and particularly the branch secretary, were also heavily involved in dealing with the effects of redundancy announcements, taking appeals to the management and occasionally resorting to works conferences involving the local full-time union officials. The other side of these developments was that collective forms of action, as reflected in membership meetings, industrial action and bargaining over company-wide policies, were downplayed, although even in 1993 there were occasions when the leaders sought mandates from the general union membership for collective resistance to the thrust of company policy. However, this rather beleaguered membership was less likely to support these entreaties than had been the case in the 1980s.

Assessment

In the context of the restructuring of work and employment relations associated with change and innovation in the telecommunications industry, the years under study had seen a reaffirmation of sectionally based economistic forms of unionism at this factory, although underwritten by successful management attempts to divide the unions from each other and to affirm a narrowly focused unionism at the factory. With the continuing uncertainty at the factory, and the experience of the redundancies and associated difficulties, the prevailing form of unionism became increasingly defensive and beleaguered.

In line with other manufacturing enterprises, the *Telecommunications Factory* management had taken steps to decentralize budgetary control and devolve the management of the labour process to establishment level. Moves had been made to establish more flexible workforces through changes to numbers employed and to forms of work organization, as well as pay policies. These changes were achieved via collective bargaining, although increasingly this took on formal aspects without the substance of a well organized union able to challenge these initiatives. MSF, as the major union, attempted to bargain for change, but increasingly the responsibility fell to very few leaders, who did not have the obvious and active support of the membership. Thus, while the unions formally remained in place, there was an increasing element of charade to their involvement and engagement with the management on the changes that were being introduced. The management at the factory effectively set the agenda for relations with unions, in the process promoting the marginalization of these unions.

One of the consequences of the defensiveness of the unions at the factory was that the union leaders became preoccupied with the question of *survival* and as a result ignored the diversity in the composition of union membership. This neglect was most clearly evident for women union members, who were simply not acknowledged by the major union. In practice, the specific interests of women members, as low-paid and part-time workers, were subordinated to the increasingly beleaguered defence of the very presence of the union at the factory. Similarly, there was almost no recognition among the union leaderships that minority ethnic groups were present or that such groups might have particular interests and concerns. The overriding preoccupation of the MSF and shopfloor union leaderships was with the rolling redundancy programmes, the seemingly endless recomposition of the workforce and the persistent insecurity and worry about the future of the factory. Such concerns relegated all other issues to the background.

In the context of the restructuring that was taking place, and the explicit attempts by management to limit the scope and scale of union representation, the union leaders became increasingly remote and isolated from the broader membership in the factory. This feature of organization was encouraged by the management, who dealt directly with the leadership, treating the leaders in stereotypical ways as uncooperative and difficult people. The management strategy at *Telecommunications Factory* was to restrict and narrow the concerns of the union in ways that made the leadership appear fairly ineffective. Thus, the MSF leaders found that they could not break out of the relatively narrow representational base of the union and open up patterns of involvement in the newer under-represented employment areas. As the committee became smaller and focused on the most vulnerable areas of employment in the factory, the isolation of and pressure on the leadership increased, until the long-standing leaders left one by one, having 'had enough'.

Faced with the management-driven agenda to divide and narrow union activity, the union leaders sought to maintain a union presence by defensive bargaining. The problem was that in the face of contracting areas of membership representation, and sectionally focused senior representatives, this was a form of organization that not only provided the conditions for a semblance of union *survival*, but reinforced a centralized form of leadership, with the convenors effectively acting in isolation from the broader membership. As a result, the union groups in the factory, and particularly the MSF leadership, remained susceptible to further managerial attempts to underwrite the separation of the central leaders from the membership, a form of top slicing.

The outcome was a paradoxical form of centralized unionism at a workplace level. The central leaders of all the unions had become increasingly isolated from their membership and from the broader trade union movement. Not only was the combine committee relatively ineffective, but the district and regional officials played little part in the process of bargaining and representation in the factory. While the central leaders attempted to maintain an organization which had a part to play in the restructuring process, they were undermined by the continuing programme of redundancies and the formalized approach to bargaining promoted by the management. The form of unionism defended by these leaders was derived from a previous period, where there was an integration between the sectional leadership and the central leaders in the factory. This form of organization could not be maintained and the result was an isolated, remote and, paradoxically, centralized form of union leadership in the factory.

6 Extending the Boundaries of Trade Unionism

One of the features of trade unionism that has received relatively little recent examination is the attempt by some union groups to extend the boundaries of unionism, particularly those between work and non-work situations. In the circumstances of change, where the certainties of the past no longer apply, trade union leaderships may begin to maintain and build the base of active trade unionism by focusing on the inter-linkages between work and home. Such a strategy aims to embed the union in a broader context of social relations than is implied by the wage relationship narrowly defined. While there has been limited evidence of such attempts among male manufacturing workers, there is some indication that women trade union members are more willing to blur the boundaries between work and home.

There are two aspects to extending the boundaries of trade unionism in the process of restructuring that are noteworthy in the debates about the changing composition and practice of trade unions. First, there is the question of how trade unions organize and operate where the majority of union members are women and the leadership is by women committed to affirming the specific interests of women members. There has been an extensive and important debate about women and trade unions, focusing particularly on the difficulties faced by women trade union members in their union membership. This debate has occurred in the context of an attempt to address questions about divisions and unities between men and women in society, with the focus on trade unions (Briskin and McDermott, 1993; Cunnison and Stageman, 1993). Such research is complemented by a few studies that look at the historical situation of women and trade unionism, where struggles by women workers have been examined (Boston, 1987). More pertinently, a series of studies, mainly in the early 1980s, documented and detailed the place of women in factory settings, including a consideration of unionism (Pollert, 1981; Cavendish, 1982; Westwood, 1984). One of the strengths of this literature has been the tracing out of the formal and informal employment and work patterns evident in manufacturing plants and the ways these take on a particular imprint with women workers. However, while there has been an attempt to locate these aspects of work and employment relations with reference to trade unions, this has been a secondary concern.

The second point refers to the relations between trade unions and the way there can be a repatterning of relations and changes in the prevailing form of unionism. These processes were evident at the third factory covered by the study, *Electronics Factory*, where the majority of the workforce was women. In an earlier study, where another plant in the same company but in a different division was studied, the process of restructuring at the plant resulted in the decline of craft-based unionism, concerned with the defence by male workers of their skills and privileges, and the emergence of a more open and solidaristic form of trade unionism based on the predominantly female general union (Elger and Fairbrother, 1991). The general point is that in conditions of a restructuring of work and employment relations, where union memberships face change and uncertainty, they may reaffirm defensive strategies, defending privilege and the type of unionism this implies, or take steps to reorganize and refocus their unionism in more open and solidaristic ways. This latter feature was in evidence at *Electronics Factory*.

In the context of restructuring and the prospect of plant closure, a form of active unionism that blurs traditional boundaries, both within the workplace and between the workplace and the community, may be able to confront the difficulties of representation in the midst of restructuring. At *Electronics Factory*, the main union, largely composed of women shopfloor workers, organized in ways that challenged the traditional boundaries of unionism. In this way it maintained a presence within the factory and ensured that management within the factory was responsive to its members' concerns. The problem was that the senior managers of the division of which the factory was a part were beyond the reach of the local union leadership and thus viewed the factory as a small and costly unit of production. This feature of corporate organization imposed a major limitation on the scope and scale of union activity within the factory.

The factory and unions

Electronics Factory was a small establishment, part of a three-site division based in the area. The factory was established in the 1930s and had long been engaged in the production of electrical and subsequently electronic automobile parts.

For most of its history, but particularly in the post-war period, the factory operated as an autonomous unit within the larger electronics conglomerate of which it is a minor part. In 1991 there were 532 employees on site, fewer than in the 1960s and 1970s. Employment began to decline further in the 1990s, and by 1993 employment stood at 404. During the 1990s there was speculation about possible closure of the factory and a move of the workforce to a larger site, six miles away, although by 1998 this still had not happened.

Beginning in the 1980s, the factory workforce was reorganized, seemingly to lay the foundation for a possible merger with the nearby larger factory. Central to this objective were two mutually reinforcing changes. First, there was a managerial reorganization towards decentralization of responsibility and a move to locate factory management decision-making within the broader corporate programme. This latter development took the form of locating key decisions about capital development and terms and conditions of employment at the larger nearby site. Second, there was a concerted attempt by management to incorporate both the union leaderships and the workers into the framework of factory decision-making via team discussion and consultation. In this latter respect, the management in effect took a decision to counter and negate the previous independence and effectiveness of the unions as collective organizations within the factory.

The factory management had long recognized a number of trade unions at the factory, with the GMB and MSF being the two main ones, covering operational workers and engineering and technical staff respectively. The GMB membership was 300 in 1991, of which 95 per cent were women, and around 280 by 1993. MSF had a constant membership during the same period of twelve supervisors and twenty-two engineering staff. Other unions recognized by the management were the AEU (with 120 members in 1991 and around 100 in 1993), the EETPU and the Association of Professional, Executive, Clerical and Computer Staff (APEX). By far the largest union at the plant was the GMB, which included almost all the women operative workers and all part-time workers (around 180).

Work and employment at the factory

The factory workforce faced increased output requirements and a period of uncertainty in the 1980s and into the 1990s. In 1987, in line with other establishments in the company, there was a major reorganization of the managerial structure and work procedures (Elger and Fairbrother, 1991). For management, this involved a delayering and reorganization of the factory management hierarchy, with the result that by 1991 the operational management comprised a site manager, two factory superintendents and thirteen supervisors. This staff was complemented by a personnel manager, support staff and a small technical staff. However, this was not an autonomous managerial structure, since the site manager reported to a divisional operations manager, based at a nearby sister establishment, and the divisional personnel manager was responsible for wage negotiations and division-wide policy.

What was distinctive about this factory was that the workforce was composed of at least 95 per cent women and had been so for at least twenty-five years. Many of the women workers had worked at the factory for many years, having started as young women on the short shifts, in the morning, afternoon or early evening, usually of four- to six-hour periods. Overall, the shift patterns were: double-day shift (6.00 a.m. to 2.00 p.m. and 2.00 p.m. to 10.00 p.m.) for maintenance workers, engineers, quality and reliability inspectors, labourers and supervisors, a mix of men and women; a single 6.00 a.m. to 2.00 p.m. operators' shift, composed only of women; and three part-time shifts (8.00 a.m. to 12.30 p.m., 1.00 p.m. to 4.30 p.m. and 6.00 p.m. to 10.00 p.m.), all women and numbering just under 200 (between 1990 and 1994). As domestic circumstances changed it was not unusual for these part-time shift workers to move to double day shifts.

The employment pattern at the factory took a particular form for the GMB membership. As indicated, from 1991 to 1993 nearly 200 GMB members were employed part-time, with 105 on the 6.00 to 10.00 p.m. shift. These staff were mainly young women, mostly with young children. According to the two principal GMB leaders in the factory, one of whom began her working life at the factory on this shift in 1975, these arrangements were convenient for childcare. In their view, 'really they are convenient hours, I will be honest with you, because they suit the person. The person does the hours that suit them' (1991). However, while this reflection on the evening shift may have been a *post hoc* rationalization, it was undoubtedly the case that a number of women were able to juggle the difficulties of childcare and domestic responsibilities around these shift hours. Perhaps of equal importance, the evening shift had been integrated into the employment conditions and arrangements at the factory, so that for many workers it was the route into day shifts or part-time mornings or afternoons.

In the past, the evening shift had been used by management to control for fluctuations in demand and the associated labour requirements. Using the shift workers in this way was possible because they had no defence as union members against management dictate since they were not recognized as union members. As stated by the GMB deputy convenor, 'If there were any lay-offs it was always the evening shift that got laid off because basically they weren't in the union then' (1991). However, in the 1970s the local union leadership negotiated equal status (on a *pro rata* basis) for these workers and secured the shift within the factory. This arrangement was convenient for the management because the evening shift became the route into employment within the factory, and presumably enabled the management to train and filter workers.

In view of the shift arrangements and the gender composition of the workforce, this factory had an unusual feel. Women came and went from the factory throughout the day. For many of the part-time workers, shifts were determined by their domestic and childcare responsibilities, so schooling, nursery arrangements and the like were frequently referred to and discussed at work. In addition, births, birthdays and retirements were celebrated publicly and enthusiastically. As a result, it was not surprising to go on to the floor and see banners, balloons and other signs of celebration. In discussion, workers spoke of the 'family' atmosphere in the factory and there was a familiarity, both among workers and between workers and management, not evident in the other workplaces covered by this study. Part of the reason for this was the length of time many had worked at the factory, with a majority of the production workforce having been there between ten and twenty years. As a factory principally composed of women workers, it was also largely free of the machismo evident in other engineering factories in the area.

The workforce had long been organized in a fairly traditional way, in work sections, under first-line supervisors and then in departments. However, beginning in 1987, modules and cellular forms of work organization were introduced (Elger and Fairbrother, 1991). The former departments were reorganized into functional departments and then work groups within the modules were functionally defined as cells, in general composed of between twenty and fifty workers, although some units were much smaller. The cell members had the right to elect a cell leader who became the contact point for the group, linking the first-line supervision with the cell. In practice these cell leaders were self-appointed and tended to be the more experienced workers, and included the local trade union leaders. While there was no substantive change to work procedures following the introduction of the cells, the attributes of cell competitiveness and self-organization, particularly on quality questions, became a feature of the factory. In addition, work procedures associated with quality control and self-inspection were introduced.

These changes also involved alterations to the wage systems at the factory. After the late 1980s, following negotiations with the unions represented at the three sites covered by the division, a single wage structure was introduced; piece-rates were ended and a flat-time payment was introduced. Operational staff were redesignated production manufacturers, and flexible work arrangements and labour mobility were introduced. In discussion, management informants illustrated flexibility and labour mobility by reference to the store keeper, who theoretically could be asked to work on the shopfloor, depending on work demands. The result was a workforce that could be deployed to meet production needs and where individual wage bargaining was not a prominent issue.

Organization and representation

The unions at the factory were organized in similar ways, and apart from MSF, representing staff supervisors and technical staff, had high levels of membership density, between 90 and 95 per cent. Each of the unions was organized around workplace steward structures, with formal responsibility for taking up issues involving the membership, at least in the first instance. Senior factory union leaders led the factory-wide negotiations and representations, working closely with the factory management, and occasionally involving regional officials.

The GMB

The main union, the GMB, was organized on the basis of two senior union leaders, the convenor and deputy convenor, supported by five line stewards, one on the night shift. These stewards dealt with line supervision and took up queries and grievances with them. The stewards, convenor and deputy were readily available to the members, although no one had full facility time; they responded to members' queries and dealt with union issues using whatever time was necessary. The convenor and the deputy convenor were readily available, on site or at home, via telephone. It was not uncommon for members to ring the convenor about problems and for the convenor and other stewards to come on to site when technically they were not at work.

The convenor and deputy convenor were both cautious about taking facility time in their activity as union leaders. They both took the view that it was important to remain close to and part of their own work groups. As the convenor stated, 'It is important to stay a working senior steward because it is important to remain part of the union. If you are put in an office, then you get removed from the members' (1993). These two union leaders were available to the members on site and off site. In addition, they were both seen to play their part as workers on the shopfloor.

The GMB steward committee was organized so that the convenor and deputy took the lead in negotiations, and the five remaining stewards not only represented their work areas but also sat on committees, such as the health and safety committee, car parks committee and pensions committee. This practice was of recent origin and was introduced with the election of the incumbent convenor in 1988. She had a commitment to active stewardship and took steps to promote it. As she said, 'I think the stewards should take more responsibility as well and unless you give it to them, they don't have it' (1991). The deputy convenor commented on this practice:

> So we make a point as near as damn it, a different steward on each committee [health and safety, traffic, pensions]. And then we have a joint shop stewards' meeting – a report back – each one of the stewards has to give a report back of any meetings they've been to. So consequently it makes the meeting more interesting because you have not got the same person talking all the time. (1991)

In addition to the frequent informal meetings and encounters, the steward committee met once a month, to review issues, receive reports and prepare for forthcoming activity. At one typical meeting in early 1991, the committee dealt with health and safety, car parks, a shorter working week and the initial preparations of the annual wage claim.

As part of the informal relations which were central to this union group, the stewards were active in collecting funds for outside bodies, such as the local hospice, bereavements, birthdays and births. This was noted by the convenor in the following way: 'We usually get things going for the hospice, the hospital. We have done quite a few presentations to different people and we have given quite a lot of money, the factory as a whole. The management join in with us. It is not just union, it is management and union joined together' (1991). While this was a union initiative, the factory management was a secondary party to it. The deputy convenor made a point of affirming this aspect of the arrangement:

> [The management] never ever stop us. They don't let us all do it together but they always let one steward. . . . Sometimes we have a cake sale or we have a tombola [a kind of lottery, especially for charity] but we do this in our time, which is in our dinner time. We do this. They give us space on the factory floor to do it. (1991)

This was a part of the union life which not only made the leaders available to members over a wide range of issues, but also extended the union boundaries, creating an open-ended view of what should concern these workers as union members.

However, the other side of this blurring of the boundaries between work and domestic life was that the union membership organized and operated in a relatively autonomous way. The roots of the cohesiveness of this membership lay in the way the local leaders of the main union had been successful in establishing an integrated membership irrespective of the variations in shift work at the factory. A crucial step in this process was the integration of the terms and conditions of the part-time shift workers with those of full-time employees. In the 1970s, the local leaders negotiated an integrated set of employment patterns and arrangements for all employees, thereby securing the evening shift as a permanent fixture and as a route into employment at the factory. This pattern was described by one of the local union leaders as follows: 'They [workers] start on the evening shift because they have got young children but then, as you know, time goes on. The families grow up so therefore as a vacancy occurs we transfer them on to days, mornings, or afternoons' (1991). The procedure was a union directed and organized one:

> We have a waiting list and when a person on evenings wishes to transfer on to days, either to full-time or part-time mornings or part-time afternoons, they put their names on the list and we have it done fairly. If he [manager] has got a vacancy on mornings we [union] have the first one on mornings and they then have the opportunity to change over. (1991)

As part of these changes, the part-time members joined the union and this also became the route along which some of the local union leaders emerged. One consequence of these practices was that the local leadership had a sharply developed sense of the concerns and problems faced by part-time workers. They took steps in their union activity to ensure that these workers were a constituent and active part of the union life in the factory, irrespective of shifts worked.

As far as the broader union movement was concerned, the unions at the factory organized and operated in a relatively isolated way. The main union group, the GMB, was not affiliated to a combine committee (although one covered the division), or to a trades and labour council, and nor did the union committee send representatives to the district committee. In addition, the union leaders had little direct contact with their full-time official, although there was regular telephone contact (once a week on average) and correspondence. None the less, it was the case that the full-time official would come into the factory to meet the union leaders at the concluding stages of the wage negotiations, and was kept informed of the course of these negotiations.

The two main shopfloor unions, the GMB and the AEU, effectively worked together, particularly in the representation of members with immediate grievances and concerns. The AEU had three line stewards and, given the distribution of workers and the consequent blurring of geographical demarcation, it was not unusual for workplace stewards to take up queries on their sections, irrespective of formal union affiliation. This practice was even more marked at a factory level, where the few AEU women members often approached the two women GMB leaders (convenor and deputy convenor) rather than the AEU convenor, who was seen as relatively traditional and not a person with whom to discuss personal and intimate issues.

MSF

The main staff union at the factory, MSF, was organized around very few people, representing a small membership in a rather defensive way. MSF had thirty-four members altogether, twelve supervisors (two women) and twenty-two engineering staff, covering all but one of the eligible technicians and related staff. Between 1991 and 1994 this membership was represented by an engineer as senior steward and three other representatives, two engineers and a supervisor. However, the bulk of the union work was done by the senior steward, who increasingly became the union, taking the lead in the inter-union negotiations about the closure of the factory. By 1994, the union was effectively led by one active member, with three workplace stewards who were relatively inactive. Part of the reason for this was that as unease and uncertainty about the future of the factory became more apparent, staff members withdrew from active involvement in the union, citing work commitments, a tougher approach to unionism by management and worries about their future prospects with the company. Nevertheless, this was the only union to organize industrial action in the plant during the 1990s. Four technicians, in pursuit of a two-year pay and grading claim, implemented a weekend overtime ban and work to rule in 1992. In the context of minimal collective industrial action, and in the face of uncertainty about the future of the plant, the management agreed to negotiations and reached an agreement whereby these four technicians received a pay increase and had their jobs re-evaluated.

A redundancy programme was implemented in 1992 and ten MSF staff were made redundant from this factory, although placed in jobs elsewhere. In addition, there were fears about the planned relocation of the plant. As the senior steward noted, 'With the proposed consolidation [of the two sites] people are very worried about their jobs. We don't know what is going to happen when we go down there. Some people will have to go' (1992). The difficulty for these members was that even by 1994 no final decision had been made about the move. It remained the subject of discussion, occasional announcements and extensive rumour. The result was that demoralization set in among the members, making it very difficult to maintain the union in an effective way.

The debilitating effect of such preoccupations on union leadership is illustrated by the senior steward, who had been in office since the late 1980s but resigned in November 1993. He was the chair of a company-sponsored committee, composed of management representatives and all unions, which considered the consolidation of the two sites. However, he ended up spending extensive amounts of time on this working party, and as a result saw the quality of his work deteriorating. This worry came to a head when he attempted to discipline a shopfloor worker over his attendance record: the main shopfloor union refused to support his decision and told him 'to back off'. In his words, he felt his job was in some danger and he was 'fed up' with the demands made on him by both unions and the company, so he resigned the senior steward-ship, although he remained a member of the union committee.

The difficulties faced by the senior steward were symptomatic of a wider set of problems faced by the membership. As employees they were very anxious about their individual futures. To counter a sense of isolation, the MSF union group was part of a corporate combine, although attending the twice yearly meetings was the extent of their involvement outside the plant. They had some contact with the regional official for the union, but this was fairly infrequent, no more than twice a month and usually by telephone. In short, this was a beleaguered and defensive union group, characterized by an active leadership attempting to make accommodations with management at the plant and across the two sites, and playing a limited role in the trade unionism at the plant.

Industrial relations

All the recognized unions, and particularly the GMB, were active, in that the local leadership had a long tradition of negotiating a range of issues with the local management – staffing levels, grading, redeployment, recruitment, dismissals and factory specific aspects of pay – as well as taking up grievances and presenting the concerns of members to management. Apart from these items, there were a number of matters which were dealt with at the divisional level – pay levels, capital expenditure, and divisional policy – and the union leaderships participated in joint forums with union leaderships from the other sites and the divisional management.

In the 1990s, with much discussion about the possibility of closure of the factory, the local union leaderships, especially of the MSF and the GMB, entered long discussions about work procedures and productivity savings. The divisional management began to look towards 'Japanese' work models and procedures (Elger and Fairbrother, 1991). Managers were sent to Japan to study work practices and organizations, while selected manual workers were sent to the Nissan plant in Sunderland. As part of these initiatives, the management, with union cooperation and agreement, introduced a set of practices relating to self-inspection and operator-led quality control. These initiatives had the consequence of reducing the number of quality inspectors in the factory, via a number of voluntary redundancies and some limited relocation.

To facilitate these negotiations, the divisional management established a union–management forum, known as the 'inner forum', attended by both staff and shopfloor union leaders and management. This forum operated as a semi-formal negotiating body where the problems and difficulties of reorganization were discussed informally. These discussions preceded more formalized negotiations. In practice, every Monday morning at 11.30 the site manager met the GMB leadership, and other union leaders, under the auspices of the inner forum, to report on activity for the week and to raise any problems with the union leaderships that had emerged in the previous week. The GMB convenor said that initially she had been very sceptical of their value, but subsequently found them 'useful' as a way of learning what was happening. As she noted, 'I will be honest with you, when it first started we were a bit dubious about it' (1991). Not only was she sceptical of the management, she also had reservations about all-union meetings:

> We were one of the first lot I think to sit down around a table of all trades because at times you did not. Somebody like me, a production worker, did not sit down with an EETPU bloke who was an electrician because you always came to loggerheads with each other but you have now what you call an inner forum and that, all the unions in the factory sit around the table together. (1991)

While this meeting was seen by the union leaderships as a 'communication' meeting, the agenda was very much set by the site manager. None the less, the local union leaders viewed it as a productive type of meeting where problems could be, and occasionally were, raised in a relatively informal setting. The routine and regular discussions between the site manager and the local union leaderships also established the basis for ongoing contact and cooperation between the unions. As time went by, these less formal negotiations and discussions became a key part of the way in which problems were dealt with, achieving a measure of agreement from the local union leaderships for the policy changes that were in the process of being implemented.

These arrangements over negotiating procedures rested on a long-term set of informal procedures in *Electronics Factory*. The workforce and the local management had worked together for many years; at least fifteen years in the case of the GMB leaders and the local management. This laid the foundation for a degree of informality in industrial relations at the factory. The fact that the union leaders were women, and the majority of workers in the factory, including the personnel manager, were women, gave rise to a seemingly more relaxed and informal atmosphere in the factory, because the women were not prepared to abide by a rigid distinction between work, union and personal relations. The outcome was a process of negotiation and bargaining which was distinctive when compared with other factories covered by the study.

This pattern of relations made for a seemingly cooperative and compliant workforce. While union leaders were involved in discussions and negotiations, there was a background of familiarity and a common interest in achieving agreement about restructuring. If the union leaders and management were unsuccessful in reaching agreement about these far-reaching changes, then the future of the factory as an operational centre was in question. Against this background a cooperative approach was developed, building on the long-standing informality that characterized negotiating relations at the factory.

Accommodative bargaining

The pattern and parameters of bargaining and negotiation at the factory were set by the management, working with the unions, and particularly the main union, the GMB. The prospect of closure of the plant and a move to the larger nearby site created a common interest in the maintenance of the plant as a profitable and viable contributor to the overall development of the corporation. While this was a difficult goal to realize, there was a *de facto* agreement that the limits of bargaining and negotiating activity were set by this recognition. The union policy was to maintain and defend the status quo, as an acceptable compromise in the defence of members' interests.

In line with developments in the Midlands engineering industry during the 1980s, and a move by many corporations to play down centralized and district-wide negotiations and agreements, this corporation had introduced plant-level bargaining and decision-making (Elger and Fairbrother, 1991). While there had been a long-standing negotiating forum for the shopfloor unions at the factory, from 1987 this committee acquired an added importance as the principal industrial relations council for management and the union leaderships, meeting monthly and attended by the GMB leadership (two seats), the AEU (one) and the EETPU (one). This was the forum which received wage claims and considered other issues, such as health and safety, working time and pensions. Throughout the 1990s, there were discussions and negotiations about pensions, since the company initiated a pension break and this caused considerable consternation among the workforce. In addition, there was extensive discussion about the implications of an agreed shorter working week, of 37 hours, and the implications for part-time workers, mainly represented by the GMB.

Following the decision by the company to consider the merger of the two sites, in the late 1980s, a working party was established to consider the detail of the proposal. This was attended by representatives of all unions on the site, as well as local management, and was chaired by the MSF senior steward from the factory. This working party provided the local union leaderships with a formalized opportunity to meet and discuss the merger with their counterparts at the other factory. It also brought all the unions at the factory together regularly, promoting a greater familiarity with each other's concerns. However, in practice this working party merely served to confirm the importance of continuing to defend the continued presence of the factory, not least for the GMB leadership, who sought to maintain the extensive opportunity for part-time working arrangements for many of their members; these members would not have the same opportunity at the other factory or easy access to the other site, six miles away.

An accommodative set of relationships thus developed between the factory management and the local union leaderships. They all faced a common fate, involving disruption and uncertainty about the immediate future. None the less, the local union leaderships frequently found themselves challenging and questioning managerial policy on shift arrangements, overtime practice, leave applications and health and safety. The result was a union leadership, particularly among the GMB and MSF representatives, prepared to question and challenge, although in the context of a clear recognition that they would not threaten the working relation with the factory management over the move to the other site. It was in these terms that the union leaderships spoke and acted on behalf of their memberships.

More importantly, the GMB leadership was able to speak with an authority that was denied the other unions and was influential on the plant management. The basis for this presence was the broad-based nature of membership activity and involvement at the plant. Thus, the local GMB leaders were able to speak with an authority in their meetings and exchanges with management. In return, the factory management looked to the shopfloor union leaders for support and assistance in preparing for the merger as well as in resisting the merger. The management encouraged an 'open door' relationship with the union leaders as a way of facilitating these links. As the personnel manager observed of management–union relations, 'Within the site they are very good. We communicate openly and resolve problems. It is an open door policy' (1993). At the same time, the GMB leadership observed that this was not an easy policy: 'You must be strong and positive. You must be accurate about what you do. You must be correct and confident. You are dealing with educated people and must be as clever as they are' (1993). This was a leadership that used the opportunities to approach the factory management in thoughtful and carefully prepared ways. Further, the two GMB leaders approached the more difficult and fractious negotiations about the future of the factory in the same manner. They were members of the working party that was developing the plans for closure and relocation and they were able to present a persuasive case for a considered move, partly in terms of the social costs as well as the viability of the factory. In the event, and for unexplained reasons, the relocation did not take place.

The result was a form of unionism which very much relied on committed and active leaders, but where there was extensive involvement and engagement between these leaderships and the union membership. In a variety of ways, through celebrations, welfare activity, charity work, informal chit-chat and discussion, the GMB leaders, in particular, maintained and developed close working relations with their members. Many had worked in the factory for over fifteen years. They had moved from part-time work to full-time, and occasionally back again. They had lived through personal difficulties with each other and they had celebrated their personal as well as work achievements together. So, in both formal and informal ways, there was an active form of participation in union affairs, which allowed these union leaderships, the GMB in particular, considerable flexibility in representing members' interests.

Assessment

The unions at *Electronics Factory* had developed close working relationships with the factory management, resulting in a practice of managerial consultation on the changes that had been introduced in working practices and technological development. Consequently, there was an atmosphere of cooperation about the restructuring that took place at the factory as well as in the division more generally. From the union point of view, particularly that of the two majority unions, the GMB and MSF, this was a policy of bargained change, where the unions pursued policies of cooperation with the local factory management as one way of retaining some influence over the scope and direction of change at the factory. The view by the local union leaderships was that if they did not do this the prospect of the divisional and corporate management closing the factory and transferring production to the nearby larger site was very high. This was a view shared by local managers in the factory.

While this approach reaffirmed the position of the GMB as the lead union, it weakened the position of MSF as the main non-manual union in the factory. MSF was a relatively small union, comprising no more than thirty-four members during the period. Unlike the other non-manual union, APEX, it was fairly active during this time, with the lead representative playing an active part in the discussions about the proposed relocation. This involvement provided the basis for increased union cooperation, in particular between MSF and the GMB, with the AEU becoming a rump union group on the shopfloor and, together with the EETPU, continuing a limited defence of craft privilege. The outcome was a recomposition of unionism in the plant, creating the base for more open and solidaristic unionism. Such an outcome was made easier by the accessibility and relative openness of the factory management, which remained committed to close working relationships with the unions (see Elger and Fairbrother, 1991).

Alongside the policy of bargained change, the local leadership of the GMB took positive steps to redefine the boundaries of unionism in the factory. This took the form of pursuing policies which explicitly and routinely blurred the rigid divisions found among many union groups between work-based issues and domestic concerns. The local GMB leadership frequently raised questions about home and domestic concerns with the management of the enterprise. While this broadened the scope of unionism in the plant, it was also the case that local leadership worked closely with the local plant management to defend work and employment practices at the factory, pursuing relatively defensive strategies. The result was a form of unionism which, while defensive on pay and employment questions, was a vital part of the working and home lives of the membership in this factory.

In effect, an accommodation had been reached between the factory management and the local union leadership, which opened up a range of issues for negotiation and occasionally dispute, but with informally acknowledged limits to this activity. This was a factory workforce which worked under the threat of closure and there was a *de facto* agreement binding all the unions and particularly the leaderships to work with the local management. On the part of management, there was also a recognition that the long-established and relatively comfortable accommodations reached at the factory would not survive the incorporation of the factory workforce at the larger site following a merger. On this basis, union leaderships were prepared to work with the factory management to defend the factory as a separate entity. It was this *de facto* agreement that underlay the accommodation between management and union leaderships, and laid the foundation for forms of accommodative bargaining, where the union leaderships pursued their members' interests, to a point; beyond this boundary there was insecurity and uncertainty.

The result was a relatively self-contained unionism, focused within the factory, with very limited contacts and connections outside. It was a factory unionism which was born out of the necessity of dealing with the prospect of major and uncertain change. Out of this concern the union memberships looked to their union leaderships to secure some semblance of security about the future, although the prospects for success were by no means certain. The weakness of this approach was that the factory union leadership looked to neither the district office nor the union memberships at the sister plants for support and assistance in confronting the pressures from the divisional management to reorganize and possibly close the plant. In brief, the factory union leaders, particularly the GMB leaders, were successful in achieving a broadly based unionism at the factory which was able to give weight to the policy of the factory management in its defence of the factory. Their success reinforced a view that they could 'go it alone'. While this was an understandable approach, it did reinforce a rather limited approach to the defence of the factory and ultimately resulted in an ongoing vulnerability to broader corporate concerns.

The distinctiveness of *Electronics Factory* lay in the major union being led by women, with a decisive female majority among the membership. The outcome was a style of unionism where the relation between home and work was much more blurred than at the other factories. In addition, the openness and accessibility of the leadership group at *Electronics Factory* was such that the membership showed considerable confidence in the incumbents, and not only gave them support but gave the leadership discretion in dealing with the difficult and complicated problems of divisional reorganization. Thus, the major union at *Electronics Factory* actively explored the boundaries of conventional unionism in noteworthy ways, broadening the base of unionism on the shopfloor, resulting in a unionism that might be the harbinger of a revived and renewed tradition of unionism in such factories.

7 STRUGGLES AND DIVISIONS

One feature of the debates about unionism has been a recognition of the persistence of trade unionism during the 1980s, despite the changes that were taking place within enterprises, as well as in the economy as a whole (Gallie *et al.*, 1996). In general, these were arguments that focused on the continued activity by union activists and their leaders, often in conjunction with full-time officials, who increasingly were relied upon because of the vulnerability of workplace union organization. However, it is important to develop the analysis further and examine both the basis of this persistence and the fluctuating circumstances of union organization. This type of examination draws attention to the complex relations between managerial policies and practices and their impact on workplace unionism, and points to the fragility of the processes of union renewal in such circumstances.

The way in which management strategies of control are implemented in practice at a factory level raises important questions in relation to trade union organization and practice. It may be, as Friedman (1977, pp. 78–9, Chapter 7) argues, that there are two broad strategies, one based on 'direct control', which suggests an immediacy in the relationship between managers and workforces, and one on 'responsible autonomy', where it is claimed that the recognition of workgroup discretion and self-motivation results in 'responsible' workforce behaviour. One strand of argument has focused on successive attempts by management to secure control over the intensity and organization of work or the failure of management to achieve these ambitions. Another focus has been the examination of the nature of job control by workers and how managements deal with such issues (Terry and Edwards, 1988). The important point to note is that managerial initiatives on worker–management relations is critical for understanding the dynamic of trade unionism.

In this study of a traditional engineering factory, designated *Heating Factory*, the argument is developed that throughout the 1980s there was an often

relatively invisible struggle taking place, whereby management pursued policies aimed at restricting the role and activity of the shopfloor unions, while
union members and their leaders attempted to draw limits to this push by
management. This contest took place against the background of relatively
active and autonomous unionism in the 1970s, when the membership and
their leaders had achieved some success in securing their collective presence in
the factory. However, as these relations became more routinized, with management seeing them as a constraint, there was a bitter leadership contest within
the unions and managers moved to secure a compliant leadership in the name
of 'social partnership'. However, in this objective they were only partially
successful, although in the course of these events the staff union all but
disappeared.

The factory and the unions

Heating Factory was located in the same town as *Car Parts,* and had been owned
by a succession of multinational corporations, the most recent acquisition
taking place in 1987 (for a more extensive history of the factory, see Fairbrother, 1996b). The factory was engaged in the production of heating units
and was subject to the fluctuations in the heating industry in general and the
housing market in particular. For most of its history the factory operated as an
independent production unit, with the site management exercising considerable independence, especially in negotiations with the recognized unions at
the plant. For their part, the unions were able to pursue agreements and raise
questions with management, which by and large were settled at the factory
level, with little reference to workers at other factories in the town or within the
corporate group as a whole.

Production was based at one site, after a merger of two sites in 1978. Prior to
the merger, production of boilers took place at the main site, where the
foundry and assembly were located. The paint and press shops were based at
the second site, where some related assembly also took place. With the decision
to base all production at the main site, new paint and press shops were built
and the assembly area was expanded. The two main workforces were integrated as a single unified workforce, subject to the same terms and conditions of
employment.

Workforce levels remained fairly constant from the mid-1970s onwards at
between 900 and 1,100 employees, with a small expansion towards the end of
the 1980s and into the 1990s. A large proportion of the workforce (although
still a minority) was of South Asian ancestry. In the 1970s there was some

evidence of institutionalized racism, with workers of South Asian ancestry ending up in the foundry and labouring areas in disproportionate numbers. These practices resulted in long-term patterns of job segregation, which were often expressed through adverse work and time allocations.

The number of women employed at the factory was small, ranging between 150 and 200 and mainly employed in support and ancillary occupations, such as clerical work, canteen work and light assembly. There had been some change in the deployment of women within the factory between the late 1970s and the 1990s. In 1979, women production workers at the main site were not permitted to work in the foundry area or most of the assembly areas. This contrasted with the practice at the second site, where women workers were employed more widely in the paint shop and assembly areas, although not in the press areas. With the move to the main site, there was an increase in the numbers of women employed, although still in small numbers. In the early 1990s more women were employed as the company recruited more sales and support staff. Throughout the whole period, the language of the factory remained both gendered and sexist, indicated, for example, by catcalls and whistling when women walked through some parts of the factory, especially the foundry.

In the 1990s, five unions were recognized at the factory: four shopfloor unions, the AEU, TGWU and GMB, with a combined membership of 700–800 members on average and the EETPU (twenty members); and the non-manual union MSF with fewer than thirty members, covering less than a quarter of eligible staff. The shopfloor unions organized on the basis of a compromise between occupations and geography, with the AEU (foundry section) organizing foundry workers, the TGWU the distribution and assembly areas, the GMB the semi-skilled and unskilled workers in the fabrication areas and the EETPU the electrical craft workers throughout the factory. A further complication came with the AEU (engineering section) representing members in the toolroom and maintenance areas.

A history of persistent restructuring

Following the merger of the two sites there were two major redundancies at the factory, one in 1981 and the other in 1984. In the first programme, 116 workers took voluntary redundancy. At that time, the market had contracted to the extent that the factory was put on a three-day week. In the second redundancy, the company initially asked for and obtained fifty volunteers. In each case, the unions became involved in negotiations about the redundancies and were able to negotiate the terms of this programme, retaining the practice of voluntary rather than compulsory redundancies.

In some ways like *Car Parts*, the factory in the 1980s was treated as a unified profit centre, with the internal organization of the factory comprising a number of cost centres which the management in the latter part of the 1980s attempted to monitor as mini-profit centres. To facilitate this development, the factory management introduced a group bonus scheme, implemented on a departmental basis. Management then began to reorganize and 'rationalize' departments and, via the establishment of production teams, attempted to redraw the boundaries of control over work processes. Although this was a period of increased production and diversification of product, it was also a period of considerable debate about the introduction of 'new' working practices and procedures, injecting an element of worry among the workforce about the future patterns of work and employment at the factory.

The local management began to prepare the workforce for a period of reorganization and restructuring, aimed at challenging long-established work procedures and allowing flexible deployment of labour. While these changes began to be introduced in the mid-1980s, it was only with the change of ownership in 1988 that there was a broad commitment to this restructuring programme, particularly among senior factory managers, including members of the personnel department, who led the programme. This restructuring began slowly and initially involved a reassessment of the technological base of the factory, particularly in the assembly areas. In the mid-1980s, at a time when the factory appeared to be financially successful, the then parent company began a process of replacing old equipment in the foundry and further mechanizing the production process. Alongside this there was the gradual introduction of new technologies in the assembly area.

With the change of ownership in 1988, there began an attempt to integrate the production at this factory so that it complemented production at other heating factories owned by the company. There was a renewed impetus for the continued introduction of new equipment and an increase in labour flexibility at the plant. Apart from announcements and information bulletins presenting the modernization of plant in terms of financial viability and security, the management at the factory began to introduce the workers to these changes in formal induction sessions.

The restructuring of labour practices also led to a breakdown in demarcated work areas, specifically with respect to electrical and fitting work. With the introduction of new technology, particularly in the press shops and the assembly areas, there were moves in 1992 by the personnel department and union leaders to establish a dual skilling arrangement for fitters and electricians, where each did a limited amount of the other's work. Initially, this was introduced for apprentices, leaving established workers alone, so that each new apprentice in either fitting or electrical work was introduced to the new technologies which had become the occasion for redefining skills. All apprentices were introduced to computer-aided manufacture and design systems, both at college and on site, and had developed the competencies appropriate for the restructured workplace.

In the 1990s, against the background of increased price competitiveness, the subsidiary heating company's operating profit fluctuated, with a loss of nearly 20 per cent in 1994. In response, the company reduced the number of sites involved in boiler production from three to two and introduced automated lines in different production areas at *Heating Factory*, particularly in the foundry in 1994. This was accompanied by efforts to increase labour productivity, introducing 'new' forms of work organization, such as cell production teams. For the workers this heralded a further round of uncertainty, since it was unclear whether boiler production would be located on one or two sites.

Organization and representation

As indicated, there were two sets of union groups at the factory. First, the four shopfloor unions were organized into a long-standing joint shop stewards committee (JSSC), which undertook all the company-wide negotiations and organized the stewards in the different sections of the factory. This committee, founded in the 1960s, had developed into an active and participative committee during the 1970s. At this time the committee was led by a partnership between the two senior stewards of the two largest unions in the factory, the TGWU and the AEU. During the 1970s, with an expanded presence of the GMB following the merger of two sites in 1979, all areas of production were divided and represented on the committee: foundry (AEU), fabrication (GMB) and assembly (TGWU), with the EEPTU covering the whole plant, wherever its members worked. Second, the staff of the union were organized by the ASTMS from the early 1970s until the late 1980s, when it effectively collapsed. During this time, it was a relatively active union, although for most of its history it was organized around a small and enthusiastic leadership. Over time the active members of the leadership group resigned from their senior representative positions, leaving a senior plant representative alone as the mainstay of the union. When he resigned his job in the late 1980s the union effectively disappeared, although a small paper membership remained.

The shopfloor committee

The shopfloor committee effectively operated as the shopfloor union of the plant, irrespective of the different union memberships, and rarely referred issues to outside union officials, preferring to settle disputes within the factory. The committee had long been a largely male preserve, in part reflecting the ethos of the plant, where women workers were seen as peripheral to the main activity. In contrast, members of Asian ancestry and Afro-Caribbean members had been elected as stewards, although not at the level their overall numbers in the plant would indicate or in senior union leadership positions. The convenor was supported by a small negotiating committee, which consisted of the senior stewards. This group reported to a weekly stewards' meeting, which was composed of between twenty and twenty-five stewards.

There were two noteworthy features to the committee which related to the gender and ethnic composition of the union membership. For many years, there had been one woman steward on the committee, representing an electrical sub-assembly area principally composed of women. While she frequently raised queries at the weekly steward meetings on behalf of her membership, there was a tendency by the others to ignore the substance of her comments. In contrast, stewards of Asian ancestry who had long been members of the committee tended not to raise issues specific to their ethnic groups, apart from occasional queries. More pertinently, there had long been an ethic in the steward committee, articulated particularly by convenors, that this was a multi-ethnic workforce and that this should be recognized both formally and informally. There was also evidence that successive convenors had been assiduous in discussing problems and factory union policy with members of Asian ancestry, particularly members who worked in strategic work areas.

The stewards were elected by their section and the senior stewards, including the convenor, by membership constituencies as a whole. Consequently, the convenor had to win at least a minimum degree of support from the stewards to ensure his continued legitimacy among the membership. There were, of course, the usual antagonisms and differences between the leadership and stewards, occasionally along individual union lines. None the less, steward support for the incumbent leadership had long been a feature of union relationships at *Heating Factory*, although this had been withdrawn on occasion.

This union organization was built around the activism of the male stewards, particularly in the foundry area. This was a strategic area for the production process and, because of ongoing pressures about work flow and payment arrangements, the workers in this area were prepared to question managerial practice and procedures. In addition, many of the workers were relatively young and not bound by established procedures and ways of relating to supervision. It was also the area where the senior convenor worked, and during the 1970s he built up a loyal following, among not only the foundry stewards but also the foundry workers.

However, this form of organization tended to marginalize the specific concerns of both the population of Asian ancestry and women. While there were five stewards of Asian ancestry on the JSSC, none was in a senior position in the union and specific concerns about language or leave arrangements tended not to be central to the stewards' discussions. None the less, the convenor was aware of the concerns of these workers, whose stewards he tended to meet separately. It was different for the women workers, who were numerically less significant and whose concerns were often ignored. This was evident in the stewards' meetings in the late 1970s and early 1980s, where the one woman steward was frequently overlooked in the discussion and where even the obvious health and safety concerns of the women, such as working in certain areas when pregnant, were regarded by other stewards as specific to women and of no major concern for the committee.

Between 1979 and 1986, the steward committee became somewhat settled and complacent. The convenor and supporting senior stewards increasingly acted without direct reference to the steward committee and the membership. Dissenting stewards were either isolated on the committee or on occasion 'encouraged' to resign. Following a rebellion by stewards and members in 1986, a number of long-standing stewards either resigned or were voted out of office, including the convenor (resigned) and his immediate successor (voted out). They were replaced by a younger group of stewards who were committed to a return to the past union practices of accountability and participation. This was accomplished by a much more assertive approach towards management, questioning the continued problems that section stewards were having in representing their members to first-line supervision, particularly over the pay arrangements, which if anything had become more complex and uncertain. The senior leadership turned its attention back to the idea of developing a cadre of committed and active 'section' stewards as the basis once again of an active JSSC. Towards this end, the senior leadership, and the newly elected young (late twenties) convenor (AEU) encouraged, for the first time in a number of years, the attendance of stewards on union courses dealing with industrial relations and health and safety at work. The style of union leadership at the time was one of openness and participation. While stewards were encouraged by the senior leaders to take up issues, the convenor and deputy made themselves available to stewards, giving support and assistance where necessary.

There was a residue of bitterness among the more long-term stewards about these changes that had taken place on the committee, and this came to a head in 1988 when a bitter and divisive strike occurred at the factory. The issue was the failure of management to meet commitments on bonus payments for one particular section of workers, namely the indirect workers (toolroom, pattern shop, maintenance and stores). In a rather astute managerial move, the company laid off the production workers and promoted disagreement among the indirect workers, with the result that the strike eventually collapsed amid recrimination and division between different sections of the workforce. The new leadership was unable to maintain support for the strike and after four weeks the strikers returned to work amid considerable feelings of bitterness and demoralization. Subsequently, the convenor, who was targeted by both management and the disgruntled former union leaders as the main initiator of the strike, resigned. The committee recomposed itself, electing a new convenor and committee.

The fall-out from the strike was considerable. Relations between the factory management and the convenor had become quite strained and personalized and shortly afterwards the convenor resigned his position. The company, aware of the weakened state of the union, also refused to recognize the now ex-convenor as a steward. Although he had the moral support of the majority of the steward committee, he was not reinstated as a steward. Subsequently, there were managerial changes, in the course of which the main protagonists in the dispute either left the company or were no longer directly responsible for the 'rationalization' programme.

Following the dispute, the JSSC began the process of rebuilding itself around the traditional issues of wages and conditions of employment. The senior leadership, the new convenor (GMB) and the deputy convenor (AEU) pursued a much more cautious policy than the previous incumbents, partly because the membership was deeply divided about the course of the dispute and its outcome. This was opportune for management and particularly the personnel department, which found itself in a changing corporate world following the acquisition of the factory by another company. This management attempted to exploit the opportunities presented by these divisions and marginalize the shopfloor factory unions.

The staff union

For the non-manual union, the ASTMS, a different pattern of development was evident. This union had long been characterized by leadership dominance, with little membership participation. In part, the class position of the non-manual workers as both management and workers meant that they had an uncertain attitude to the union (Carter, 1986). This was reflected in the relatively low membership of the union in the early 1970s, about 50 per cent of eligible staff. The union was led by a young male technologist who worked in the research area, where the core of the membership were employed. In 1975 the union was involved in a short strike over a management proposal on redundancy selection. Following this, over half the membership resigned, encouraged by a management view that the secretary had 'manipulated the Strike to his own personal benefit' (Internal document, n.d.). It was not clear why the membership took this view.

Even so, the union maintained a relatively active profile up to the mid-1980s, principally because of the commitment of the senior steward. He pursued issues on behalf of his membership in the plant and he was active in wider union circles beyond the plant. In addition, he gave the union a high profile on health and safety, not only because of his union involvement but also because of his job in technical services, where he was a major participant in developing an asbestos substitution programme in the 1970s. As a trade union leader, he openly worked with the convenor and deputy convenor of the JSSC to develop complementary approaches, particularly on health and safety questions.

However, in the early 1980s the senior steward began to withdraw from active leadership of the union, partly because of a senior management policy to promote him to more senior grades and thereby compromise his leadership. While he attempted to maintain his earlier levels of involvement this became more difficult, so he reluctantly took a decision to play a less active role in the union (Interview, 1986). For a time the momentum of the union was maintained, first with a set of leaders drawn from technical services and then with an attempt to build a leadership core at the main factory in the late 1980s. The technical services leadership collapsed in 1985 when they argued for a ban on overtime work over the introduction of a merit-based method for awarding salary increases but failed to gain significant support. The result was that the ban was not recognized by many union members and it eventually collapsed amid feelings of bitterness and betrayal by different sections of the membership, resulting in a further 50 per cent resigning from the union. With the shift of the leadership to the main factory, there was a partial revival of interest by the membership, but this collapsed in the aftermath of the 1988 dispute involving shopfloor workers. The divisions engendered during this dispute also divided the staff over the principle of union solidarity, and signalled the end of staff union activity in the factory, although approximately 30 staff remained in formal membership.

The limits of bargained change

Following a change in ownership of the factory in the late 1980s, the personnel department acquired a more prominent set of responsibilities within the factory, initiating programmes aimed at achieving a more malleable and compliant workforce. As part of realizing this objective, the personnel department began to take on direct responsibility for most negotiations and bargaining in the plant, even on individual items and problems. Related to this shift in focus, management, via the personnel department, took steps to structure union activity in ways that spoke of 'partnership' but in fact were management led and controlled. It was against the background of these initiatives that the senior leadership of the JSSC began to work with management and pursue a policy of pragmatic accommodation (Jones and Rose, 1986).

The initial step by the management was an attempt to by-pass the local elected union leadership and deal directly with regional officials. The background to this development was that in the early 1990s, following the restructuring initiated in the late 1980s, the personnel department (the personnel manager, employee relations officer, training and health and safety officer and support staff) began to take on a more prominent set of responsibilities, not only for this factory but also for the other factories in the subsidiary company. In the light of this, and as part of an attempt to establish uniform procedures and practices across the division, the personnel manager and the employee relations officer began a policy of by-passing the senior union leadership at the factory and meeting the full-time union officials in the area. In turn, these officials saw this invitation as an opportunity to play a more active role in a major factory in the area, even if it undermined the local elected leaders.

The company management was of the view that dealing directly with the regional union officials, very much removed from the day-to-day concerns of the factory, would reinforce the company position and approach. Further, it was an approach which members of the personnel department thought would change the outlook and practice of the union committee in the plant. This approach was summed up by company officials: 'the Union must become more of a "policing" function, acting as a guardian of the new Culture and therefore instinctively being part of it, rather than as a critical bystander promoting division between the Company and employee' (Internal document, n.d.). One possible outcome was that the JSSC would begin to lose its previous autonomy within the wider union movement and become an adjunct of the full-time union officials, who would take responsibility for union policy in the factory.

However, the senior staff in the personnel department were apprehensive about this development, anticipating that an over-reliance on regional officials might stimulate a more active and independent union leadership in the factory, in part in opposition to the control of the regional officials. The personnel department also saw a danger in a possible future Labour government, which might have the effect of stimulating a more active approach to bargaining. Somewhat naively, they thought a Labour government was likely to underwrite union activism within workplaces, which could undermine the relatively 'cosy' relationships with the regional officials. In these circumstances, the personnel department began to promote what they defined as 'integrative bargaining', based on a reorganization of the work procedures (cell production and team working). This was coupled with a major technological upgrade in the foundry to reduce staffing levels and to promote a shift in union power away from the foundry workforce and towards what the management saw as a more 'positive' membership elsewhere, particularly in assembly.

A crucial aspect of the introduction of cellular forms of production was the replacement of piece-work wage bargaining with flat-rate wages. This form of production was part of a management aim to remove the basis of union organization in the factory. Reflecting on the introduction of the cellular form of work, a representative from the personnel department commented:

> We are attempting to move away from a piecework system which inevitably means that people go like the clappers in the morning to get the production rate up, as it were, and then do less in the afternoon. And the idea behind that is to make sure we have the right first time built-in quality. (1993)

What was not stated was that the shopfloor union leaders had built the union over and over on the basis of the strong sectional identity that came with piecework bargaining, section by section. All the major disputes in the 1980s had centred on attempts by management to qualify and dilute these arrangements, and thereby undermine the union organization in the plant.

Faced with these developments and against the background of the continued aftermath of the 1988 strike, the union leadership began to take steps to reposition the shopfloor union committee at the factory. There was a clear recognition by the senior leaders that the strike had undermined the union base in critical ways. As noted:

> The strike was three or four years ago and the people that broke the picket line are still here. When we are trying to build it the union is only as strong as the workers and the members are still divided and there are still people who will not speak to other people [as a result of the strike]. (Convenor, 1993)

In these circumstances, and in the awareness that the management at the factory was attempting to narrow the focus of the union and restrict the wage bargaining activity of the stewards, the JSSC leadership began to emphasize the traditional concerns of the membership as a way of ensuing a continued reliance on and identification with the union activity and representation at the factory. In addition, the steward leaders began to distance themselves from their regional officials and emphasize the relative autonomy of the union committee within the wider union movement.

In 1993, the shopfloor leaders negotiated an agreement on labour utilization and new technology, building on earlier and less precise agreements. This agreement covered staff in maintenance and other service areas in the factory and aimed to define the limits of dual skilling. Central to the agreement was an attempt to protect the position of older workers who did not want to be retrained in the use of electronic equipment. Underlying this concern was the issue of status and whether it was possible to negotiate staff status for maintenance and related workers, as new technology was introduced. It is in these respects that the shopfloor unions accepted the basic thrust of the restructuring as part of an attempt to secure a continued future for workers at this factory, as well as to re-establish the basis of workplace unionism.

Alongside these types of negotiations the senior leadership encouraged stewards to take up section-based and section-focused issues, addressing the production supervision in the first instance, rather than the personnel department. In part, this move was helped by the way in which personnel staff were increasingly drawn into divisional negotiations and responsibilities, making the more hands-on approach within the factory less possible and practical. As a result, there was a complicated process of establishing and re-establishing the basis of negotiation and bargaining at the factory. In this, the union leaders were active in influencing the direction and focus of these arrangements, as part of the means of rebuilding the union presence at the factory.

The outcome was ambiguous and uneasy. On the one hand, the union leaders were aware of the vulnerability of their position, although they believed they were having some success. As noted by the deputy convenor, 'The union is less powerful because of the environment we are in plus the effect of the strike that took place [1988] and we have gone out of our way to try and rebuild the factory union ... and I think we are getting that way' (1993). On the other hand, as indicated, the union leaders saw the factory managers, via the personnel department, as seeking to shift the balance of relations between management and the unions in their favour; as far as the factory union leadership was concerned, the rhetoric of 'partnership' was that and little more.

The union leaders recognized that the key dimension of their strategy for recovery was to relay the foundation for active and participative steward-based structures. In this respect, the difficulties they faced were twofold. First, membership remained divided about the activities that took place in the strikes of 1988, as well as their outcome. These divisions remained salient, even five years later, and made it difficult for union leaders and activists to build the sectional identities that were critical to this form of unionism. Second, the company managers were astute in attempting to shift the focus of management practice from a rather adversarial relation to one where there was an appearance of 'partnership' and cooperation.

Even so, a slow process of union recovery appeared to be taking place. The union leaders, supported by the steward committee, moved to reaffirm a factory-focused form of unionism. In part, this involved distancing the union committee from the regional full-time officials; in part, it involved re-emphasizing the specificity of union organization and action at the factory, as if the factory was not part of a wider division within the company. The outcome was a partial recovery of a sense of a factory union consciousness, which allowed the leadership to gain a critical perspective on the management rhetoric of 'partnership' and cooperation.

Assessment

The union history at *Heating Factory* was marked by fluctuation and struggle, where the staff union had collapsed and effectively ceased to operate by the mid-1980s and the shopfloor unions had developed active and relatively open forms of unionism at some periods, followed by relatively remote forms of leadership at others. By the 1990s the JSSC operated in a bargaining terrain that was dominated and set by the personnel department. The result was a one-sided partnership, where the union leadership acted as if there was little alternative but to accept the terms and conditions of employment set by management.

The management at *Heating Factory*, as part of the overall approach by the parent company, had decentralized budgetary control and devolved the management of the labour process. One aim was to establish the basis for a more malleable and compliant workforce at the factory, involving a revived personnel department in the 1990s, the deployment of the workforce in teams and related forms of work organization, experiments with pay systems and the elaboration of a corporate culture focusing on the individual worker. A second aim was to demobilize the shopfloor unions at the factory, by drawing boundaries around the legitimate concerns of 'responsible' union leaderships. The main mechanism in this process was to restrict the activity of the section stewards and to deal with the senior leadership in isolation from the stewards.

By the 1990s, the union strategy pursued by the local leadership was one of apparent rather than real compliance, seeking to influence and adapt the changes via factory collective bargaining. Although the factory management had expressed some preference for dealing directly with the district officials, the overarching approach was to negotiate directly with the JSSC leaderships, as the most likely way to ensure compliance from the unions. In turn, the JSSC leadership saw this managerial approach as a way of securing the long-term future of the unions in the plant, in the face of corporate rumour and uncertainty about the viability of *Heating Factory*. It was also the case that the JSSC leadership used the opportunity of local bargaining as a key step in rebuilding the presence of the union in the factory.

At a number of points during the history of the unions at the factory, the union activists and leaders had been successful in developing relatively participative and open forms of organization, reflected in the issues taken up as well as the style and methods of organizing and operating as trade unionists. These distinct patterns of unionism were also underwritten in a paradoxical way by management practice and procedure. For much of the history of the JSSC, the management dealt directly and exclusively with the JSSC (and the staff union in its earlier period) in formalized and regulated ways. In these circumstances, there was the space for union activists and their leaders to develop active and participative forms of unionism. It was only when the factory managers began to initiate policies aimed at reorganizing the work practices and employment conditions that they began to look for a changed relation with the unions in the plant. The previous pattern of relationships was predicated on the recognition that there was not a necessary overlap between the interests of the workforce and those of management, on working conditions, patterns of work organization and the terms and conditions of employment at the factory. However, towards the end of the 1980s and into the 1990s, it became important for the factory management to secure compliance and cooperation from the unions for the changes that were envisaged.

During the 1990s, the union leadership faced major difficulties in rebuilding the union as a unified and solidaristic organization. The critical point about the 1988 strike was that the membership divided in terms of skill and area of work. It was in this respect that the ongoing animosities following the strike had a material dimension to them that was not easily resolved by the passing of time and a reconsideration of the strike itself. For the union leaders, both the convenor and deputy convenor, as well as the majority of the committee, one part of the problem was that they had all been supporters of the strike and thus found it difficult to sympathize with those who had opposed it. None the less, the factory union leadership had taken steps to move beyond the divisiveness of the strike and affirm the importance of solidarity and unity, principally by promoting a factory union consciousness in the context of the managerial policies of the 1990s.

Alongside the divisions associated with the aftermath of the 1988 strike, the union membership remained divided on gender lines. In practice, the interests of women members at the factory were subordinated in the context of sectionally focused concerns defined in terms of the dominant male ethos. Although there were periods when the union committee organized in participative and relatively open ways, there was no guarantee that the interests of women members would be recognized. Despite the relative openness of the steward committee, women were in effect invisible and not central to the union concerns. Paradoxically, many of the women members worked in the same area, but this did not mean that the female steward for the section was 'heard' at the steward meetings.

A more complicated history was evident in relation to the ethnic composition of the workforce. Although there was evidence of informal racism at the factory, the union leadership recognized the importance of establishing an accommodation with the substantial number of workers of Asian origin. These members were recognized as an integral component of the membership. Not only did they play a part in the committee, but successive convenors had long acknowledged the importance of this section of the membership at times of industrial action. This was illustrated by the ongoing informal dialogue between the convenor, together with other factory union leaders, and this membership. All the same, there were occasions when racist sentiments were expressed by the majority union membership, over such issues as special leave arrangements and the like. Usually, the senior union leadership acted quickly to defuse the complaints and maintain the relatively harmonious pattern of relations in the factory.

One way whereby the union leadership dealt with the gendered, racial and skill divisions in the factory was to develop the union committee on the basis of the steward form of representation, with each steward responsible for his or her own section. Steward constituencies were defined by working patterns and arrangements, which were imposed by the factory management, and in this respect the JSSC was a critical factor in building a sense of union purpose and solidarity. Rather than play on the divisions and distinctiveness of these constituencies, as was the case at *Car Parts*, the activists and senior leadership emphasized the importance of developing a unity of purpose. However, this was a tentative accommodation, and in circumstances where management played on the divisions in the factory, particularly on skill differences and the way they were reflected in pay levels, as was the case in the mid-1980s, the vulnerability of this form of organization became evident.

The outcome was a form of unionism that reflected the flux and flow of pressures on unionism during the 1980s and into the 1990s. These unions, including the staff union when it was active, were relatively self-contained, developing a pattern of unionism which was factory-based and focused. The JSSC leadership, in particular, embodied the union within the factory and took the lead in promoting a unified approach by the stewards and their members in the early period. In this respect, it was important that the management pursued an approach towards the unions that was predicated on formalized procedures and practices, providing the opportunity for the union leadership to develop participative and engaged practices by activists and to a lesser extent members more generally. This was an effective form of organization, reflected in the successes of the union in securing an orderly settlement of wage negotiations, making advances in addressing the hazardous and dangerous working conditions at the factory and developing an activist profile in the broader union movement in the community. It was only when management began to play on the implicit divisions within the workforce that the vulnerability of this form of organization became apparent.

The problem for the union leadership was that the factory management continued to seek a narrowing of the union agenda and concern within the factory. In pursuing these goals the management promoted policies designed to undermine the shopfloor union committee, within both the factory and the broader union movement. While there were limits to the success of this strategy, the factory management had been partially successful in that the shopfloor unions were in a weakened state when compared with earlier periods. However, the local union leaderships were not acquiescent to these strategies: they took steps to maintain and refocus the union presence within the factory. Building on past practices, the shopfloor union leadership continued to promote a form of factory union consciousness among the activist membership, and in particular the section stewards. Thus, while it was a union group that continued to face a vulnerable future, it was also one where there were attempts to relocate and reposition the union in the light of the changing circumstances of worker–management relations at the factory.

Unions at Work

The fate and fortune of the unions studied were worked out in terms of the changing patterns of workplace relations at these factories. Faced with the restructuring that was taking place in the manufacturing sector, the vulnerabilities and uncertainties of trade unionism became apparent. In all cases, there were attempts by union leaderships and activists to protect and sustain unionism. In a number of cases, particularly among the staff unions, this proved impossible, and these unions disappeared except in name. Elsewhere, different strategies for survival and resistance were pursued, in part in relation to traditions and experiences, both within unions and between union memberships and management, and in part in relation to the specificities of the restructuring that was taking place.

One difficulty that was apparent in all cases was that the threats to union organization and operation were not only in terms of immediate worker and management relations, but also in relation to the less discernible exigencies associated with corporate plans and strategies for particular factories and spheres of production. Acquisitions by the parent company might have had knock-on effects on particular plants and corporate reconstruction might have meant that plants were sold on or closed down. More than this, such developments also took place in the context of the ongoing uncertainties in the West Midlands, which impacted disproportionately on the manufacturing sector. While it may have been important for these unions to consolidate their strengths and address these political challenges and developments beyond the workplace, the pressures were such that without exception these union groups were forced back on to their own resources and activities for survival.

The immediate terrain of unionism in these factories was set by managerial initiative and policies of control and labour regulation. In the broader context of the changes that took place in the West Midlands and the internationalization of manufacturing during this period, managements pursued policies of labour reorganization. These policies included a reduction in staffing levels, in some cases the relocation of workforces and the restructuring and reorganization of workforces, in terms of employment relations and work organization. Such initiatives were often prompted by wider corporate imperatives and informed by concerns to control labour costs and achieve flexible compliance.

One focus in this process of manufacturing reorganization in the region was a concern with the detail of management–labour relations, reflected in managerial approaches to the control and organization of labour. The four factories studied had long histories in the region. They were organized in relatively conventional and traditional ways, focused on operational managements, where first-line supervision was pivotal in the organization of a compliant and controlled manual workforce. However, in the 1980s, there were tentative moves at these factories, with implications for manual and non-manual staff, to move beyond the traditional patterns of worker–management relations and to develop managerial styles and work-related procedures associated with HRM. But in all cases these were hesitant and unevenly implemented patterns of managerial organization and approach. The outcome was that during the 1980s and into the 1990s, manufacturing trade unions faced changing work and employment relations; in the context of changed policies and practices, established relations were not simply reproduced but involved an alteration between different occupations and forms of trade unionism.

In the manufacturing sector, as evident in these four factories, management had taken steps to decentralize budgetary control and devolve the management of the labour process to establishment level. There had been moves to establish more flexible workforces through changes to numbers employed and to forms of work organization as well as pay policies. What is noteworthy about the restructuring in this region is that many of these changes were achieved via collective bargaining. Unions had frequently bargained for change, albeit reluctantly and in circumstances not of their choosing. This ranged from the physical reconstruction of workplaces, accompanied by moves to reorganize work procedures and related arrangements, to the more mundane and incremental change evident in these factories. In some cases this was associated with the effective demise of unionism in the plant, in the sense that, although unions were still recognized, they were merely shadow organizations when compared with the past.

The union groups in the four factories were markedly different in a number of respects. At *Car Parts*, the major union was highly centralized, whereas at *Electronics Factory* and *Heating Factory*, at a number of points during their history, more participative forms of organization were evident. In the case of *Telecommunications Factory*, a more mixed pattern of relations was evident, where the assault on the unions by management resulted in union leaderships who were increasingly isolated from their memberships, principally because of profound uncertainty about the future for all these workers, irrespective of union position or area of work. These distinct patterns of organization were also underwritten by management practice and procedure, particularly in the case of *Car Parts*, where there was a long history of cooperative relations between the senior union leaders and personnel. None the less, there was evidence elsewhere that managements set the agenda for relations with unions, in the process affirming particular aspects of trade unionism. Overall, management seemed concerned to maintain the long-standing bargaining relationships in each plant.

These studies confirm the way in which the dynamics and character of change are conditioned by the specific ways in which the labour–capital relation has been institutionalized and expressed. In each case this relation was expressed via internal organization and segmentation, as well as in terms of the general relation between managers and workers. So, for example, the staff workers and shopfloor workers were differentiated from each other by job tasks and location, a pattern that was reinforced by the history of relations between staff and shopfloor workers. Despite moves to harmonize and remove some of the more obvious conditions of employment that distinguished these groups of workers, there remained in each factory a marked segmentation between different groups of workers. However, it should also be noted that the specific details of these relations were overlain with the continued persistence of a distinction between management on the one hand and workers on the other.

Significantly, the collective organization and activity of workforces themselves contributed to the recomposition of worker relations and the renewal of trade unions. The organization of staff and the shopfloor into separate unions within each of these plants simply reinforced the distinctiveness of each group. Even where the JSSC was relatively open and inclusive, as was the case in both *Electronics Factory* and *Heating Factory* (at different times during the 1970s and 1980s), there was little attempt to incorporate and include the staff unions by the JSSC. The realities of social life in the factories underwrote these patterns of separation, despite moves by senior management to remove the more obvious signs of differentiation in the form of eating arrangements, sickness benefits, leave arrangements and the like. Where a degree of solidarity was attained it was generally at the behest of the staff union leadership and usually defined by the shopfloor leadership as a recognition of the positive attributes of individual staff rather than an acknowledgement of the common condition of staff and shop floor workers.

The bargaining relationships evident at each factory were rooted in sectional forms of work and employment organization, which only began to break down in the 1990s. It could be argued that sectionalism both allowed the possibility of unity and reinforced division. However, this took a number of different forms depending on the lines of division and distinction, as well as the consciousness and forms of group identity associated with sectionally based and organized memberships (see Kelly, 1988, pp. 145–6). The differences between these union organizations thus lie in a complex articulation of unionism by leaders and their members. These relations are developed in the context of industrial relations practices and procedures and managerial organization and approaches. A competitive sectionalism (where members are functionally divided, represented by stewards who restrict their concerns to the section) constitutes the organizational basis for centralized forms of union leadership, whereas a beneficial sectionalism (where members are similarly functionally organized but their representatives act in concert with other stewards, irrespective of section) provides the basis for participative forms of unionism. It is in this respect that it is possible to claim that different forms of unionism are associated with specific types of sectionalism, and thus to characterize the form of unionism at *Car Parts* and *Telecommunications Factory* as centralized and that at *Electronics Factory* and *Heating Factory* as participative and member-centred.

Sectionalism is the grist for these forms of workplace unionism, which can be moulded and fashioned in one way or another. To this extent, neither bureaucratic nor democratic forms of workplace unionism are inevitable; there is clearly a cross-cutting set of tensions which in the complex circumstances of work and employment relations may allow centralized or democratic forms of unionism to emerge. It is this set of relations and practices that constitutes the politics of workplace unionism. This is an argument that sectionalism can be creatively developed to lay the foundation for democratic forms of unionism. Where steward democracy is qualified and negated, stewards and their members can only rely on the strength of their own sections or fall silent. Where democracy is evident it is likely to be built on the back of sectional practice and organization. This is not without difficulties. There may be a tendency to rely on informal union relations, which may not always be the most effective way of dealing with problems. It may result in occasionally individualistic and non-supportive action by one steward or membership at the expense of others. At the same time, it may allow for a regular turnover of central leaders and the uncertainties associated with such changes. More than this, it may mean that central stewards are readily accessible and supportive in ways that are not evident in bureaucratized unions. Finally, and most crucially, it is under the circumstances of sectionally based union practices and relations that a milieu is provided for collective organization and action, the core of democratic practice.

The pattern of union renewal in this sector had become one of survival, as the precondition to a more comprehensive relocation and rebuilding of unionism in these factories. The leaders of these union groups all found themselves in beleaguered positions, where they faced sets of developments that were seemingly beyond their control and where members faced a future of some uncertainty. Even where senior leadership had forged a close and collaborative relationship with the factory management, the membership was not protected from the harsher aspects of the restructuring that took place during the 1980s and the 1990s. These leaderships had limited success in recruiting new generations of activists to broaden and extend the representational base of the union. With the partial exception of the female union leadership at *Electronics Factory*, members were unwilling to come forward and help to develop the union. In some cases the inability to maintain and rebuild workplace unionism resulted in the effective end of the union form of representation for sections of the workforce in these factories. The problem was that the managerial agenda was such that the unions were placed in defensive positions where there was little prospect of collective resistance to the developments that were taking place.

There are two sides to the survival strategies pursued by unions in these factories. Some union leaderships either sought out or had long pursued an accommodation with management, and complied with the implementation of managerial programmes of reorganization and recomposition. These leaderships sought to ensure the presence of the union in the factory on the basis of a minimalist agenda of members' interests. The problem was that this resulted in a hollowing out of the union and left collective representation as a charade. In addition, in the context of continued corporate developments and economic restructuring, there was a hardening of the managerial approach to unionism and there appeared to be little that these union memberships could do to resist. In these circumstances the prospects for union renewal were limited.

However, leaving the analysis at this point would be misleading. What this ignores is the dynamic of collective organization and representation in the context of the wage relationship in these factories. As two of the union groups, at *Electronics Factory* and in particular at *Heating Factory*, demonstrated, there is an ongoing vitality to unionism, which the few often turn to and in the process rebuild (in the case of *Heating Factory*) or maintain (in the case of *Electronics Factory*). As indicated, this not only entails a process of maintaining unionism, it also involves a process of reorienting the focus of unionism in relation to the concerns and interests of members, as well as the circumstances of work and employment, and the politics of these relations. It may be that the test for union activists and leaders is to recognize and acknowledge the importance of developing strategies of renewal, rather than to acquiesce in a defensive manner to the managerial approaches that are being implemented, as if they are inevitable and immutable. One part of this recognition is the articulation of a union consciousness, rooted in an understanding of the strength of collective organization and power; another is a proactive response to the sense of powerlessness that has accompanied the restructuring of the manufacturing sector over the past two decades. It is in these respects that the possibility of union renewal remains a possibility, even in these beset factories.

PART III
UTILITIES

INTRODUCTION

In Britain, since 1976, privatization policies have been introduced as part of an attempt to transform the state sector by revising the terms and conditions of employment as well as restructuring work relations. These have involved job losses, increased use of personal employment contracts, blurring of recruitment demarcations stemming from harmonization and the spread of casualization from manual to white-collar occupations (Ferner, 1989; Colling, 1991; Ferner and Colling, 1991; Fairbrother, 1994a, b; Pendleton, 1997). While these developments pose a major threat to trade unions, this restructuring of the social relations of production can provide unions with opportunities to reconsider and develop their unionism anew.

Privatization policies are concerned with both the transfer of publicly owned assets to the private sector and the 'commercialization' of the state sector. These policies have taken a number of different forms: sell-offs, externalization and contracting-out. Initially, privatization involved and was identified with sell-offs, but increasingly sections of the public sector have been externalized (offered to an outside contractor without any in-house bids) or contracted out (the moving of projects or clusters of activity to outside contractors). The Conservative governments of the 1980s changed regulations to minimize in-house bids, and thereby to introduce an extensive and comprehensive form of privatization throughout the public sector.

The implementation of privatization policies has involved a managerial reconsideration of industrial relations, as privatized managements attempt to recompose their enterprises to meet the changed circumstances in which they now operate. According to Ferner and Colling (1991, pp. 405–6), approaches now range from 'hard-line industrial relations', with the prospect of industrial conflict, to a preference of some managements 'to maintain stability and continuity with the earlier public enterprise traditions'. They note that in some cases the moves towards 'hard-line' policies are not peculiar to the privatized corporations and may be rooted in other factors, such as technological change and market deregulation. Privatization offers contradictory incentives for managers both to minimize costs and to sustain and improve quality; as a result, there is no single management approach towards the recomposition of work and employment relations in these enterprises.

The scale of privatization

Privatization policies are part of a more general pattern of restructuring and reorganization of the British state. The scale of privatization in Britain has been immense. It has included the sale of corporations and the contracting-out of service functions. A wide variety of rationales has been used by advocates of privatization, including value for money, popular capitalism, the requirement to cut the public sector deficit, the introduction of competition and the supposed higher efficiency of the private sector (Martin and Parker, 1997).

The areas subjected to privatization include:

- *Utilities*: British Telecom, Cable and Wireless, all electricity generators and distributors as well as the transmission grid, British Gas, water companies.
- *Transport*: British Airways, British Airports Authority, Associated British Ports, British Rail, National Bus Company, local bus companies.
- *Production companies*: BP, Britoil, Enterprise Oil, British Aerospace, Jaguar, Rolls Royce, British Steel.
- *Public administration*: income tax, social security, national insurance and driver and vehicle licensing computers; legal advice to central and local government; architects and designers; housing management; driving test examination; school inspection, nursery school inspection; civil service and teachers' pension schemes.
- *Defence*: ordnance factories, naval dockyards, atomic weapons establishment, management of bases, firing ranges and ammunition depots, personnel selection and recruitment agency.
- *Local services*: refuse collection, street cleaning, school meals, school cleaning.
- *Health services*: hospital cleaning, hospital catering, hospital laundry.
- *Other*: Amersham International, National Engineering Laboratory, National Physical Laboratory, Public Services Agency, Highways Agency (details supplied by Public Services Privatization Research Unit (PSPRU), 1996).

One result is that over sixty multinational groups are now involved in the British public service. Thus privatization has had the effect of transferring the ownership of substantial sections of the British state from the public to the national and international private sector.

The features of privatization

Over the past decade, the privatized corporations have been acquired by a group of multinationals, which now dominate the UK privatized public services. This process has been twofold, involving the purchase of privatized firms (currently under way in the privatized electricity industry) or the acquisition of responsibility for public sector functions (as in the case of housing management privatization). The result has been a very complicated pattern of relationships and connections, with an increasing concentration of ownership by multinational corporations.

These developments can be illustrated with reference to the electricity sector, where London Electricity has explored the possibility of financing and running a hospital in another part of the country. At the same time, Leeds General National Health Service Trust initially began selling power from its power plant and subsequently sold it to Générale des Eaux (a French multinational whose main business was water, but which also had interests in catering, communications, construction, education, energy, environment, health, housing, property and transport). This French multinational also owned the largest chain of private hospitals in the UK. A further illustration is provided by one of the largest waste management companies in the USA, WMX Technologies, which acquired the refuse collection of one local authority, an architects' department of another, a water company and a major accident and emergency hospital (PSPRU, 1996, p. 1). Such manoeuvres point to the complex web of corporate relationships that have begun to emerge both within and between the utilities.

What is equally significant is that there is a concentration of ownership emerging in the utilities sector, with the same companies recurring in Britain and elsewhere, within three main clusters of public service enterprise: water, energy, telecommunications and transport; environmental services, healthcare, prisons, housing, social services; cleaning, catering, computers, finance and security. These companies have pursued a variety of approaches, including specialism in some areas of activity, take-overs and extending the range of their services. A relatively small number of multinationals have been involved, and these companies operate over a wide range of public services in more than one continent.

Privatization: a global phenomenon

During the early 1990s, public bodies were increasingly excluded from the tendering process, thus further encouraging the transfer of public services and resources into the multinational private sector. However, this is not a peculiarity of Britain and is evident around the world. This approach to economic regulation has become a feature of nation state policy as states attempt to reposition themselves within global markets. In the case of Britain, deregulation was part of a programme to lay the foundation for a marketized economy within Britain and an international presence beyond. The move towards privatization is part of the move to internationalize economies. In this respect, states have unleashed a pattern of development in which the state has been the prime mover in opening up public services to international control and organization, laying the foundation for the extension of an internationalized private services sector in ways that were not anticipated in the early 1980s.

In the many debates about globalization, there has been much comment on the role and function of the state, ranging from the irrelevance of the state (Ohmae, 1990, 1995) to the continuing importance of the state as a manager of national economies (Hirst and Thompson, 1996). What is absent in such accounts is a consideration of the implications of the changes taking place in the form of the state. Conversely, when changes in the forms of labour in society are the subject of enquiry, the implications for state form and the internal organization of the state and its own labour process are equally absent (Sabel, 1994). Even in those studies where the state as such has been the focus of attention, the implications of radical state restructuring for its own employment, labour organization and employee acquiescence or resistance have received little detailed consideration. Moreover, this is almost equally true for works that celebrate the new entrepreneurialism of the state (Osborne and Gaebler, 1992), welfare provision in terms of post-Fordist analyses (Hoggett, 1991) and more critical perspectives (Jessop, 1994).

The neglect of labour as both an agent and recipient of changing global state relations therefore has a twofold nature. The social relations of labour, it is argued, are no longer bound by or defined by the nation state, with the result that a 'borderless' world of capital may be in the process of emerging (Ohmae, 1990, 1995; Dicken, 1992; Sklair, 1995; Boyer and Drache, 1996). Although this particular line of argument can be questioned, one aspect which has evoked comment is that for workers there is now a vulnerability in employment relations which organized and unorganized labour have found difficult to address (Elger and Smith, 1994). Thus, assessments range from a celebration of the importance of globalization, on the one hand, to a focus on its invidious effect on workers and the uncertainty and unevenness of their response and resistance, on the other.

The 'new' privatized management

The focus of this part of the book is on the patterns and implications of these developments in the privatized utilities. The privatization of state enterprises provided an opportunity for the state to lay the foundation for services and products to be offered to the public on a commercial basis, albeit in monopolistic market conditions (Ramanadham, 1988, pp. 3–25; Young, 1990, p. 537; Whitfield, 1992, pp. 65–104, 127–69). Associated with these initiatives were attempts by successive governments to restructure the labour process so that it was no longer organized to provide goods and services to the public on the basis of some notion of need, but in terms of efficiency and cost-effectiveness (Whitfield, 1992, pp. 128–31). The assumption was that a traditional state labour process, predicated on formalized notions of consensual work and employment relations, was not sufficient for the commercialized climate of the 1980s and 1990s.

Management structures of the traditional core areas of the privatized companies have been transformed in decisive ways. This has involved moves from functional forms of organization (for example, billing, sales or engineering) to geographical structures (at the level of the district), in the case of water and electricity and more recently gas, and to the establishment of a comprehensive divisional structure, in the case of telecommunications. While this development has been noted by many, there has been little reference to what decentralization means in practice (an exception is Colling, 1991, p. 127; see also Fairbrother *et al.*, 1996).

With the establishment of privatized utilities, the new corporate managements embarked on a programme of decentralizing managerial authority: that is, 'the *delegation* of power and authority to lower levels, with ultimate responsibility remaining at the national level' (Martin, 1991, p. 268). Often mistakenly described as a process of devolution, which refers to 'the *transfer* of power, authority and responsibility from a national to a sub-national level' (*ibid.*), decentralization was the guiding principle of the managerial restructuring which took place in these large privatized utilities. This *delegation* of power and authority became the means for the achievement of more malleable and compliant workforces in the face of dramatic change and reorganization in these industries.

More recently, there has been an increasing emphasis on human resource management and forms of total quality management. This rhetoric and the introduction of practices associated with the HRM agenda have been used to legitimize the decentralization of management in these corporations and to rationalize a more explicitly 'business' framework, apparently based on consensual managerial approaches. In part, this managerial approach has provided the basis for integrating workforces more closely into the business ethos of each corporation, as well as laying the foundation for work intensification. The emphasis in these initiatives has been on managerialism and the commodification of employment relations (Tuckman, 1992, pp. 21–2).

Such developments have had an impact on unionism within the privatized enterprises. There were relatively long traditions of unionism in these sections of the public sector. In general, these unions organized and operated in relatively centralized ways, negotiating with equally centralized public sector managements. The result was a distanced form of organization, with relatively little activity at a local level, apart from negotiating the implementation of national agreements and representing members on grievances and related personal difficulties. With privatization, and the processes of change that were involved in these changes of ownership, unions faced difficulties, as the past patterns and forms of representation had less purchase. Workers as union members faced 'new' managerial approaches and styles. These enterprises increasingly operated in market environments where the past certainties of state employment no longer applied. In these circumstances, there were pressures on unions at a local level to re-examine the basis of union organization and operation, although the uptake and outcome were very varied.

The study

The redrawing of state boundaries in the form of privatization has been extensive and comprehensive in the UK. However, changes in ownership *per se* did not necessarily imply a reorganization and recomposition of these enterprises, and it is important to consider the period before privatization and subsequently to understand the full impact of the process of privatization. In the lead-up to privatization it has been common for these state enterprises to initiate processes of change, including managerial recomposition, staff reorganization, institutional changes and staff down-sizing, as part of the preparation for privatization. It is also the case that following privatization some enterprises continued the process of restructuring, while others continued to organize and operate as quasi-monopolies in the private sector.

The various patterns of privatization meant that worker experience of this process was likewise varied. Initially the brunt of change, in the lead-up to privatization, and subsequently, fell on the manual staff, with the non-manual staff less affected by these processes of change. However, in time all workers were caught up in this process, as they experienced institutional change, reorganization and recomposition of managerial hierarchies, and eventually changed patterns of employment, including extensive contracting-out and out-sourcing. Such developments impacted on the unions recruiting and representing these workers. These unions, usually organized on an industry basis, differentiated by occupation and grade; but with privatization and the distancing of the state from the organization and operation of these industries, these unions faced an unclear future, as they sought to re-establish their basis of representation in these industries.

In addressing these issues, the study focuses on three core utilities – telecommunications, gas and water – and examines three companies: British Telecommunications plc (BT), British Gas plc (gas) and Severn Trent Water plc (water). These companies were privatized at different times during the 1980s, BT in 1984, gas in 1986 and water in 1989. In the case of gas and, particularly, water, the companies and the government were subject to very active campaigns against privatization by trade unionists in these industries. While these campaigns did not halt the moves towards privatization they did cause delays to the initial timetable. With privatization there was a varied pattern of internal corporate reorganization and restructuring. In the case of BT and the water industry, there was what has been referred to as a radical restructuring of the way these companies organize and operate, whereas initially there was very little change in British Gas (Ferner and Colling, 1991; see also Fairbrother, 1994b). However, by the mid-1990s this had changed and British Gas was embarked on a comprehensive reorganization, spurred by its loss of a monopoly position.

8 'RESPONSIBLE' REPRESENTATION: BRITISH TELECOMMUNICATIONS PLC

The privatization of utilities involved changes in ownership but did not necessarily lead to managerial reorganization and changed relations between management and unions, at least in the initial period. In the case of the privatization of British Telecommunications (BT) in 1984 there was little substantive change in labour–management relations until the late 1980s. To an important extent this created an impression that privatization did not necessarily herald major change and that the established relations between union leaderships and the company could be maintained. There were, however, major issues for unions to address, such as staff reductions and the moves by the company to establish itself as an international corporation.

In the context of apparent continuity of relations with management, union leaderships, especially the British Telecom section of the CWU/NCU, saw no major reason to review and revise patterns of organization or modes of operation. This view was particularly evident at a local level, as local leaderships began to address the implications of privatization. In the main, local union branches were organized on a geographical basis, focused on local leaderships, where at least the branch secretary and often additional local leaders had 100 per cent facility time. These local leaderships were usually based in central union offices, shared by more than one branch in the case of the engineering sections of the union. The result was that the unions developed a form of unionism based on active and skilled local leaderships, who developed an expertise in taking up grievances and dealt with the district management in their area of responsibility, and where members could rely on this leadership to deal with their personal and individual difficulties.

The outcome of these sets of relationships was a form of *responsible* unionism, characterized by an established and relatively stable local leadership who spoke on behalf of a relatively quiescent membership and who had acted with the confidence that they could bring their leaders to account at the regular membership meetings and periodic elections for union office and post. These leaders often became 'experts' in negotiation and representation, taking initiatives with management, and while they often took steps to maintain their relationships with the membership, formally as well as via informal links and relationships, they had an important degree of independence and discretion in representing their members.

As a form of *responsible* unionism, this pattern of union organization and representation in the CWU/NCU branches in the West Midlands was maintained throughout the post-privatization period. There was little incentive to review and reconsider this form of unionism, although increasingly it became difficult for local union leaderships to maintain close representational relationships with members. The problem for the local leaderships, particularly in the engineering sections, was that managerial reorganization during the 1990s resulted in attenuated managerial structures, with managers responsible for extensive geographical areas or regions. In this circumstance, the local leaderships, continuing to benefit from the facility time arrangements for union negotiators, followed the contours of managerial reorganization and in effect became 'professionalized' union leaders speaking on behalf of dispersed and spread out memberships. These issues are examined in relation to three CWU/NCU branches in the region, two engineering branches and a clerical branch.

Unions in the Birmingham region

The focus of the research was on the Birmingham area, covering the range of BT activity in the locality. These activities comprised engineering work, both servicing and repairing, in BT installations as well as in businesses and residences. There was also a substantial workforce concerned with sales, billing, administration and engineering support. These workers were often employed in the large tower blocks owned or leased by BT in the inner-city areas of most major cities. Formally, and in practice, there was a distinction between the engineering sections of the industry and the clerical/administrative areas. In the main, the engineering section of the business was composed of men located in the areas where equipment was or working from depots and increasingly homes. As BT reorganized and repositioned itself, following privatization, the clerical and administrative staff, composed mainly of women, became more central to the business, beginning to qualify the image of the industry as predominantly male.

The workforce was spread throughout the region, increasingly organized under a series of discrete managerial hierarchies. One of the consequences was that the engineering staff, previously organized as part of a geographical region, were located under different managerial hierarchies, with senior management often located in far removed parts of the country. While similar developments took place in the clerical and administrative areas, they were not as noticeable, since the workforce continued to be grouped and based in large work areas, in tower blocks and the like. This workforce was organized into three CWU/NCU branches in the Birmingham area, two from engineering and one covering clerical staff. The branch leaderships worked closely together, with the two engineering branch offices based in the same room of the same building.

The two CWU/NCU engineering branches had long organized in the region. The larger branch had 1,750 members in 1991 and 1,200 in 1996, with a 93 per cent union membership density. Members worked in switching and transmission, maintenance and installation. Most of the members (about 95 per cent) were male and long-term employees of British Telecom. They were spread over 110 workplaces, which ranged in size from one worker to 150. In contrast, the second branch in the region covered only 310 members in 1991 and fewer than 200 by 1996. The British Telecom members in this branch worked in such areas as electrical power, plumbing, accommodation and drawing. It covered only eighteen workplaces and had a 95 per cent union membership density, almost all male (over 80 per cent). There was a concentration of members in one workplace, about eighty in 1991 and sixty in 1996, with the remainder of the membership spread among the other seventeen workplaces.

The smaller branch recruited members in both British Telecom and the postal service. For most of the 1990s, the branch was maintained by an active branch secretary, elected in 1991. Via a creative use of facility time arrangements, this secretary had 100 per cent facility time allowance, and thus was in a position to continue to service his small membership. The continued existence of the smaller branch was the result of an informal arrangement between the two branch secretaries to maximize the facility time allowances and to work together in the left-wing political groupings within the union, although the membership decline in the smaller branch pointed to the eventual prospect of a merger. With the resignation of the branch secretary of the smaller branch in 1996, the two branches merged under the leadership of the other branch secretary.

Formally, there was a similar pattern of organization and representation in the clerical areas of the union. Here, the branches were composed of clusters of clerical and administrative workers based in the large telecommunication buildings in Birmingham and surrounding areas. The clerical branch had a membership of 1,287 in 1991 which had remained constant through to 1996. Most of the membership worked in billing, sales, personnel sections and computing, with some located in engineering support. Although the branch faced some difficulty in recruiting in the retail area, it had a consistent 85 per cent union membership density. Most of the membership were women (80 per cent), employed at workplaces where the membership numbers ranged from one to 600. There was a relatively high turnover of members, with approximately 45 per cent having been employed for fewer than five years.

Restructuring and divisionalization

Since privatization in 1984, British Telecommunications plc has gone through a series of reorganizations, involving a series of redundancy programmes, product diversification and an emphasis on market position. As part of the restructuring of the 1980s and 1990s, there was a series of disputes, with a major strike during January and February 1987, over attempts by management to link pay, productivity and labour flexibility. The implementation of the settlement following this dispute was not straightforward and subsequently involved a series of difficult negotiations at a local level. This was followed by a major reorganization in 1991, known as Project Sovereign, which divided the corporation into a number of business divisions based on customer groupings. Further reorganizations followed this initial stage, as the corporation attempted to refine and develop the logic of divisionalization.

The management structure was maintained more or less intact until 1991, when the company, under Project Sovereign, reorganized the business into five major divisions: personal communications, business communications, worldwide network, global communications and group headquarters. Each division operated as a separate business unit, with a four-level senior management structure. The result was that staff in each of these divisions worked to new and discrete managerial hierarchies within the business. While there were further reorganizations, the basic structure remained intact, although there was an increasing corporate emphasis on international developments. In 1997, BT entered into negotiations with MCI (an American long-distance telecommunications carrier) on the establishment of a joint venture company, named Concert. While there was extensive development and progress towards the establishment of the joint venture company, the project collapsed when WorldCom, a relatively unknown telecommunications player, made a successful surprise bid for MCI. By 1998, the business was organized into two principal divisions: Global Division and BT (UK). Of these two divisions, BT (UK) was the group company for the United Kingdom, and subsequently reorganized into ten separate divisions. Further, in 1998, BT reached an agreement with American Telephone and Telegraph (AT&T), the major American long-distance carrier, to establish a joint venture which is expected to come into being in the summer of 1999 and absorb BT's Global Division.

At a managerial level, these changes had a decisive impact. The pattern of managerial reorganization was an initial recomposition of managerial structures in the early 1990s, from geographically based centralized arrangements to devolved forms of management. However, these forms of management were not very effective or well integrated into the overall managerial hierarchies, and with the implementation of Project Sovereign there was a recentralization of the divisionally based management hierarchies. One result was an inconsistency of policy application across the divisions, with the implication of further restructuring of the operational and financial arrangements of the corporation (Colling and Ferner, 1992; Ferner and Terry, 1997, pp. 93–4).

With the establishment of the divisional structure, the number of managers overall was reduced and managers were given three-year rolling contracts, with personal contracts for the two senior levels of management, and further extensions within the managerial grades over time. Equally importantly, the new managerial hierarchies have encouraged an approach by managerial staff which emphasizes the independence and distinctiveness of each division. As a result, managerial staff have begun to press staff to identify with the division, work within the division remit and restrict their activities to the division. This approach contrasts sharply with the pre-privatized period as well as the early years of the corporation, when staff were positively encouraged to take a more holistic view of the work they were doing, noting the full range of work that had to be done. While staff worked within their grades and their competencies, there was a recognition that areas of work were interdependent and that tasks could not necessarily be confined to the immediate job in hand.

This point is highlighted by one local union leader, reflecting on the impact of Project Sovereign as early as 1992:

> The divisions are now becoming more independent of each other. Staff now do not like to do work for other divisions, except where there is a service level agreement. They treat divisions like 'customers'. At one time, when there was a concern from management for the whole business, if one engineer was doing a test at a telephone exchange and if asked to look at something else he would do so, but now he would not because it is not in the budget figures.

These features of the divisional organization developed in the corporation during the 1990s became more pronounced, but continued to be qualified by staff and 'old-style' managers. At the local level, many were long-term employees of the corporation, particularly in the engineering sections; they had come into the corporation as young workers, doing apprenticeships and working 'on the tools', and in a number of cases achieving promotion to the first few levels of management. These staff were familiar with each other from the past, and came out of backgrounds where work was organized for the whole business under a unified managerial hierarchy at a local level; they sought to retain some of the more positive aspects of these relationships in the new corporation. At an informal level, there was cooperation across the divisions, particularly by staff attending to jobs at the interface between the various divisions. However, this was much more restricted than in the past and rested on informal relationships.

Such features of work organization and relationships were not evident in the predominantly female clerical and administrative grades within the divisions. In these areas, there was a very high turnover of staff, with around 40 per cent of the staff in the Birmingham region having worked fewer than five years for the corporation. One result was that the informal relationships evident in the engineering areas had not been developed. The clerical and administrative areas of employment were moulded by the reorganization of the corporation in relatively unproblematic ways, as far as corporate management was concerned. The aim was to reduce staffing levels, increase productivity and, where appropriate and possible, contract out areas of work that were not regarded as central to the work of the corporation.

The divisionalization of the company became quite pronounced during the mid-1990s, and by 1996 difficulties had begun to emerge. Managerial structures both within and between divisions had become relatively fixed and rigidities had begun to develop in work routines and practices. One consequence was that it had become difficult to develop work across divisions. In response, a task force had been set up within the corporation, charged with exploring ways of encouraging more cooperative ways of operating across the divisions. This was not widely welcomed by divisional management and the problems of this form of corporate organization were likely to become more pronounced, with implications for work organization and practice.

The advent of managerialism

Alongside the moves towards divisionalization, there was a senior management attempt to elaborate a distinct managerial ethos, aimed at defining the corporation as a modern and managerially progressive enterprise. The old style staff approach associated with the gradual progression of staff from the depot to the supervisory and managerial levels fell away, as new staff were recruited directly into the corporation. At the lower levels of the managerial hierarchies, staff remained in place, although increasingly facing glass ceilings. However, these were managements where there was increasing emphasis on new managerial principles, associated in particular with the public embrace of the principles and practice of HRM. Still, this was a tentative development, in that most attention was given to increased communications within the enterprise, reflected in cascade forms of team briefings, the production of glossy internal publications and regular surveys of staff about conditions and experience within the corporation. Thus, the twin aspects of the so-called 'new' managerialism emerging in the privatized utilities were evident: on the one hand, there was a much more assertive and cost-conscious management and, on the other hand, management was encouraged to develop a more 'humane' and less bureaucratized approach to its relations with staff.

For staff, the changes were very much seen as part of the advent of a 'new' corporate management, largely unsympathetic to the concerns of staff. In the words of one engineering union branch official, 'Management is under pressure to push things through. . . . It is a macho-style, more aggressive, more sharp-suited. . . . Under Project Sovereign, a lot of the old civil service management were cleared out. We were left with managers with MBAs; people who do not understand the business' (1992). While it could be claimed that here the scale of the change was overstated, since substantial numbers of the 'old' staff remained in post, particularly at the lower levels, there was a change in managerial style and ethos, best exemplified by the appointment of 'new' style managers, referred to above.

In addition to the changing management style, many managers were no longer familiar with the telecommunications industry, having been recruited and trained outside the business. They were not the familiar managers of the pre-privatized era, recruited from within the industry and socialized into the mores of a statutory corporation. These developments had an impact on the way in which work was organized in the corporation. There was an increasing emphasis on commercial relations both within the enterprise and between the enterprise and the external world. These developments were described by one BT branch secretary in the following terms: '[TQM] is a favourite buzz word with . . . managers . . . always talking about internal customers and customer first. "We all have a duty to provide our best service to the customer" ' (1992). Such initiatives were part of the reorganization of BT as a major international corporation, and no longer a statutory authority principally located within the UK. These developments were very much part of the creation of an ethos of modernity and globalization. Privatization heralded a change in both practice and ethos.

In practice, the corporation embarked on a programme of reorganization, presenting these changes to the union representatives as part of a 'new' transparency in relations between management and unions. However, behind the facade, for unions this was business as usual: staff numbers were being reduced, work routines and demands were becoming more pressured and the union representatives were finding it difficult to counter these developments. The style of the managerial approach was especially evident in the programme of staff reductions, particularly in the engineering areas. With the reorganization of the corporation into zones or divisions, the divisional management adopted the practice of briefing union representatives about planned reductions. The union representatives received the information at briefing meetings, organized on the cascade principle, from the top down:

> I would receive information at a meeting which would include the use of overhead projectors; they may well give me a hard copy at the end of the meeting. It may well come through a week later with the minutes of the meeting. Yes there would be information available on current staff in post and their projected targets for the end of the financial year. . . . This would include a breakdown of managerial, engineering, clerical and other grades. . . . This may be broken down into release figures, those volunteering to go, retirements, people reaching the age of 60 and being told by their employers they no longer require them to work till 65, transfers out of the division into another division that they can cease (I say that rather tongue in cheek) and redeployments. (1994)

In one case, in the building services section, management announced that the targets for staff reductions in the coming twelve months were from 718 (1994) to 504 (1995) and, by November 1994, 75 per cent of the target had been reached. This was accomplished by voluntary departures and a degree of movement between the engineering grades and the clerical ones.

For management, these procedures were a more acceptable and staff-friendly way to deal with the changes that were being implemented by the corporation. These were not 'announcements' but 'consultations'. For the union representatives who attended these meetings, the briefings were a more 'glossy' but no more acceptable way for such management announcements to be made. As union representatives, they worried about a deteriorating staff morale and increased work intensification, but they felt there was very little that they could do to address these developments. The result was that there was a cynicism among the union representatives about both the style and the content of the 'new' managerial approach that was evident in the corporation.

Organization and representation

Past forms of trade unionism in British Telecom assumed that there was a necessary hierarchy of concerns, with local leaders administering a branch and attending to routine individual cases and the national leadership negotiating pay and the uniform conditions that applied throughout the corporation. Complementing these arrangements, the union branches were organized into area structures and the national level of union organization. Although formally the annual conference (comprised of branch representatives) was the sovereign body for policy-making, the day-to-day links between branches and the national body were provided by the branch officers, via committees, individual contact and representation. The outcome was a centralized union, where national negotiators reached settlements which applied throughout the country and local leaders attempted to implement the detail of these agreements as well as taking up individual grievances and problems. Over time, the full-time officials, in the case of the CWU/NCU often drawn from the right wing of the labour movement, acquired a predominance within the union, and it was not uncommon for many of the left-wing branch officers to challenge these officials on the floor of conference as well as in other union forums.

With the move towards privatization, involving the break-up of national negotiations, the CWU/NCU, like other BT unions, was forced to consider the development of organizational forms that allow for a more broadly based participation locally or suffer the marginalization of their organization at this level. However, in considering possible ways of reorganizing and developing their union, the CWU/NCU branches were concerned to retain their organizational integrity and not simply mirror managerial structures. The engineering branches were led by small numbers of officers, who had relatively generous facility time arrangements, calculated on the basis of membership numbers. Most members worked out of depots or from similar worksites in telecommunication buildings, and they looked to the branch officers for information and guidance. In turn, the branch officers worked in the union offices, and often visited the main depots and buildings to make themselves available to the membership. Similarly, the three senior offices of the clerical branch had a set of offices in one of the BT office blocks in the centre of the city. From this site they serviced a widely dispersed membership, located in BT office blocks in the city and immediate environs.

As a way of strengthening their branches, these senior lay representatives spent considerable time developing ways of making themselves more accessible to their members, particularly those working in small numbers in relatively isolated work areas. This involved the exploitation of such facilities as computer resources, as well as mobile telephones. In these two engineering branches, the leaders established comprehensive databases which allowed them to communicate very quickly with the membership, often countering corporation newsletters with union responses within hours. In addition, according to these senior union lay representatives, members using their work computer facilities were much more likely to raise questions and queries with their senior union lay representatives than was the case in the past.

In the case of the clerical branch, the leadership was composed of an executive, with the three senior officers having full facility time in 1991, although reduced to two and a half days by 1996. While these three senior officers were based in the union office, in the centre of the city, they had worked out a rota of workplace visits. Over time, these union surgeries became important ligaments in the construction of a union consciousness. In addition, the two senior leaders were active participants at the national levels of union activity, representing the branch membership and as delegates to union committees, especially the National Women's Advisory Committee in the case of one of these branch leaders. Via such patterns of representation, the branch leadership tied the branch into a broader perspective of union activity and organization.

The major threat to the integrity and the future of the CWU/NCU branches in their current form arose from a senior managerial attempt to restrict the level of facility time available to branch officers as well as an attempt to end cross-representation. Under British Telecom facility arrangements there were specified time allowances for designated branch officers, usually the branch secretary. British Telecom also provided accommodation, telephone, fax, stationery and heating. Increasingly, however, divisional managers argued that with the fall of union membership following staff cut-backs, facility time should also be reduced. In the case of one branch officer, the time allowance was cut from five days to two and a half days per week in 1992. The management justification for this was that branch membership had declined, and thus there 'was less work for the branch secretary'. In fact, the branch membership had fallen from 411 (1985) to 263 (1992), with an increase to 302 in January 1993, following the relocation of members from other branches. Paradoxically, however, it was the divisionalization of BT that enabled this leader to maintain full facility time by covering designated areas and occupations within the new divisional structures, in addition to his branch membership.

In a comment about these developments, the branch officers in the three CWU/NCU branches said that they felt they 'were at the sharp end' (1996). They felt that the head office of the union was less than helpful, in that the union nationally seemed to be acquiescing to these threats to branch representation, rather than developing a counter-position that supported the branches. While the national approach rested on an assessment of the politics of defending what may have been seen as a relatively generous facility provision, the effect at a branch level was that the senior branch officials were critical of the lack of support they received from head office. In these circumstances, the memberships of each union branch had agreed to fund the increased expenses by branch officers as they attempted to represent their members on a range of committees and in different parts of the country. The branch officers of the three branches also met each other on a more regular basis than previously to consider how they might begin to address some of these problems. It was in this context that these branch leaderships began to consider merging their branches, as a way of pooling resources and strengthening representation in areas with few members in one or the other branch.

It is important to note that the managerial and senior technical staff were also unionized, as members of the Society of Telecom Executives (STE). Because of the change in corporate organization and the implications for work and employment, this union took a series of steps to develop a form of representation and organization to meet the changed circumstances of BT senior staff employment. While the branches continued to be organized in relatively conventional ways, with a branch executive and officers, they had been reorganized in 1992 to reflect the divisionalization of the business. Branches were composed of sub-branches, each organized along divisional lines. The logic was to create a structure that could be adapted so as to accommodate any further reorganizations of BT. Although this reorganization placed the STE branch, and its regional support office in the city, in a relatively favourable position to meet the changed circumstances of BT as a privatized corporation, the branch was relatively inactive at a local level. The membership of the branch faced substantial managerial delayering, the advent of personal salary contracts and continued managerial reorganization. In these circumstances, and because many branch members supervised CWU/NCU members, the branch conducted its affairs with little reference to the CWU/NCU branches.

Industrial relations at a local level

The reorganization and restructuring of management had a major impact on industrial relations at a local level. In the pre-privatized era and for a few years afterwards, the formal arrangements for industrial relations at a local level were maintained. The principal union representing both engineering and clerical staff was the NCU and after 1995 the UCW, while the STE represented the managerial staff. These two unions were both centralized, reflecting bargaining arrangements and priorities. In the main, for both management and the unions, the focus of negotiations was at the national level, where uniform terms and conditions of employment were negotiated. While there was a lively involvement in negotiations at a local level, this was usually to implement the detail of national settlements, negotiate specific terms and conditions for particular local circumstances and take up grievances and related problems that emerged at this level.

There were two important aspects to the pre-1990s arrangements. First, while there were management hierarchies for different aspects of work and the unions were organized accordingly, there was a regional industrial relations structure, which meant that there were formal and informal negotiations that applied to the whole area. The NCU in the area was distinguished by the nomenclature of different branches, such as 'Birmingham Internal' (dealing with staff employed working on internally located equipment in exchanges) and 'Birmingham External' (dealing with lines and equipment located in customers' buildings). These branches were party to the Birmingham and district joint consultative committee, and constituted the trade union side on this body. The union leaderships in this earlier period also played an active part in negotiating with managers across different departments, as well as dealing with the regional and relatively locally based district management for the area. In this respect, industrial relations were characterized by a degree of uniformity and cohesiveness within the region.

However, it must be noted that there was a parallel set of arrangements for the clerical and administrative staff. These divisions were long-standing, in part going back to a time when the clerical staff were organized and represented by civil service unions (until 1984, when these unions merged with the forerunner of the NCU) and partly because they were predominantly female sections of the workforce in a largely male industry. As with the engineering section of the workforce, these were centralized unions, which had also developed a local remit of activity, conducting negotiations over local issues and concerns.

With the privatization of the corporation and, more importantly, the lead up to and implementation of Project Sovereign, there was both a narrowing of the remit of industrial relations at a local level and an increased remoteness of negotiations from the workplace. The most obvious and immediate consequence of the divisionalization of the corporation was that negotiations became focused within the divisional structures, often at a considerable remove from the locality. The section of the corporation which became 'business services' was responsible for estate management. At a managerial level the division comprised a number of districts within three major areas. The principal negotiations over terms and conditions of employment occurred at the area level, with the consequence that union negotiators and local leaders often found themselves travelling long distances across the country to meet the area or national management teams. In another division, the branch chair said she was a member of a zone which covered the country as follows: '[It] goes from as high as Stoke and involves everything south, including all of Wales, but not London' (1994). She also ended up travelling across the country and representing a very dispersed membership.

The divisionalization of the corporation created different managerial hierarchies, capable of deciding specific terms and conditions for the divisions as well as varying the terms and conditions of employment within the framework of national agreements. This facility, coupled with the remoteness of managers, resulted in a narrowing of issues that could be dealt with at a local level. The negotiating forums at a local level were disbanded by management and replaced with a series of 'coordinating committees' in each division, for different sections of the workforce. These committees were located away from the workplace, covering widely dispersed workforces, organized according to the divisional split. One consequence of this arrangement was that the local negotiators also represented a dispersed membership, so that the closeness and intimacy of the past was broken. These arrangements resulted in a rather distanced form of negotiation. As one union officer remarked in relation to the announcement of corporate plans for staff reductions at the coordinating committee meetings:

> we are no longer able to say 'you can't do that because' and they will sit there and listen to us. I think it's because – more often now than in the past – people are giving us presentational material . . . and we're just like the end of a chain of dissemination. But also because the company clearly no longer sees that they want the union to have any part in its decisions. (1994)

In addition, where local issues were raised this was now often with managers, who had neither the authority nor the competence to deal with them. These union representatives increasingly faced managers who either would not or could not negotiate or bargain.

The outcome was that a management structure and a union movement which had been organized to settle grievances at a local level and to reach local agreements at a local level could no longer do so. The paradox was that the devolution of managerial structures to the divisional level resulted in the reaffirmation of centralized and remote managerial structures and associated bargaining arrangements. While local union leaderships had been opposed to these arrangements, with the imposition of the new managerial structures and associated bargaining forums they had little alternative but to participate and attempt to open up negotiating platforms removed from the intimacy and interplay of locally based and focused structures. Over time, this resulted in a restructured and reorganized pattern of industrial relations within the corporation.

The emergence of 'responsible' representation

The years following privatization were initially marked by a relative continuity of bargaining procedures, with the corporation initiating an extensive managerial restructuring in 1994 which recast these arrangements in significant ways. At first, the bargaining procedures were maintained intact, with the result that branches began to adjust to the new routines of a commercial environment, without any impetus to examine how they organized and represented members. However, the reorganization of managerial hierarchies and the establishment of associated bargaining arrangements dramatically changed the terrain for union organization and activity. No longer could unions organize on a geographical basis, developing issues and problems as they affected individual members and groups of members in the immediate locality. The thrust of these changes was such that a geographically based unionism was no longer sustainable.

New bargaining forums were established for each division, based on a hierarchical principle that negotiations should be division-based, via area and national structures. The consequence of this decision was to move formal multi-union negotiations away from the local area and into the divisions, often covering large geographical areas. This development signalled the end of the multi-union geographical district committees, which attempted during the 1970s and early 1980s to develop a union profile in the city, taking up specific issues but also questioning British Telecom policy and practice in the city and environs. For some time there were vigorous efforts to maintain the inter-union city-wide structures, but they gradually fell into abeyance as hard-pressed leaderships down-graded their importance in the new structures.

The changed bargaining arrangements also made it difficult for the CWU/ NCU leaders, at a branch level, to deal with management in the new structure on any other basis than individual, manager to union leader and vice versa. However, a further consequence of establishing managerial hierarchies from the area level upwards was that negotiations often took place in distant geographical offices, rather than in the immediate offices in the city. All the senior branch leaders frequently travelled outside the city to meet low-level managers, representing their members on individual grievances and problems. In addition, much discussion took place via telephone as branch leaders attempted to maintain a service to the membership.

Local union leaderships had begun to face a set of difficulties that signalled the end of separate branches in the city. Increasingly, union negotiators had to deal with many more managers than previously, located in different divisions, and in some cases in geographically distant offices. Local managements began to indicate that they might no longer be prepared to recognize union leaderships based in different divisions. While this did not result in actual decisions to prevent cross-representation, in terms of allocating funds for negotiation structures and arrangements, managers had informally indicated to local union leaders that they thought cross-representation should end.

None the less, the CWU/NCU union branch leaderships had become quite skilled at identifying local grievances faced by members, such as the implementation of new work procedures at depots or the introduction of changed hours of attendance following the adoption of market-type customer care programmes. These leaders showed initiative, by-passing the formal requirements for cross-representation and developing, within the branches, representatives from each of the divisions, able to represent divisional members with their management. This was an attempt to anticipate and counter the informal comments by managers that cross-representation should end. The leaders were also prepared to create situations where, as branch officers, they were formally requested to assist a group of members who were not in the same division as themselves. On one occasion, a group of women members working in a customer reception office informally approached one of the branch leaders for assistance in a dispute with the office manager about hours of attendance. These workers then threatened industrial action, which allowed them to call in this branch leader formally to open negotiation with a hitherto reluctant office management.

With the beginnings of divisionalization, the branch leaderships faced a changed set of conditions, which stimulated reorganization and the emergence of distinctive forms of unionism in this industry. The basis of unionism at a local level, the social relations of work and employment at the immediate point of production and service, began to change, with consequences for the traditional modes of union organization in the area. As the production process and associated activities undertaken by British Telecom changed, the distinctions between clerical work and computer-based engineering work became blurred. This was accompanied by a shift from large depot bases, where workers reported and received directions about work, to more decentralized work stations, and in some cases mobile vans.

These developments eroded the distinctions which formed the basis of the traditional divisions in union organization, between largely male engineering branches and predominantly female clerical branches. This blurring of job demarcations was described by one clerical union branch official with reference to four engineers taking on reception work:

> I think that the move of them into the clerical hierarchy is actually the start of the blurring of the line between clerical and engineering work of this sort . . . those people are probably doing work which is obviously clerical work not engineering work. The technical work that they have to do is now quite limited. I think that if we felt that there is a new job that has been created and I walked in there and sat with them for a bit I would say 'Oh yeah, well this is clerical work' because there is not very much that they are doing that is technical any more. (1994)

In the light of these types of development, the branch leadership of the clerical branch and the smaller engineering branch sought to persuade their members that a unified branch would be more effective and result in more comprehensive representation for the membership. Jobs were changing and the rationale of the past no longer applied. The implication for branch coverage was obvious to the branch leaders: 'we will have merged branches and we won't have clerical and engineering constituencies which we are forced to have at the moment because it won't be easy to define whether a job is a clerical one or engineering' (1994). Over a period of three years there had been a number of attempts to merge the branches, in line with developments in the union elsewhere in the country. However, these attempts came to nothing, as the predominantly male engineering members resisted what they saw as a dilution of the basis of branch membership and practice.

One of the contributory factors that undermined the need for urgency in such a reorganization was that the branch leaders had become more removed and distanced from their members. The basis of branch leadership began to shift, from a more directly accountable leadership to one where leaders increasingly acted as 'responsible' representatives. It had long been the case that the branch leadership comprised a small group of personnel with facility time to represent and carry out the duties of branch officers. When negotiations were localized and when the membership was based in large depots and related workplaces there was an ongoing set of accountable relations between members and leaders. While it is important not to romanticize the degree to which this generated forms of genuine membership participation, it is equally important not to undervalue the ongoing relationship between leaders and members in this situation.

In contrast, following the managerial reorganization and recomposition of the corporation following privatization, the basis of union leadership shifted decisively. Increasingly, leaders were forced to participate in structures and to represent members in forums that were removed from the locality and where the activity in one division no longer necessarily impinged on that in another. The result was a form of *responsible* representation where union leaders, of whatever political ilk, spoke on behalf of members in these rather removed forums. In these circumstances it was not possible for union leaderships to develop or maintain the close reciprocal and accountable relations that many union leaders aspire to realize. It is in this respect that the privatization of British Telecom was associated with the further development of a particular form of union leadership, at least in the case of the CWU/NCU.

Assessment

The three CWU/NCU union branches were all similar in one important respect: they were all organized and operated on the basis of *responsible* leadership. In this respect, the branches were all led by well established, long-serving leaders, who also had a significant presence within the divisions in which their branches were located. Such a form of leadership had its roots in the centralized patterns of organization that had long characterized the CWU/NCU in the West Midlands. In this respect the branches were very much integral parts of the national union organization, and the branches organized and operated as such.

This form of organization was evident at the branch level. Each of the main branch leaders had assembled a facility time package, partly in terms of the branch allowance but also in relation to their respective responsibilities on the zonal and national coordinating committees. As the BT managerial hierarchies were recomposed and reorganized in the period following privatization, these branch leaders also relocated so that they could continue to represent their memberships in what was seen as an effective way. Part of the impetus for affirming this form of unionism was that British Telecommunications plc increasingly positioned itself as one of the major telecommunications corporations in the modern world. These staff were facing the uncertainties and pressures that were associated with the internationalization of the telecommunications industry, and wanted the assurance of forms of unionism where experienced and reliable leaderships attempted to grapple with the changes that were taking place.

In the face of the waves of redundancies that occurred, and complementing the managerial reorganizations during the same period, it is hardly surprising that the members acquiesced to the increased remoteness of their local leadership. The question for the members was whether they could rely on their local leaders to represent their interests within both the union and the corporation. The national executive had successively retained an authority within the industry, leading the union as a nationally focused and organized union. As the local leaders consolidated their positions within the corporate bargaining structures they also developed a national presence within the union.

Thus the refocusing of local leadership concerns, away from the immediacy of the day-to-day activity in the locality to the broader perspective of divisional representation and bargaining, became a strategy for ensuring the continued presence of the union in the industry. However, the cost of this approach was that the conditions for membership involvement and participation in union affairs, at the local level, were undermined. It was not that the leaders and their supporting activists were unaware of this patterning of representation. Rather, in the context of a corporate policy that affirmed the international face of the industry and patterns of managerial reorganization, a form of unionism that underwrote a representation by established leaders, both locally and nationally, was seen as appropriate. It is in these respects that the CWU/NCU unions became exemplars of the modern form of *responsible* unionism.

9 REMOVED FORMS OF REPRESENTATION: GAS

As with BT, the privatization of British Gas signified little substantive managerial reorganization in the first few years (Ferner and Colling, 1991). The privatized corporation continued to organize and operate much as it had in the pre-privatization period, as a monopoly provider of gas services. This was a management approach where the concern was to maintain stability and continuity with the earlier public enterprise traditions (Ferner and Colling, 1991, pp. 405–6). It was only in the early to mid-1990s that the corporation began to reorganize in an extensive way, leading to the break-up of the industry into a number of contiguous divisions, in the first instance, and then in the late 1990s into a series of functional divisions and eventually corporations, the main one being TransCo, the provider of gas delivery. In addition, the corporation during the 1990s began to refocus its concerns as both a nationally focused company and increasingly a corporation that operated in international energy markets.

The unions, both the GMB (as the principal manual union) and UNISON (and its forerunner in this industry, NALGO), responded to the privatization of British Gas by maintaining their then current forms of organization and representation. This was in the context of a managerial strategy of continuity in the core areas of the business: 'the traditional industrial relations ethos of public enterprise on the whole persists, or re-asserts itself after a period of instability: well-organized unions, at least for non-managerial staff, strong bargaining relationships, and management by agreement' (Ferner and Colling, 1991, p. 405).

In the lead-up to and immediately following privatization, the unions, as was the case in other utilities, were organized around either full-time officials, particularly so in the manual areas, or branch secretaries, in the case of NALGO and then UNISON, who were in effect the union. This form of unionism was rooted in the bargaining arrangements in the industry, based on the Whitley form of representation and organization. The focus was on a form of responsible unionism, with minimal membership involvement and activity in these unions. In view of the stability of managerial relations, and the maintenance of bargaining arrangements in the industry, these union forms persisted. It was in these circumstances that, until the early 1990s, there was a limited stimulus to the unions to reorganize and reconsider their presence in the corporation.

In the 1990s there was a process of work reorganization, particularly in the manual areas, as well as the beginnings of an extensive managerial reorganization as part of the fragmentation of the former monopoly corporation. The local union leaderships and their members faced a managerially driven pattern of change in which the terrain of unionism was recast. These developments provided the opportunity for a reconsideration of the form of unionism in the industry, where the concern became how to provide for a more active and participative form of unionism at a local level. In this way, the unions were drawn into debates about the relevance of the traditional forms of responsible unionism that had long characterized the industry.

The research revealed two patterns of trade unionism: one where unions remain organized around established leaders, particularly full-time officials or long-established senior lay representatives, who have adapted their activity in the light of the changing structures of relations between unions and employers; and a second, where the patterns of membership participation are in the process of generating new lay power bases, thereby establishing the basis for union renewal. The paradox is that the restructuring and reorganization of these utilities underwrote the importance of continued *responsible* leaderships and at the same time created an opportunity for unions to reorganize and open up a range of opportunities for broader membership participation in negotiating and other structures. The difficulty for the unions at a local level was to realize the opportunities presented by this paradox.

These issues are explored with reference to five NALGO/UNISON branches and a GMB steward committee in the West Midlands region. In the case of the NALGO/UNISON branches the principal focus is on one which covered a large area to the west of Birmingham. It was organized around a branch executive committee, led by a long-standing branch secretary. The GMB committee comprised the senior stewards for an area north of the city. This committee worked closely with the full-time official responsible for gas. In both cases, these union groups experienced the difficulties and uncertainties that came with the restructuring of the gas corporation in the early 1990s.

Restructuring the gas corporation in the West Midlands

Following privatization in 1986, there was little change in the way the gas corporation was organized, although it operated as a corporatized enterprise, rather
than as a statutory authority, as in the past. The first major change came with the
Gas Staffs and Senior Officers (GSSO) review in 1992, aimed at delayering
management, which in the West Midlands resulted in a decentralization of
functions from the regional headquarters to eight districts, each with its own
management organization. As part of this restructuring, there was a reorganization of functional activity under the auspices of designated district managers,
reporting to a 'quasi-autonomous' general manager, and away from the previous
regionally based structure. Originally, the regional management structure had
been organized on the basis of functional managers, with managerial hierarchies
below them. This changed in 1992 with the establishment of operations managers, who each covered four districts, and below them multi-functional
managers, with a general manager in charge of a district. The critical point in
this review was that it laid the foundation for a move away from centralized
forms of regional organization, towards the creation of district forms.

Subsequently, in 1994, the company was reorganized into business units,
each with its own management structure. This ended the district form of
managerial organization and created a vastly different terrain for unions in the
area. Following the reorganization of the company nationally, the area was
divided into a series of business units. This involved the reorganization of the
workforce into six business units (TransCo, Public Gas Supply, Support Services, Service, Business Gas and Retail). These divisions increasingly operated
as separate and distinct units. The situation was further complicated in 1996
with the announcement of the 'demerger' of the company into two entities.

Alongside these developments, there was a major down-sizing of the corporation between 1994 and 1996, with the exit of nearly 25,000 staff from
British Gas as a whole. This reduction in staff was disproportionately focused
on the manual workforce, and there was speculation that there was a prospect
that such staff were in danger of being dramatically reduced or removed
altogether from the corporation, with increased employment of contract staff.
In the West Midlands, during the 1990s, the old regional headquarters was
dismantled and each business unit was reorganized with its own managerial
structures (and headquarters). This resulted in considerable anxiety among
staff about their future in the business units, and the company. Thus, these
staff, manual and non-manual, faced unclear futures because of continued
speculation about the future of business units and the prospects for the two
semi-independent corporations established in 1996.

In the main, the gas workforce was employed in district offices, the size of which ranged from a few persons in depots to several hundreds in the case of staff located in the regional headquarters office. Manual workers had traditionally worked out of depots, but increasingly were working from small fully equipped vans based at home, and at depots in the case of larger vans which could not be parked in residential areas overnight. In the 1990s, there was extensive relocation of non-manual staff, as numbers were reduced, accompanied by the extensive refurbishment and renovation of offices on an open plan basis (in one office covered by the study only sixty of the previous 120 jobs were made permanent). This was a period of considerable uncertainty and anxiety for management and workforce alike, as the impact of the reorganization was worked through at a local level.

These rounds of reforms created a situation where staff were unsure what was happening and increasingly expressed a lack of confidence in management. For one local gas union official this created difficulties:

> Management changes frequently. There are movements between the different functions which has an impact on staff. Managers have poor training and because of the frequent moves they don't get to know their staff. This causes problems. When I go to see them they admit to not knowing the proper procedures or how to sort things out without too much fuss. (1993)

Such developments introduced an unpredictability and uncertainty into the relations between unions and management.

These developments were further complicated by the changes in the way in which management organized and operated, especially in face-to-face contact with gas workers. Critical to these initiatives was a rhetorical and practical embrace of delayered forms of management, usually associated with HRM principles and practice. This resulted in a 'new' managerial style where the emphasis was on consensus and harmony, with the advent of managerial practices aimed at encouraging an openness about decisions taken in organizing and operating offices. While there were variations in the degree to which managers adhered to this approach, there was a general move in this direction. The problem for management was that at the same time that a more open management approach was encouraged, staff reductions were imposed.

Thus, as part of these developments there were indications that workers faced increased pressure and tension at work. Management began to enforce the formal rules relating to sickness and absenteeism in ways that pressured staff. As one union branch secretary observed:

> Absenteesim is now linked to sickness. Managers have initiated changes in engineering involving manual and non-manual. In the past, staff could have a day off without comment. Now managers are attempting to highlight absenteeism by naming depots with high sickness levels. For example, if somebody has a broken leg then they are requested to come and work at a sedentary job. There has been a great reduction on days lost through sickness. (1992)

Under a rhetoric of HRM, these managers sought to tighten up the rules relating to working time. The result was a feeling of resentment among staff at what were seen by many as petty-minded and two-faced approaches to worker management by managers. It was also the case that staff felt increasingly pressured by these developments.

These developments were implemented in the area covered by the study on a top-down basis, with successive layers of management inducted into the new approach to differing degrees and in successive periods. In one office in the region, the development of a managerial approach associated with HRM was symbolized by the location of the office manager's desk in the middle of the open plan office, with a large round boardroom style table for meetings with other senior staff in the office. This ergonomic feature created the appearance of open management. It also created a situation where union representatives were in close proximity and visible to management.

Representation and organization

The two principal unions in the industry, the GMB and NALGO/UNISON, were well established in the region, having organized in the area for many years. In the early 1990s, in the case of the then NALGO, the five branches comprised four area-based branches, covering large geographical areas and many workplaces (with memberships between 500 and 600) and a large regional headquarters branch (approximately 1,400 members). The main manual union in the area, the GMB, had in the gas industry long been a full-time-officer dominated union group. With the reorganization and recomposition of the company, the full-time officer, with the senior stewards in the area, promoted more active forms of workplace representation, thereby beginning to qualify the historical dominance of the full-time officials. In contrast, the NALGO branches faced the problem of shrinking activist bases, with the responsibility for branch life and activity falling on the shoulders of a few members, and particularly the branch secretaries.

The GMB

For many decades the form of workplace unionism in this sector was full-time officer focused; this official was central to all the major negotiations in the region, as well as the union organization in the area. To an important extent this officer had long been, and in part remained, the face of the union in the area. In the late 1980s, it was acknowledged by the regional level of the union that communication with members was not good, and that it had become desirable to develop more active forms of union representation at a district level. In part, this recognition arose from an awareness that members' work routines were changing in ways that were likely to make the continued organization of the union as a relatively centralized and remote structure more difficult to maintain. Under the reorganization that had begun to take place, workers no longer came into depots where there was always a reasonable expectation that they could raise issues with union representatives and exchange views with each other; as a result, the union leadership had begun to consider alternative ways of involving the membership in union activity.

The GMB in the West Midlands area was an old and established union grouping, organized on the basis of a steward structure, located in the depots and related workplaces across the area. Prior to privatization and until the early 1990s in the privatized corporation, these stewards formally held the responsibility for representing members at a local level, as well as playing a part in the district committees in the region. In practice these were relatively formalized sets of arrangements, with the lead taken by the full-time officials. These officials were often drawn from the gas industry and over time acquired a prominence within the area, as the effective face of the union. They took the lead on the negotiating committees; they spoke on behalf of the stewards and members; and for most purposes they were the union. This form of representation and organization was rooted in the particularities of the industry labour process, the form of labour organization and activity that had been developed over the previous two decades. These manual workers worked out of depots, in teams, reporting back to supervisory staff at periodic intervals. This was a fairly quiescent form of organization, resting on the energy, goodwill and competence of the officials. The members were relatively passive, seeing themselves as served effectively by full-time officials.

With the advent of more decentralized forms of management, the depots became the focus for negotiations and bargaining over fringe benefits and employment conditions. Following this development, the full-time officials and leading local activists attempted to put some flesh on the embryonic steward structures in the depots. For many years, stewards had been named in depots, but in practice this was largely a nominal procedure, with many stewards playing little part in representative structures or negotiating procedures. In these circumstances, it was unsurprising that the full-time officers in the industry tended to retain their prominence and dominance within the representative and organizational structures of the union.

These pressures stimulated the beginnings of a review of the representational and organizational structures of the union. A number of the full-time officials began to recognize that they no longer represented the membership for which they were responsible in the 'old way'; it was necessary to reconsider, in more focused ways than in the past, how to cover the range of queries and problems raised at a local level. The solution was to stimulate steward structures at a local level and to create combine committees for each division, usually composed of senior stewards from each district, at district and area levels. In most cases, though these developments built on existing arrangements and practices, the appearance of continuity could be deceptive. As stewards became more practised and as senior stewards took on more effective leadership roles within their area, the traditional relationships with full-time officials began to shift.

One full-time officer reported how the manual union organization was being negatively affected by the switch from depot-based work organization to on-site reporting. He went on to note that this did not lend itself to 'good trade unionism in terms of meeting members' (1991). In this case, the full-time officer recognized that past practices would not suffice and the district initiated a practice of special steward meetings to address problems and issues as they arose. This innovation complemented an election system, introduced in 1988, for members of the regional joint committee, so as to achieve more directly accountable forms of representation on this committee. In addition, the negotiators at a regional level placed a request for facility time for senior stewards to brief stewards on the progress and outcomes of bargaining and negotiation. In these respects the district union committee attempted to move away from almost exclusive reliance on the full-time officer.

For many, among both the full-time cadre and the lay representative structures, these were not comfortable developments, representing as they did a questioning of, and sometimes a challenge to, past relationships. Not all full-time officials were relaxed about the apparent changes in their relationships with lay representatives. Conversely, many lay representatives found themselves taking a lead in negotiations, both formally and informally, which would have been unimaginable a few years earlier. While there was little evidence of conflict between full-time officials and lay representatives over these developments, it took time for each group to have confidence in the redistribution of responsibilities. Indeed, most of the full-time officials were encouraging these developments in principle, as a way of making their own jobs manageable in the face of the managerial restructuring that was taking place in the privatized corporations. As one official commented:

> There have been changes in the management structure in the region, involving decentralisation. There are now eight districts which in many ways are autonomous and away from the regional structure. In some ways it is better for us [GMB]. The representatives are drawn from the eight districts and it allows us to get closer to the members. Previously there were four areas so now it is much better. (1993)

These changes were associated with the development of a senior steward system of representation, which was welcomed: 'The union structure previously was wishy-washy. It was changed some years ago with the appointment of Senior Stewards. They are now proving their benefit as they can deal with problems that before people would ring me direct about' (Full-time official, 1993). The senior stewards also responded positively although cautiously to these developments as a bit 'nerve-racking'. In this way the representational and organizational structures of the manual unions, and particularly the GMB, had begun to change.

NALGO/UNISON

Similar sets of developments occurred within the main non-manual union in the industry, NALGO/UNISON. The membership of UNISON and its predecessor in the industry, NALGO, had long been organized via branch structures, with informal representation from the dispersed workplaces where many worked. These branches often covered wide geographical areas and many workplaces. Branches were grouped into regional structures, participating in the regional bargaining forums. From there the branches had representation on national structures, both within the union and on national bargaining committees.

In 1989, after a major reorganization within the union, twelve NALGO branches in the region were reduced to five merged branches: a headquarters branch (1,500 members at the time), two branches each based on one gas corporation district, a large branch covering three districts and another branch covering four districts and some regional offices outside the headquarters. The branches were organized under a district gas committee, with each branch nominating to the committee on a *pro rata* basis, with some additional representation from two ex-headquarters-based branches. There were thirty-one members on the committee, which decided union policy for the region and participated as the major union in the trade union side of the regional joint committee (the other union being APEX). Contact with the other main union grouping in the industry, the GMB, was on an *ad hoc* and infrequent basis.

The large branch to the west of Birmingham had long been organized on a geographical basis, covering the different divisions that made up British Gas in the area before and after privatization. The branch officers and particularly the branch secretary provided the basis for branch activity, which was primarily concerned with political and administrative union matters, acting as a conduit for national policy and practice, and monitoring and taking up individual cases. Originally the branch covered three districts, which after 1994 became largely irrelevant as the business unit structure was established, becoming the primary basis for membership identity and reference. The branch increasingly represented a fragmented workforce, based on divisions and the further disaggregation of British Gas in 1996.

The branch membership covered administrative and engineering staff working in depots, offices and showrooms, across a large geographical area. They were engaged in activities associated with the functions of distribution, commercial and business work, domestic supply, housing development, administrative services and other services. The membership was 550 in 1990 and through attrition and reorganization had fallen to 400 in 1996. The spread of membership ranged from two or three in showrooms to 120 in the district office buildings. During 1996 the main challenge was to meet the problems arising from isolation and fragmentation of the company, which was both a functional disaggregation, as business unit structures, and a geographical one, within the region.

The branch was organized on the conventional basis of a set of officers and an executive. Throughout the recent history of the branch there had been an attempt by the leading officers to develop the executive representation so that it reflected the different workplaces and functions covered by the branch membership. This informal constituency arrangement meant that most (but by no means all) areas of the branch membership were covered. One of the practices introduced by the branch secretary was to reorganize the agenda of the monthly executive meetings so that reports were received about the different units. In this way an attempt was made to ensure the basis for participation by the different sections.

In 1994, after the establishment of the business units, the senior branch leadership decided 'to put far more onus on individual stewards to stand up and be counted' (1994). Previously, the stewards in the branch had acted as ciphers for the senior leadership, particularly the branch secretary, distributing union circulars and notices and referring any problems directly to the branch secretary or one of the other relevant senior officers. The subsequent development was described by the branch secretary with reference to one district office where the representatives after 1994 began to 'take ownership' of the union activity in the district. They formed a core activist group who 'came out of themselves' as representatives. These stewards met as a group, took up issues with local management and developed a more active relationship with the senior branch leadership. The branch secretary noted that there was still an unevenness across the branch but that, on the basis of business unit reorganization, the branch as a whole had a more independent activist base than was ever the case previously. As the branch secretary noted, 'out of adversity came some good' (1994).

The organization of meetings on the basis of business units was an important development, providing an example of the way that branches were developing in the gas industry. Since branches were not functionally based but geographical on a regional structure, the way the different sets of negotiations and activities were integrated into branch life became a matter of importance. The difficulty was that the branch operated on the basis of report only, with little attempt to provide further integration of the different activities within the units. One of the pressing problems for the branch was that managers increasingly opposed cross-representation, on budget grounds, challenging the past practice of cross-division participation and cooperation between units.

The main concern in the branch was to retain membership levels, with recruitment playing very little part in the branch activity. The maintenance of membership was complicated by the different practices and futures within the various units which made up the branch. In a number of instances, branch officers were frustrated in their recruitment (and other union activity) when they were prevented from going into offices covered by a different business unit from their own. Some of the business units were rather 'bullish' and not well disposed to NALGO/UNISON. There was a further complication which had made it very difficult for the branches to address the question of recruitment, since the branch, like many others in the gas industry, did not have a record of its membership for a number of months in 1995 and 1996; the consequence was that non-members could not be identified. This came about because of difficulties created by British Gas in returning the check-off lists to the union nationally. As a result, very little was happening on recruitment, or on other union activity. The branch executive was very much taken up with reorganization both at work and within the union, leaving little time or opportunity to address branch-specific issues. At both individual and group levels there was uncertainty about jobs, with members of TransCo reapplying for their jobs towards the end of 1995. These were not propitious times for activity to build up or consolidate the branch membership.

This form of representation was found wanting when the union attempted to deal with the consequences of reorganization in the 1990s and a shrinking membership base. The pressures following reorganization of managerial hierarchies, relocation of staff around the area into reconstituted district offices, according to division, and the reduction of staff levels impacted on these representational structures. Branch secretaries, for example, found themselves in the unenviable position of shouldering the burden of branch representation both within the locality and more generally within the union, with little support from other members. In circumstances of insecurity and uncertainty, it was not surprising for previously active members either to leave the industry or to withdraw from active involvement in the union. The remaining members were often reluctant to play more active parts in the union.

Despite these difficulties the NALGO/UNISON branches were relatively successful in maintaining an ongoing presence in the region. These branches faced common sets of problems concerning the activist base and branch resources. In almost every case there was evidence that the activist base was small and shrinking, in the context of staff reductions:

> Things are getting harder. It is becoming more difficult at work. We lost 10% of staff before Xmas because of the voluntary severance programme. This has meant increased pressure on staff remaining. . . . There is now far more pressure. People are worried because of rumours about sections that may be sold off. To date British Gas have not made anybody compulsory redundant. These are worrying times for the majority of staff. (Branch secretary, 1992)

As a result, union members were not as willing or able to devote time to union activity. As the branch secretary noted, the branch committee, 'is as important as it was before but it is not as effective as before. People do not have time to devote to union activities. People are pressured' (1992). Still, the branch leaderships continued to encourage the further development of branch organization, particularly the establishment of sub-branch structures, to facilitate representation from the different divisions. Most branch offices were under-resourced, primarily as a result of declining membership, which in turn created uncertainty about the appropriate levels of administrative support within the branch and concerns about the best ways of delivering it. There was a general view that the level of servicing and assistance available at a regional level was inadequate and failed to meet the needs of the branches. In part, this had arisen because of the mismatch between the geographical location of the NALGO/UNISON region and the evolving company structures and locations.

In the face of the reorganization that began in the early 1990s, the then NALGO branches in the region began discussing the possibility of merging all the branches into one regionally based branch. With the establishment of UNISON, and especially the move towards a functional business unit structure in the region, the branches continued to consider the prospect of merging to form a regional gas branch. The merger proposal was to organize as a regional UNISON branch, mirroring the old regional gas committee. The plan was to have an executive comprising the three senior officers, chair, secretary and treasurer, other branch officers and the five chief stewards for the business units. Below this level of organization a steward committee was to be established for each business unit in the area, comprising at least one steward per office and more where appropriate (although there were problems with retail, where there was not one steward per showroom). These committees would be responsible for industrial relations in their business units, while the senior branch officers would have administrative, policy and political responsibility for the organization and operation of the branch. It was hoped that the monthly stewards' meetings would begin to act as an area joint stewards' committee, in which stewards would inform each other of developments in each business unit, planning joint approaches where appropriate, developing branch policy and practice in a mutually supportive and acknowledged way as well as reporting back to the bi-monthly branch executive.

However, there was uncertainty what these changes might mean in practice. The difficulty was that the branches were fragmenting in relation to industrial relations structures, which were no longer straightforwardly comparable. In addition, it remained unclear what the regional support for the new branch would be, with sections of the leadership concerned that the branch should have a dedicated full-time officer and administrative support. These worries, however, did not inhibit the move towards a regional branch, especially since two of the five branches were effectively without a representative structure by the mid-1990s, following job restructuring and reorganization, as well as substantial relocation of the former regional headquarters staff. In the event, four of the five branches merged on 1 October 1996, with the headquarters branch scheduled to join the new regionally based branch in 1997, largely because this branch had not finalized its financial records and arrangements in time for the merger.

Industrial relations

With the fragmentation of the corporation into business units, industrial relations procedures were also divided and broken down. In fact, the negotiating structure covering the region became extremely complicated, with a series of reorganizations which made it difficult for union branches to adjust to the new circumstances. At a general level, the previous centralized structures were replaced initially by six and then by three separate negotiating arrangements, defined by function and status. One consequence was that for the unions recognized by the company the bargaining arrangements for representation and participation in the business units were remote and non-accountable, at least in any formal sense. In one service business unit, one of the only two offices in the country was located within the study area covered by one of the non-manual union branches. This office had approximately sixty permanent staff and just under 200 temporary staff, and in these circumstances it was not easy for the staff to play an active part in these negotiating structures.

Beyond the workplace, a series of regional business unit committees were established to coordinate and lead negotiations at a regional level. Union branches sent appropriate representatives (employees of the business units) to these committees. The representatives did not represent the branch in any strict constitutional sense, although they were in place by virtue of their branch membership. The committees only really operated in one case, that of TransCo, whereas the others were more or less moribund. In the case of TransCo, the regional committee meetings fed through to the national committee level. These committee representatives then reported back to the members, although not for the ratification of decisions but for the purposes of keeping members informed. What is perhaps more important is that these representatives reported back to their local office negotiating committees, although on an *ad hoc* basis, since accountable structures were not really in place.

In the business units, apart from TransCo, a number of union branch members and senior stewards were on the relevant national committees, but as nominees of the regional committees (effectively defunct) and not from the branch or steward committee as such. The result was attenuated patterns of union participation in the business unit union committees, and thus in relation to the differing bargaining arrangements in each business unit. The problem at the branch or committee level was that this was a form of representation which was formally indirect, and which relied on the integrity and enthusiasm of the particular representatives in keeping the branch and the business unit membership informed of what was happening either regionally or, more importantly, nationally.

The restructuring of the gas corporation was accompanied by a changed approach by the company management to the organization and conduct of industrial relations. Following the principles of HRM, the company had moved to provide information to staff in distinctive ways. This presentation of information generally took the form of formal presentation from the national level down, using overhead projection hand-outs and written commentary. Generally this took place at regional or national level and did not involve the branch directly or immediately. At a local level, with the move towards forms of HRM management practice, these developments gave the appearance of more openness in the provision of information.

One of the advantages of the new managerial approach was a management commitment to forewarn negotiators about items that were to be raised on the negotiating forums in TransCo, the district-based local forums, the area forums, covering seven or eight districts, and the national forum, for the whole division/company. At a local level this was an important development, since negotiators were in a position to prepare for negotiations in ways that had not been so in the past. As one UNISON participant noted:

> What's happened so far is that prior to every meeting [of the local forum] we've had advanced notification of what's going to be on the agenda . . . if we've asked for any information, such as staffing levels, overtime, work throughout the month, or whatever it may be, we have that given to us before the meeting . . . it does seem to be a more open approach by management. (1996)

However, there was a deceptive side to these procedures, since staff often learnt about the developments that were taking place in the corporation overall by public announcements to the media as well as formal presentations. This created a situation where there was considerable uncertainty among the staff about the way in which the corporation as a whole was changing and the implications of these developments, but where detailed information of staffing levels and practices, by district, was provided. The difficulty for the local union leaders was to do more than note these developments.

Following the privatization of the gas corporation there was a marked increase in the number of items subject to negotiation and discussion, although initially the formal bargaining procedures remained unaltered. Most issues were settled at a regional level, with the district-based form of consultative committees remaining largely moribund. In the early 1990s, however, the corporation began to switch attention away from the region, giving district managers considerably more autonomy and responsibility than in the past, particularly over the deployment of labour. Accompanying this decentralization, there was a managerial attempt to focus the first stage of bargaining and negotiation at this level via the district committees. Most recently, there had been an extensive fragmentation of bargaining arrangements, to connect with the newly established business units and with the new employing units established by the disaggregation of British Gas.

The division of the company into business units transformed the negotiating arrangements and structures, with dramatic implications for union organization. Broadly similar arrangements were set up in each of the business units, involving district or equivalent joint negotiations, as well as area and national joint negotiations. In the case of the GMB, the steward structures were reorganized so as to facilitate representation in these new arrangements. The UNISON branches also reorganized so as to link with the new bargaining arrangements, usually setting up *de facto* branch business unit structures. These procedures were formalized with the establishment of the merged branch.

Following the reorganization of the company into business units, the manual unions were able to build on the steward form of organization to establish negotiating committees, composed of senior stewards. These committees were developed to link into the bargaining forums that had been established for each business unit. The earlier encouragement and development of steward structures in the depots and related workplaces facilitated the development of accountable negotiating arrangements. With the establishment of more active steward committees, supported in most cases by the local managements, senior stewards were more comprehensively resourced, in a number of cases, not only with office facilities in the reconstructed offices, but with mobile telephones so that contact could be maintained between local management and the senior stewards. As a result, with the shift to more removed bargaining forums within the business units, these senior stewards were able to utilize these locally provided facilities to lay the foundation for contact between senior stewards, as well as between senior stewards and their members. None the less, despite these innovations the union was still led by full-time officers, with district officers taking the lead in the negotiations, according to the business units for which they were responsible.

Paralleling these developments, and with the shift to more decentralized forms of management in the early 1990s, the local non-manual union leaderships began to take up issues which had previously been dealt with at a regional level of negotiations, such as those relating to the implementation of quality management procedures. In addition, the incidence of problems referred to branch secretaries in the region increased dramatically. When the branch secretary of one branch was first elected, she dealt with only one discipline case in the first year. Three years later, over twenty-four discipline cases, many concerned with sickness records and absenteeism, were referred to her, with twelve going through more than one stage of the procedure. In addition, in 1993, this branch secretary dealt with two cases of sexual harassment for the first time.

Beyond the branch level, a series of regional business unit committees had been established during the 1990s to coordinate and lead negotiations at a regional level. The branches sent appropriate representatives (employees of the business units) to these committees. These representatives did not represent their branches in any strict constitutional sense, although they were in place by virtue of their branch membership. For example, in the case of TransCo, one of the major business unit divisions in the area, the regional committee meetings fed through to the national committee level, in the form of representation as well as policy. These committee representatives then reported back to their branches, although this was for information and on a voluntary basis only. What is perhaps more important is that these representatives reported back to their local office negotiating committees, although on an *ad hoc* basis, since the accountable structures were not really in place. The problem at the branch level was that this was a form of representation that was informally direct, but that formally relied on the integrity and enthusiasm of the particular representatives in keeping the branch and their business unit membership informed of what was happening either regionally or, more importantly, nationally.

The branches were preoccupied with the development of bargaining and negotiation procedures, and this was reflected in the comments by branch leaders about information and support from the national level of the union. At a general level, the branches were positive about the energy service group of UNISON and the educational and information programmes that had been developed. These were seen to provide the basis for developing the union branches in ways that would enable them to address the challenges in the energy industry. The branch leaderships expressed concern about the relationship between the branch and the regional office. This was not necessarily a criticism of the expertise of the regional officers but a more general observation that they appeared to be organized so as to service local government and health service groups of UNISON rather than the energy sector.

Removed forms of representation

The pattern in gas was that the division of the company into business units had transformed the negotiating arrangements and structures, with dramatic implications for union organization. Business units had been established, involving district or equivalent joint negotiations, as well as area and national joint negotiations. One of the most striking features of recent years has been the growth of collective bargaining at local levels. Many of the branch and steward respondents, and all the regional officials, commented on this trend. Examples were given of the difficulties many had in refocusing their activities and developing their negotiating skills on such issues as pay. The key problem faced by local union representatives was that, without exception, management set the agenda for, and the terms of, local negotiations. This was a consequence of two main factors. First, management had more resources available to it at local level than did union representatives and, second, many union representatives felt uncertain about the relationship between national or company level bargaining and local level negotiations.

There was also an inherent tension between local and national/company levels of collective bargaining in the utilities. Business units were remote and non-accountable where they were organized across large geographical areas. The unions in the gas corporation were faced with complex and significant problems in adjusting to the fragmentation of collective bargaining across the various service groups. At branch and steward committee level, it was often difficult to gain a picture of an overall strategic approach to this complex of arrangements. It was only where considerable emphasis has been placed on educational and briefing programmes that branch officers and leading stewards saw themselves positively contributing to both local level negotiations and the broader service group approach. Some branch representatives and stewards saw themselves as isolated and removed from national/company level negotiations and a few were 'overwhelmed' by the demands placed upon them by local bargaining.

The other side of these developments was that for UNISON, in particular, there was a crisis of representation, in that the activist base of the branches was shrinking, putting further pressure on the over-worked branch officials. As one local leader noted:

> I think the problem is more on the trade unions than on the management . . .
> because certainly with the restructuring at the moment, there's been a lot of
> reps, a lot of the established and experienced reps, have gone on voluntary
> redundancy, and so the trade unions have been left high and dry in many
> areas, all their reps have gone, so there are void areas of trade union
> representation. (1996)

While such pressures were also evident among the GMB areas of representation, they were experienced more sharply by the local UNISON branches.

Alongside this, the UNISON branch officers increasingly dealt directly with the national union office, and no longer with the regional officials. The problem for these officers was that with the shift to divisional forms of corporate organization, the regional officials found it difficult to connect with the new corporate structures that were being developed. As one branch leader noted about the regional office:

> I can't even remember the last time I went into the regional office of
> UNISON. We seem to have been left on our own. We go straight from the
> local level . . . to the national. I mean there seems to be no regional
> assistance as we used to have. There is nominally a Gas Officer at a regional
> level but we never go to [this person]. (1996)

The corollary at the national level was that national full-time officials increasingly relied on lay representatives to provide adequate representation at the local level. In the case of UNISON in 1996 there were only 3.5 staff employed in the energy services group responsible for gas. In a situation where there was a contracting activist base in the local areas covered by the union, the pressures of representation fell on fewer and fewer shoulders.

There was some limited evidence that the GMB senior steward committees also experienced difficulty connecting with the new management structures that were being put in place. The differences with the UNISON arrangements were twofold. First, the senior steward representative structure was a fairly malleable one, in that stewards were district-based and could regroup according to the changes taking place. Second, there was a flexibility in the job remit of the GMB officials that enabled them to work with the regrouped steward committees that was not available to the regionally based and tied officials of UNISON. Thus, while the GMB committee members faced uncertainty about the future, as the corporation(s) reorganized, they were also in a position to respond to and meet these changes. The main problem for this union was to extend its representative structures beyond the former British Gas corporation, and its successors, to the contract firms that have become a feature of gas services.

The consequence of these developments was that remote forms of union representation had become more evident, especially in the case of the UNISON membership. After a period where both local manual and non-manual union leaderships had become more actively involved in localized bargaining and representation, as a response to the devolution of managerial hierarchies and the reorganization of the local labour process, further corporate reorganization qualified these trends. With the divisionalization of the corporation into business units, and the relocation of negotiating forums, the unions went through a further period of adjustment and adaptation. The consequence was that the union form of organization in the corporation was characterized by dual forms of representation, one based on branches and part of the political and administrative structures of the unions, the other based on the negotiating hierarchies in the corporation, involving representatives from each division or business unit. These negotiating arrangements sat uneasily within the past union structures and were in a continuing process of evolution. The result was removed forms of union organization and representation.

Assessment

The approach by the unions in this utility was reactive rather than proactive. Prior to privatization both the manual and non-manual unions had organized around full-time officials, on the basis that the memberships were relatively quiescent. Over time the form of unionism that emerged was one where the memberships were reliant on these full-time officials. There was little tradition or experience of membership involvement and participation, even in the manual unions. The result was a unionism that was ill-equipped for the managerial changes that were eventually introduced following privatization.

With privatization, there was little change to established management–staff relations, especially in the non-manual grades. However, in the 1990s, the senior management of the then British Gas corporation introduced a series of changes which effectively transformed the terrain of unionism in the industry. There were two aspects to this reorganization: a fragmentation of the formerly unified corporation and the repositioning of sections of the corporation within the national energy markets as well as internationally as part of an emergent international market. For the union branches and committees there was an attempt to promote a broader pattern of membership involvement and participation as a way of countering the negative effects of these changes. Such a response was most evident in the GMB, where the full-time official sponsored a more active form of steward representation than had been evident in the past. Similar moves occurred in the then NALGO branches, although the combination of a dispersed membership and a membership which saw itself as 'white-collar' and different from the manual workforce limited moves in this direction. In addition, the relevant full-time officials had a less involved relationship with their memberships than was the case with the manual unions.

With the further restructuring of the corporation in the mid-1990s, the differences between the two union groups became more apparent. In the case of the GMB, the promotion of more active steward arrangements enabled the union to maintain a presence within the successor companies of British Gas. As part of this development, there was some indication that the steward committees, particularly the convenors, were in a position to qualify their traditional reliance on full-time officials, not least because of the fragmentation that occurred within the industry, and the practical impossibility of continued full-time officer dominance. In contrast, the UNISON branches faced continuing difficulties as the activist base contracted and the remaining branch leaders came under more and more pressure from managements to restrict and curtail their union activity. One solution was to pool the resources of the union branches, in part in compliance with UNISON rules, and merge the branches. However, this solution was only partial, in that the activist base remained small and the leaders faced difficulties reconciling the union structures with company structures and arrangements. The result was a form of unionism that provided neither for membership involvement and participation nor for effective and reasonably resourced representation by increasingly beleaguered leaderships.

10 PARTICIPATIVE REPRESENTATION: WATER

In contrast with privatization in gas and telecommunications, the process of restructuring in the water industry was relatively sudden and comprehensive. The privatization of the water industry in 1989 involved the immediate break-up of the water authority, with the establishment of a series of regionally based water corporations. Managerial hierarchies were recast and layers of management were given responsibility for the development of these regionally based corporations, in marketing and sales, and production activity, as well as in relation to industrial relations. This was a comprehensive process of restructuring which recast the terrain of management–labour relations in substantive ways.

As with other utilities, the patterns of unionism were based around forms of responsible leadership at both national and local levels. This was a centralized form of unionism, where union leaders, at both national and local level, spoke on behalf of a relatively uninvolved and quiescent membership. The focus of negotiation and bargaining was at a national level, and unions in the industry had developed a top-down form of representation where the local leaders were effectively ciphers for policy initiatives and responses developed by the national leadership. While this was a form of unionism rooted in the structure and organization of the industry in the pre-privatization period, with the privatization of the industry the conditions for it no longer applied.

On privatization of the industry, the established bargaining and negotiating arrangements were reconstructed, in part driven by the managerial restructuring that took place and in part by the proactive responses of the unions and, for the non-manual staff, by initiatives taken by the NALGO/UNISON leadership, nationally and regionally. Each water company management developed an approach to industrial relations, which in some cases, such as Severn Trent plc, involved working with regional union leaders, full-time and lay, adapting and developing past practices and arrangements for the new situation in which they found themselves. In other cases, such as Northumberland Water plc, the management moved to marginalize the recognized unions, and place the management in a dominant position in the privatized company.

For the NALGO/UNISON memberships in Severn Trent plc the privatization of the industry provided the opportunity to reconsider the past forms of union organization. This was an occasion for reviewing the centralized patterns of leadership in the area and to initiate more participative membership arrangements. These were contested developments, by management as well as within the union. On the one hand, the 'new' corporate management sought to create a set of arrangements that would permit the corporation to develop in the circumstances of privatization, unhindered by union concerns and preoccupations. In this respect there was a strong impetus to lay down formal procedures for industrial relations over a relatively limited range of subjects. On the other hand, the established union leaders in the region faced the problem of defining and opening up issues for their membership in ways that were novel and no longer relied on an established and resourced London-based national leadership. In this respect the union leaders faced an opportunity to renew their unionism, and provide the conditions for a broader membership involvement than had been the case previously. It is this complex of issues that is examined in this chapter.

The water industry in the West Midlands

The restructuring of the water industry at the time of privatization, in 1989, was relatively sudden and dramatic, signified by the establishment of ten regionally based water companies. This involved the break-up of centralized national management structures and thus raised major questions for the unions. Managements, which had been socialized into the relatively consensual ethos of nationalized industries, found themselves adopting new enterprise-based approaches and structures, in which workforces were reorganized to meet the requirements of integrated regionally based corporations, and where it became necessary to develop new bargaining arrangements and procedures. As these new corporations began to establish themselves in the commercial world of the international water industry, they were subject to take-overs (Northumbrian Water) or considered take-over (Severn Trent Water and Wessex Water on South West Water) and diversification (North West Water and Norweb). Not surprisingly, in these varied circumstances, corporations approached union–management relations in a variety of ways, from the marginalization of unions (Northumbrian Water initiating unilateral changes

Table 10.1 *Workforce numbers for Severn Trent plc, 1991–1995*

	Water and sewerage services	Other
1991	7054	470
1993	7445	3074
1995	6531	4097

Source: Severn Trent plc (1995, p. 46).

in terms and conditions of employment) to the continued recognition and involvement with unions (Severn Trent adopting a bargaining approach to change).

The water company studied covered the whole of the West Midlands region, and more. In the 1980s, prior to privatization, many jobs were lost as the company reorganized in readiness for privatization, while there was a further loss of jobs as a result of transfers undertaken during the privatization process. (Some employees, for example, moved across to the newly created National River Authority.) At the time of privatization, there were approximately 7,500 staff, over half non-manual and nearly 10 per cent women. About 5 per cent of the workforce was employed on a part-time basis, working in clerical and support areas, with most of these staff being women. Following privatization, Severn Trent Water plc increased its employment numbers, as indicated in Table 10.1.

Between 1991 and 1995 there was a decrease in the numbers employed in the core business areas of water and sewerage by 7.5 per cent, while there was an increase of 871 per cent in 'other' areas of activity over the same period. This expansion occurred in the following areas and countries: waste management (United Kingdom and Belgium); operating and consultancy expertise (North America and Europe); customer service software (United Kingdom and the United States of America); and the development of water and sewerage facilities for properties in the United Kingdom. In the early 1990s, the staff worked in widely dispersed areas, across thirty-four major locations in the vast geographical area covered by the company. There were a number of relatively large clusters of staff of around 150, although there were also areas of employment where relatively few staff were employed. The range of activities included highly technical work, to do with the treatment of water and sewerage, billing and related activities, as well as the organization and operation of the water and sewerage facilities across the region.

The privatization of the water industry in 1989 was the occasion for two strikingly different responses from manual workers and non-manual staff. At Severn Trent the manual workers had been socialized into a more accommodating acceptance of change, partly as a result of the major cuts in their numbers during the 1980s and partly because their full-time officers believed that they were not prepared to question these developments more forcefully. With privatization, they continued to rely on their full-time officers. In contrast, a number of lay activists from NALGO were major participants in the campaigns opposing privatization and this experience was drawn upon in their subsequent activity in negotiations with management. Building on this experience, non-manual staff in the region became more actively involved in their union, possibly reflecting the novelty of insecurity and work reorganization and the search for some sort of respite from the dramatic reconstruction of the industry.

The company

Following privatization, the company pursued a relatively modest programme of acquisition and internal reorganization. The core business remained water and sewerage, with a modest degree of diversification and the reorganization of discrete areas, such as the laboratories, as separate subsidiary companies. In addition, the company purchased a number of outside companies, although, when compared with the policies of other water companies, this was also relatively modest in its scale. By 1996, the company was one of nine British water companies operating in an internationally based market. It had established a subsidiary company operating in the environmental sector, and based on the laboratories in the former parent company. In addition, it had acquired subsidiaries in Central and South America as well as Western Europe.

In brief, the company pursued a relatively consistent and limited policy of consolidating the 'core' business, unlike the extensive and in some cases unsuccessful diversification programmes undertaken by other water companies. None the less, the company did pursue a modest degree of diversification and acquisition, which placed the corporation in a stable and secure position within the UK and the international water industry. This was a strategy based on the belief that modest growth, based on the 'core' business, was the basis for long-term success. Central to this programme was the evolution of a 'vision' or 'mission', which concentrated on the development and improvement of its 'core' business, incorporating aspects of HRM policies and practices.

The company identified its purpose in the following terms:

As a world leader in the provision of water and waste services, Severn Trent plc's strategy for growth focuses on using and developing its expertise in the management of resources and assets and in providing a high level of service to its customers. The company will continue to use these skills to strengthen its existing businesses and to add value to other utility and utility-related operations. (Severn Trent plc, 1996, p. 5)

The management 'challenge' was to improve profitability and sales, deliver customer service, develop commercial skills and reduce costs.

Within the 'core' business there was considerable reorganization and restructuring after privatization. At an operational level, Severn Trent plc reorganized away from functionally focused structures to ones that were district or geographically based. These districts, fifteen in all, were given an important degree of budgetary and managerial autonomy, so that local managers were able to pursue their own remits, albeit within a corporate determined framework. District managers took the opportunity provided by this reorganization to pursue distinctive policies, such as a questioning of prevailing flexi-time arrangements, job mobility practices and the redeployment of staff to meet changing priorities.

Following privatization and the recomposition of managerial hierarchies in the water company, there was a move both to monitor work efforts more closely and to establish the mechanisms for encouraging a committed and involved workforce. The impetus for the close monitoring of work effort came from the corporate management as well as statutory and regulatory requirements. A senior engineer identified these developments in the following terms:

we have certain targets that we have to meet, from the regulator's point of view, so therefore we need to monitor the situation to make sure we are providing that or we are providing that service, and that has a knock-on effect and to do that you need to get [information and data] for the whole company, so every department in every district has to monitor it and so on. ... There has been a great increase in that sort of thing since privatisation, certainly privatisation and regulation and the levels of service required by legislation and the regulator. (1992)

One of the outcomes of these developments was that the relations between management and the workforce began to change. During the early 1990s, following establishment of the privatized companies, procedures were put in place for increased data collection and work monitoring as part of a requirement to meet statutory and related obligations, but also in terms of establishing the corporation as a market-based and market-focused enterprise.

Accompanying these developments, the corporate management encouraged the development of HRM practices which focused on sets of mutual responsibilities between the corporation and the workforce. Central to this initiative in the early 1990s was the promotion of team briefings throughout the company. According to one senior engineer the aim of these briefings was as follows: '[They were] set up to meet the need to keep people informed but also they were set up with the clear view that it was also a feed back on the effects of policies decided from high up and how people on the ground as it were felt about it, how things were working' (1992). These arrangements had been initiated by the personnel department and were seen as a way of 'getting the message across' and a way to ensure that management could learn about the impact of corporate policy on the workforce. Overall, such initiatives were presented by the senior management as part of the development of a responsive and forward-looking management. These developments were cast in terms of features of a modern management working to the principles and practices of HRM.

Representation and organization

In the early 1980s, there were fifteen NALGO branches covering the areas within the Severn Trent water area. As the corporation reorganized during the 1980s, the local union leadership, at the instigation of the regional NALGO full-time officer, initiated a process of branch reorganization and consolidation in the region. In the first instance, in 1986, the branches were rationalized into five, covering four geographical areas and the headquarters buildings. These were further reduced to three branches in 1990, when the headquarters branch was merged with two contiguous geographical branches in the west of the region as one branch. The two other branches remained unaltered. Following this, there was informal comment among branch leaders in the region about the desirability of a further merger to create one branch for Severn Trent plc, at some time in the late 1990s. The main barrier to the further consolidation of the NALGO branches was the reluctance of the established leaderships in the two smaller branches to lose their pre-eminence as senior branch leaders in the area. Nothing happened until the merger to establish UNISON, and on 1 July 1996, a single UNISON branch for the region was established, composed of three NALGO branches and the six small NUPE branches in the region.

The merger of branches during this period had implications not only for the size of the new branch but also for the relationship between the branch

217

leadership and members, including locally based activists. The headquarters NALGO branch merged with the two western geographical branches on 19 January 1991, resulting in a branch of 1,648 members (77 per cent union density). The membership was spread over forty to fifty workplaces, organized into fourteen districts. With managerial reorganization in 1989 and 1990, a local joint council (LJC) was set up in each of these districts. This provided the base for workplace activity at the workplace level. Although NALGO provided the largest union group on each LJC, with representatives from relevant workplaces in each district, there was only a loose connection between this level of branch representation and the branch executive.

The establishment of the merged headquarters branch was seen by the branch secretary as a positive development. As stated: 'The merger allows a pooling of abilities to get over difficulties of post-privatisation. We now have experienced people throughout the area and have pooled our expertise. Our publicity benefits from the pooling of resources. It raises the profile of the branch' (1991). The formal branch structure involved a branch executive committee, which consisted of representatives elected at the annual general meeting, irrespective of the area where they worked. In 1991, there was provision for ninety steward positions within the branch, although only seventy positions were filled. Meetings of the branch executive committee were scheduled for four times a year, although extraordinary meetings could be held if deemed necessary by the senior officers. On average, forty of the stewards and officers attended the executive committee meetings. While this was a relatively low attendance, the locus of activity within the branch was not the executive committee meetings, but the specialist committee meetings. The finance and general purposes committee was the main committee of the branch, and composed of representatives of each LJC, although the coverage was far from complete, as only seven of the fourteen LJCs had regular representation.

The branch secretary saw this reorganization as providing the basis for a more participative branch structure, when compared with previous arrangements. He noted: 'We are better organised than previously, although we have a long way to go but it is working. Now we have to rely on activists in the branch for example on the pay campaign the information was spread by notice by local representatives. This is new and there are a lot of committed reps' (1991). Previously the branches had been organized around a few branch officers and there had been a very minimal representative structure in place in each of these branches.

However, the pattern of representation and involvement was partial. The composition of the branch executive was skewed towards the headquarters staff, with the annual general meeting held in the headquarters building, thus providing the opportunity for these staff to attend the meeting and play an ongoing part in the branch. The full-time branch administrator was also based in the headquarters building, further affirming the pattern of representation within the branch. One consequence of these arrangements was that only seven of the senior LJC stewards attended the branch executive meetings as committee members; the others had more *ad hoc* relationships with the branch leadership, via the branch secretary and the regional full-time officer. This pattern of representation and participation made for an uneven form of representation, with most activity focused on the headquarters. However, following the merger, there was a net increase of the branch membership of 10 per cent between 1991 and 1992, as the branch established its prominence in the region.

The branch secretary was very aware of the problems associated with this pattern of representation. He had been the branch secretary of one of the smaller branches involved in the merger, and was elected secretary of the newly established merged branch in 1991. Together with the regional officer, he took steps to encourage a broader pattern of representation and participation within the branch. They both were of the opinion that the newly merged branch would provide the core leadership grouping of any later merged branch, and were concerned to broaden participation within the new branch and to maintain 'good' relations with the leaderships of the two remaining NALGO branches. One important development was that the branch was able to use its resources to expand administrative and organizational support. As a result, the branch began to develop in ways that meant it no longer relied on the regional officer, as had been the case with the three branches prior to the merger.

In developing participation and forms of accountable representation within the branch, they faced the problem of a membership spread over a large geographical area, with undeveloped traditions of trade unionism in many of the outlying areas. The branch secretary, who worked in one of the southern districts, but travelled to the headquarters building, to the branch office and to attend meetings a number of times a week, was very familiar with the problems of distance, both geographically and in the form of underdeveloped traditions of trade union consciousness and awareness. He noted: 'Communication is a problem. Some people are not prepared to be full stewards. Our problem is to make sure that members feed information about developments in their workplaces into the branch. This is not the same as day-to-day information but it is important' (1991). The branch secretary approached the question of developing tighter forms of trade union awareness and forms of participation and representation in a relatively informal way, relying on face-to-face contact and personal encouragement, rather than reorganizing the branch in a constitutional way so as to ensure at least formal involvement from each district and area covered by the branch.

In contrast, the other two branches were much smaller, one covering the eastern part of the region and the other the northern. The eastern branch, the second branch covered by the study, contained only 504 members in 1991 and covered three districts, with thirty-two workplaces in total. While the membership was just as diverse as the larger branch and spread over an extensive geographical area, it was relatively easy for this branch secretary to visit each district and encourage a more participative approach to both negotiations and involvement within the branch committees. As the branch secretary stated, 'Mostly the reps deal with members. Only if a member has a problem that the rep feels that they cannot handle do members come to see me' (1991). The branch executive was composed of twenty-two persons, including the officers. With the move towards district-based negotiations and the establishment of the LJCs, the branch leadership encouraged the development of constituency forms of representation, based on the LJCs and, to a lesser extent, area and function of work. As a result, there was a representational basis to a broad pattern of involvement with members in this branch, reflected in the relationship between representatives and members, as well as the involvement of representatives on the branch executive committee. This committee met monthly and on average fifteen members attended.

The reorganization of the branch executive committee led to an important change in the way the branch conducted its business. Reports from the LJCs became standard agenda items. Trade union secretaries from the LJCs developed the practice of reporting problems and issues that were coming up in their districts to the branch executive committee. There was a more informed and detailed discussion of these issues at a branch level than previously, enabling more participative forms of union leadership to begin to evolve. These discussions at the branch executive committee meetings were both a means to achieve more participation within branch life and an indication of increased participation at these meetings and in the districts.

Overall, the establishment of LJCs was the occasion for some members to become active participants in local negotiations. This was vividly illustrated by two bargaining schools for NALGO district committee members in the newly established bargaining structure. The fifty-seven members in attendance included most of the long-standing active union members in the area before privatization, as well as a substantial minority (nearly a third according to the full-time officer) who had played no consistent active role in the union until that moment. Indeed, one of the features of the two schools was that nearly a quarter of the members in attendance were women, which caused comment from three or four of the most senior union officials, who were used to predominantly male schools, particularly on bargaining issues. Through locally based negotiating committees these members became involved in local union activity, often for the first time in their union lives. Issues that were previously overlooked, such as a concern with increased workloads or work routines, acquired a new importance and relevance because members raised them as problems with their local representatives on the LJCs.

Bargaining arrangements

Following privatization of the water industry, the regional levels of the manual and non-manual unions were, for the first time, directly involved and responsible for pay bargaining. This meant that union officials, both full-time and lay, were faced with the problem of drawing up pay claims, presenting their cases and responding to managements who were equally inexperienced. The relation between these levels of union organization and the national headquarters began to shift, so that regional leaderships began to make new claims on national resources: for example, for assistance in preparing pay claims. More generally, nationally based and focused bargaining arrangements were disbanded with privatization. In their place, Severn Trent plc proposed new sets of arrangements, based on district managerial structures. Each district had a local joint consultative committee for each of the three negotiating groups, dealing with local issues.

The negotiating structures within Severn Trent were complex, involving three sets of union groups. Following privatization, the reorganization into districts and the end of national bargaining were accompanied by a series of changes in bargaining and consultation arrangements. There were seven recognized unions in the company: GMB, APEX, TGWU, NUPE, AEU, NALGO/UNISON and EETPU. These unions initially operated through three main negotiating committees, covering 'industrial' staff (GMB, TGWU, NUPE/UNISON), 'craft' staff (GMB, TGWU, EETPU, AEU) and non-manual staff (APEX, NALGO/UNISON, NUPE/UNISON), although by 1993 the 'industrial' and 'craft' committees had merged together, as the first step in the company's attempt to establish single table bargaining.

The formal negotiating structure was composed of a set of relationships from the district level of the organization to the company level:

Table 10.2 *Regional joint negotiating committee, Severn Trent plc*

Union	Company
NALGO *(four representatives, including the regional full-time officer)*	*Personnel manager*
NUPE *(one representative, the full-time officer)*	*Personnel–industrial relations officer*
	Finance manager
APEX *(one representative, the full-time officer)*	*Operations manager*
	Senior district manager

- *The company council*: senior management industrial relations team and trade union side.
- *District committees*: fifteen district committees, with a management and a trade union side (local joint committee); four/five support services units.

At the corporate level, negotiating committees were established for pay and conditions of employment for non-manual and manual staff. This followed a period of extensive negotiations between the union officials and the newly established management team for Severn Trent plc. The main committee for the non-manual staff was known as the regional joint negotiating council (RJNC), and was composed as shown in Table 10.2. This committee usually met four to five times a year, although at the time of pay negotiations and other complicated negotiations, these formal meetings would be accompanied by a series of semi-formal and sub-committee meetings and negotiations to try to settle disagreements.

The membership of the corporate NALGO/UNISON negotiating team was carefully constructed to include the branch secretary for the eastern branch, a long-serving and influential NALGO member at a regional level, despite the fact that the headquarters branch had the numbers to prevent his election. Since NALGO was the largest union for the non-manual staff, it was the lead union in the negotiations. The members of the committee prepared carefully for the meetings, sounding out members on pay claims and other matters, as well as discussing the claims and progress of negotiations with each other. This latter contact was mainly by telephone, although there were relatively frequent meetings both before and after negotiations. The membership of the NALGO/UNISON team had been active within NALGO for a number of years, were familiar with each other and had a lot of respect for the NALGO/UNISON full-time officers. The result was a cohesive committee, whose members occasionally argued with each other, but which overall presented a united front to management in the formal and semi-formal negotiations that took place.

Severn Trent plc proposed new sets of arrangements as an independent private corporation, based on revised district managerial structures, with each district establishing a local joint consultative committee for each of the three negotiating groups. Following privatization, and with the advent of wage bargaining at the company level, these negotiating committees acquired an added importance within the company. The council dealt with overall strategic planning for the company and a joint negotiating committee of the council considered issues of pay and working conditions. Below this level of negotiation, the company established a series of local joint committees (LJCs), in accordance with the reorganization of management structures on a district basis. These district managers were given the responsibility for staff management at this level. From management's point of view this reorganization and the establishment of the LJCs were aimed at developing the district's 'ownership of their own issues', and broadly reflected company policy aimed at the 'empowerment' of the local management and workforce.

For the unions, these developments heralded a substantial redefinition of union organization and activity. Following privatization, the regional levels of manual and non-manual unions were, for the first time, directly involved and responsible for pay bargaining. This meant that union officials, both full-time and lay, were faced with the problem and difficulty of drawing up pay claims, presenting their cases and responding to managements who were equally inexperienced. It meant that the relation between these levels of union organization and the national headquarters began to shift, so that regional leaderships began to make new claims on national resources, such as assistance in preparing pay claims.

This reorganization of bargaining procedures and arrangements provided an opportunity for locally based union groups to challenge local managements through a judicious use of the new bargaining structures, clearly illustrated by one NALGO/UNISON branch. In 1992, management began to alter the terms of the corporate flexi-time agreement in a seemingly *ad hoc* way in three recently established districts, each covered by the union branch. This policy became apparent at a branch executive meeting when the three district trade union secretaries reported that their managements were questioning current agreements. After a long debate about how best to proceed, the executive decided to single out the one district where they judged the branch had the strongest presence on this issue and to negotiate an acceptable alternative agreement. During the month interval before the next branch executive meeting, the branch negotiators reached a new arrangement on flexi-time that was acceptable to the membership and the executive. The executive then initiated similar negotiations at the other district committees, arguing the case of comparability.

In this way they achieved a set of agreements that frustrated the management attempt to restrict the use of flexi-time throughout the area.

The company approach to negotiations was a combination of traditional and 'new' styles of management. On the one hand, consultation and informal discussion were used by many managers in their dealings with union representatives, and these union representatives responded in kind. In large measure this represented the continuation of practices that had long been evident in the water industry. On the other hand, the company did not hesitate to 'force' the issue in negotiations, testing the willingness of union memberships to support their leaderships in negotiations, particularly at a company level. This was most evident with the non-manual staff, where the company refused to settle the negotiations at an early stage, thereby pushing the negotiators into the consideration of, and balloting for, industrial action in 1991, 1992 and 1993. While the ballots were supportive of the leadership position, settlements were reached before any industrial action was undertaken. In a more limited way this approach and style of bargaining continued through to 1996.

During the 1990s, the company culture appeared to shift towards an HRM model of management. To an important extent this turned out to be a largely rhetorical development, particularly at the lower levels of the managerial hierarchies. It was also the case that, in line with the corporate approach to negotiations, especially over wages and terms and conditions of employment, the company would 'press' the union negotiators in the annual negotiations. The result was that there was a formality to negotiations that belied any moves towards new managerial styles and forms of management in the corporation.

The union representatives were increasingly involved in taking up individual cases with management. There appeared to be a tightening up by the local managers on so-called fringe benefits, relating to the payment of allowances and leave arrangements, discipline cases, grading disputes and the like. In one case, a branch executive member was 'harassed' by local management while on maternity leave. As the branch secretary commented:

> I dealt with a case for a member – she is actually on our executive committee – who is off on maternity leave. She was pestered by Severn Trent when she just came out of hospital and was also hassled on the day the child was born by their demands for a return of keys and all this sort of thing – with local management and with industrial relations, telling them to bloody well lay off and leave her alone. (1992)

This example was one of a number of such cases, suggesting a general approach by the local management in the company. Often such cases resulted from a literal interpretation of the rules and regulations of work and employment.

There was variation in the way in which local managers approached individual cases and local negotiations. This variation was interpreted by a union leader as career related:

> Some managers have got better in that there are some managers around who really wielded the big stick to let people know that they were there and what power they had and who have mellowed and who don't feel the need to do that now and therefore relations have got better and you see a reduction in things like disciplinary cases in certain areas and indeed grievances in certain areas. But then you get people who are on a different rung on the ladder and maybe where that other manager was two or three years ago so it's very mixed. (1992)

The outcome was that there was an ongoing stream of individual cases that were dealt with by branch secretaries and the LJC secretaries, which reflected what often appeared to the union activists as a rather arbitrary and *ad hoc* approach by local managers in their relations with their workforce.

More generally, there was evidence that the more formal relations between the union negotiating teams and the corporate management had established a routinized and regulated relationship with each other. In this respect, some of the mistrust between the two sides was less evident by the mid-1990s when compared with the period immediately following privatization. In the words of one branch secretary, 'There has been a willingness to show trust, one side in the other' (1992). However, at a local level, the patterns of relations between local managers and their workforces were both uneven and varied. Thus, while the corporate level relations between the union representatives and senior management had settled down, there were times at which the caution expressed by the union leaders towards the company management was reinforced by the continued practice of local managers towards their staff.

Participative forms of representation

The advent of privatization and the establishment of the new company provided an occasion and the impetus for the union leaders to re-examine the way in which branches were organized and operated. There were two sides to this response. On the one hand, the leaders took the initiative to break the culture whereby the branches were in effect organized around very few experienced leaders. In this respect, the management initiative to develop a district-based form of managerialism, with associated bargaining forums, provided the opportunity for the branch leaders to encourage the emergence of district-based workplace stewards. In this respect, these developments indicated an outward-looking leadership, keen to encourage a broad-based participation in union activity, including the representation of members both directly to local managers and to lead negotiators on the local district committees. On the other hand, the establishment of formal negotiating committees at a corporate level stimulated the development of a relatively formalized and routine set of relations between the branch leaders and the senior company personnel. This development, after a period of dispute and acrimony between these leaders and company senior staff, reinforced the branch leaders' positions as prominent and leading personnel within the union. In the circumstances of broad geographical branches with dispersed memberships there was the potential for these leaders to become relatively removed from the immediate day-to-day concerns of the membership. That this did not happen was testimony to the commitment by these leaders to forms of active participation by members within the branches.

Following privatization, the union groups in the area went through a process of reorganization and reassessment of how they organized, resulting in a more participative form of unionism than had been the case previously, as well as a more leadership-led union. The establishment of a negotiating structure, based on LJCs at the district level, provided the occasion for these formerly remote forms of union representation, based around one or at most two active members, to reorganize in a more comprehensive and participative way. The LJCs became the base level of negotiation and the NALGO membership in this company responded in positive ways, with previously inactive members coming forward as members of the LJC union side. However, there was an unevenness in this process, with eastern branch much more successful in establishing a participative practice than the branch based on the headquarters staff and the western areas. The reason for this difference appears to have been the way in which the branch secretary of eastern branch was able to facilitate and assist the embryonic union committees on the LJCs in his area. In contrast, the branch secretary of the headquarters-based branch had fourteen LJCs to aid, a much larger geographical area to cover and a greater hesitancy among the membership about active union involvement and engagement.

However, the development of an activist-based membership was not an easy accomplishment. There were problems and difficulties in encouraging members to come forward and then to be in a position to represent members and negotiate with managers. As one union secretary stated, the main difficulty

'I would say is having enough people specifically trained and able to represent members' interests. We are quite well off in some areas and really stretched. You know we have one or two one-man or one-woman bands in some areas so in some areas this is our biggest problem' (1992). The question was how to achieve a critical mass of activists across the region and located in the often dispersed and somewhat isolated workplaces that characterize these types of companies. In part, this involved active encouragement and resourcing from the branch officers; in part, it involved the development and articulation of a union consciousness that gave these people the confidence to act as union representatives with inexperienced union members and occasionally arbitrary and punitive local managers.

The main mechanism for developing an activist and participative membership was via the development of the local negotiating committees. In this respect, the union leaders encouraged a traditional form of union involvement and activity: that is, securing and protecting the terms and conditions of employment of the membership. This was very much a deliberate strategy, as noted by the branch secretary of the regional headquarters branch:

> we wanted to get people interested, to feel part of the branch ... and I think that probably the single, the two things that have helped in that respect are the channelling of more things on conditions of service issues through local joint secretaries and 'Streuth' the [branch] newsletter that goes out and I think these two things have enabled us to keep people feeling that they are part of a unit. (1992)

For members the salience of the union was not the activity of the branch leaders or the resources available to the branch office, but the ability to be able to express concern, present a view or have a problem dealt with at their workplace. For these branches this meant a district-based structure, resting on active representatives at this level.

However, there was a paradox to these developments, in that the establishment of Severn Trent plc and the development of the new negotiating structures created the conditions for a more prominent role for the senior union leadership in the company. Previously, the branch secretaries and related officials had been the 'rank and file' of highly centralized union structures. They had acted as conduits from the national levels of the union, and they had represented their members in the union structures as well as on the Whitley committees of the time. With privatization, these same leaders began to take on more responsibility, negotiating directly with management and negotiating novel items such as pay agreements. Thus, they began to acquire the expertise and familiarity with negotiations and bargaining that had long been denied them. They acquired a renewed legitimacy as leaders and were in a position to exercise this newly found authority in debates, arguments and discussions with the membership. Part of this was a learning process, discovering the nuances of negotiation, bargaining and representation at a senior management level; part of it was the recognition that they were the senior lay union representatives in the newly established corporation.

Thus, this was a form of union organization where the tensions between a participative form of organization and activity and a more formalized and potentially remote leadership were marked. Clearly, there was a possibility that these leaders would acquire an autonomy, rooted in their relations as lead negotiators and active participants within the wider union structures of NALGO/UNISON which could begin to impact on their relations with members. However, both sets of leaders took steps to resist such a possibility by focusing and locating much of the union activity that took place in these branches at the district level. In this respect they steered a cautious path between participation and remoteness, in the context of the pressures and uncertainties that characterize post-privatization companies.

Assessment

In contrast to the other two cases, the water industry was disaggregated on privatization, creating a distinct set of conditions for the restructuring and reorganization of the industry that followed privatization. Each of the separate water companies was charged with the establishment of its own procedures and approaches to work and employment relations. As a result, different patterns of relations emerged in each of the corporations over time. In the case of Severn Trent plc the management approach was to create the basis of continuity and cooperation with unions in the privatized company. As such, the management recomposed its managerial hierarchies in line with the establishment of the new company and introduced bargaining forums at different levels of this managerial structure.

Faced with this development, the union leadership in the area, encouraged by the regional full-time officer, began a process of merger, recomposing the branches so as to pool resources and focus activist behaviour, and the encouragement of a workplace steward representative system. While the intention of the full-time officer had been to encourage the creation of one branch, for the corporation, with sub-branches for the specific areas of the new company, the existing leaders, particularly in the east and north of the region, were reluctant to lose their separate branch identity. As a result, three branches remained in place until 1996 when a single UNISON branch was established for the NALGO and NUPE memberships. It is unlikely that this development will make much difference in practice.

The development of the workplace-based steward system was the striking achievement of these branches. In the past, there had been talk of developing this form of representation. However, these suggestions were still-born because, until the restructuring that accompanied privatization, there was little that such representatives could do other than act as ciphers for regional and national policy. It was in these circumstances that the branches tended to be dominated by branch secretaries and/or chairpersons, with relatively little activity below them. When members wanted to play a part in branch activity it was generally as a branch officer, and occasionally as a regional officer (in education and the like) alongside the principal officers of the branch.

With the recomposition of managerial hierarchies and the establishment of localized bargaining forums, leading to the main negotiating regional forum, the branch leaderships moved to establish a localized workplace representative structure. As a result, there was a broadening of the participation and involvement of the activist membership in ways that had not happened previously. Although there was an unevenness and in some cases a tentativeness in this initiative, the basis for a broader activist engagement in branch life was laid. Unlike the developments in the gas sector, there was no separation between the union structures and the industrial relations arrangements. The outcome was that the conditions were created for a more involved membership in branch life.

It is still important to express a caution about the import of these developments. The central branch leadership retained a pre-eminent role in the branches, in part affirmed by the representational relationships within the union, as well as the industrial relations procedures and practices in the company. In addition, this company, like other utility companies, began to diversify and develop their concerns, placing a premium on resources and the development of policies that looked beyond the specific remit of water and sewerage treatment. In this respect, one of the ironies was that the central branch leaderships, who dealt directly with the senior company management, retained much of their authority within the branch, and from time to time acted in ways that minimized the scope and scale of membership involvement in union activity. All the same, these were branches that had undergone a more comprehensive process of renewal than was evident in the other utility sectors.

UNIONS AT WORK

The past decade has been a period of change for the three companies covered by the study. In each case, there has been a process of diversification and restructuring, as these utilities began to focus their activities both within the UK and internationally. The companies no longer operate within a UK remit, and they have all begun to play a prominent role within the international industries of which they are a part. It is reasonable to assume that this pattern of change will continue, and become even more significant. There is the prospect that these companies will become involved in take-overs, further purchasing of public sector bodies and new ventures both within the UK and internationally.

The corporate managements of the post-privatization companies have challenged past practices in relatively fundamental ways, encouraging decentralized local managements within the newly established corporate frameworks. At each of the companies, with increased financial accountability at lower levels of management, there has been a comprehensive move to create 'new' managements concerned with deploying their workforces in conformity with their budgets and customer requirements. As part of these initiatives, cost and profit centres have been established in each corporation.

For staff, these developments have had a profound impact on their terms and conditions of employment. In every case, there has been extensive job loss, among all sections of staff, as these privatized enterprises reposition themselves in the new conditions in which they find themselves. The pattern and sequencing of job loss affected the manual workforce, often in the lead-up to privatization and immediately afterwards, with the non-manual staff experiencing these uncertainties more recently. Alongside these job reductions, there is evidence of work intensification, an increase in stress levels and a decline in staff morale as the impact of falling staff levels and changed work procedures began to impact on the remaining staff (PSPRU, 1996).

As part of the managerial organization of these companies, there has been a move to change their workforces, laying the foundations for a restructured labour process. Key to this have been attempts to individualize work routines and relations as well as to encourage forms of worker identification with these changes. There has also been a generalized attempt to introduce forms of flexibility into these enterprises. This includes a questioning of the demarcations between manual and non-manual jobs as well as between crafts and specialisms. In BT, for example, where these developments were most evident, the craft specialisms of engineers have been questioned, as well as the traditional demarcations between clerical work and engineering in computer keyboard areas.

These developments have been accompanied by extensive changes in the bargaining and negotiating arrangements in each of these companies. Managements have begun to elicit workforce support for the restructuring that is taking place through consultation procedures. The most common innovation has been to establish procedures for team briefings, generally on the basis of a cascade system from senior management down (informants, from each company). In these sessions, local managers have attempted to engender a workforce concern with the corporate ethos of each company.

For trade unions for which historically the focus has been on national bargaining arrangements and standardized and uniform terms and conditions of employment, such developments raise acute questions. As these conditions were qualified and questioned, with the move towards more devolved forms of bargaining, local union memberships found themselves in positions where they either addressed these new circumstances or became by-standers to the changes that were in the process of taking place (McIntosh and Broderick, 1995). At another level, what appeared to be happening was that variegated patterns of negotiations were emerging in the utilities, ranging from a continuation of the long-standing individual consultation that had marked this sector to more assertive forms of negotiation.

In the post-privatization context, local union leaders and their members faced major challenges to established practices as well as new opportunities to represent and articulate the concerns of the workforce. Previously, the union branches in each of these industries had organized in more or less conventional ways, usually serviced on a relatively active basis by regional full-time officials, with the result that many of the manual branches had evolved ways of working where they were heavily dependent on full-time officials. This tendency was reinforced by bargaining arrangements which placed a premium on the involvement of full-time officials. These forms of organization had the twofold advantage of allowing coordinated approaches to management initiatives, both within unions and between unions at regional and national levels, as well as direct negotiation with key management decision-makers, regionally and nationally. The consequence, particularly in water and gas, was relatively quiescent forms of local trade unionism.

The other side to these developments is that managerial decentralization was accompanied by a centralization of control within these organizations. The paradox is that devolution took place within centrally determined frameworks, whereby change was implemented which gave the appearance of autonomy without the substance that such developments might at first sight suggest. None the less, as part of the enhancement of local managerial authority, these moves were accompanied by the revival or establishment of district consultative committees, particularly in the case of the gas union branches and those in water. To meet the challenge of managerial restructuring, local unions in these industries sought to utilize these committees to question and object to managerial initiatives, with a view to restricting the implementation of centrally determined but locally enforced policies. In the case of the BT union groups such an opportunity did not present itself.

The unions in these utilities were faced with a dilemma, either to continue organizing with an emphasis on full-time officer involvement or to reconstitute their unions around more active forms of lay member involvement. Where the emphasis was on the former type of unionism, it proved very difficult for unions to stimulate local activity. In general, full-time or centrally based officials either did not recognize the way this form of union involvement was a disincentive for membership participation, for members to organize in ways that empower themselves, or found it a threatening prospect. At the same time, an unreflective commitment to decentralized forms of unionism can result in uneven and uncoordinated union activity, leaving the local membership exposed to managerial initiatives, at both local and national levels. Thus, while limited membership involvement was not a significant problem in the past, the restructuring of these companies following privatization created circumstances where local union activity has become more necessary. The problem for unions is how to generate this activity, whether locally or nationally.

The patterns of union centralization were reflected in the forms of branch organization evident in this sector. In the main, branches covered large numbers of workplaces and memberships. Negotiations were usually undertaken by branch officials or referred up the union hierarchy. Branch executives were not based on discrete membership constituencies according to area or function; instead, they were elected by the whole membership and acted as representatives of this membership. Apart from the annual general meeting there were few opportunities for the membership in any particular workplace to exercise accountability and control over their representatives. This was a form of union organization where the branch executives were relatively remote and removed from workplace memberships.

The most frequent problem faced by branches was that the branch organization no longer connected directly into negotiating structures. This, most clearly, was the case in water and telecommunications, where some union branches covered two separate employers (post and telecommunications) or where branch organization was no longer coterminous with local bargaining arrangements or corporate level arrangements. Specifically, in the case of water this meant that branch secretaries, before privatization the principal local representatives for local negotiations, had to cede authority to a layer of new local representatives elected to participate in local bargaining committees.

In other utilities (particularly gas), local consultative structures had been long-established but effectively moribund for a number of years. As part of the recomposition of managerial structures in these industries, there was a concurrent devolution of managerial responsibilities over bargaining and work organization. These changes and developments provided the stimulus for the beginnings of locally based and focused unions. In the case of non-manual unions this involved a much broader range of members for the first time. Significantly, this included many women members taking on representative and bargaining roles at the local district level. For manual unions a reliance on full-time officers survived, although whether this can be maintained when the district level negotiations become established as the routine way of addressing most union issues, at least in the first instance, is doubtful. Overall, this pattern of union renewal suggests that in these utilities forms of workplace-based unionism were beginning to emerge in ways that suggest a radical departure from the previously remote and centralized forms of unionism typical of these industries.

There were also indications that this was an economistic form of unionism, which places a pre-eminence on *responsible* branch leadership, actively involved in the bargaining structures and committees that have come to characterize these utilities. As these committees become established and as the trends towards divisionalization and business unit forms of organization increase (especially in gas and telecommunications), local union leaderships (*qua* negotiators) begin to act in relatively autonomous ways. The outcome is that the links of accountability are no longer as evident as may have appeared to be the case in the initial stages of privatization.

The focus of union concerns and activities is quite uneven at this stage. The trends and patterns of change appear quite diverse. One key factor in this is the part played by management in creating the conditions and the occasion for a reconsideration of the way local unions organize and operate. Initially, following privatization, there were signs of differential patterns of change in these three industries, although, more recently, it appears that similar processes of managerial devolution and decentralization are occurring in the core traditional areas of all these industries. The way in which local unions respond to these developments depends on the traditions of unionism in these industries and the ways in which they are challenged by these changes. As a result, there is variation in union responses to these challenges and the forms of unionism that are emerging.

PART IV
PUBLIC SERVICES

Introduction

Since 1980, the British state as an employer has changed in complex and contradictory ways. In the context of increasing difficulties with private capital accumulation, growing trade union militancy in the state sector and a shift in government ideology, governments began to impose more stringent financial regimes on state services and to restructure the control of the work process. The result, in key areas of the state administration, was a qualification of the bureaucratized relations of the past, with their layered relations of responsibility and attenuated lines of seniority. There has been a recomposition of managerial and worker relations through the establishment of marketized state labour processes. In addition, the boundaries and organization of the state apparatus have been redefined. The result is a permeable set of relations defining the public sector, where there is a mix of responsibility between public sector enterprises and the private sector for the provision of public sector functions. A further complication is that sections of the public sector have entered into market relations with each other, for the provision of public sector goods and services.

Background

Historically, the modern state apparatus was constructed during the nineteenth century as a bureaucratized set of institutions where policy-makers could rely on a neutral generalist administrative staff to implement state policy, irrespective of the government in office. While there was always an underside to these arrangements, where administrative staff, particularly at the senior levels and in the policy-making areas, were socially and politically conservative, these state functionaries worked with successive governments in cooperative and supportive ways. There was an opaqueness to management–labour relations in these centralized and hierarchical arrangements. The internal organization of the state apparatus was layered and rule-bound. An elaborate set of procedures was established (known as the Whitley system of consultation) to ensure the orderly and consensual settlement of grievances, as well as the representation of the interests of different sections of the state hierarchy.

These consensual relationships were also affirmed by the privileging core sections of state workers, via security of employment, pension entitlements and reasonably high status. The result was a relatively cohesive set of relations, where governments set the terms and conditions of employment, in formalized and administrative ways, but where there was the appearance of a unified and cooperative management and workforce.

During the 1970s these established arrangements began to break down. As policy-makers began to face up to the increasing problems of capital accumulation, there were attempts to impose wage restraint via formal agreements with unions, paradoxically underwriting the increased relevance of trade unionism to state workers. The result was increased union militancy by state workers during the 1970s, based on periodic membership mobilization. For union leaderships this meant a direct engagement with state policy, questioning the successive incomes policies during this period, which impacted disproportionately on the public sector. One feature of this period was that union leaderships began to question state policy directly, on incomes policies and on other state policies concerned with the provision of state services and provisions. For the governments of the period, the dilemma was how to implement state policies on state services as well as on incomes policies without creating the conditions for direct challenges from increasingly active state sector unions.

The managerial state

Faced with a restless state workforce and committed to economic deregulation, successive governments in the 1980s sought to redefine their relationship with the state apparatus and place the responsibility for the control and organization of the state workforce on a newly defined state management. Internal relations were reconstructed and presented in technical terms in order to distance governments from the implications of restructuring, while shifting responsibility for more direct control over the state labour force from government ministers to internal management. The outcome was a paradoxical depoliticization of the state apparatus. On the one hand, direct government engagement in management and labour relations in the state sector was minimized; on the other hand, the opaqueness of the traditional managerial relations in the state sector was stripped away as the reconfiguration of managerial hierarchies proceeded.

The emergent managerial state has three features to it. First, this is a 'managerial' state, where policies are presented in a 'depoliticized' way, as technical or non-political solutions, such as the provision of health care, the organization of education, the provision of state benefits or the implementation of economic policies relating to balance of payments problems, trade imbalances and low productivity levels. Second, there has been a reconfiguration of managerial hierarchies within the state, with the result that the relations between management and labour have been recast away from the impersonal rule-bound management of the past, so that direct parliamentary control of labour relations becomes a thing of the past. Third, and related, there has been an individualization of work and employment relations, with the elaboration of more flexible forms of working and labour markets in the state sector.

The reforms within the public sector were top-down, recasting the forms of control and organization in these sectors. During the 1980s, successive conservative governments transformed the state sector from a centralized and layered set of institutions, characterized by standardized conditions of work and employment, to managerial and commercialized employers. The outcome was a restructured labour process and a change in the dominant mode of control of labour in these sectors. Class relations at the point of production were recomposed, so that the differentiation between a middle class and a working class became more apparent (Carter and Fairbrother, 1995).

Central state

The British central state has been fragmented and managerial hierarchies have been recomposed. The first phase of these reforms occurred in the early 1980s, with the *Financial Management Initiative* aimed at giving devolved managements more discretion and responsibility, particularly over budgetary and operational matters. These were relatively limited reforms, in that they did not address the structural organization of the civil service; they were an internal reorganization of a bureaucratized employment structure.

These reforms were followed by an institutional reorganization of the civil service from 1988 onwards, known as *Next Steps*, establishing a series of semi-autonomous management units, or agencies. This second phase of reform began the reorganization of the civil service as a series of *de facto* business units or organizations, with their own managements, recruitment policies and terms and conditions of employment. By 1996, nearly three-quarters of the permanent employees in the civil service worked in agencies, subject to their own management hierarchies, with responsibility for establishing distinctive terms and conditions of employment. There were 102 agencies (and two departments operating on *Next Steps* lines) covering more than 350,126 permanent employees, 71 per cent of the civil service workforce (Government Statistical Service, 1996).

From a relatively anonymous position within an extended administratively controlled hierarchy, state managers were transformed into highly visible and identifiable actors involved less and less in a collective labour process and more and more in the control and supervision of the work of others. This signified the ending of the characteristic civil service, comprising standardized work and employment conditions within centralized and hierarchical structures. These were the first stages in the creation of commercialized employment structures, within which there was a more highly visible state middle class and working class.

Local state

Paralleling the changes in central government, there has been a long-term move by central governments to extend their control over the organization and administration of local government since the 1960s onwards. This centralization of control, particularly over finances, was accompanied by a shift in the forms of control within local government administrations, from administrative modes of organization to more managerialist-based approaches to control. There have been both moves to decentralize the provision of services as well as to reorganize the local state in the form of business units, often occurring within the same local authority and irrespective of the political group in control. Local state work was organized on the basis of managerially accountable departments, along functional lines. In many authorities this was accompanied by decentralized service provision, with some of the functions in over 60 per cent of all local authorities organized in this way by the mid-1990s (Miller, 1996, p. 62). Additionally, there has been a widespread introduction of externalization and out-sourcing, much of it driven by central government ruling.

Contracting-out was a key policy mechanism in the re-regulation of labour in this sector, initially impacting disproportionately on manual workers, and then extended to non-manual groups. In 1979, local government authorities were encouraged to consider contracting-out arrangements for sections of their workforce, particularly cleaning and refuse collection (Whitfield, 1992). The formal stage of contracting-out began with the passage of the Local Government Planning and Land Act in 1980, which introduced compulsory competitive tendering (CCT) into local government housing maintenance and road construction/maintenance (Foster, 1993, p. 50). Throughout the 1980s these arrangements were extended and elaborated, by legislation and government/administrative rulings. By the mid-1990s, contracting-out, and the associated arrangements of externalization and out-sourcing, had become a predominant feature of the local state.

There have been major changes in the organization and operation of local government, partly as a result of legislative initiatives and partly as particular local government authorities put their own stamp on these developments (e.g. McIntosh and Broderick, 1996; Miller, 1996, pp. 118–34). One result is that the past bases for collective organization and work relations have been qualified. The impact of these changes has varied according to occupational level. For manual workers, the early changes were accompanied by new attempts to regulate and control the organization of work, through a further range of measures such as work study and job evaluation. This was followed by the fragmentation of the local state on business unit lines, the decentralization of line managements and the introduction of managerial approaches associated with consultation, rather than negotiation (Kessler, 1991). Overall, the result has been a radically restructured local state.

The marketized state

The marketization of central and local state administrations has had a diverse impact. Marketization (restructuring by exposure to the market, either directly through competition and privatization or indirectly through the process of market testing and related activities) has led to a reconfiguration of class relations within the state, with implications for labour representation and collective state worker activity. The primary focus for this rearticulation of class relations was the recomposition of the labour process with the explicit defini- tion of a 'frontier of control' between a 'new' stratum of managers and a proletarianized workforce, comprised of both the manual and lower strata of the non-managerial non-manual workforce. In this respect, the 'frontier of control' was made more explicit and public. With increasing problems of private capital accumulation, developing trade union militancy and a shift in government ideology, governments since 1979 sought to impose a sharper financial regime on state services and to restructure the control of the work process. State structures were fragmented, so that the unities of the past no longer applied. The responsibilities of middle and junior managers have been recast to enforce the acceptance of responsibility and accountability. From relatively anonymous positions within extended administratively controlled hierarchies, managers became highly visible and identifiable actors involved less in a collective labour process and more in the control and supervision of the work of others.

The reconfiguration of the state apparatus aimed, in part, to undermine the basis of collective organization, thereby weakening trade union influence within the state. During the 1970s and the 1980s the public sector unions had emerged as potentially powerful and influential groupings, reflected in the patterning of major disputes, which, almost without exception, occurred in the public rather than the private sector. In view of this, one of the intentions of the governments during this period was to undermine and marginalize unions in this sector. One strand to this approach was the successive legislation during the 1980s and into the 1990s aimed at restricting the activity of unions as well as relaying the organizational basis of unions, via rules relating to union elections and other arrangements. A second strand was to create public sector enterprises where managerialism prevailed and union influence was minimized.

The study

The central point of these observations is that in the context of the profound restructuring of the social relations of service and public sector provision, the conditions and circumstances of union organization and practice also change. Against the backdrop of highly centralized traditions and forms of unionism in the public sector, and given the specificity of the restructuring of social relations, there is then the possibility of distinctive and different forms of unionism emerging. However, it is also possible that the basis for a localized and active form of unionism will be denied as union memberships and their leaders bow to the apparent inevitability and dominance of public sector restructuring. These are the prospects that will now be explored.

The ways in which the public sector unions have reorganized and laid the foundations for a different form of unionism are examined with reference to the civil service and local government. In the case of the civil service, three unions are studied, the CPSA and NUCPS (now PCS) in the Benefits Agency and the IRSF (a constituent of the PTC and then PCS) in the Department of Inland Revenue. During the 1990s, the Benefits Agency was established and the Inland Revenue was reorganized into executive offices. These changes in the terrain of civil service organization posed major challenges to both sets of unions. In the case of local government, three local authority branches were studied, all located in one metropolitan authority. The focus was on union activity within social services, and the branches comprised a city-wide NALGO/ UNISON branch and two NUPE/UNISON branches. The metropolitan authority restructured and reorganized in substantive ways during the 1990s, creating problems for these unions. A further complication arose as a result of the merger between the two unions in 1993 to form UNISON. The ways in which these branches experienced and responded to the changes in the public sector are presented in the three following chapters.

11 SIGNS OF ACTIVE TRADE UNIONISM: THE BENEFITS AGENCY

Civil service unions developed during the twentieth century as highly centralized bodies, serving relatively quiescent memberships in effective ways. In consequence, there was a limited involvement by memberships in their unions at a workplace level, at least until the 1970s, when a number of public sector unions began to reorganize so as to stimulate more active forms of unionism at a local level (Fryer *et al.*, 1974). In the 1980s, the fragmentation of the civil service and the devolution of department responsibilities to local and district managerial levels were accompanied by related changes in bargaining and negotiating practices. It was in these circumstances that local union leaderships and activists began to take the first steps towards revived and renewed forms of unionism.

In the main, the civil service unions were founded as staff associations, recruiting from within specific grades, occupations or areas of work. A major impetus for union organization was the establishment of the Whitley system. A key feature of this form of negotiation was that these embryonic unions came to mirror the structure of management organizationally and in the way issues were examined and considered, in particular developing consensual approaches to negotiation. Significantly, this resulted in management and unions approaching the new circumstances of employment in ways that both drew upon past experiences and relationships and sought to develop opportunities to redefine employment relations in distinct ways.

Throughout the 1970s and into the 1980s, these centrally organized unions began to address these changing circumstances by looking at their traditional forms of organization, rooted in a fifty-year history of civil service trade unionism. In the case of the benefits section of social security, the national union leadership of one union, the then SCPS, took steps during this period to refocus the union organization, and in particular to develop workplace organization. As the union noted:

due to the inevitability of continuing Government action through incomes
policy and public expenditure curbs the Society [SCPS] will require in the
future a strengthened organisation at workplace level, both for effective
collective bargaining purposes and in the event of the need for industrial
action. (Drake *et al.*, 1980, Appendix D, p. 79)

Among the national leadership and the activist element of the membership
there was an increasing recognition of the need to provide the base for a more
active and membership-involved union than had existed in the past. Following
on from this, the union commissioned outside experts to review the organization and operation of the union form, which had much in common with the
relatively autonomous forms of steward organization in the manufacturing
sector, particularly engineering (Drake *et al.*, 1980, 1982).

In the case of the CPSA there had been a less formal shift to a workplace
representative structure of organization. During the 1970s the union had
developed more active forms of representation, partly as a result of the larger
numbers of members at a local level and partly because these members were in
the lower grades, and subject to routine and standardized forms of work and
employment relations. These features provided a baseline for collective organization that was often absent in the higher-grade SCPS, with its dispersed and
hierarchically located membership. In addition, the CPSA was the subject of
ongoing activity by different political groupings in the union, who focused on
the offices for support and sustenance. As a result, during this same period a *de
facto* form of workplace representation had developed in many of the offices
covered by the CPSA.

During the 1980s, the union leaderships and their memberships faced a
dramatically changing set of work and employment relations. At the behest of
government initiatives, two sets of changes were introduced. First, during the
early to mid-1980s, managerial hierarchies were recomposed in the context of
financial devolution and, second, in the late 1980s and the early 1990s, a
programme of institutional fragmentation occurred with the establishment of
agencies throughout the civil service. For unions there was a choice between
emphasizing and developing more participative forms of organization and/or
retaining and developing centralized forms of leadership in the face of the
fragmentation that was taking place. These are the questions that will now be
explored.

Public sector reform

During the 1980s, successive Conservative governments initiated a major restructuring and reorganization of the state sector. A range of policies was introduced, aimed at challenging the uniform and standardized conditions of civil service work and employment, not least to remove the basis for collective organization and action by civil service workers. The result of such policies was the commercialization of relations in this sector. One aspect of this commercialization was a restructuring of managerial hierarchies, away from a rule-governed bureaucracy and towards a public sector defined by a managerial ethos, shifting from rules and centrally determined procedures to management discretion and some autonomy for local management in relation to the 'management' of staff in offices.

With moves towards the decentralization of managerial control and organization, there has been a major reorganization of operational managerial activities, with increased line management and financial responsibilities at localized levels throughout the public sector. However, the decentralization of day-to-day operations occurred within the framework of budgetary control and strategic decision-making at headquarters level. This was reflected in the introduction and use of increasingly complicated financial indicators and controls. One consequence was that the moves to establish a degree of autonomy for local management were within clearly defined and prescribed parameters.

This restructuring of the social relations of public sector production and provision has had major implications for labour. It is in these contexts that managers have sought, with few exceptions, either to incorporate the local union leaderships into this patterning of change or to define managerial prerogative in such ways that collective worker organization is made irrelevant to the process of change. The result is that a range of issues are now subject to negotiation at a local level, but on terms that have largely been set by local managements. Such developments both create problems for union memberships and open up possibilities.

So as to unravel the complicated processes of change at work, two civil service districts in the Benefits Agency in the West Midlands are examined. The focus of the study is on the ways in which the public sector unions reorganized and laid the foundations for a different form of unionism. Two unions are studied, the CPSA and NUCPS (now PTC). The changed terrain of civil service organization posed major challenges to both unions. In the case of the branch membership in the Coventry area, the NUCPS during the 1990s had around 200 members and the CPSA 400, nearly 80 per cent of the eligible membership. In the second area, near Birmingham, the NUCPS branch membership was around 150 (and slowly increasing) and the CPSA membership ranged from 250 to 260 members. In both NUCPS branches, the proportion of women members was around 60 per cent, with the CPSA branches having a higher proportion, near 80 per cent. With the founding of the Benefits Agency, these unions faced both opportuities and difficulties.

The Benefits Agency in the civil service

From 1968 to 1988, the provision of social security was organized through the Department of Health and Social Security, and subsequently in the Department of Social Security (DSS), a typically centralized and hierarchical civil service department. This department was under the responsibility of a minister, advised by senior civil service staff. In 1991, these arrangements were ended when one section was transformed into the Benefits Agency, a corporatized body, under the control of a chief executive, with a remit to devolve and decentralize management organization and practice (more extensive versions of this history are presented in Fairbrother, 1994a, 1996a).

The DSS was established out of the combined department covering both health and social security, the Department of Health and Social Security (DHSS). This was accompanied by an internal reorganization of the DSS area of operations on a regional basis, building on earlier reforms in the department, with each region covering the local offices that administered social security in the community. The section of work covered by the department had been subject to a series of reorganizations, aimed principally at creating a more capital-intensive labour process and reducing the reliance on an extensive clerical workforce.

There were two aspects to these changes. First, the department was subjected to the programmes associated with the *Financial Management Initiative* (FMI), introduced throughout the civil service in the early 1980s. This programme of reform was associated with the introduction of management information systems and procedures for assessing the provision of services in financial terms. The department was reorganized around cost and budget centres. One outcome was an increased emphasis on management control and responsibilities. Second, and related, there was a series of attempts throughout the 1980s to re-establish the basis of benefit provision, away from labour-intensive clerical procedures to computerized procedures. This development involved a switch from a set of procedures based on piecemeal service provision to the administration of benefits on a 'whole' person basis.

These initiatives were only partially successful, with the reorganization of service procedures subject to public criticism (Committee of Public Accounts, 1989, p. iii, para. 2; Social Security Committee, 1991, p. 26, paras 85–7). In the early 1990s, the restructuring took a more dramatic turn with the ministerial decision to implement the recommendations of the Ibbs Report in 1988, entitled *Next Steps*. This inaugurated a new phase of public sector restructuring, with the report advocating that sections of the civil service were and should be recognized as enterprises (agencies), operating on a *de facto* commercial basis as corporations. With the acceptance of these recommendations, a process of corporatization was inaugurated which meant the reorganization of sections of the civil service, with their own management hierarchies, recruitment policies and terms and conditions of employment.

Following the decision in 1989 to establish agencies in the DSS, there was an extensive reorganization of the benefits labour process. It was a planned process of change, aimed at creating a new managerial structure, composed of management personnel who had immediate responsibility for the provision of benefit services. The purpose was to remould the Benefits Agency in ways that signified a break from the past. As reported:

> the most important thing of all was to change ourselves from being a hierarchical bureaucratic organisation concerned with our internal processes, into one that actually began to think about everything from a customer point of view and customer perspective, so we did an awful lot of things right at the outset to get the customer focus right. (Senior manager, 1992)

This involved the redesignation of managerial responsibilities at a district level, with the creation of the post of customer service manager, as well as defining claimants as customers.

The outcome of this process of change was a restructured service, drawing on commercial principles. As one informant observed, 'it's very much to do with having a sharper, more business, more commercial orientation and bringing in some of the kind of market principles' (Senior manager, 1992). This ethos of change was embraced by those who planned the establishment of the Benefits Agency, and it was put into practice after the launch of the agency in April 1991.

The decentralization of management

The key element in this restructuring was to decentralize managerial responsibility for operational matters to a district level. The aim was to secure a compliant and much reduced workforce that could be expanded or contracted according to provision requirements, deployed where required and employed on a variable time basis. To achieve this flexible and compliant workforce, the managerial hierarchies in the benefit area were recomposed so that local managerial staff had operational responsibility for staff deployment and activity. In effect, these developments amounted to the recomposition of the social relations of benefit provision in Britain.

This process began in the 1980s, building on the FMI reforms, as the Permanent Secretary of the DSS observed:

> We have steadily delegated an enormous amount of tasks to them [district managers] which they wanted to have, like local recruitment, the ability to run their own accommodation budget, repairs and things like that, the ability to organise their office. We have put them on a cash budget instead of a head count budget, so they have cash income and can deploy how many people in how many grades they want within the budget given to them. They have enormous freedoms. (Social Security Committee, 1991, p. 15, para. 8)

The claim was that a decentralized managerial structure would enable the provision of services in an 'efficient and effective' way. As the then Chief Executive observed:

> Our stated aim in the business plan is to devolve as much power as we can to those local managers [district managers] and we have already started by devolving personnel functions and have asked local managers to tell us what other functions we need to devolve to make life easier, to enable them to deliver the service more effectively. (Social Security Committee, 1991, p. 15, para. 8)

These managers were seen as the front-line for the changes heralded by the *Next Steps* programme.

The decentralization of managerial responsibilities involved a centralization of office management structures. With the creation of districts, local offices were grouped together into districts, as the base organizational unit in the Benefits Agency. As already indicated, the district managers were recruited from the former layer of office managers, on the same grade. These former office managers acquired the responsibility for two or more offices, and

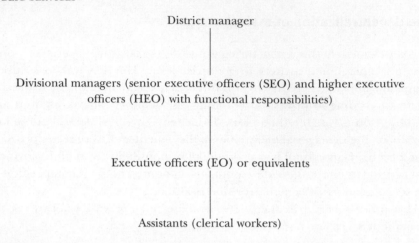

District manager

Divisional managers (senior executive officers (SEO) and higher executive officers (HEO) with functional responsibilities)

Executive officers (EO) or equivalents

Assistants (clerical workers)

Figure 11.1 Employment hierarchy in the district management units, Benefits Agency

functions and responsibilities formerly exercised at a regional level were devolved to them (Social Security Committee, 1991, p. 35). As a result there was both an intensification of managerial work and the centralization of managerial responsibility at a local level.

The benefits offices were grouped into an area form of organization, composed of district management units (DMUs), comprising two or more offices. These units were organized in a hierarchical way (see Figure 11.1). The principle underlying this form of organization was to allow larger numbers of benefit staff to be grouped together. These changes heralded the reorganization of local offices in a more centralized yet partially devolved way. On the one hand, offices were grouped together to create district offices, under the responsibility of a principal officer; on the other hand, senior staff were given greater discretion and responsibility for both staff and financial issues.

Work within the DMUs was also reorganized, though not uniformly across the districts. Because managers had considerable discretion, as indicated above, some district managers retained a traditional form of work organization, while others began to organize work procedures and the related arrangements in the office. For example, in one office the work of checking and adjudication (previously organized as a separate unit), was devolved to quality control command, involving twelve EO grade workers under an HEO. Alongside this, a customer service command was created, gathering a range of difficult and previously independent functions together, under the direction of a part-time EO, whose principal activity was to liaise with the public.

Each DMU was organized as a cost centre and a bargaining unit. At one and the same time, this laid the foundation for a degree of financial independence that was previously unusual, and created the conditions for variation between districts. Initially this was reflected in a distinction between districts where managers were willing to exercise their increased discretion and those where managers refused to accept responsibility for their own budget, because they were unable to comply with the requirements indicated in these budgets.

This change involved a structural reorganization of management and of related negotiating procedures. The outcome was that these new managers pursued different managerial approaches towards their staff and unions, ranging from the cooperative and consensual to the provocatively conflictual. Thus there was a paradox to these developments, in that the decentralizaion of managerial responsibility also led to increasing intervention from the area management as district managers looked for guidance on a range of issues for which they had acquired new responsibilities.

Unions in the Benefits Agency

At the time of the study, two unions organized the vast majority of workers in the Benefits Agency: the NUCPS representing ancillary and support workers, executive officers, higher executive officers, senior executive officers and principal grades; and the CPSA covering administrative assistants, administrative officers and some executive officer equivalent grades. These unions organized in very similar ways and have long been characterized by relatively remote and non-accountable national leaderships.

The restructuring of the civil service resulted in a decentralized managerial structure and practice in the emergent agencies. For unions in the civil service, with their long history of organization, and their hard-won commitment to uniform terms and conditions of employment, these developments shifted the terrain of their activity in profound ways. In this respect, these unions faced questions about the balance between national and local negotiations, and between the terms and conditions for one agency compared with another, and about the thrust and implementation of government policy within an agency and across areas of state service and provision. Thus, it is not surprising that union memberships have been caught up in debates and argument about ways to organize in these areas and policies to pursue.

The reorganization of the DSS, with the establishment of the Benefits Agency in April 1991, threatened the unions who organized workers in the former department; these unions faced a new and in some cases aggressively confident management. Policies were implemented, particularly at a local level, which were clearly aimed at undermining what managers saw as the privileged status of the two main unions in the benefits section. Facility time was restricted, managers were less forthcoming in their dealings with local union leaders and the regional level of the Whitley structure was abolished on the grounds that most, if not all, locally based problems would be settled at a local level. In the face of these challenges, unions at a local level reorganized and recomposed themselves, often in novel ways, reflecting their diverse experiences as non-manual workers who could no longer rely on past procedures and forms of organization.

In effect, the creation of the Benefits Agency signalled a shift in the frontier of control between workers and management (Goodrich, 1920). Previously, offices were organized in a bureaucratic form, as rule-bound impersonal structures, in relatively uniform and standardized ways. One result was that at a local or office level there were relatively few grievances or problems that could be or indeed were settled. The union form of organization in the DSS (and its forerunners) was also centralized and relatively remote for most members, since the internal union reforms of the early 1980s in the case of the SCPS were relatively ineffective and unevenly implemented. There were exceptions to these arrangements, particularly where a small number of active union members in offices attempted to force a shift in decision-making from regional or national levels, on at least some issues, such as overtime working during the mid-1980s. However, these exceptions were very limited.

In the past, each social security office had its own Whitley structure. When the Benefits Agency was set up, offices were grouped in twos or threes and the Whitley structures reorganized accordingly. In one office, for example, there were twenty NUCPS staff and almost double that number of CPSA staff. There was an office Whitley committee, comprised of a management side and a trade union side, with two representatives from the NUCPS and two from the CPSA. This committee dealt with a range of issues, such as staff reductions, increased workloads, the practicalities of the attempts to computerize work procedures, pay queries and appraisal. In this office, the union representatives worked closely together, although the NUCPS representative tended to take the lead, in part playing on his more senior status within the office. The Whitley committee met monthly and was regarded by the union leadership as relatively effective, particularly in recent years, as the opportunities for substantive local bargaining began to open up.

With the establishment of the agency, a process of combining offices and resituating the office Whitley committees began. This brought together union memberships and leaderships, who had little experience of working together, were active in varying and non-complementary ways or were drawn from different and sometimes antagonistic political traditions. The branch leaderships attempted to coordinate activity between offices, gave support to office Whitley secretaries and tried to provide an indirect link with the regional Whitley structures. The link with the regional or area level of managerial organization was made much more difficult by a view within management, following the establishment of the agency, that there was no longer any need for negotiations at a regional level. It took time for the union leaderships in the area to re-establish themselves as the recognized spokespeople for the membership in the area, with access to regular meetings with area management. In this way, the branch leaderships began to rebuild their representational structures, after initial hostility from management to the idea of area or regional negotiations.

The further complication in this process of reorganization was that agencies continued to be established for different functions of work. One representative described the process in late 1993:

> Over the last few years they [management] have been separating out what was just DSS as separate Agencies. Now they had already separated out 'contributions' into a 'Conts Agency'. So we had to have separate reps for that because they have their own industrial relations structure there. Similarly they separated out fraud work, although it is not a separate Agency but organisationally it's separate. And during the last year they have been separating out what used to be called 'liable relatives' work. It's now 'child support' of the infamous Agency to be and again it's a separate structure and we have been trying to get some reps organised for that. (1993)

These changes were initiated by management, often in response to government decision. The unions were forced to follow these developments and establish representative structures for these areas of work within each branch (in the case of the then NUCPS union) or separate branches (in the case of the CPSA) or fail to participate in the newly established bargaining arrangements. In this respect, this was a managerially defined development which served to stimulate a broadening of the representational base within these union branches.

The reorientation and development of the representational base in these branches was also part of a political agenda among some of the union leaderships. In another office, political affiliations and involvement were associated with the development of a vibrant union presence in the office. The broad left, including Militant Tendency, had a leading presence, and the major question was the effectiveness of the unions in confronting what was seen by most members as a major assault on terms and conditions of employment. The two unions were organized in the office: NUCPS covering the executive officer grade and above (on average fifty-odd members during the first part of the 1990s) and the security and telephone staff (eight members), and the CPSA (with over double the membership) recruiting the clerical staff. Of the two unions, the NUCPS had the major presence, playing a leading role in the main negotiating forum, the Office Whitley, and taking the initiative on most issues involving the two unions, including the establishment of an effective representative structure in the office. Between 1985 and 1988, the chair of the committee, a member of Militant Tendency, had increasingly acted as the senior steward in the office, on behalf of the CPSA as well as NUCPS members. It was acknowledged by most others on the committee that his activity in the office, and more generally in the branch, had laid the foundation for a union presence capable of meeting and surviving the challenge of Next Steps.

Thus, this was a period of union reorganization, within each union as well as between unions. These union leaderships attempted to utilize the opportunities that began to open up for local negotiation and bargaining during the 1980s and 1990s. With the establishment of the agency structures and the concomitant recomposition of managerial hierarchies, union memberships faced considerable uncertainty about the organization of work as well as their future in these offices, as market testing and related forms of contracting-out of services were mooted. In such circumstances, union leaderships attempted to recompose and resituate unionism in these offices, establishing a more activist base, and promoting a consciousness of trade unionism.

Industrial relations

The two main national unions in the Benefits Agency had participated in the Whitley structures that governed bargaining and negotiation within the civil service since 1918. From the early 1970s, as the importance of the public sector grew (within the broader economic framework of decision and policy), the ways in which successive governments dealt with civil service employees also became more pressing. In these circumstances, the unions began to shed their staff association past and elaborate publicly a trade union consciousness. This was reflected in the conduct of negotiations within the Whitley structures, as well as engagement in strikes and related activities in pursuance of their goals.

With the ending of effective national negotiations during the 1980s, as a result of government restructuring of the public sector, there was a shift in the locus of bargaining from a national to a more devolved level. The locus of bargaining and negotiations became focused on departments/agencies rather than the civil service as a whole. Increasingly, work organization and employment conditions were decided at the department/agency level, building on trends evident in the 1970s, but given a boost with the implementation of the Next Steps programme. Integral to these developments, negotiating structures were developed at the district level of the Benefits Agency, along with agency-specific negotiating hierarchies. These new negotiating structures and arrangements reflected the recomposed managerial hierarchies within the civil service.

One key feature of the changes was the decentralization of negotiating structures to the district level of the Benefits Agency. One union representative observed:

> There has been much more devolution of authority to ... these district managers. So much more of what goes on depends on their approach and personality. For example the manager of [one office] a very clever capable woman ... after initially appearing to be a bit of a dragon ... has actually been as nice as pie to the unions in [the office] whereas we have had a hand-picked evil bastard really in [another office] and it has taken us since April to cut him down to size. He nearly cut us down to size on a few occasions. (1992)

This development took place within the framework of agency-specific negotiations and structures. The parameters for these negotiations were set by the business plans developed by the Chief Executive and senior management of the Benefits Agency. These plans set the framework within which negotiations occurred, and they were given force via managerial decree and policy. It was within this framework that the Benefits Agency unions sought to play a part in restructuring.

With the establishment of the Benefits Agency, branches were reorganized, especially in the NUCPS, with a reallocation of offices to other branches and the creation of smaller branches based on contiguous district management units. Before the agency, branches were composed of a number of offices, often seven or more, usually spread over a large geographical area or around a large city. The branch coverage in the West Midlands ranged from seven offices spread over a twenty-mile radius (CPSA) to eleven offices spread over a sixty-mile radius (NUCPS). The branch secretaries complained that this geographical spread caused considerable problems. It was not just a matter of keeping in contact with the offices, or encouraging links between offices, but in at least three offices in each of the four branches the branch leadership was unable to develop representative structures. The result was that office managers had a free hand to recruit, vary the terms of employment (within the limits set by national agreements) and reorganize work procedures, more or less as they saw fit. In addition, the branch executives, composed of officers and representatives from each office, were limited by the lack of any regular representation from these poorly organized offices.

The management throughout the region attempted to restrict unions through a resort to the constitutional procedures of the Whitley arrangements. Existing agreements were reviewed by managements in the districts; agreements they did not want were dropped. This was illustrated by a management imposition of restrictions in facility rights in these offices, when the overall amount of facility time available throughout the region was sharply reduced. The result was that facility time to pursue issues at a regional (subsequently area) level was ended on the grounds that no issues would ever reach area management level, and thus there was no need for a facility allowance. At the same time a strict limit of twenty hours per week per union per district was imposed for district level activity. This restriction had the effect of reducing the number of representatives on the trade union side in the offices, and the outcome that when union representatives attended a Whitley meeting, a week's time was used.

In the two to three years after the establishment of the Benefits Agency there was a struggle in the offices, via negotiations and procedures, between a management increasingly committed to the principle of managerial pre-eminence and union memberships who sought to influence and constrain the exercise of managerial authority. There was a general onslaught by the district and area managers on union rights and prerogatives. In the first instance, this resulted in a loss of confidence among some sections of the union members, who sullenly and cynically began to comply with managerial dictate and to withdraw from active involvement in their unions. For a period, this left the leaderships within offices and at a branch level relatively exposed as they continued to question and negotiate with management. This, however, over-states the patterning of relations within the offices, since, paradoxically, this struggle provided an opportunity for union leaderships in the Benefits Agency to rethink their unionism. In one office, the local leaders from both unions worked closely together, questioning management decisions and reporting to members, and thereby developed a sense of collective involvement in these events. In some cases union leaders built on past experience to extend and develop their union organizations, so as to meet the new circumstances of agency organization.

The beginnings of union activism

During the 1990s, building on the changes that took place in the 1980s, and addressing the implications of agency status, the union members in the former DSS were relatively active. They were prepared to challenge and question the developments and changes that were taking place, questioning the occasionally high-handed approaches adopted by managers, expressing concern about managerial initiatives which introduced further market-type relations into social security work, such as market testing and contracting-out, or occasionally participating in national union campaigns over government policies relating to social security provision and work. Crucial to these developments were the local union leaderships of both unions, who increasingly took on the role of workplace representatives, encouraging members, responding to queries and taking up issues with managers. Although there was an unevenness to this, from office to office, and in terms of the slow process of developing and expressing a trade union consciousness about work and employment relations in social security, as well as managerial and government policy, it was nevertheless the case that a process of union activism in these areas of employment had begun.

One indication of these developments came with the rising prominence of the local union leaders as representatives based in offices and districts, rather than as representatives defined by formal position as branch officers of trade union side members on a range of committees and related bodies. The point of this distinction is that there was evidence that the local union leaders located and identified more closely with the actual detail and practice of managerial policy or the implications of government regulation and requirement in the office than had been the case in the past. In part this was the consequence of the decentralization of managerial responsibilities to the district level, and in part because of the increasing pressures and difficulties faced by workers in these offices. These were not easy offices in which to work, and in this respect there was a fertile ground for union organization and activity.

There was an increased sophistication to the way in which local union leaders worked in the districts and the locality in which the offices were grouped. With increased differentiation among the workforce, in terms of employment arrangements or work procedures and activity, or on occasion by employer, specific sections of the workforce faced different sets of problems or expressed differentiated concerns. One feature of this development of local-level trade unionism was the greater willingness by local union leaderships to disaggregate the concerns of their membership. This was illustrated by the move in a number of union committees to acknowledge and address the interests of women members: for example, successfully pursuing a policy of extending the opportunities for part-time work. One office, in Birmingham, went from no part-time workers to fifty-nine out of 280 in the six years up to 1992. The unions negotiated parity with full-time workers, and part-time workers saw this negotiating initiative as a successful union action. According to the branch secretary, the part-time workers had become very supportive of the union as a result. In this way the local union leaderships took steps to consolidate and develop the base of unionism in these offices, with some success.

There was also evidence that union memberships were willing to engage in forms of collective action that expressed their concerns about managerial policy and government requirements in this area of employment. Dating back to the 1980s, these were areas of employment where there had been uncertainty among the membership about the practical consequences and implications of the institutional changes taking place in social security. Such developments ranged from the redefinition of local managerial staff in the offices and districts as *managers*, as well as the institutional reorganizations associated with the establishment of agencies in social security, to the market testing of work areas and the contracting-out of some clusters of work. One example of the preparedness of members to resort to collective action came in an office in Coventry over the question of market testing. In April 1993 there was a proposal to market test a very small work area, stationery, involving two union members. These two members, on the advice of the local union representatives, refused to fill in the forms required by management and set off a process of non-compliance with the requirements for market testing by most of the 400 union members in the office.

The local union representatives in the Coventry office were critical to the incident over market testing. They had long had a policy of opposition to market testing, reflecting the national policy of each union. The uncertainty for local union representatives everywhere was what this policy of opposition might mean in practice in any particular office. In the case of this office, the opposition had been loud and vocal, discussed at committee and membership meetings, and raised with management. However, in the event of implementing market testing in the district there was less certainty. When the two staff from stationery sought advice about the completion of the preliminary forms for the market testing process, the local representatives took the opportunity to defend the two union members and to develop an office-wide campaign of opposition. One local union leader summarized the position as follows: 'the first visit of the market testers to the office – our attitude was they walk in, we walk out. We arranged everything. We'd got everything set up. It was planned to the word and planned to the minute, over the previous week' (1993). These plans involved notifying management of the joint union opposition, holding meetings of the senior representatives to plan an approach to the forthcoming visit and beginning to talk to members about possible responses. On the day of the visit, the senior representatives met the market testers, expressed their opposition, held a representatives' meeting, attended by over twenty floor representatives, notified management that they intended to recommend a walk-out by all staff, called a car park meeting of all staff (attended by over 300 people) and agreed a suspension of work for the rest of the day, the afternoon, leaving senior management to deal with over forty claimants. Subsequently, the management agreed to delay market testing at the office, and a fortnight later the national negotiators for social security secured an agreement that staff participation in market testing at the office would henceforth be on a voluntary basis.

The notable feature of this action in the office was that it built on the long period of seemingly limited and small examples of union mobilization and activity in the office over the previous decade. During the latter part of the 1980s and into the 1990s, there had been a number of examples where staff had walked out and closed the office for short times because of management action and government policies towards social security work and provision. In addition, these local representatives, like others in the area, had been prepared to argue with management and to recommend walk-outs and related action. These were contested actions and there were times when the local representatives were hard-pressed and, indeed, resigned their positions because of the difficulties and pressures involved in building a sense of trade unionism in this way.

More generally, in the period following the establishment of the Benefits Agency, there was an upsurge of union activism within the offices covered by the study. This was a period where members' meetings on the office floor, petitions, walk-outs, strikes and other forms of collective activity were not infrequent occurrences, illustrated in one office where there was some form of. collective action every quarter over a three-year period. In this period, the union leaderships in the area used the opportunity provided by introduction of FMI and the preparation for agency reorganization to promote union interests in a broad range of concerns and issues, and thereby helped to develop a consciousness that these were issues and concerns which were properly the province of union activity. At the same time, there was evidence that the members were responsive to these entreaties and on occasion were prepared to act unilaterally and then approach the local representatives for support.

All the union groups covered by the study reported a much greater willingness for staff to meet and consider industrial action than at any other period they could remember. In some cases, staff were prepared to walk out unilaterally and question the right of the managers to behave as they did. In addition, union meetings were well attended compared with previous periods. There was greater membership interest in union activity, and a process of developing union activity in more participative and involved ways had begun. Such developments did not occur overnight and had to be worked at, particularly by the local leaderships.

There were two aspects to these developments in the benefits offices: an increased willingness by members to act as trade unionists and activity by local representatives to encourage members to define problems as union problems. These were contested developments, and involved division among the representatives as well as members. While the members of both unions were much more likely to refer issues and problems to their union representatives than in the past, this was not a uniformly agreed position. The pressures on staff in these offices were major, in carrying out work activity, in dealing with claimants and in attempting to keep workloads manageable and under control. For many the question was how to 'get by'. In addition, local managers were under pressure and were prepared to take steps to marginalize union representatives and to define problems and difficulties as managerial concerns and not those of the trade union. However, despite these caveats, overall there was a much greater willingness by the members to define difficulties they faced in the course of their work as union problems, as illustrated by the market testing example. This might involve referring apparently arbitrary managerial decisions to the union, such as allocation of work or difficulties with maternity arrangements.

In these cases the union representatives sought redress by negotiating with the newly responsible managers at a district level. Often this involved working out procedures as they went along. For many representatives, acting as *de facto* workplace stewards was a novel experience, especially since many representatives learnt their unionism in the committees that characterized so much union work for most of the 1980s. As a result there were differences among the representatives, with some seeking accommodations and compliance with management decision, while others, and particularly those who were politically active, occasionally in the Labour Party and often in one of the smaller left-wing groups, were prepared to challenge and question management. Even so, just as the members developed a union consciousness in terms of their work and employment experience, as well as in relation to the broader political understandings that many have, so too did the representatives build a sense of trade unionism in these offices in terms of concrete managerial approaches and decisions and work and employment experience.

These developments in the local offices were not part of an anarchic process of union activity, although they occurred in an apparently uneven and varied way from office to office. It was not that each office or district pursued its own concerns and interests, without reference to each other or the union nationally. The development of a more activist approach to unionism by these memberships occurred within the framework of agency-level policies and programmes. The union sections within the DSS reorganized so as to negotiate and represent their memberships at the agency level. Within this framework of bargaining and negotiation, memberships in offices also began to pursue these concerns at a local level. To this extent, the early 1990s was a period in which union memberships within the Benefits Agency began to promote an activist base, with an important degree of independence, but firmly within the framework of a national union structure.

Assessment

The broadening of the representational base of each of these branches and the encouragement of workplace-based action by the branch leaderships was part of the refocusing of the unions in the Benefits Agency. In each branch there was evidence of deliberate attempts to extend representational structures. Moreover, in each year of the study, the members in each of these branches were involved in various forms of industrial action, including stoppages. It is in these respects that a more participative and active form of union organization began to emerge.

The background to the attempts to establish representative structures and procedures in new agencies and separate areas of work lay in early attempts by the unions to establish workplace steward structures and arrangements in this area of employment. In the case of NUCPS (or the SCPS as it then was), this involved a national-leader initiative to transform the way the union organized and operated. Specifically, it involved a commissioned three-year review of the union (Drake *et al.*, 1980, 1982). However, these attempts to graft a steward form of organization on to well established centralized civil service unions were not without difficulty.

In the comprehensive review for the SCPS there was an acute awareness of the restructuring of work and employment relations, but little consciousness of the specificity of these social relations and what they might mean for collective organization and activity. Rather, it was thought that the idealized model of collective organization in the factory setting could be grafted on to the particular circumstances of public sector employment, with its blurred boundaries between waged worker and manager, the continued relevance of nationally defined terms and conditions of employment and the dispersed and varied circumstances of work situations. There was little recognition of the distinctiveness of work and employment relations, the specificity of managerial hierarchies or the persistence of public sector traditions of organization and activity. Hence, amnesia on the social and historical origins of these models of change resulted in a forced programme of union reconstruction and reorganization.

What happened in practice was that the initial attempts in both unions to establish participative representational structures were principally located within the electoral framework of each union. Representatives were part of the means whereby the national union leadership organized campaigns and related activity. They were also part of the electoral machines that organized in each union. However, with the managerial recomposition in the 1980s and the 1970s, these embryonic representational structures came into their own, and the local leaderships took steps to extend the representational base of each of these branches so that they could begin to deal with the 'new' managements that emerged during this period.

This upsurge in local union activity within the civil service varied from office to office. For a time there appeared to be a process of union renewal taking place, in the sense that the locus of unionism was beginning to shift towards the local level. The condition for this development was that local management gained an independence and relative freedom of decision-making that meant that union leaderships could begin to bargain and press their cases at this level. The supposed independence of local management was an illusion; this was a decentralized managerial hierarchy, still very much under the control of the 'new' agency's senior management structures, which had been put in place during this period. These agencies were organized and operated as corporate structures, in business units, with the locus of power and authority remaining with the chief executive and board of management for each agency (or equivalent).

There was another side to the corporatization of the civil service. The advent of agency structures meant that unions within each agency could develop approaches that were agency-specific and not aimed at the civil service as a whole. The agencies had the authority to establish agency-specific terms and conditions of employment, within parameters set by governments for the civil service as a whole, and the important negotiations take place at an agency level. As a consequence, union memberships within specific agencies had the potential to address these developments, in the course of the negotiations and bargaining that took place within each agency, both formally and informally.

The outcome was that unions within the agencies began to reorganize, to stimulate and encourage a revival of local unionism in some cases and the creation of locally focused and based structures in other cases. In social security this regrouping initially resulted in the appearance of relatively autonomous union groups within offices, taking on management in a variety of ways. Not surprisingly, this was a contested development, as some local leaderships saw their newly acquired autonomy qualified in the interests of overall agency membership. This was part of the struggle within these unions about the appropriate models of unionism in the corporatized civil service, focusing on the appropriateness of centralized or decentralized forms of representation and involvement.

While the potential for a more activist base was established within these unions, principally by the local leaderships in the branches, it was within the framework of a form of union organization structured to negotiate and represent the membership at local, area and national levels of the emergent agency structures. The central point is that in the context of the profound restructuring of the social relations of service provision, the conditions and circumstances of union organization and practice also began to change. However, this was within limits and these union bodies remained very much integral parts of nationally organized unions. In part, this reflected the complicated arrangements, involving both the decentralization of managerial structures and the continuing centralization and control over budgetary arrangements and policy initiatives in these agencies. Still, it remained the case that the remote and centralized union structures of the past no longer had a salience and were no longer relevant. In this respect, the foundation for the process of union renewal in these areas of employment was laid in the 1970s, as a result of national union leadership initiative and the subsequent recomposition of union hierarchies in the 1980s and 1990s.

12 MANAGERIAL DECENTRALIZATION AND ACTIVE TRADE UNIONISM: THE INLAND REVENUE

The implementation of strategies of change took a distinctive form in the Inland Revenue. The introduction of FMI into the Inland Revenue in the mid-1980s laid the foundation for a reconstituted management structure, though it initially appeared that the Inland Revenue would be exempt from the Next Steps programme, principally because of the nature of its activity. The Inland Revenue was also closely tied into the Treasury, operating under the general direction of the Treasury ministers, which meant that any reservations about revenue control had a force that was not evident in other departments. Even so, in the 1990s the Inland Revenue was subjected to the strictures of the *Next Steps* programme by being reorganized as a *de facto* agency, with the establishment of executive offices (for a more detailed account of this history, see Fairbrother, 1994a, Chapters 7 and 8).

Altogether, five principal unions were recognized by the Board of Inland Revenue: the IRSF, the Institute of Professionals, Managers and Specialists (IPMS), the CPSA, the NUCPS and the Association of First Division Civil Servants (FDA). These unions were all members of the Council of Civil Service Unions, and they faced similar problems during the 1980s and into the 1990s, responding to the restructuring that was taking place in broadly matching ways. However, this did not mean that they were always successful in coordinating their activity on Revenue matters, let alone other civil service concerns, in harmonious and cooperative ways. Although a number of unions were recognized by the Inland Revenue, the principal union was the IRSF (part of PTC after 1995 and then PCS in 1998).

This restructuring of the Inland Revenue during the 1980s and into the 1990s transformed the relations between management and staff in decisive ways. There was a move to individualize and question the standardized work and employment relations of the past, with the introduction of Revenue-specific procedures and practices. New layers of staff acquired the trappings and authority of management, while other staff faced an intensification of work, as well as increased job uncertainty. It was in this context of change that the IRSF experienced the tensions and opportunities of civil service restructuring.

The IRSF had long organized as a department-based and department-specific union. As with other civil service unions, it was a centralized union, with the national leadership exercising considerable control and influence over locally based memberships. In this respect it was a union form of organization where the national leadership had acquired expertise and experience as negotiators and representatives, acting on behalf of a largely quiescent membership, and thus gaining a reputation as an accommodative union (see Hyman, 1989, pp. 180–3). Nevertheless, this was also a union that had long had the embryonic structures of locally based negotiating forums. These structures provided the opportunity for the membership in this union, more so than other civil service trade unions, to organize and act at a local level as the reorganization of management proceeded. Thus, in the 1980s the union leadership and active sections of the membership faced a series of dilemmas, which could be presented starkly as a choice between affirming a more locally based and active form of trade unionism or one where the national leadership continued to prevail. However, in practice the way such dilemmas are resolved is more complicated than is suggested by a straightforward choice between two models of unionism. It is the working out of these dilemmas, particularly at a local level, that is the focus of this chapter.

The Board of Inland Revenue

The Board of Inland Revenue administered and collected direct taxes, and was organized with a head office in London and tax and collection offices throughout the United Kingdom. The tax and collection offices were, in effect, the basic unit of the Inland Revenue, with direct responsibility for the administration and collection of taxes in a locality. Between 1991 and 1996, staff in post (full-time equivalent) fell from 65,717 to 54,906.

The Board was constituted by an Act of Parliament in 1849, and from 1909 was responsible for the administration and collection of direct taxes: mainly income tax, corporation tax, capital gains tax, inheritance tax, stamp duty, development land tax and petroleum revenue tax. As such, the Inland Revenue had long had a distinctive ethos, reflected in department-specific grades and pay levels. While entrance examinations had been introduced into the Inland Revenue, like other areas of the civil service, there were significant variations in salaries for similar jobs in the civil service throughout the nineteenth century, with Inland Revenue staff near the bottom (Humphreys, 1958, pp. 20, 22–3). More significantly in the long run, the Department of the Board of Revenue retained its department grading structures, thereby reinforcing a view that this was a distinct section within the civil service. None the less, salary scales approximated the Treasury grades by the 1930s, and this has remained the case into the 1990s.

Throughout the 1980s and into the 1990s, the focus of government policy was on budgetary control and the introduction of management information systems. Initially this was under FMI, but it was eventually superseded by the *Next Steps* programme and the establishment of executive offices within the Inland Revenue. Under FMI this involved three related developments. First, the Senior Management System was introduced, a procedure of target setting and review involving senior managers, directors and the Board. The result was a statement of intent for the Board, similar to the mission statement of other enterprises (see 'Departmental statement' in Inland Revenue, 1987, 1988; 'Inland Revenue's purpose and aims' in Inland Revenue, 1990, 1991, 1992; 'Inland Revenue job, aims and values' in Inland Revenue, 1996). Second, management information systems were introduced, usually as part of the computerization of the bulk of revenue work during this period. Third, line management budgeting was introduced, covering the whole of the department by 1987/8, and giving line managers increased discretion over the deployment of budgets at an office level.

When the *Next Steps* programme was announced in 1988, it appeared that the Inland Revenue would be exempt from this comprehensive programme of change. The importance of the recognition of direct control over revenue collection resulted in a government decision to keep the Department of Inland Revenue formally within the civil service, as a core area of state activity. However, on 25 July 1990 the Chancellor of the Exchequer took the first steps towards establishing executive offices in the Inland Revenue with the announcement that internal managerial delegation and accountability within the department would be extended. He also stated that there would be a review of the department, to examine how it could be restructured and its work reorganized (Hansard, 25 July 1990, *239–241*w). On 17 February 1991, the department published its *Next Steps* programme, the 'action plan'. By April 1992 it had established thirty-four executive offices to assess and collect tax, or to provide relevant support services for this work, which, with the Valuation Office Agency, covered 96 per cent of the department's staff (Inland Revenue, 1992, p. 3). Each executive office was organized on the basis of an enhanced managerial structure, under the management of a controller, appointed by the

Chair of the Board of Inland Revenue. However, open competition for the senior post of executive officer was deemed inappropriate for this version of the *Next Steps* programme.

By October 1992, fourteen regional executive offices had been set up, each with a collector in place, covering tax and collection across Great Britain. The remaining twenty executive offices covered such activities as accounts, capital taxes, claims and enforcement, financial services, pensions, solicitor's office and training. The controllers of these executive offices were appointed by the chair of the Board. They were responsible for the preparation for annual operating plans as well as the reports of overall performance against these plans. As with agencies, each executive office had a framework document which set out its relationship to the rest of the department. These developments were part of the increasing commodification of public service work in this and other sections of the civil service. Market testing was introduced into department activity in the late 1980s and was extended during the 1990s. This was preceded by feasibility reviews in the late 1980s covering actuarial advice, payment of travelling and subsistence, and pay arrangements. In 1989, a rolling programme for market testing began, which included in-house catering, the contracting-out of the project management of the records office at Peterborough and a switch from the Inland Revenue data network to the contracted-out government data network (Inland Revenue, 1990, p. 27). By 1992, market testing had become a key and seemingly permanent feature of the department's activity. Work had been contracted out, including bulk records storage and the delivery of employer's budget packs.

Thus, contrary to initial expectations, the Inland Revenue was brought into the centre of the *Next Steps* programme, as an agency in fact, if not in name. In effect, there was a substantial reorganization of the social relations of revenue collection, along agency lines. This programme of change amounted to the 'corporatization' of the Inland Revenue. A central feature was the establishment of an Inland Revenue managerial structure, giving managements at all levels of the Revenue a novel degree of operational and budgetary authority.

Managerial procedures

Throughout the 1980s a number of changes were introduced which had a dramatic effect on staffing levels and work procedures. These included budgetary and management information systems, the utilization of information technology and work measurement and efficiency scrutinies. In 1987/8 line management budget systems were extended over the whole department.

Beginning in 1986, with the publication of a memorandum to office managers about the allocation of their time to budgetary matters, by April 1987 over 1,300 managers were operating their own budgets, deploying resources in line with operational objectives. Since then further changes have been implemented, aimed at targeting and monitoring costs and expenditure. This pattern of change included the development of information and budgeting systems. One feature was the development of an information system for the allocation of clerical staff between regions and offices.

A theme that acquired increasing prominence towards the end of the 1980s and into the 1990s was management planning. There was a sense in which the department attempted to coordinate the different developments taking place in operations, financial control, staff organization and training and 'customer' relations as integral features of managerial planning and organization. Publications related to this development argued that the Revenue required 'business-like' planning (Inland Revenue, 1990, p. 24). In a management plan produced in 1990, unit costs were specified for the department's main functions, and input/output budgeting information was presented as part of the development of managerial planning in the department.

Central to these plans was line-management budgeting. Throughout the 1980s, managers in charge of local offices had their own budgets. Gradually this was brought into relatively close alignment with overall department managerial objectives, with the introduction of management information systems. Associated with these developments, the department examined the way work was organized, introducing new procedures, including work measurement programmes and studies of clerical work associated with the introduction of computer-based systems. There were also studies of the scope for delegating work to lower levels in the taxation and collection offices, typing and secretarial services, and the storage of records and forms. The department also carried out a number of efficiency scrutinies.

Overall, staffing levels in the Inland Revenue fell dramatically over the 1980s and into the 1990s, from 78,312 in 1980 to 54,906 in 1996. This was largely the result of computerization and the reorganization of procedures. During the early 1980s an extensive computerization programme was implemented in the Board of Inland Revenue. By 1988 the tax records of all employees had been transferred on to computer, 93 per cent within the computerization of the Pay As You Earn (PAYE) system (Inland Revenue, 1987, p. 19). For most staff this meant that desktop computer terminals had become their basic work tools, with a consequent substantial reduction in work with paper records, although such records remained a feature of this type of work. Procedures were also implemented for the automatic transfer of cases between offices, thereby providing more up-to-date and comprehensive profiles of tax-payers' liabilities and payment records.

Work and employment

With the introduction of FMI and the developments associated with *Next Steps*, a relatively clear strategy of change in work and employment practices was mapped out. The aim was to reorganize local offices so that a layer of staff – the district inspector and other senior staff – became responsible for the budgeting of the office. In effect, this meant redrawing the management–worker divide in these offices. At the same time, this shift in emphasis was a formalization of an already existing division which often took a gender form in the office, with men managing and women working. While the impetus for these changes came from outside the office, the way in which they were implemented depended crucially on the practices and commitments of the local management and workforce.

Managements were increasingly placed in a position where they were responsible for budgetary matters over a range of items in quite unprecedented ways. While this did not necessarily mean a discernible change in managerial style, there was evidence of managers feeling their way in these processes and, in the course of doing so, often invoking a range of practices that made it difficult for the union membership to meet the challenge of these new arrangements. Managers often viewed these changes in terms of long-standing relations with their less senior staff, both as subordinates and often as women.

For management, these changes had mixed results: on the one hand, managerial structures were decentralized, with local managers acquiring a range of responsibilities that they had not held previously; on the other hand, there was a closer degree of monitoring by one level of management of another. Area or regional managers were now more likely to visit district offices to consider the office performance and whether offices were meeting targets. There was thus a greater degree of managerial autonomy and discretion at an office and district level; at the same time these managers had become more directly accountable to senior levels of management over budget performance and targets.

At a more general level, management was made more accountable through the individualization of employment contracts and the introduction of performance-related pay. During the 1990s, the first steps were taken towards the implementation of personal employment contracts for managers, including bonus arrangements for managers if they met agreed targets. These developments were associated with the establishment of cost centres for each office, delegating responsibility for sections to an increasing number of managerial staff. This resulted in some managers taking a relatively 'hard' line towards office staff in their attempts to meet targets and comply with budgetary restrictions.

The majority of people employed in the Inland Revenue offices worked in clerical jobs, at visual display terminals, 70–80 per cent of them women. They were employed on case work, following through records, updating and modifying assessments and dealing with the routine of taxation and collection. Work was rigorously defined:

> We all have clearly defined jobs in the sense that work is graded. You can literally open a book and see at what level this type of enquiry should be dealt with, whether it should be dealt with by a Revenue Assistant or a Revenue Officer. . . . It's fairly clearly defined. There is no sort of 'Well I don't know whether to give this to Bill or to Mary', you know. It's either Bill's job or Mary's job and that's it. (Revenue officer, 1992)

She went on to say: 'I can't delegate any of my work to anybody else. It's my work and that's it. Only somebody of an equivalent grade could do it' (1992). Most people worked as clerical workers, dealing with enquiries. Others worked on the telephones, answering queries, while yet other staff were employed at the counters, dealing with the public face-to-face. A smaller number of workers were employed as inspectors and investigators, with the latter often visiting enterprises.

The restructuring and reorganization of the Inland Revenue meant that these workers experienced considerable change and upheaval during the 1980s and particularly the 1990s, which was reflected in their worries and concerns as workers. One of the main work worries was the workload that was evident in these offices. Many spoke of low staff numbers: 'There is not enough staff to do the work', and on this item one local IRSF branch official remarked:

> The basic problem is that there is too few staff so we have always got arrears of work. We never ever get the job finished. We never do all aspects of the job. That is the basic problem, whatever section you are on, and whatever time of the year, there is too much work. [It leads to] stress, people leaving, being off sick, all the time. Pressure on them to skimp the job, not do it properly, just to get the figures done. (1992)

As management acquired more authority and discretion over the organization of work in the offices, workers worked to monthly targets. Most respondents identified the pressures of work as of even more immediate concern to workers in these areas than pay. Workers in general took their work seriously and worried about not giving a proper service to the public. They found it increasingly difficult to provide a quick service, so that in their face-to-face dealings with the public they were often frustrated by their inability to respond adequately to the requests that were made of them.

Comprehensive reporting and appraisal procedures had been introduced, so that workers were assessed by their line managers, who set annual targets. During the first part of the 1980s work measurement programmes were introduced, covering executive and clerical work in local tax and collection offices. According to the branch secretaries, workers were increasingly likely to raise questions about these reporting procedures with the office secretary, because of the way these procedures had been slowly tied into pay and promotion procedures.

There had also been a general tightening up of employment practices on absenteeism, sickness and other related issues. The rate of absenteeism in these offices had been increasing, particularly as a result of stress and the pressures generated by seemingly unmanageable workloads. At the same time, managements showed an increased willingness to question workers about absenteeism and to discipline them for breaches of the absenteeism procedures. There was an increased concern by managements to monitor time-keeping and attendance records. Workers were more likely to be questioned about sickness and asked to see Inland Revenue approved medical staff. Further, there was an increased concern with inefficiency procedures: the time period before someone could be dismissed for inefficient work practices was reduced from nine months to four months.

Thus, the Inland Revenue staff worked in an increasingly pressured work environment. They faced a more assertive management at an office level, willing to press the workforce on output, work procedures and output. In turn, these managers faced escalating demands over office output and related targets. These were not easy offices in which to work, and many of the strains and tensions evident in the Benefit Agency offices were also apparent here.

The union in the West Midlands

By the 1990s, the major union in the Inland Revenue, the IRSF, was the only department-based union in the civil service. Its membership in the West Midlands was dispersed across a number of offices in the region, with concentrations of staff particularly in the large population centres such as Birmingham and Coventry. The union was organized into a number of branches, usually covering large geographical areas. These branches were serviced by a regional officer who had played an increasingly direct and active part in office activity, causing some disquiet among branch leaderships who felt marginalized.

The Coventry and District Taxation Branch, for example, covered an area from Nuneaton and Hinkley in the north to Stratford-upon-Avon in the south. It comprised eight offices, responsible for the administration and assessment of income, capital and corporation taxes. This branch paralleled the management structure, covering non-industrial staff, with 500 members spread over eight offices. In Birmingham the taxation branch was primarily based in one building, in which ten taxation offices are located, although other offices were located outside the main building and beyond Birmingham, in Ludlow, Solihull, Burton upon Trent and Redditch. During the early 1990s, this branch had around 1,290 members, the majority of whom were revenue assistants and revenue officers, with no more than 100 inspectors and 150 technical and related staff.

The spread of membership did not make it easy for either the full-time officer assigned to the region or branch officers to organize and coordinate the activity of members. In a number of offices the membership was relatively inactive and the office representatives were either inexperienced or passive. This was evident in the larger branch where the membership was spread over twenty-six workplaces, over a thirty-mile radius from the centre of Birmingham. The membership in these workplaces ranged from two to 113. The geographical spread of members and their dispersion over a number of workplaces made it difficult for members to participate in union activity. One branch officer stated about the membership in the furthest workplace:

> [There is a] lack of contact with people in [Western Town], there is the difficulty of them getting to meetings . . . they themselves are isolated. It is not as if there is 500 people out in [Western Town]. I mean there is 47 out in [Western Town], there is not many of them. [They are] just stuck out there. . . . [Northern Town] is not so bad because transport is better there, on a railway line, but at [Western Town] there is no railway. (Branch officer, Inland Revenue, 1992)

Many office leaderships faced the added difficulty of dealing with managements with increased discretionary powers, which in a small remote office could inhibit union activity. The result was that there was often an unevenness from office to office in terms of membership involvement and activity.

One way in which the IRSF nationally attempted to support and develop both office representation in the region and the branches was by the establishment of a regional office in Birmingham, staffed by a regional officer and a secretary. The first regional officer was appointed in 1988 in the face of opposition from some of the branch secretaries in the region, who saw the appointment as a way of restricting their activity as the leading lay officials in the region. In effect, this development undermined the activity and involvement of the branch secretaries in the Whitley committees, since it became more common for office secretaries to deal directly with the regional officer and for the regional officer to take the lead in the regional committees. These arrangements meant that the branch secretaries concentrated more on the administrative and representational structures within the union and less on the formal negotiating committees. However, in practice, the branch secretaries were also participants in the Whitley arrangements, as office secretaries and as members of the regional Whitley committees. In this way they bridged the potential gap between the negotiating structures and the forms of union internal representation and organization.

Dilemmas for the union

With the beginnings of the implementation of FMI in the Inland Revenue in the early 1980s, the IRSF, both locally and nationally, saw an opportunity to re-examine the form and activity of the local office union structure. Members in offices had long been organized on the basis of office committees for negotiating purposes, and in branches for union political and administrative activity. Such a dual structure resulted in particular styles of unionism. There was a long-standing tendency for members to be represented by office secretaries and the regional counterparts in the Whitley. It was through the office committees that grievances and related issues were addressed, and when not settled forwarded to the regional and national Whitley structures. In contrast, the branches were the base units of the union for the purposes of administration, including recruitment and the provision of union services, as well as politically, in terms of elections and representation within the union.

At the time of the introduction of FMI, many office committees were moribund, having not operated as negotiating committees for many years and effectively consisting of an office secretary in name only. The remit of these committees was relatively limited, and they tended to act as conduits for national decisions, seldom taking on an active role in pursuing the interests of their membership. One of the reasons for this situation was that relatively few items could be negotiated and dealt with at a local level. The practices of the past, whereby the union membership relied on competent negotiators at a national level, had been carried over into the early 1980s. With restructuring in the offices, many union office committees faced problems in publicly redefining the remit of the committees, so as to make them more effective and representative (Fairbrother, 1994a; see also Fairbrother, 1991).

Under the long-established Whitley procedures for these meetings, practices which had been accepted in the past by the union side took on a sinister aspect, as intimidating occasions for many office secretaries. In one taxation office, many local Whitley meetings were held in the office of the district inspector, who had made it clear that he expected the office secretaries (or union representatives) to meet him in his office and not in one of the meeting rooms in the building, and further that the representatives should bring their own chairs to the office for the meeting. Not only was the venue felt by some to be inappropriate and intimidating as the district inspector's personal office, but the practice with the chairs was thought to be demeaning. In the main, office secretaries were young women, employed as revenue executives or assistants, while the managers were middle-aged males, at least two grades above the office secretaries. The patronizing and controlling attitudes typical of such males were often carried over into their negotiations with the office secretaries.

Since the mid-1980s the local branch leaderships had faced a number of difficulties in confronting the challenge of FMI. During the 1980s, and particularly after 1986, union branch secretaries in the regions took steps to develop and support the office Whitley structure. Office secretaries were encouraged to attend locally focused schools aimed at developing the skills and approaches necessary to deal with FMI. In addition, office secretaries were encouraged to meet each other, often at the initiative of the branch secretaries, to discuss developments in different offices. In this period, branch secretaries and their executives were confident about the union organization and the ability to meet the changing circumstances in which they operated. This was a period when the changes associated with FMI had just been introduced, particularly the decentralization of budgetary responsibility to district managements. The union successfully revived the office Whitley structure and branches were beginning to shift their concerns, from administering and relaying the national decisions of the union to members, to a concern with coordinating and planning activity across the offices. In some instances this meant that branch secretaries gave support to inexperienced office secretaries, developing educational programmes for union representatives and refocusing branch agendas on office activity.

By 1990, the confidence among the union leaders in the late 1980s had begun to dissipate. The branch executives, and particularly the branch secretaries, had lost some of their capacity to coordinate and plan activity across the different offices. In part, this may have been a consequence of the appointment of the full-time officer in the region, who began to organize union activity directly with the office secretaries, thereby by-passing the branches. While the branches had never had a formal involvement in negotiations, this had not been a problem in the mid-1980s when they began to take on the temporary appearance of workplace steward committee. In a number of branches it had become more difficult to fill all the officer positions, and in one case the branch secretary also acted as treasurer and publicity officer because she had been unable to persuade any other members to do these jobs. Alongside this, office secretaries found it increasingly difficult to broaden their remit of concerns, away from housekeeping issues 'about the colour of the toilet paper' to questions about reporting procedures, pay and the like.

Two years later, when the executive offices were introduced, there were signs of a further revival of activity as the office union organization began to face an increasingly rigid office management. Managers began to demand more from the office staff, and where staff were not completely intimidated there was a return to the union: more people were willing to play active parts in the branch organization. Branches which had difficulty filling executive and officer positions two years earlier had members volunteering to take on different tasks. The difficulty for members at this level was to address effectively the increasing attempts by management to restrict and curtail union activity. At the same time, the union nationally continued to affirm the importance of organizing as a centrally controlled union, which from the point of view of many locally active union members often undermined these initiatives.

The *Next Steps* programme posed a set of questions for the IRSF which it found difficult to address. In particular, the emphasis on managerialism raised the question of the relationship between local and national trade unionism in acute ways. For most of its history, the IRSF has organized as a nationally focused union, with relatively minimal involvement by members in their workplaces. In general, negotiations took place at a regional or national level, and as a result, the branches, which were organized geographically, played a minimal role in bargaining. With the implementation of the *Next Steps* programme, the IRSF faced a changed negotiating terrain, in which local managements gained greater discretion, thus providing an opening for local memberships to begin bargaining over substantive issues for the first time. On 7 February 1991, the Chair of the Board of Inland Revenue wrote to the General Secretary of the IRSF to inform him that the Valuation Office (within the Inland Revenue structure) would be established as an agency and that *Next Steps* principles would be applied to the rest of the Department of Inland Revenue. The IRSF responded to this announcement at a national level, reaffirming the role of the national leadership and thus devaluing the importance of local activity and initiative.

Decentralized managements and active unions

The reform programme in the Inland Revenue posed a set of questions for the IRSF that it found difficult to address. In particular, the programme, with its emphasis on managerialism, raised the question of the relationship between local and national trade unionism in a very acute way. In general, negotiations took place at a regional or national level, and as a result the branches, which were organized on a geographical basis with an administrative and political remit, played a minimal role in bargaining. Beginning with the FMI programme, and continued with the *Next Steps* programme, the negotiating terrain was changed, giving local managements greater discretion and opening up the potential for local memberships to begin bargaining over substantive issues for the first time in their history.

At a general level, the Inland Revenue illustrates many of the trends towards the restructuring of the civil service. The aim was to reorganize the management structures in the Inland Revenue Department so that it became a managerially controlled section of the civil service. Local management in the Inland Revenue, as in other civil service departments, acquired considerable discretion over staffing and conditions of employment. For workers in the department this meant considerable concern and worry, with increased workloads and uncertainties about their terms and conditions of employment. At the same time, these workers faced managements who had begun to act in more confident ways, demanding commitment and loyalty from their workforces for the changes that had occurred and were planned for the future.

These developments opened up the way for managers to redefine the way in which work is done and the terms on which work is remunerated. They had acquired considerable discretion over staffing and conditions of employment, and they were beginning to exercise this discretion. These managers sought to exercise their new prerogatives in ways that elicited staff support, though in a number of instances this was in idiosyncratic ways. For workers these developments raised questions about their responses to the advent of managerialism in the Inland Revenue. In this process they began to look to their unions for support.

For the union activists in these offices, the changes provided an impetus to renew the basis of the union organization in the offices, building on the office committee structure and developing embryonic workplace steward structures and practices. One outcome was that in a number of cases office secretaries and other committee members began to act much more consciously as *de facto* workplace stewards, responding to members and taking up issues with managers, in some instances, and the branch officers or the regional officer in others. While such developments were not without difficulty, there was evidence that, in most offices, the office secretaries in particular began to take on a more public union mantle and make the initial steps towards the development of a collective union presence in these offices. At both procedural and substantive levels, these committees began to redefine their relations with management in terms of distinctive sets of interests and concerns between union members on the one side and local management on the other. These activities included recruiting new members to the committees, establishing cycles of union meetings, opening up negotiations with management and questioning their often assumed and unquestioned views about managerial discretion and prerogative.

In 1991 and 1992, partly in anticipation of the moves to organize the Inland Revenue along agency-type lines, there was evidence of a managerial attempt to reassert control over work and employment procedures. In one office, the branch secretary reported that the office management had taken steps to present a more unified approach among the managers in relation to the monitoring of work procedures and practices. At the same time, the local office managers began to tighten up on the reporting procedures used in the office. The result was that the staff in this office felt that they were under much closer control and scrutiny than had been the case previously. Faced with these problems, and in response to membership complaints, the branch secretary, who was also the office secretary for the 150 members in the office, took steps to try to develop a more active and comprehensive floor-based representative system. She was aware that many of the representatives were inexperienced and nervous about taking up issues directly with managers, and in an attempt to address this problem she encouraged these representatives to attend off-site educational programmes specially designed to address some of these concerns and developments. Over a couple of years, there was evidence of increased union involvement by some of these representatives, taking up issues on behalf of members and playing a more active role in the committee activity that characterized much of the union work in these offices.

The attempt by local managers to assume the prerogatives of more assertive and on occasion aggressive managements was evident elsewhere. In another example, in 1993, an office manager used the opportunity of the publication of the *Citizen's Charter* to remind staff about their presentation to customers and their relations with the public. This was done in rather heavy-handed way, with the manager gathering together all the staff who dealt directly with the public and telling them how to speak and how to present themselves. He gave the staff instructions to wear name badges, speak 'properly and clearly' and conduct themselves in ways that were a credit to the office. The reaction of the staff was upset and anger. They complained to the branch secretary, who was then faced with the problem of trying to persuade them not to walk out and instead to make a formal complaint about the behaviour of the manager. In the event, the latter course was agreed but, as the branch secretary noted, the manager in one speech transformed a group of 'quiet' union members into aggrieved trade unionists who were prepared to walk out because of the way he had treated them; they were no longer willing to accept managerial dictate without comment. Subsequently, the branch secretary obtained a formal apology from the manager and a more active trade union membership (Interviews, 1993).

These two examples indicate that local management in the Inland Revenue had begun to adopt a more authoritative style of management, thereby implementing the prerogatives implied by the *Next Steps* programme. In this respect, these managers took steps to increase managerial supervision and monitoring of work organization and procedure. Faced with these developments, the local union leaders looked to the union form of organization in the offices to build and develop a union response to these developments. There were signs that the unions in these offices, historically relatively inactive, had begun to take steps to renew their organizations and to open up a broader set of issues that previously they had been unable or unwilling to pursue.

The branch form of organization was pivotal in the process of establishing an active union presence in the offices in the region. As with many civil service unions, branches typically covered a number of workplaces, constituted on the basis of the district unit. As such, the branch drew its executive membership from a number of workplaces, and provided a focus for workplace members as well as a representative forum for negotiating. Thus, the branch form of organization countered the distance and dispersal of membership and provided links between workplaces. A limitation on this arrangement was that there was often no constituency basis to representation on the committee, with the result that inactive memberships or remote workplaces were usually under-represented on the committee.

Increasingly, the regional office or local executive office became the focus for workplace and union branch activity, reflecting the realities of managerial decentralization. As one branch secretary noted, in a comment about the issues that were being raised at her branch committee meetings:

> Budgeting problems have come up now ... more so, because [Inland revenue] budgets have been devolved to local offices. And power as well as money has been devolved to local Executive Offices, the regional offices, and we are much involved with what they decide and what they discuss, because they are much more able to ... hire and fire people and do all sorts of things. So these things have come up on the agenda, which we did not have before. (1992)

This occurred in the following context:

> [Before regional offices] were there and they were working and were making decisions but they were not autonomous and now they are and now they can actually make decisions about numbers of staff employed in the region, just as districts can now make decisions about the staff employed in particular districts ... they ... have their own budget and can make their own decisions about far more things, opening hours, time the switch boards come on, you know the time the switch boards are open. All this sort of thing. So therefore we have to be more involved. (1992)

This suggests that for workers the introduction of FMI and the advent of the *Next Steps* heralded both more immediate and direct forms of control and new opportunities for collective organization. It is in these circumstances that members have begun to look to their union to provide the means for collective organization and action in the workplaces. Office committees were more likely to address issues concerning the way their work was organized than in the past. Branch executives were more likely to be composed of people who saw their role as more akin to that of a workplace steward who spoke for members on the basis of consultation and discussion. In addition, with the devolution of managerial discretion over operational activity at district and regional levels, the branch executive committees became the forum for an exchange of views about such decisions, for the sharing of information between workplaces and for representation at a regional level. One possible outcome was that the form of unionism prevalent in the Inland Revenue would be recast in distinct and imaginative ways.

This renewal, however, occurred in the context of the union attempting to reaffirm its integrity as a department-based and focused union. In these circumstances the union nationally has attempted to maintain and consolidate its control over workplace forms of union organization. This was reflected in the policies elaborated by the union as well as in the organizational change that has begun. As indicated, a regional officer had been appointed, with the effect that the relative autonomy of the branch form of organization had begun to be compromised, as the regional officer began to take over some of the representational activity that was formerly the province of the branch executive and particularly the branch secretary. Instead of the branch organizing as a political unit, concerned with the coordination and development of office activity, there was pressure on the branch leaders to restrict their activity to the administration of union affairs at this level of organization, acting as a cipher of union policy for the regional and national levels of the union. Insofar as this happened, the potential offered by this particular form of branch organization was compromised.

Assessment

The dramatic restructuring of the state sector created a new terrain for union organization and activity. These developments challenged the basis of the centralized and department-based ISRF. This union could no longer operate as it did previously; however, this did not mean that it debated and reorganized in seamless or uncontested ways. Assessing and making sense of the political and economic restructuring of the state sector was fraught and hotly debated, with many in the union adopting a wait and see approach, before reluctantly changing modes of organization and operation.

The history of the IRSF was somewhat distinctive, in that this union had long organized on a department basis and, with the introduction of FMI and the decentralization of management responsibilities, the union adapted to the changed circumstances. Long-standing committees were encouraged to broaden the remit of their concerns as the union attempted to address the changes taking place at this level of the managerial hierarchies. This set of developments was encouraged by the national leaderships, although, as is often the case, local and regional leaderships also saw an opportunity to qualify the centralized basis of representation in the union. Consequently, the 1980s were marked by dispute within the union about the ways in which it should develop so as to address changing relationships at work.

The process of reorganization was, first, to give local leaderships (usually the branch officers) a degree of independence and autonomy unusual in the IRSF, or other civil service unions. Faced with increasingly assertive and often arbitrary managements, developing more 'hands-on' approaches towards their staff, within a rhetoric that 'managers must manage', union leaderships and their memberships embarked on a period of active unionism at a local level. During the 1980s, these leaderships took steps to secure local negotiations on a broad range of work and employment issues. As part of this development, memberships became more assertive, no longer prepared to acquiesce to managerial dictate, more ready to complain aloud and to walk out of their offices because managements appeared arbitrary or aggressive or both. This was a period of increased union activity within offices, which has continued in a limited way in the Inland Revenue under the *Next Steps* initiative.

The IRSF model of unionism, department or agency based and focused, is likely to become the norm within the civil service unions in the next few years. At a general level, unions in the civil service now operate as 'federal' bodies, composed of a series of parallel but distinct union groupings, agency by agency. These new representative structures rested more securely on an activist leadership at a local level, when compared with the past, but they also organized and operated as agency-specific union bodies. The national executives of these unions thus comprised a membership whose prime experience and reference point was the representative union structures in each agency or cluster of agencies. Thus the merger between the NUCPS and IRSF was also a sign of the future, with the retention of the IRSF mode of organization and operation within the broader federal structure of a large civil service union covering all grades and represented in all areas of civil service employment.

13 REBUILDING TRADE UNIONISM: LOCAL GOVERNMENT

One of the distinctive features of trade unionism in the local state is the centrality of the branch form of organization. Local authority union memberships have long been organized as members of relatively large geographical branches covering a multitude of workplaces, not unlike other areas of the public sector. In general, branches were and remain defined by employer, the local authority as a whole or a unit of employment, such as social services. However, unlike in the civil service trade union branches, there was usually a close relation between the branch as a political and administrative unit within the trade union and the representational structure for negotiations and bargaining with employers. While this had not always been the case in the unions which came to constitute UNISON, with the establishment of this trade union in 1993 it became the norm.

Prior to the establishment of UNISON, the two constituent unions that organized in the local state, NALGO and NUPE, had taken steps, in the 1970s, to establish forms of workplace representation as a key element of branch organization. In each trade union, the national leadership, supported by regional officials and key sections of the activist membership, promoted workplace steward structures. These initiatives were introduced in a more comprehensive way in NUPE, and this union was seen by other public sector unions as a pace setter (Drake *et al.*, 1980, pp. 95–6). At the time, the NUPE leadership's promotion of such representational arrangements was a response to the emergence of local bargaining and locally negotiated bonus schemes, in local government and elsewhere in the public sector (Fryer *et al.*, 1974). While these initiatives were introduced in a period when national negotiations still prevailed and local authority managements were centralized, the developments inadvertently anticipated the much more comprehensive decentralization of managerial structures within local authorities during the 1980s and 1990s.

By the 1990s the restructuring and recomposition of local government managerial hierarchies in decentralized and partially devolved ways had begun to take place. In this context, and against the background of earlier reorganization, the local government unions faced a choice between maintaining a centralized form of representation, at both national and local authority levels, or refocusing union organization and activity in more devolved ways. Crucially, this is a choice founded in a pattern of union organization where there has long been a structural disengagement between national leaderships and local leaderships, and, moreover, between leaderships at the regional/local branch officer level and the departments within local authorities (Fairbrother, 1994a, pp. 167–8; Foster and Scott, 1998a, pp. 139–40). This can mean that local union bodies are organized to interpret national agreements or negotiate over specifically local matters or, as is the case in local government, interpret local authority agreements or bargain over departmental matters and concerns. Regional and/or national levels of union structures are organized to address the macro-concerns of trade union life, rather than the detail of the local and the immediate. While in practice relationships are more complicated than just suggested, there is often a broad patterning of relationships which comply with these distinctions. Moreover, there are often specific issues which bring out these difference sharply and forcibly (Heery and Kelly, 1994, pp. 1, 7, 11; Heery, 1998a; comment by Foster and Scott, 1998a, pp. 140, 147). For local union leaderships and their memberships, there is thus a choice of action and organization, which may reinforce the authority of regional leaderships (less so national leaders) or affirm the autonomy of local leaderships and activists. Further, there is a question of how and under what circumstances memberships are integrated into union organization and activity.

The focus of this chapter is on the way local union memberships in one local authority dealt with the restructuring that took place in the late 1980s and 1990s in the context of their relations with management and regional officials. This authority, Metropolitan Council, was a large metropolitan council under Labour Party control for most of the 1980s and 1990s. As with most authorities, Metropolitan Council provided a range of services, with education, housing and social services accounting for the majority of the workforce. The workforce was organized in terms of departments, under the formal responsibility of a chief executive or director of department. While it could be argued that this local authority constituted a particular case of change and development, it is the aim of the chapter to unravel the social processes of change in this sector, irrespective of the particularity of this authority. In the course of this account, comparison is drawn with the developments in the civil service.

Reaffirming a managed local authority

During the past twenty years, there has been a persistent move by central governments to extend control over the organization and operation of local government administration and provision of state services (for further details, see Fairbrother, 1996a). A key feature in the implementation of these policies has been a steady centralization of control within local government structures, establishing hierarchical managerial structures within local government and between local government and central government. Managerial controls were introduced into local government during this period, signified most clearly by the establishment of centralized structures for policy formulation as well as the organization of local state work into managerially accountable departments, along functional lines (Bains Report, 1972; Pattison, 1973; Cockburn, 1977). For manual workforces, these changes were accompanied by attempts to regulate and control the organization of work, through such measures as work study and job evaluation (Terry, 1982, 1983).

During the 1980s, there was a new twist to these policies, aimed at decentralizing local government provision within a centralized set of financial arrangements. Thus, building on policy reforms during the 1970s, central government during the 1980s initiated policy changes that would meet the twin objectives of controlling local government finance while permitting local management control over the organization and provision of services. The result was a transformation in the social relations of local government provision and services, from a decentralized form of administration and organization to one where these services were provided via a fragmented and devolved set of arrangements.

One of the strands of reform during the past twenty years was to affirm the tendency towards a 'managed' local authority, in which the managers were increasingly responsible for operational and administrative activity, as well as policy formulation, with the elected representatives reduced to the role of 'overseers'. Managers became increasingly interventionist over their areas of responsibility, creating managerial structures that were little different in principle and practice from the *Next Steps* agency structures in central government. Thus relatively independent managerial hierarchies were put in place in the different departments and sections that comprised local authorities, with a remit to provide services in 'efficient and effective' ways. The result was an increasingly 'managed' labour process within authorities, transforming the social relations of service provision in important ways (Farnham and Horton, 1993).

As part of the restructuring of local government, successive Conservative governments promoted the transformation of service provision, including privatization, contracting-out or externalization of services, market testing and the reorganization of service provision on an agency basis. Of particular importance and a central strand in the marketization of local government provision and organization was the process of competitive tendering for specific functions and services (Cutler and Waine, 1994). As Foster and Scott (1998b) argue, the introduction of competitive tendering procedures in local government was part of an attempt to weaken the autonomy and discretion of local government. Initially, in the early 1980s, these polices focused on manual workforces in construction and maintenance, but they were extended subsequently to a wider range of local government services, coupled with the extension of managerial practices and a progressive depoliticization of local government, via contractual and related arrangements. In the 1990s, these developments were extended, with the elaboration and promotion of the idea of the 'enabling' state 'choosing services from a plurality of agencies' (Foster and Scott, 1998b, p. 122). The articulation of this notion was accompanied by the extension of procedures and practices associated with the further marketization of the local state. These developments were clearly evident in Metropolitan Council.

Management in Metropolitan Council

Metropolitan Council had over 30,000 employees in total, and was one of the larger metropolitan authorities in the country. It had long been dominated by the Labour Party, acquiring a reputation for relatively conservative politics, although the different sections of the authority varied in approach. The area covered by the authority was a traditional manufacturing area, which had gone through major changes during the 1980s, related to the restructuring of manufacturing. None the less, it remained a major manufacturing conurbation, when compared with Great Britain as a whole. It is within this context of change that the authority pursued policies of reconstruction with the encouragement of inward investment and the use of extensive European Union aid.

Throughout the 1980s and into the 1990s, Metropolitan Council faced problems typical of most local authorities in England and Wales. It experienced problems with financial restrictions and controls, aimed at both limiting local government expenditure and directing local government finances in particular directions (Doogan, 1997). In line with the restructuring that was taking place in local government in general, during this period the council reorganized and recomposed its managerial hierarchies, underwriting department operational autonomy and resulting in the elaboration of the principles and practice associated with 'new public management' (Farnham and Horton, 1993). One feature of these developments was to decentralize and disaggregate managerial structures and responsibilities, with discretion to provide services according to proxy market criteria, as well as to establish market relations with external providers. There was an emphasis on separating policy activities and administrative organization and responsibility, as well as distinguishing between the purchase of services and the provision of those same services. The so-called purchaser/provider split has come to characterize most aspects of local authority service provision. Increasingly, local authorities have drawn on aspects of human resource management to inform managerial practice and organizations. Accompanying these developments in the sphere of management–staff relations, there was an increasing use of performance measures, to assess, evaluate and control service provision.

These developments were clearly illustrated by the pattern of managerial organization in social services in Metropolitan Council. The formal structure from 1992 onwards is shown in Figure 13.1. The work of social services workers was organized in terms of three principal groups. First, workers were organized in teams. This was clearly illustrated with reference to homes for the elderly, where a team manager was based in an area office and was responsible for an officer-in-charge based in a home, who in turn was responsible for a social services team of perhaps a dozen people providing residential care. Second, there were field workers, often working in multidisciplinary teams: for example, with adults who had experienced learning difficulties. Third, administrative workers, clerks and related support staff also worked in teams, reporting to an administrative officer based at each location, who in turn reported to an administrative team manager.

In 1993, 6,666 persons (full-time equivalents) were employed in social services, nearly half in non-manual jobs. They were spread over more than 250 workplaces throughout the city area, employed in such diverse jobs as children's homes, elderly persons' homes, social welfare centres, day nurseries and nursery centres, adult social education centres, social work teams, home care and central administrative activity. Over the previous years a number of these areas had become part of the private service sector, as the council relinquished control of residential homes for the elderly, under legislation associated with compulsory competitive tendering.

While there had been no major reorganization of the managerial structure for this department in recent years, the way in which work was organized had undergone considerable change, with implications for the management of the workforce. In the early 1990s, the major policy development for social services

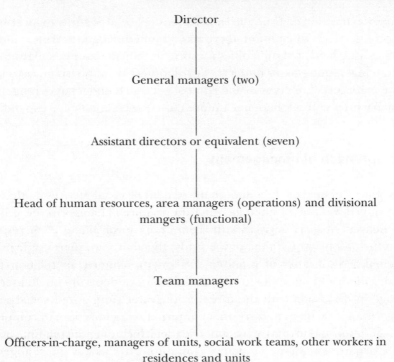

Director

General managers (two)

Assistant directors or equivalent (seven)

Head of human resources, area managers (operations) and divisional mangers (functional)

Team managers

Officers-in-charge, managers of units, social work teams, other workers in residences and units

Figure 13.1 Managerial hierarchy in Social Services, Metropolitan Council

was in community care, aimed at achieving two stated objectives: 'to give clients a better quality of life in a less institutionalised environment' and 'to achieve lower costs in service provision' (CIPFA, 1989, p. 32). The government endorsed the broad principle that local authorities should have the primary responsibility for the coordination of social service provision (apart from the mentally disabled), although this should involve a wider range of agencies. Uncertainty remained about the extent to which there would be a shift of financial and related resources to local authorities to meet these objectives (CIPFA, 1989, p. 33).

These changes, especially in the area of community care, were part of a transformation in the character of social services work, shifting from the provision of services to the administration and coordination of care work. Central to these initiatives was the split between purchasers and providers in social service work, implemented under the community care legislation of the early 1990s (the Children Act 1989 and the NHS and Community Care Act 1990). Under this legislation the responsibility for residential and nursing homes was transferred from the Department of Social Security to local authority social services. In addition, there was a limited budget provision for these services, which created difficulties for local authorities as they sought to meet operational requirements under the legislation. The emphasis on costs underwrote managerial supervision and control over such budgetary arrangements, as managerial staff became much more closely accountable for expenditure.

The approach of management

The policy pursued by the senior management of social services in Metropolitan Council was one of implementing the required changes to the provision and delivery of social services with a minimum involvement of or resistance from the unions. At the time of the study, the above two pieces of legislation imposed a distinct set of requirements on the council, in relation to the organization and structure of the social services department. Rather than engage in discussion with the three unions which organized social services staff, the approach was to carry out an internal reorganization, to comply with the legislation and to inform the union leaders, including the full-time officers, at the department joint consultative committee. In this way the changes were presented as inevitable and irreversible.

Following the passage of this legislation, the senior managerial structure was reorganized into two divisions, each under the authority of a deputy director. This, however, was presented as a limited change, in the following terms:

> It is only radically different at senior management level because at the middle management levels we already did have quite a specialist operational structure but at the top levels we had very broad general management. Now we have cut down if you like on the broad areas and focused the managers more than they were previously, but they are still called . . . General Manager. We have a General Manager for Community Care and a General Manager for Children and Families who operate at Deputy Director of Social Services level. (Senior manager, 1992)

This reorganization of the senior managerial hierarchies within the department was of significance, in that it was part of a general change in social services in particular and local government more generally.

The decisive development in this type of employment was the decentralization of managerial responsibilities and control. Such developments occurred against a background where this was and remains an area of employment of extraordinary complexity, like most of the public sector. There were variations between skilled and unskilled manual labour, routine manual and technical workers. These workers were overseen by managers at various levels, including middle and senior management, and the relevant committees of the city. Between these two classes were lower-level managers and supervisors, together with a range of professional workers, such as social workers and others. The result was that even within social services there were functional, sectoral and vertical differences in work and employment experiences (Carter and Fairbrother, 1995; Carter 1995).

During the late 1980s and particularly in the 1990s, there was a tendency towards clarification of the managerial and supervisory relations within areas of employment such as social services. The decentralization of managerial responsibilities signified the emergence of a more transparent set of relations between these managers *qua* managers and the workforces they supervised; in this respect the opaqueness of past supervisory relations within the layered hierarchies of public sector employment was qualified, although still a feature of this area of employment. These changes were driven by policies to define and promote forms of managerialism within local government, exemplified by human resource management practices and the policies of the central local government agency responsible for negotiating wages and conditions, the Local Government Management Board. On the one hand, there was an attempt to promote more flexible forms of work and employment within local government, reflected in attempts to end detailed and 'rigid' job remits. On the other hand, there was a devolution of responsibilities for setting terms and conditions of employment to the department level of the local government organization.

The senior management of the social services department embraced these developments. On jobs there was a recognition that past patterns of differentiation between staff were beginning to change. As one senior manager noted, 'The manual workers are still pretty low status. There is a shift in attitude towards them and it is wanting them to be higher status, especially in residential work for children. So there is some move to "professionalism", if that is the right word, for some of the manual workers' (1992). These patterns of development were seen as part of an ongoing process of change in these areas of employment. As stated about home care work, 'It is just a shift. Again if you take the home care service, previously known as home help service, there is a functional shift towards more personal care rather than domestic work. Right. You get that sort of shift but it is within a framework that existed for some considerable time' (Senior manager, 1992). In this context, there was an intensification of work and jobs were changing. These developments were seen as part of a broad process of change which impacted directly on the content of work within the social services department. As a senior manager stated in a comment about these shifts:

> We have still got the same range of jobs, although the focus of the jobs is changing somewhat, for example, there is more focus on the work that is done by home care assistants for people in their homes and there are more jobs being worked in the field compared with say institutional care, you know things like that. These are important shifts in local authority social services work. (1992)

Such developments occurred in a context where there was an intensification of work and employment in process. Not only had the relations between management and workers changed, but over time in this area of work there had been a change in work content, towards a more comprehensive engagement with those sections of the community who are reliant on or in contact with the social services department. A home care worker of twenty-six years' standing commented on her work history: 'When I first started it was just house work but now of course we are doing more or less nurse's chores now ... the job has got so intense and personalised' (1996). Although such changes had taken place in this area of work and elsewhere, there was not always a recognition that for many workers it was seen as a job where there had been an intensification of work in an increasingly pressured area of employment.

The changes that took place in social services were part of a wider framework of change within local government and the public sector more broadly. Clearly, there was a general pattern of change taking place in the content of jobs, but it was also the case that the direction of these changes was underwritten by government policy and legislative changes to the nature and character of managerial and employee relations in this sector.

Unions in Metropolitan Council

Before 1 July 1996, six branches organized in Metropolitan Council, five ex-NUPE branches and one ex-NALGO branch. Three of the six UNISON branches represented staff in social services and related areas, comprising a section of the former NALGO branch, covering the whole of the authority, and two specialist NUPE branches, one dealing with social services and the other with homecare. In 1995, all six branches became embroiled in a long drawn out and contentious debate over merger, partly reflecting political divisions within the leaderships, with a neo-Trotskyist-led leadership in the ex-NALGO branch arguing for union-wide constituencies in the name of democratic accountability, but also as a way of securing political dominance over the branch, since no other group organized across the full range of departments. The other more moderate branches argued for the retention of a sectional organization based on occupational functions, such as homecare. In 1996, the branches merged to form a single UNISON branch, although the previous branch leaderships remained responsible for their areas of negotiation and representation.

The three main branches in social services were organized as follows. The city-wide ex-NALGO branch (City Branch) had a membership of just over 8,000 in 1993 (of which approximately 1,000 were retired members), out of a potential membership of 18,000. Over 60 per cent of the membership were women, and although there was a sizeable ethnic minority membership, the actual proportion was unknown. The senior branch leadership claimed that sixty or seventy members were activists, in the sense that they participated in union activities, and took the initiative in developing a sense of unionism among the membership. Nevertheless, this was a difficult branch to organize, since it covered well over 1,500 separate workplaces, across all departments. To address the problems of organization that resulted from this membership distribution, the branch had developed a comprehensive department-based representational structure, particularly in social services and housing. These sections were led by department convenors and a steward-based form of representation.

The aim of the branch leadership was to 'organize from the bottom up': from workplace stewards via department-based steward representative structures to a city-wide executive. The aim was 'to have a steward in every workplace', although in practice there were many workplaces in the city which remained under-represented. However, where a department-based steward structure was developed, there was a platform for relatively autonomous organization within the branch. In the case of social services, the stewards were organized on a department basis, with chief steward and deputy, elected by the membership at the annual department meeting, responsible for day-to-day activity in the department and negotiations. More generally, departments were represented on the executive on a proportional basis, following elections at the department annual general meeting. In practice these representatives generally included the chief steward. This was a membership-based structure, organized by departments.

The branch executive, elected by the membership at the annual general meeting, contained seventy-two members, and an officer group of seventeen.

The two key officers were: the branch secretary responsible for the work of the executive, dealing with administration, the formulation and implementation of policy, as well as the politics of the union; and the branch secretary responsible for service conditions, who worked to the branch service conditions committee. This committee contained approximately thirty stewards (usually the senior stewards), two per department (at least one woman) and the branch officers. The committee dealt with council policy on service conditions, city-wide negotiations and representation on the joint trade union side.

The result was a dual structure of representation, the first based on a steward form of representation within departments, such as social services, and the second based on the idea that an accountable executive should be based on the mass membership meeting (of 18,000!). Where a department was well organized, with an effective representative structure, as in social services, there was a pattern of representation and accountability, from the membership to the senior representative areas. However, in the smaller, less well organized areas this pattern of representation was not as clear cut, although activists within these departments were able to play a part in the broader city-wide structures, if elected at the annual general meeting to the branch executive or as an officer. As a result, there was a disjuncture in the branch between the principles of mass membership representation and department-based forms of representation.

In contrast, the Homecare Branch was a specialist occupational branch, representing homecare workers in the city. The branch had a membership of some 1,800 out of a potential membership of 2,200. Nearly all the members were employed on a part-time basis (80 per cent) and most were women (90–95 per cent). The branch membership was ethnically very mixed, with members of Vietnamese, Afro-Caribbean, Asian, Irish and English ancestry. While the leadership identified no more than twelve to sixteen members as activists (the steward committee), the members were diligent in attending branch meetings and remaining in contact with the leadership, despite the fact that most workers seldom met other staff, including supervisors, in the course of their work. The pattern of work and employment was characterized by a high degree of worker anonymity and isolation.

In order to understand the patterns of representation in the branch it is necessary to appreciate the particular circumstances of work and employment in the homecare area, as low-paid and mostly part-time. Most of the members worked from home, with little direct contact with each other or with supervisors. Since 1988, new contracts had been in force, ensuring 'flexibility', so that many members worked two hours in the morning and two hours in the evening. The split shifts and the nature of the work meant that these members had to travel considerable distances, often on a decaying public transport system, to and from their places of work in private residences. Many of the homecarers dealt with up to ten calls a day and the mobile carers as many as seventeen calls a day.

The branch members faced an intensification of work, coupled with a managerial approach aimed at ending the old contracts, which specified fixed hours of work and guaranteed bus fares and mileage allowances to and from work, unlike the new contracts. With half the workforce on the old contracts, individual managers challenged these arrangements by withdrawing the travel allowance for their section of the workforce and reinstating it when the union leadership formally complained. As the branch secretary stated:

> It has really gone on in the last few years because of the intensity of the job.
> . . . Some of these managers, I am being honest, they are bastards. They
> are. . . . Hospitals are closing, and old people's homes are closing. They
> [management] are putting them back into the community so this is where
> we are getting more intense work. I mean 'Close that home. We'll put them
> into the community. The home cares will see to them'. (1996)

For the branch secretary these were endemic problems and issues by the mid-1990s, and much of her time was spent receiving complaints from members about these arrangements and arguing with management about the retention of the old contracts. In this she was assisted by the regional full-time official responsible for the branch, who also made representations to the social services management and the councillors on the social services committee.

Branch representation focused on the two lead officers, the secretary and chairperson, both of whom were on full secondment: because of her contract of employment the secretary was only paid for twenty hours a week, although she was a full-time union officer. The branch had an inner-city office, used by the secretary and chairperson. While the office was formally accessible and available to members, because of the work patterns of members and costs of public transport much of the branch business was conducted over the tele-phone, from the officers' houses, at any time from 6.30 a.m. to 11.00 p.m., as well as on weekends and public holidays. It is in this rather unusual way that branch life and activity for the members had been established and main-tained.

In addition to the two senior officers of the branch, there were fifteen steward positions, although only twelve were in post. Each steward represented at least one of fourteen geographical areas across the city and there was also a steward for the night watch staff. Two of the twelve stewards were male (one of Asian ancestry). The stewards met once a month with the senior branch officers, in a council meeting room. In practice, the stewards dealt with members' queries and concerns, often by telephone, although this tended to be somewhat *ad hoc* because of the work situation of both stewards and members. As a result, the queries and concerns of branch members focused on the two senior officers.

The branch had been relatively effective in building up a sense of branch life and activity. This was reflected in the degree of contact between the officers and members, the range of cases taken up and the attendance at meetings. This last point is illustrated by the attendance at the annual general meeting, usually held on a Saturday afternoon, and attracting just under 200 members on average. It was clear that without the enthusiasm and the activity of the senior officers and the area stewards, the branch would have been relatively moribund, not because of membership lack of interest, but because the circumstances of employment in this area of local government life created particular difficulties and potential obstacles to union activity.

The branch leadership had a close and accessible relationship with the full-time officer assigned to the branch. This regional officer often drew the attention of the branch leadership to wider developments that were taking place in the city, and without such support, there was a possibility that the branch leadership, understandably, would have become immersed in the particularities of homecare work and would not have seen the broader pattern of developments. The contracts of employment that had been imposed on homecarers were not unusual, although the impact within the homecare area had been particularly sharp. However, this broader context of change was not always acknowledged by the branch leaders, who of necessity dealt with the consequences of change in their areas of responsibility.

The third branch, Social Services Branch, comprised 3,000 members out of a potential 6,000. Members in this branch worked in social services, mainly as manual workers, although for historical reasons related to disquiet with NALGO, a significant number of members worked in the administration, professional, technical and clerical grades. While the vast majority of members were employed by the authority, a small number worked in the voluntary and private sectors. The majority of the members were full-time, although there was a growing part-time membership, and an increase in casual employment. The job categories covered by the branch included domestics, care assistants, cooks, social workers, children's home workers and managers and residential home workers. There were a large number of part-time and casual workers, although not a majority.

The branch was organized on the basis of a branch executive, comprising sixteen members. There were also eleven senior steward positions, and they were entitled to attend the branch executive meetings. In addition, some stewards doubled up as branch officers. A number of the officers had facility time: the secretary (100 per cent), the chairperson (50 per cent), the vice chairperson (two days currently shared by two people) and the community care officer (two days). This last position was created to deal with the changes occasioned by legislation and council policy in the care field. The steward structure was defined partly by function and partly by geography. Hence there was a senior steward for the children's homes. However, because of the issues that had arisen in the elderly care area and the restructuring that had taken place, particularly around privatization proposals, there were two senior stewards for this section, one for the north of the city and one for the south. There were also four senior stewards for the fieldwork areas, covering social work and related occupations. The point about this arrangement was that the branch was prepared to be flexible about the numbers of senior stewards in post, and was prepared to recognize more if the workload was thought to warrant it.

Underpinning the representative structures, the branch had an activist base of about a dozen who came into the branch office, helped with the routine of branch business and attended meetings. According to the branch secretary:

> Activists are people who I see mainly. People who actually bother to come to this office, who actually want to try and get involved, who help out with the mundane 'stuffing of envelope tasks' to actually going out and representing people at disciplinaries. If you broaden that out I suppose it's still not many. Some people I don't see at all but who do the business. Example – we've got a welfare officer who never comes to any meetings. We never meet her here but I pass all the welfare work on to her and she does it and I have never had any complaints and there's quite a lot of work involved in that. (1996)

Thus, there was a range of commitment in the branch: some worked closely with the branch officers; others were probably equally active, working with members in supportive ways, although they were not particularly visible.

Branch activity was organized around a series of overlapping and sequential meetings. The branch held monthly members' meetings and monthly branch committee meetings, attended by the officers and senior stewards and open to others. In practice, very few members attended the members' meeting, at most a dozen, apart from the general meeting, where attendance was larger but still in tens rather than hundreds. The attendance at the officer committee meetings was on average about half the eligible members, although this was attributed to the difficulty of organizing time to attend meetings when shift work was so prevalent in the branch.

Meeting the challenge of management

The local authority was one of the larger metropolitan authorities in the country. It had long been dominated by the Labour Party, acquiring a reputation for relatively conservative politics, although there was variation in approach between different sections of the authority. In the early 1980s the Conservative group on the council gained power, and cancelled check-off for the NALGO membership, resulting in a major haemorrhage of membership. It was only in the mid-1990s that the branch began to move back towards the levels before check-off was cancelled: to 8,000 members, still well below the 50 per cent mark.

During the 1980s and early 1990s, the local authority was caught up in the problems associated with fixed budget grants and had to deal with cuts and financial restrictions. These policies were the occasion of bitter disputes between the unions and the council, with union opposition led by the ex-NALGO branch, supported by the two social service area NUPE branches. In addition, the manual workforce was subjected to the compulsory competitive tendering (CCT) programme, with some externalization, although not on the scale found elsewhere. One of the consequences of this differentiation was that there was a view among the NUPE/UNISON leaderships that the non-manual workers did not appreciate the magnitude and impact of the restructuring that was taking place in local government. This lack of understanding, they felt, led to rather principled but unsustainable opposition to the restructuring, resulting in occasional hardship and inequity for manual workers as they bore the brunt of a rather conservative compliance with government policy.

The restructuring that took place, partly arising from government requirements and partly from the council's own programmes, such as moves towards neighbourhood offices in the housing department, had an impact on the UNISON branches. These branches had been caught up in negotiations and lobbying about the proposed budget cuts, year in, year out. Some branches were affected more than others, so that the Social Services Branch had to negotiate over proposed redundancies, as well as the down-grading and redeployment of staff, following an externalization programme for the residential homes for the elderly. There were persistent worries about the impact of legislation, particularly in the community care area, as well as in relation to CCT. These initiatives created persistent problems for the ex-NUPE branches, and members in these branches were involved in a series of campaigns, and occasionally tendering activity, in relation to such proposals.

To meet these problems, the Social Services Branch leaders, along with those of the Homecare Branch and the social services section of the City Branch, had introduced a practice of joint stewards' meetings, aimed at sharing problems and developing common policy. This initiative began with the establishment of UNISON, and was seen as putting the principles of unity into practice, but it was acknowledged that while such meetings had been held, they were relatively infrequent. The branch leaders were also involved in working with the other UNISON branches in a range of meetings, with councillors and senior local authority officials. The leaders used these meetings to establish common approaches to the council, although in practice the meetings among the union leaders from the social service areas dealt with more substantive issues.

The problem was that in the case of the two smaller branches there were relatively few activists, indicated by the number of stewards and by participation and involvement in branch activity. Nevertheless, these two branches, and particularly the Homecare Branch, had developed a style and mode of operating that resulted in a relatively effective system of representation. In contrast, the City Branch had a comprehensive representative structure within the larger departments and on the basis of city-wide membership involvement, but in practice the attendance at membership meetings was minimal, and the department representative structures were not integrated into the branch executive in any direct way, except via the service conditions committee. In the debates in 1996 about merging the branches into one UNISON branch there was a dilemma between developing a city-wide branch with a membership-based representative structure, irrespective of department, or developing structures which formally integrated the department-based and other employer representative systems into a federal-type branch, based on sub-branches. In the event, a city-wide branch was agreed and put in place in 1996.

The regional office, the branches and management

The management approach to the unions in social services was one of calculated indifference. At the department level, negotiations with unions was led by the head of human resources for social services ('previously known as personnel manager'); for wider issues, the lead was taken by the local authority head of human resources. With devolution of the implementation of agreements to the authority, these levels of management were increasingly involved in a broader range of negotiations than had been the case in the past. In part as a response to these developments, and in part as a recognition that the unions were reorganizing so as to raise issues and questions, as well as to negotiate the implementation of national agreements at the local level, the management introduced more formalized arrangements at a department level. There was a managerial instruction that at least one of the deputy directors should always attend the department joint consultative committee (JCC), as well as other senior managers 'in sufficient numbers to show the unions that we need to take the JCC seriously and use it productively' (Senior manager, 1992).

Such developments were part of a broader pattern of managerial recomposition that was taking place in social services, with local managers taking on more and more responsibility. These changes were very much ongoing and part of the fluctuating 'frontier of control' in local government. As a senior manager commented:

> you have more locally responsive services, the closer the decision maker is to the customer. That's the theory. Where we've got to do the work is getting the budgets devolved with the power and responsibility and we think we have done it up to a certain extent. We've got cost centre management for a considerable number of managers but not yet for all managers. Well I think it is having a good impact in the sense that managers welcome the opportunity to make more decisions, have more discretion, more responsibility. (1992)

In other words, the department management, at all levels, increasingly had authority to exercise responsibility over work and employment questions, and the negotiating arrangements had been adapted accordingly.

As a consequence, the regional union office began to reorganize to establish a more formal relationship with both management and the union branches, so as to provide a platform for a more coordinated and perhaps controlled union response to managerial initiatives. There were three officers responsible for the city branches, and they recognized the increasing importance of a coordinated and planned officer approach to the city management. The senior regional officer introduced the practice of regular 'team' meetings composed of the three officials to review work in progress, identify issues and problems and plan responses. In the context of the past autonomy of regional officials in this union office, this was a rather novel and cooperative development.

However, there remained strict limits to the involvement of regional officers in union branch activity. Partly reflecting the different trade union traditions of each branch, the ex-NUPE branches continued to maintain close working relations with the regional officials, while the ex-NALGO union branch maintained a distanced relationship from the regional officers (although they were a city block apart). More importantly, as the managerial recomposition proceeded, lay leaders in all social service branches increasingly dealt with local managers directly and as part of the steward and related representative structures in each branch. This development provided these lay leaders and activists with the platforms that either maintained a distance from the regional officials or promoted increased local activity within the branches, with the by-product that local leaders often developed more proactive approaches to the regional officials than had been the case in the past (an aspect that was welcomed by these particular officials). In this respect the structural disengagement that was evident between national union officials and local leaders was replicated, in part and in a more complicated way, at the regional level. Each level of the union had separate spheres of responsibility, and relations between the department lay leadership and the regional officials were worked out accordingly.

The difficulty came when local managers attempted to side-step the lay leadership in these branches and deal directly with the regional officials. The onus was then on the regional officers to resist the temptation to deal directly with the managers, with little or only formal reference to the lay members and their leaders. This was a matter of principle and consciousness rather than a necessity, rooted in notions of accountability and control. As a regional officer stated, 'I won't go in above people's heads and I won't subvert the role of the lay officials, not at all, never ever. There is no reason for me to do that and I won't do it' (1996). But the sting in the tail was also acknowledged: 'Having said that if I want to progress matters, if I want to handle things in a proactive way then I would feel free to take, to raise those issues with the appropriate branch not just wait for those things to come to me' (Regional officer, Metropolitan Council, 1996). Thus it was a tenuous relation and stance, which very much relied on the approach and attitudes of the regional officers concerned.

The city had a complex range of formal and informal negotiating arrangements, involving the UNISON members as well as other trade unions represented in the city. To coordinate branch responses and approaches to the city, the UNISON branches, on the instigation of the regional office, established a UNISON liaison forum. These meetings were attended by representatives of all branches and the full-time regional officers. At these meetings, in practice often pre-meetings before more formal discussions with councillors and senior council staff, a common approach was worked out, or areas of disagreement were flagged up so that the union side was prepared for the negotiations with the council. Obviously such meetings were important when the council was preparing and presenting the budget arrangements for the coming year. The budget was preceded by formal presentations and informal discussions about the proposed plans. These were very much part of the overall negotiating process in the city, since these formal and informal occasions were used by the council to indicate where financial cuts might fall and the implications for council staff, while the union representatives clearly indicated possible responses. These arrangements were formalized via a trade union forum in the city and associated committees.

Within social services, there was a view among management that the lay leaders were not serious about engaging with managers over the reorganization that was taking place. It is this that may explain why local managers continued to look to the regional office as the source of reliable consistency:

> They [the unions] have obviously been in discussion about reorganisation but that is at what I would consider to be a superficial level. The unions have tended to go for the status quo on the whole, I think, because they don't get deeply involved in some of the issues because then they would have to take more responsibility for them, do you know what I mean? So they are not in deep, some of them are tokenistic. (Senior manager, 1992)

The complaint was that the union leaders were simply concerned to 'protect numbers of jobs, ensure no compulsory redundancies' (Senior manager, 1992).

From the union leaders' point of view, the managers used the opportunity of reorganization to redefine and substantively to diminish service provision in the area of social services, with closures of facilities and the redefinition and dilution of social service jobs. This view was affirmed in a graphic way by a set of tortuous negotiations in 1992 and 1993 over access to emergency social service support. The situation was that the management wanted to end general social service admission teams, comprised of a range of qualified staff who would deal with and assess all admissions, and then pass them on to specialists, with retrained administrative staff who would conduct the preliminary assessments and refer the case immediately on to specialist staff. For management this was cast in terms of ensuring 'that the public has direct access to the specialist services as soon as possible' (Senior manager, 1992). For the local unions it was job dilution: 'New referrals would be dealt with by what they call an access response team, essentially consisting of re-graded admin. workers and they would deal with all incoming referrals and make a decision whether a referral was an emergency' (Branch secretary, 1992).

Of course, it was more than these comments suggest. For management it was also about funding and salary levels. In the context of budget restrictions, including the non-filling of 10 per cent of jobs in the council as a whole, and filling only twenty-five of 138 jobs allocated to deal with the implications of the legislative changes in social services, these were compelling factors. For the union this was about not only job protection but also the quality of service provision. As such issues arose, the lay leaders of the unions were involved in a range of negotiations about staffing, individual grievances, pay levels and allowances, as well as the quality and objectives of service provision in a relatively beleaguered area of public sector employment. It was in this context that the lay leaders in each of these branches sought to develop union approaches that enabled them to address the widening raft of issues in local government.

Assessment

In Metropolitan Council, UNISON, as the pre-eminent local government union, faced an uncertain future in which different models of unionism were invoked and contested. On the one hand, there was an argument for the further development of executive-led steward structures, where the basis of union representation and participation was rooted in the negotiating and bargaining structures of local government in the authority. In this respect, there was formal acknowledgement of the occupational and functional basis of union activity and membership involvement in union activity, so that the healthcare workers, for example, constituted a relatively cohesive section of the workforce and had built their unionism on this recognition. On the other hand, it was argued by the activists within the City Branch that the strength of the union lay in developing a membership-based form of representation and organization for the membership as a whole. They argued for a redefinition of the boundaries of unionism, addressing economistic questions as well as policy and political direction at both local and national levels. Rather than looking to the regional office for support and sustenance, the strength of unionism at a local level lay in the articulation of a clear and focused political agenda.

The evidence suggests that the union structures and consultative arrangements, both within the departments and across the authority more widely, underwrote the centrality of the chief stewards and branch officers for negotiation and representation. In part, this was because these arrangements suited the department managements as well as the councillors, and reflected the way the unions organized and operated in at least two respects. First, the union branches had long organized at the authority-wide level, with relatively little attention given to the workplace or local level of union activity. However, with restructuring and the decentralization of managerial responsibilities, there was pressure on union leaders to encourage the development of local organization and activity. Second, the leaders in these branches were uncertain how best to involve dispersed, fragmented and often isolated members in branch activity. This was seen as a problem of consciousness – members do not want to be involved – as well as an organizational problem, given the nature and character of work and employment in these areas.

The problem with a union form of organization that was rooted in bargaining and negotiating structures was that it could result in overlooking the broader pattern of developments promoted by the authority as a whole. Where this was recognized, there was scope for a critical left political leadership to promote an outward-looking analysis of local state policy that questioned the context and focus of bargaining and negotiations. In this respect, this is an attempt to situate trade unionism in the broader context of political developments at the local and national state levels. Within the context of the local state, it involves promoting inter-union workplace activity across the authority as a whole. At a more prosaic level, it also involves affirming the political influence of organized and cohesive political groups, able to speak on behalf of both active and quiescent memberships.

In a variety of ways, these different aspects of unionism were evident in Metropolitan Council. The outcome was a sharp debate between the branch leaderships, covering the social services union memberships, in the lead-up to merger of the branches in 1996. The two ex-NUPE branches, organized as executive-led branches, successfully advocated the continued recognition of the negotiating structures, as the basis for union representation in the areas they covered. In conjunction with the social services shop steward organization within the ex-NALGO branch, these arrangements were maintained within the new city-wide branch established in 1996. While the establishment of the city-wide branch and the rejection of a proposal to establish sub-branches for social services and the like was seen by many participants as a victory for the former leadership of the ex-NALGO branch, it was a somewhat Pyrrhic accomplishment. Membership involvement continued to be via the functional negotiating structures and associated forms of representation, and the city-wide leadership remained disconnected from the nitty gritty of membership participation and involvement at a workplace level.

At the same time, the regional office had taken steps to establish a more integrated form of organization than had previously been the case. The creation of team-based forms of organization was part of an attempt to organize the regional office so as to address the reorganization of senior management and the articulation of authority-wide policy more effectively. However, there remained a disjunction between the regional office and the city-wide elected union leadership, as the regional officers sought to deal directly with the authority management on the basis of the negotiating arrangements for different functions and to counter the rhetoric of the political groups which dominated the ex-NALGO branch. The outcome was a perpetuation of the persistent disengagement between the two levels of union organization, despite attempts by regional officers to establish the basis for more cooperative relations between them. For the regional officers the problem was 'politics', and for the left political activists it was the urge for full-time officials to 'control' the membership. More importantly, the roots of the tension between the two levels of organization lay in the structural disengagement between the two areas of union organization and activity.

The point to note in the relations that defined the different levels and areas of union activity is that senior management, supported by councillors, set the scene for union organization and activity on the authority. This was a management that promoted the decentralization of operational and budgetary control as a way of by-passing an uncooperative union leadership. In the name of statutory compliance, management initiated reorganization and recomposition of social services and other areas of local state work. The focus on department-based structures was promoted by senior management and the branch leaderships either located themselves wholly within these arrangements or attempted to transcend the specific and focus union activity at a city-wide level. In both cases these were limited strategies.

It was in the circumstances of organizing on a departmental basis that the local leaderships laid the foundation for more actively involved forms of unionism, based on the specific developments taking place in each department. In all the branches there had been a slow development of workplace steward forms of representation and activism. Clearly, these initiatives took time to embed within the structures of unionism in the authority. It was not easy or straightforward to develop the union arrangements and practices that would enable the membership to confront the developments taking place in local government. Not only did leaders have to wrestle with past practice, but their political analysis was not always rooted in the complexity of social relations in and against the state, and, indeed, in and against the union as a political organization. It was out of these sets of concerns that these unions took steps to renew their concerns and forms of organization and activity.

PUBLIC SERVICES

In local government, unions face major challenges, with a profound questioning of the traditions and history of centralized national forms of unionism. These old forms of unionism no longer suffice, and previously confident and controlling local leaders have been forced to examine their past practices and to consider how to organize anew, or face a seemingly irreversible decline. Such a reappraisal has not been and will not be easy, but there is a prospect of success with unions beginning to renew themselves locally, with consequences for the way unions organize both regionally and nationally. It is in this respect that the developments within the local state are a harbinger of the future, indicating the possibility of further decline or the prospect of renewal.

UNIONS AT WORK

The restructuring of the state sector over the past two decades has transformed work and employment relations in this area in distinctive ways. This process of change involved both the redrawing of state boundaries, via privatization, including the various forms of contracting-out and out-sourcing that have come to characterize these areas of state activity, and the managerial recomposition and institutional fragmentation of the state as employer. These changes were part of a repositioning of the state within the economy and had major implications for work and employment relations in the state sector.

While there was a common pattern to the restructuring in different areas of the state, there were distinctions evident between the civil service and local government, partly reflecting the different traditions, forms of organization and histories. In the case of the civil service the process of restructuring began with a recomposition of managerial hierarchies, which involved the devolution of operational responsibilities and the recentralization of budgetary control and financial management. This was followed by the institutional fragmentation of the civil service with the establishment of agencies (or their equivalents) in the 1990s. In contrast, the restructuring of local government was more seamless, involving the maturation of managerial forms of organization begun in the 1970s and extended to include comprehensive programmes of out-sourcing and reorganization of employment relations. The outcome was a transformed form of state employment characterized by the increased predominance of 'managerial' control and organization of labour in this sector.

The recomposition of the public sector brought into question past managerial and employment practices. One thread running through these developments was the emergence and development of decentralized forms of local management, qualifying the previously centralized forms of organization and operation in the public sector. With increased financial and operational accountability at lower levels of management, there was a comprehensive move to create 'new' management structures and to recompose managerial hierarchies. One consequence of these changes was that the relations between state managers and state workforces became more transparent, indicating the changing nature of class relations in this sector. Increasingly state managers looked at proposals aimed at deploying their workforces in conformity with budgets and a perception of customer requirements. However, these developments were qualified in key respects, in that the remaining public sector was still required to organize so as to meet legislative requirements relating to public service provision in the community.

The impact on state workforces was profound. Overall there has been an intensification of work and employment practices, as staff faced changing and increased demands on their time. In the case of local government these developments took place as part of the process of compulsory competitive tendering and related practices. Equivalent, although more diverse, changes took place in the civil service, although the outcome was the same. Alongside these developments, the standardized forms of employment in the civil service were qualified with the establishment of agency forms of management and employment. As indicated, there is evidence of work intensification in these areas of employment, increased stress levels and a decline in staff morale, not dissimilar to the developments in the privatized utilities.

The broad restructuring of the public sector has stimulated a re-examination of the way that unions in this sector organize and operate. The formerly centralized unions have had to deal with the detail and implications of the decentralization of managerial structures and the consequences of the process of depoliticization that is under way in this sector. Increasingly, these unions are dealing with state managers, who have the authority and discretion to deal directly with their workforces. In this respect, there is a decisive change in relations between these unions and the state management, in that they no longer deal directly with governments, even as a last resort, on the determination of the terms and conditions of employment in this sector. While this is not to suggest that governments are no longer a feature of the complex of relations between state unions and state managers, it is to acknowledge that these relations are now more attenuated than they were in the past.

As part of the restructuring of state work and employment relations, the recomposition of managerial hierarchies has involved a decentralization of managerial decision-making and policy formulation. In this respect, these centralized unions have faced a situation where the decisions that have a bearing on work and employment are no longer made at a national level but are worked out in a variety of complicated ways both locally and nationally. As a result, there has been increased scope and possibility for local union groups to address and develop locally focused negotiations and bargaining arrangements. Such developments have provided these union memberships with the platform for a refocusing and reorientation of union organization and activity. While these developments were varied and uneven, they occurred in a context where there had been little opportunity for local leaders and activists to develop their trade unionism within the broader structures of these trade unions. With the developments of the past two decades, such opportunities became apparent.

With the restructuring of the civil service, bargaining and negotiating arrangements were changed by management. The past certainties and pre-dictabilities of the Whitley form of negotiation ended, and unions found themselves in more complicated and adversarial relations with managements. These managements no longer act as immediate mouthpieces for the govern-ment of the day, since there has been a distancing by governments from direct responsibility and accountability for the operational activity of state bodies. Increasingly, there is a sense in which managers bargain with trade union representatives over the particular terms and conditions of employment, agency by agency. However, there was only a limited discretion available to these managements, as the agencies remained under the rubric of the public sector, subject to the indirect mechanisms of control indicated by business plans, financial regulation and the provision of service.

At one level, the depoliticization and decentralization of managerial struc-tures in this sector provided the opportunity for these locally based union groups not only to reorient the embryonic forms of workplace unionism that had been promoted in the preceding decade but also to build the representa-tive structures of such organization. The impetus for this was provided by the managerial restructuring that took place, but the focus and detail came with the experience gained by the local leaders and activists in these workplaces. In this respect, it was striking that these developments did not take place with the active support and encouragement of the wider trade union; indeed, the fragility of the developments was underwritten by the lack of connection between change at a workplace level and the disengagement of the national unions from these developments.

In the case of local government, the historical focus of negotiations at an authority level served to sustain a centralized union structure where the branch officers played their part as key actors in the process of union representation in relation to local authorities. This was the principal point of contact between union representatives and managerial staff. Such an involvement meant that these officials were likely to acquire the expertise, the experience and the familiarity to represent and negotiate on behalf of their membership with management. The other side of these procedures was that there were strong inhibitions on the emergence of actively involved and participative member-ships, partly because of the scale and scope of local authority employment as well as the relative absence of local bargaining forums. None the less, there has been a relatively long recognition by local leaderships and national activists in these unions of the importance of locally based representative structures, and there have been attempts by unions to establish such structures.

The shift in bargaining and negotiating arrangements has been from the level of the local authority to that of the department. Both manual and non-manual unions have long organized as relatively centralized and hierarchical bodies so as to connect with the local authority bargaining structures. One consequence of this has been that these unions had relatively ineffective steward structures representing the specific concerns of members on either a geographical or functional basis. With the shift towards decentralized bargaining arrangements, following on from budgetary and financial decentralization to the departments, these unions have attempted to follow suit and develop departmental and locally based forms of representation. In doing this, these union groups put in place a process of change which has involved a more integrated and planned approach by local leaders and regional officials in their relations to local government managers and officials, as well as a more secure base for workplace-focused organization and activity. Such developments are at the beginning and have been complicated by the merger of the two major local government unions, NALGO and NUPE, but it can be expected that these trends are likely to continue and be developed in due course.

At a general level, a complicated process of union reorganization has been taking place in this sector, from a form of unionism where centralized effectiveness prevailed and predominated to one where there was the possibility of more participative and involved forms of unionism emerging. In the past, these unions had addressed the diversity of membership circumstance by centralized bargaining and representation, which did not place a premium on member involvement and activity. With the restructuring of the public sector, unions in this sector faced a different range of possibilities. Such developments provided the platform for a process of union reorganization and renewal, although this was not a straightforward process, nor one without contention and debate.

PART V
THE POLITICS OF WORKPLACE
TRADE UNIONISM

14 DILEMMAS AND PROSPECTS: THE FUTURE FOR TRADE UNIONS

The recent history of trade unionism in advanced capitalist countries has stimulated debate about the nature of the problems faced by unions and their responses (Hyman, 1994; Johnston, 1994; Kelly, 1997; McIlroy, 1997; Boxall and Haynes, 1997; Bronfenbrenner *et al.*, 1998; Peetz, 1998). One strand of argument emphasized the importance of centralized union structures, in the course of which there is an undervaluation of the importance of locally based trade unionism (Willman *et al.*, 1993; Undy *et al.*, 1996; Heery, 1998a). Complementing this account, a second strand of argument holds that trade unions can no longer rely on the Labour Party in office to provide the conditions for a return to political prominence (McIlroy, 1995, pp. 408–14, 417–21; 1997, pp. 121–2). The future is clear: it is to emphasize the importance of centralized, effective trade union organization, achieving a fruitful and productive balance between active workplace trade unionism and forward-thinking centralized leaderships (Terry, 1996; McIlroy, 1997). In contrast, Gallie *et al.* (1996) argue that the situation is more stable than suggested at first sight, that while unions have faced difficulties, at a workplace level there remains a relatively secure membership base, still attracted to unions. It is this factor and the compliance of employers that continue to sustain unions, rather than positive initiatives by union leaderships and representatives.

Faced with a hostile climate at all levels, trade unions, both individually and as part of the TUC, have attempted to respond positively. Union modernization has come to the forefront of trade union concerns (Williams, 1997; Heery, 1998b). A number of activities have been proposed, ranging from the promotion of union services to members to the employment of trained organizers, not only to recruit members but also to develop union structures and representative practices. As part of these developments, individual unions, as well as the TUC, have looked elsewhere at competing models of union organization and practice, particularly the United States of America, Australia and the

Netherlands. These initiatives have been part of debates about the precise form of trade unionism that should be encouraged and developed, usually presented in terms of a contrast between the service model of organization and one that emphasizes organization (Bronfenbrenner *et al.*, 1998).

The argument here is that the choice facing union memberships is between a form of trade unionism that accommodates to employer policies, including those of governments, and one that poses a more direct challenge to such policies and strategies. The first is likely to entail further sophistication in the development of bureaucratically effective forms of trade unionism, whereas in the second case workplace-based union structures are likely to become more prominent. In either case, trade unionism will continue to display a tension between pressures towards bureaucracy and those towards democracy. More recently, the argument has been advanced that a strong organizational base, including active workplace memberships, provides the basis for successful engagement in social partnership policies and practices between trade unions and employers (Boxall and Haynes, 1997; Heery, 1998b). However, the weakness in these accounts is the failure to acknowledge that collective organization requires integrated and mutually reciprocal relations at all levels of the union; otherwise this form of organization is predicated on the possibility of structural disengagement (Foster and Scott, 1998a, pp. 139–40, 146). It is the construction and reconstruction of the collective identity and practice that distinguishes the union form of organization and operation. The realization of this objective is not an easy task, and the dilemmas arising from these tensions will be the key issues for unionists into the next century.

Patterns of organization and representation

Twenty years of restructuring highlight different trends and patterns in union responses. On the one hand, restructuring in manufacturing has generally been met by a reaffirmation of an economistic remit. Unions have been concerned to address issues and problems within the workplace, rather than to look to the complex of relations that underpin the patterns and forms of economic restructuring. Even where government policies can be seen to be detrimental to specific industries, such as the automobile industry, union memberships have tended to pursue a narrow range of policies and concerns, although national leaders have often been engaged in lobbying against such policies. On the other hand, unions in the public services and utilities, particularly during the privatization periods, have addressed state policies more directly and explicitly. While the latter development opens up opportunities for unions to broaden their remit beyond narrow economism, it does not necessarily mean that this breadth will be maintained. However, forging workplace union practices in these conditions may increase the likelihood that unions will be able to maintain this spectrum of concerns.

Manufacturing

Trade unionism in manufacturing has a relatively long and active history. In particular, there has been a history of active workplace trade unionism which in the 1960s was regarded as vigorously exemplifying many of the developments that had come to characterize British industrial relations (Terry and Edwards, 1988). This model of workplace trade unionism, based principally on the engineering industry, owed much to the traditions and patterns of trade unionism and industrial relations in the West Midlands. It is a model where the focus of union activity was the workplace, usually based on shop steward committees taking up the immediate concerns and grievances of union members and attempting to represent the members' collective interests to managements. This means, however, that for many union memberships there was no necessary correspondence between union branch activity and trade unionism at the workplace; the steward committee is factory or site based, whereas union branch organization was geographically organized, involving stewards from many workplaces in the area.

The research presented here supports the proposition that the forms of worker organization are rooted in a complex interplay between work and employment relations on the one hand, and bargaining relationships on the other. The restructuring of the manufacturing sector in the West Midlands was achieved by and large via collective bargaining. Trade unions bargained over change, from the physical reconstruction of workplaces, accompanied by moves to reorganize work procedures and related arrangements, to the more mundane and incremental change that has occurred in many engineering factories. While occasionally this has been associated with the demise of trade unionism (occurring in one case study plant), elsewhere the union committees sought to address change in relatively traditional ways, giving limited attention to their forms of organization. Such patterns of trade unionism were found to develop towards either bureaucratic or democratic forms, with features in each set of arrangements making one form of organization more likely than the other.

The trade unions based in the manufacturing sector tended to cover one or a few workplaces. Whether manual or non-manual, they were organized on the basis of shop steward or workplace steward structures. In this respect, the prevailing form of workplace organization was built around the sectional steward, representing a shop or work group within the workplace and sitting as a member of a steward committee which decided union policies and practices for that site. The trade union representatives were able to maintain their networks of support despite the trends towards managerial advantage and control. Moreover, the issues addressed by these unions continued to be those they had long addressed: pay, discipline, redundancy, leave arrangements and the organization of work. It was noteworthy that these union groups tended to ignore questions relating to state policies and practices, and very few people (often only two or three) played an active part in their union's policy-making forums. Thus, while existing forms of workplace organization and operation were maintained, there was very little indication of a broadening or a redefinition of trade unionism along the lines looked for by some commentators.

Over the past few years, trade unionism in these manufacturing plants developed in uneven ways. To illustrate, the *Electronics Factory* union membership pursued a policy of self-contained accommodative bargaining so as to secure their futures as further restructuring was planned and implemented. In the case of unions at *Telecommunications Factory*, a similar policy was elaborated, but by the mid-1990s the unions at this factory were shadows of their past selves. The paradoxical feature was that although the main workplace union leadership had been assiduous in cultivating links with outside union leaderships, via the combine committee, their actions actually confirmed the distance between the membership and the leadership at the factory. In the context of the massive restructuring that took place at the two factories it was very difficult for the memberships to maintain a presence within their factories and simultaneously to extend their presence beyond these factories. The result was a defensive accommodation between union leaderships and factory management, although these arrangements were qualified at *Electronics Factory*. Here the leadership of the principal union had pursued a policy of blurring the boundaries between work and home which put the union leaders in a stronger position to maintain and encourage an active presence within the factory.

The other two cases illustrate different patterns of trade unionism. In the case of the *Car Parts* manual union, a policy of centralized economistic bargaining was maintained and developed as the 1980s and 1990s proceeded. This resulted in a trade unionism that continued to play a part in influencing the direction and development of employment policy in the factory. In contrast, the manual unions at *Heating Factory* attempted to develop a more participative form of trade unionism during the 1980s, which was seen by the factory management as a challenge. After a series of bitter disputes in the second half of the 1980s, the union leadership was gradually drawn into local social partnership type arrangements, where management publicly advocated these arrangements and set the parameters of action and the union leadership felt obliged to comply with these initiatives. The result was a shadowy form of trade unionism where the leadership and the membership no longer questioned the factory management, at least on major issues.

Overall, there was evidence of tentative steps towards union renewal at these four factories, although it took a particular form. In the first place, the restructuring that occurred in this sector was in the context of corporate and managerial strategies on which unions had little purchase or influence. The decline of the manufacturing sector in the region had its roots in industry developments in the United Kingdom and, more generally, the internationalization of major corporations over the past twenty years. In this context, the form and direction of the restructuring within workplaces was driven by local managements within frameworks set elsewhere. As the union leaderships in these workplaces sought to maintain their presence in these beleaguered circumstances, their strategies were very much those of survival. These unions in the manufacturing sector were mostly organized on the basis of steward forms of representation and involvement. It was this form of organization that was maintained during this period and provided the bedrock for the continued presence of unions in the factories. The outcome was an accommodative form of trade unionism, where leaderships were prepared to work with the grain of managerial policy and direction. Although these arrangements did not preclude the emergence of more active and critical local leaderships, this did not happen in these factories in the first part of the 1990s (see Gall, 1998, p. 151). Even where union groups attempted to redefine the boundaries of trade unionism, it was within the parameters of a managerially defined restructuring that was still in progress.

Privatized utilities

With the advent of privatization policies, the centralized unions in this sector faced a challenge of some magnitude. The form of restructuring was set partly by the state (by dismantling and disaggregating the former state enterprises in the case of water, or by leaving them largely intact, as happened in the gas industry) and partly in the light of corporate decisions relating to the way these privatized enterprises pursued their interests. While, in principle, unions face a choice between accommodating to these changes or attempting to challenge them, in practice this choice is not clear-cut (Fairbrother and Waddington,

1990). The difficulty for the trade unions organizing in this sector was that at the time of privatization the prevailing form of trade unionism was highly centralized, with little evidence of active and engaged local union organization and representation. In this respect, this was a distinctive form of trade unionism when compared with unions in the manufacturing sector. While there was a prospect that when faced with major change and uncertainty about the future, union leaderships, both locally and nationally, would pursue accommodative policies, as a way of ensuring the continued presence of the trade unions in these industries, there was little evidence of this, particularly at a local level. If anything, there was an increased emphasis on developing more active and participative forms of trade unionism aimed at addressing the problems faced by workers in the post-privatization situation.

The traditional forms of trade unionism in this sector were characterized by centralization, remoteness and the representation of members' interests by experienced but relatively inaccessible leaders. In some unions, particularly in the manual sector, trade unionism was structured around the full-time officer, while in the non-manual unions senior lay officials played leading roles in local activity. With the changed terrain of work and employment, coupled with revised bargaining structures, a number of the union branches and committees began to reconsider the way they organized and operated. In general, the initiative for this came from the senior lay representatives or the full-time officers.

One feature of the pattern of union organization in *British Telecom* was the continued affirmation of stable and responsible forms of branch leadership for the main union, the CWU/NCU. Here senior branch officials acted on behalf of the union, where members played a limited active role in branch life and the officials represented the branch (rather than the members) in the negotiating structures and arrangements. However, the social relations of the branch were more complicated than this suggests, and the members were familiar to and in contact with the branch officers. They faced uncertainty about their futures, as the industry restructured and reorganized work procedures and arrangements, and they expressed their concerns to the officers. The problem was that these corporate initiatives were imposed from above, by senior executives, although implemented and put into practice by local managers. In this circumstance, the members were helpless and saw themselves as victims of remote and distant forces over which they had little control or influence. Faced with this type of managerial approach, the branch officers became the union at the local level and in this respect they experienced first hand the difficulties and problems of dealing with a transnational corporation. It was a form of organization encouraged by the national union leadership, who dealt directly with senior corporate staff and saw a 'professionalized' and responsible branch leadership, speaking on behalf of members and representing the branch at different levels of the corporate structure, as the most appropriate organizational response to the restructuring that was taking place.

Faced with a broadly similar pattern of privatization, the response by the local union leaderships in the gas industry, the former *British Gas*, was different. Initially, there was very little substantive change in the organization and operation of the corporation. Bargaining arrangements and personnel practices bequeathed from the period of state ownership were maintained with little change. Thus, until the early 1990s the base union groups in the industry, either branches or steward committees, tended to underwrite a relatively remote form of leadership, thereby reproducing the pattern of representation evident at the national level within the localities covered by the unions. However, with the moves towards forms of divisionalization and disaggregation of the newly established corporate entities that comprised the former *British Gas*, the unions began a process of reassessing the way they organized and operated within the privatized corporation. The spur for this was the prospect that the established form of union organization was out of step with the new bargaining arrangements and that there was the prospect that the local level of union organization would collapse. This assessment provided the opportunity for a process of reorganization where union groups began to build the basis for participation around the bargaining arrangements in the industry.

The contrast with the water industry was striking. Here the national structure of the industry was dismantled at the time of privatization and a number of autonomous regionally based corporations were established. For both management and the unions operating within the industry, this was a new and difficult situation. They had to establish and learn how to relate to each other over a complete range of bargained items and issues. In these circumstances the principal union, UNISON (formerly NALGO), pursued a policy of developing a steward-based representative structure, promoted locally, in the districts and at a regional (or corporate) level by the regional officials. The outcome was a form of representation rooted in the bargaining structure of the company, but capable of extending the definition of union organization and activity within the company and the union. To a limited extent, the local union groups in the water industry did this, in particular opening up discussions with the company about corporate policy and practice, as well as developing bargaining relationships with local managements at a district and office level.

The argument is that there was a pattern of leadership-led and leadership-focused union renewal in process in privatized companies, centred on a local

level of union organization (Fairbrother, 1994b). The roots of this development lay in the way in which local-level union leaderships attempted to
relocate themselves within these privatized companies, against the backdrop of
managerial restructuring and reorganization. Local committees in each of the
privatized companies studied took the initiative to reorganize and lay the
foundation for renewed forms of trade unionism at this level, centred in the
main on the established branch leaderships, since the national union responses generally failed to connect with their own immediate and pressing
concerns at a local level. While the aspirations of the local leaders were to
construct more participative forms of trade unionism, outcomes varied in
practice, depending on the managerial reorganization that was implemented
in each area and the negotiating structures that had been put into place. There
was thus a process of union renewal, centred on the authority acquired by local
leaders in their active participation and involvement in decentralized bargaining structures and arrangements. This was not a straightforward process; nor
was it confined to the local level. A complicated pattern of reorganization was
in process, involving localized forms of union organization as well as the
reconstruction, in uneven and varied ways, of relations between local union
groups and regional and national levels of these unions (see Foster and Scott,
1998a, pp. 140, 146).

To explain the diverse patterns that were evident, two sets of relations should
be considered. First, one patterning of relations was apparent, between the
non-manual unions, particularly NALGO (subsequently UNISON) in water,
which had taken the opportunity to reconstitute the union around lay power
bases, and the manual unions, illustrated by the GMB in the gas sector, which
had begun to reorganize around its senior area convenors. The problem was
that the previous forms of representation set the terms for renewal, by
extending an established lay representative system or a full-time officer-based
form of organization. Second, contrasting forms of lay representation also
structured the pattern of change. In the case of the NCU (subsequently the
CWU), with its relatively centralized form of national organization, the senior
lay branch officials effectively reproduced this form of representation at a
lower level. As they had been drawn into the newly established bargaining
arrangements of the divisionalized company they developed locally based but
centralized forms of representation. In contrast, the NALGO branches, with
their long traditions of lay representation and minimal full-time officer support, had begun to extend these patterns of lay representation in the new
circumstances of privatization. In these diverse ways privatization heralded the
beginnings of varied forms of union renewal in these seemingly unlikely
circumstances.

The public sector

Developments in the public sector were complicated. In the civil service, the formerly centralized unions faced increasingly decentralized managements. Unions in local government faced an increasingly fragmented managerial structure, raising organizational problems for unions used to negotiating and dealing with centralized local authorities. Both situations raised important questions for forms of trade unionism long characterized by centralized bargaining and representation.

Civil service

The restructuring of the 1980s provided the occasion for a re-evaluation of the traditional form of trade unionism in the civil service. These unions had long been centrally organized, providing a framework for local union activity, whereby branches responded to nationally initiated policies. Although these unions continued to be critical of the moves towards agencies and the associated decentralization of managerial structures, for union members the restructuring at an office level was an opportunity to recast their involvement. The problem, as noted in other studies, was that the developments at an office level in the civil service reproduced the patterns of 'structural disengagement' between local and national levels of trade union organization and activity (Fairbrother, 1994a, pp. 166–9; Foster and Scott, 1998a, pp. 140, 146).

Local civil service trade unions began to open up a range of new issues. These included staffing levels, the allocation of overtime work and the refurbishment of offices. While these were not startlingly novel areas of negotiation and bargaining, the local leaderships were often involved in such negotiations for the first time in their working lives. In addition, these unions, with large numbers of women members, have begun to move decisively to open up questions relating to equal opportunities and sexual and racial harassment, as well as the consideration of atypical forms of employment in terms of membership rather than employer interest. The opportunity for this was provided by the reorganization of bargaining arrangements at an office level rather than at regional or national levels, as in the past.

In these civil service trade unions the focus of such changes was on the branch secretaries and their executives. In the past, it is fair to note, many branch secretaries acted as ciphers for national union policy, transmitting policies downwards and reporting membership responses upwards. While this oversimplifies what were more complicated relationships, it none the less captures one of the major dimensions of the traditional form of trade union organization in this sector. With the decentralization of managerial structures and the decentralization of bargaining arrangements, these officials found themselves in a position to play a more active role in negotiating and representing members' concerns than previously. It is on the basis of these new-found opportunities that it has become possible to develop more participative forms of unionism than was the case in the past.

In these circumstances there were signs of pressure from members, as well as local activists, for the development of more responsive forms of trade unionism. These moves, however, were very tentative, often confined to grumbles and complaints about the reorganization and intensification of civil service work. The problem was that these unions did not have the mechanisms or the means whereby members could readily raise issues that stewards could begin to identify and address collectively. For this to happen a more participative form of trade unionism was required, but these unions, buried in the traditions of the past, with their large fragmented and dispersed memberships, found it very difficult to transform rhetorical commitments to participation and involvement into concrete measures designed to enable such a transformation to take place.

The emergence of more active and broadly based forms of trade unionism at a local level occurred within the residual forms of these centrally organized unions. What appears to have happened is that there was a shift in the locus of trade unionism, from the centre to the local level, although the paraphernalia of centralized union forms of organization remained in place. The point is that for members the focus of their trade unionism was gradually shifting to the office level, while the national leaderships had barely begun to grapple with the task of providing support for these memberships in the changed environment of agencies and decentralized managerial structures. The problem for the unions was how to coordinate the activity of the branch form of organization while at the same time enabling trade unionism at the local level to develop and flourish. The result was that trade unionism in this sector had begun to evolve in more participative and locally based ways, although in appearance they remained centrally organized and directed trade unions.

Local government

In the case of local government, the historical focus of negotiations at an authority level served to sustain a centralized union structure where the branch officers played their part as key actors in the process of union representation in relation to local authorities. This was the principal point of contact between union representatives and managerial staff. Such an involvement meant that these officials were likely to acquire the expertise and experience to represent and negotiate on behalf of their membership with management. Because of the scale and scope of local authority employment, and the way branches were organized on the basis of implementing national agreements, it was hardly likely that actively involved and participative memberships would emerge and develop at this time.

During the 1970s, there was both an expansion of local government employment and the beginnings of a shift towards a decentralization of managerial responsibility from the authority level to that of the department. Such changes had important implications for union organization and operation. Whereas in the past the branch officials were principally responsible for the majority of negotiations and consultations in the authority, increasingly this was becoming impractical. It became more likely that the detail of such negotiations would begin to preclude such officials, although there were signs that valiant attempts were being made to retain this involvement. Further, authority-wide union officials were likely to rely increasingly on department briefings to allow them to present adequate cases. There was thus a paradoxical pattern of change, towards decentralized local bargaining on the one hand and the retention of forms of centralized representation and bargaining on the other.

In the case of local authority unions, where there has been a long tradition of service and condition negotiations at an authority level, these changes raised acute problems for branch officials and full-time officers who attempted to service regions. Whereas in the past the branch officials were principally responsible for the majority of negotiations and consultations in the authority, often with some involvement from regional full-time officers, this had become increasingly impracticable. It was no longer possible for such officials and officers to retain a familiarity with the detail of such negotiations, although there were indications on the part of many of noteworthy but largely unsuccessful attempts to retain an intimate involvement in such negotiations. As a result, complicated relations developed between authority-wide union officials in their preparation and presentation of cases at the authority level. The problem was that many of the department representatives were inexperienced and, in the case of business units, unions found it very difficult to find members willing to become involved in negotiations with their 'new' managers, although, as indicated, there were exceptions to this general pattern.

Alongside such changes at the level of negotiations and consultation, there were signs of a more widespread involvement in day-to-day union activity as a result of the different patterns of trade unionism in the departments. To the extent that this analysis is correct, it is likely to be the case that if unions become embedded in these devolved and decentralized processes of representation and negotiation, then the prevailing forms of trade unionism will find it more difficult to maintain an effective presence in the local state. The outcome was a fragile accommodation between a membership facing increasing uncertainties and a leadership, particularly at regional and national levels, which was ill-equipped to recognize and acknowledge the importance of encouraging more devolved and decentralized forms of representation.

There was an on-going aspect to the fluctuating relations between local activists/representatives and the branch officials, partly reflecting the different traditions of trade unionism in the sector. Additionally, the regional full-time officers were part of this process, although often at one remove. In the context of debates about the most appropriate forms of unionism for this sector, this was part of a development to reorient and refocus unions in the light of the changing cirumstances of representation and negotiation. In effect, as with the civil service, there was a shift in the locus of unionism from a centralized practice to more localized forms. The problem was how to recognize and acknowledge the circumstances and realities of localized representation and negotiation while ensuring a planned and co-ordinated approach across the local authority, as well as from one authority to another. Although these were sharply contested dilemmas, there were signs that these union groups had begun to address such difficulties, albeit in uneven and hesitant ways.

Unions in the state sector

In the state sector, the restructuring was promoted by successive governments and senior state managers. In general, managements pursued relatively cohesive and thought-out strategies under the guise of human resource management, to individualize workers rather than explicitly to marginalize unions. These policies were part of an attempt to lay the grounds for an acquiescent and commodified workforce, prepared to accept the restructuring that was taking place. On occasion, in all these areas, managements acted to restrict the scope of union activity by questioning, and in some cases restricting, the use of union facility time. The danger of these initiatives was that union leaderships could be drawn reluctantly into agreement with the general thrust of these strategies, cooperating because to do otherwise would threaten their continued activity. Moreover, union leaderships occasionally found themselves representing memberships attracted by the self-realizing features of human resource management, although facing increased managerial control over working time.

Even so, while these were beleaguered union memberships, they were far from cowed by the array of policies pursued by union managements. Although varied in degree and implementation, the state sector was the site for a raft of walk-outs, small stoppages and membership meetings in the 1990s, with many workers taking part in such action for the first time. In addition, there was a healthy cynicism among local union leaders about managements' claimed objectives in their pursuit of consultation and teamwork procedures. They saw these initiatives as very much a gloss to legitimate attempts to control and reorganize workforces at a local level. Even where members were reluctant to support their leaderships actively via industrial action, such as strikes, the leaders themselves showed little reluctance to challenge and question managerial policies and to organize, often covertly, displays of resentment and opposition from workers.

The renewal of trade unionism in the public sector is taking place in relation to the shift in managerial organization and relationships. There has been a refocusing of bargaining relationships from centralized to locally based arrangements, with management strategies aimed at redrawing the employment relation, via out-sourcing, contracting-out and casualization. Unions have responded to the altered terrain of bargaining relationships, which in effect *invite* workplace union organization and activity where little existed before. As Heery (1998a, p. 362) notes, this points to an explanation of 'union behaviour in terms of the structure of collective bargaining and the prior strategic choices of employers'. However, this is only one component of a wider set of changes that are taking place.

As a result of this composite of relations, there is often an uncertainty and an unevenness in responding to the changed union milieu of the public sector. It is for this reason that there has been argument about the trends at work, whether patterns of renewal or retreat are in evidence (Colling, 1995; Terry, 1995). Indeed, in view of the readily available evidence, it often makes sense to argue that retreat rather than renewal is more likely. However, this is to draw conclusions on the basis of flimsy indications of union change. Rather, a struggle is taking place within the unions organizing in the public sector about the form of trade unionism that is in the process of emerging. These developments are taking place in terms of the complex interrelationships between the workplace and the union beyond. While it is premature to argue that a particular form is actually emerging, it is reasonable to suggest that there is a process of change taking place which may result in a more participative and inclusive form of trade unionism.

When faced with changed managerial structures and work and employment relations, the union committees in these sectors looked anew at the ways they organized and operated. While different models of trade unionism were invoked in practice, ranging from forms of 'social movement' unionism to more economistically dependent unionism, it was also the case that more participative local union organization had begun to emerge, based on forms of workplace representation (Foster and Scott, 1998a, p. 147). It was in these varied ways that the foundation was presented for a process of union renewal in this sector.

Union form

These developments bring the question of union form and union renewal back into the centre of debates about trade unionism. In the context of restructuring, a reliance on centralized and hierarchical forms of trade unionism no longer suffices. The choice in the late 1990s and into the 2000s, therefore, will be between a form of trade unionism that accommodates to government policies and restructuring and one that poses a more direct challenge to them. The first is likely to entail further sophistication in the development of bureaucratically effective forms of trade unionism; in the second case, workplace-based union structures are likely to become more prominent. In either case, trade unionism will continue to display a tension between pressures towards bureaucracy and those towards democracy. The dilemmas arising from this tension will be the key issues for unionists in the near future. It is in this respect that unions once again return to the centre stage of debates about democracy, both within unions and as part of broader concerns within the liberal democratic state.

In Britain, the dominant form of trade unionism during the post-war period has been 'responsible unionism'. Such trade unionism is defined as comprising hierarchical organization, membership involvement exemplified by formal representative structures and procedures, and a commitment to reformist politics. This type of trade unionism has been advocated by Flanders (1970) and, in the 1980s and 1990s, by Kelly (1987, 1988). It is a trade unionism rooted in the particular circumstances of post-war Britain, when unions aspired to partnership with Labour governments to achieve social reconstruction. Crucially, it is also a trade unionism which allowed for what became known as 'constructive' working relationships with successive Conservative governments of the period.

This prevailing form of trade unionism allows a tentative resolution of the tensions between bureaucracy and democracy and permits unions to fulfil their part of the partnership with government in the construction of social democracy. Bureaucracy has long been noted as a feature of trade union organization (Lipset *et al.*, 1956, pp. 82–124; Michels, 1962). Recently this type of analysis has been interrogated by Hyman (1989), who argues that bureaucracy must be defined as a social relation characteristic of the union form of organization. To develop this analysis further, it is necessary to consider the circumstances under which bureaucratic forms of organization develop in terms of the material and historical circumstances of trade unionism.

For Hyman, union bureaucracy is a 'social relation pervading trade union practice at every level: a social relation corrosive of the foundations of collective solidarity' (Hyman, 1989, p. 181). He identifies three sets of relations: a separation of representation from mobilization; a hierarchy of control and activism; and the detachment of formal procedures of policy formulation and decision-making from members' experiences. This leads, he argues, to a situation where 'workers' organisations which are defined and constituted through struggle tend also to contain and inhibit such struggle' (Hyman, 1989, p. 181). In developing this analysis, he refers to a process of internal union democracy, indicated by a hierarchy of activism and involvement throughout the union characterized by the predominance of white, male, relatively skilled and higher-paid workers in more secure jobs. This, for him, mirrors the ways in which the working class more generally is ranked and stratified, and has significant political consequences.

It has been common to define union democracy with reference to the processes and procedures of membership involvement in trade union decision-making and organization. Following this line of argument, the emphasis has been on the bases of opposition within unions (Lipset *et al.*, 1956; Martin, 1968, pp. 205–20), as well as on electoral procedures within unions (TUC, 1983). This emphasis directs attention away from the bases of participation and involvement in unions and thus the foundation of an active or mobilized form of trade unionism. It is an argument for a form of democracy which is modelled on the parliamentary model of liberal democratic states, with particular reference to ballot procedures. Emphasis is given to the individual franchise, secret ballots and periodic elections. It is a view of democracy where the elected person is most frequently seen as a representative for a constituency rather than as a delegate of a constituency. As a representative the spokesperson has the authority to speak on behalf of the constituency without direct reference to that constituency, although there always remains the possibility of recall at elections. Thus, the emphasis is on procedure and representation.

Other views of democracy have focused on the basis of membership participation and decision-making and by implication on a distinct and alternative form of trade unionism (Cohen and Fosh, 1988; Fairbrother and Waddington, 1990). The emphasis in this form of organization is on widespread debate and discussion, accountability and membership involvement. Such organization suggests a layered structure, where each level has distinct and related spheres of influence and responsibility but where there is the possibility of mutual interaction between each layer of activity. In practice, such democracy is built around meetings, mandating and advising delegates, report backs and the collective determination of policies and activities. It is signified by ongoing debate and dialogue at all levels of the union. This is a form of democracy which is founded on the continual interaction between workers and their delegates. It runs counter to the parliamentary model of liberal democratic states as it is founded on the forms and practice of collective organization and action.

The issue for unions is whether to organize and operate in bureaucratically effective ways or on the basis of collective participation and involvement. There is a complex interrelationship between these two forms of trade unionism, worked out in terms of the policies and practices pursued by all unions. This tension was pointed to by the syndicalists at the turn of the century when they advocated forms of trade unionism marked by federally organized structures based on participative workplace groups (Unofficial Reform Committee, 1912, pp. 25–7). Implicit in this type of analysis is the argument that a process of union renewal is always on the agenda in terms of the revitalization of existing forms of organization, new variants of union organization and activity to address new contingencies and a heightening of union debate and activism. While there is no clear-cut and straightforward path for unions, the central tension within unions is expressed in terms of pressures for hierarchical accommodative forms of trade unionism and workplace-based union activism.

The bases of workplace unionism

It is now possible to assess where these developments might lead and what forms of trade unionism might be emerging. This draws attention to the possibilities and conditions for union renewal: that is, union restructuring towards more participative forms of trade unionism rather than the reaffirmation of hierarchical representative forms of trade unionism (Hyman, 1979; Cohen and Fosh, 1988; Fairbrother, 1989b, 1994a, b, 1996a; Carter, 1997;

Foster and Scott, 1998a, b). If more active forms of trade unionism are to develop at a local level, then union members and their leaders must be in a position to exercise choices about their future. This is clearly made easier where the membership is relatively cohesive (although not necessarily socially homogeneous) and grouped in reasonable numbers (for example, in local authority areas of employment compared with the fragmentation in the manual areas of the water industry), and where proactive rather than defensive policies can be pursued (the civil service compared with most manufacturing enterprises).

Union memberships are faced with a choice either to pursue proactive policies or simply to respond to the agendas set by both the state and employers. The experience in the public sector illustrates this point. Here trade unions faced a crisis of representation, in that the previously centralized and remote forms of trade unionism no longer sufficed. Nevertheless, some trade unions have been able to act in proactive ways. Relative to past practices they have begun to take up the opportunities offered by local bargaining, campaigning and negotiation. While many of the issues are mundane and predictable, and located within established bargaining agenda, it is none the less the case that these are union groups which previously had little or no opportunity to deal with such items as staffing levels or refurbishment. Such responses are more than they seem at first sight; they are part of an attempt by these local memberships to prepare for the future, to lay the foundation for more active and forward-looking unions than existed in the past. It is in this sense that they are proactive union memberships, opening up possibilities in hitherto non-active local union groups. In contrast, the unions in the manufacturing sector, and most of the manual union memberships in the utilities, have not taken the initiative to redefine and open up union issues and questions in new ways. They have resorted to past procedures and responded in predictable ways to the agenda-setting by their managements.

The problem faced by many unions is that a cycle of dependency has been built up over a long period of time, which, in the conditions of job uncertainty, contracting membership levels and confident managements, has been very difficult to break. Where union groups have been organized in hierarchically participative ways (workplace steward committees in the engineering sector) or have been reliant on the active intervention of full-time officials (manual unions in the utilities), it has been difficult to take steps to lay the foundation for more collective forms of union organization and action. Hierarchically participative is that form of organization where there is an opportunity for members to play an active part in union activity and procedures but within a vertically organized political structure where decision-making is effectively the prerogative of the few. None the less, where workplace union groups have been able to open up a broader remit of workplace-based issues and where they have been able to build forms of union organization that allow a wider involvement of membership in union activity (local government and civil service), there is the prospect of more proactive forms of trade unionism emerging.

A more comprehensive view of union renewal, however, goes beyond the straightforward comparison just presented. The argument is that the processes of change in the three sectors are both mediated at a workplace level and part of a broader patterning of change that is taking place at both state and corporate levels. In this respect, the process of renewal involves a complex relationship between the local and broader levels of union engagement and interaction. Once these features are taken into account it is possible to move beyond the narrow focus of much of the debate to date and consider the processes of renewal that may be at work in contemporary trade unionism at the end of the twentieth century.

In the context of the restructuring that is in process in the three sectors, the base point of trade unionism is *survival*. While this appears to be a rather dramatic statement, the way changes are mediated at a workplace level means that the very existence of union groups and organization can be threatened, as was evident in some of the cases reported above. The question is how union groups can survive when faced with the array of managerial strategies and approaches, not necessarily aimed at the removal of unions from the workplace, but often directed at the marginalization of union groups. In such circumstances, the problem is not only to maintain the formal base of union organization but to give some substance to the notion of membership involvement and engagement in union activity. Otherwise, the result is the shell of an organization and often the cynicism of potential members. Faced with this situation, it is common to look outside for assistance and guidance. However, the urgings of officials and national leaders or the strictures of political groupings do not necessarily achieve this objective, although they may help (see Gall, 1998). It is necessary to note that in a variety of ways the *survival* of workplace unions critically depends on members themselves, albeit on one or two activists who are willing to maintain and pursue the semblance of trade unionism in the most unpropitious conditions. In this respect, the key aspect for *survival* is the affirmation and development of the workplace structure as the basis for union organization and activity.

One feature of the process of union renewal evident in both the privatized utilities and the public sector is the way the pattern of restructuring that has occurred implicitly places a premium on refocusing and redirecting trade unionism in these sectors. Such concerns may involve the *reorientation* of national and regional forms of union organization as well as the stimulation and encouragement of local organization and activity. In both sectors, the past was characterized by minimal workplace organization and activity and it was only under the conditions of managerial recomposition and the development of associated bargaining structures that such organization was developed. Of course, it is difficult to interpret the significance of such initiatives, apart from noting the emergence of local union *leaderships* and *activists* where there were few previously. It is possible to play down the novelty of such initiatives. Indeed, they can be devalued by presenting them as a well trodden path, evident in the manufacturing sector in the past and now extended to the public sector, in particular (Heery, 1998a, p. 362). While this may be so, the point to make is that the current phase of union renewal in the public sector is occurring under very different and distinct circumstances when compared with manufacturing in the 1950s and 1960s. Not only is the state in a process of restructuring, in the UK and elsewhere, but it is also the case that the state remains a key player in the changes taking place, for the public sector (by definition) but also for the privatized industries and the private sector more generally. More than this, the circumstances and conditions of trade unionism remain central to state policy and programmes, and to this extent the *development of workplace unionism,* albeit within national frameworks of organization and concern, will remain a distinctive feature of unions in the next century.

However, for a mature form of renewed trade unionism to emerge it is necessary to begin to consider the way forms of union organization and activity can be *developed* at a workplace level and whether this can be done in *mutually supportive* ways between the local and the union beyond (see Foster and Scott, 1998a, p. 147). The question is whether union groupings can develop proactive rather than reactive forms of trade unionism (although the interrelationship between reactive and proactive is much more complicated than is often assumed). Clearly, these are not easy paths to follow, because of the complications of history, tradition, the particular circumstances of work and employment relations, and the complex relations implied by state policies and corporate strategies, at local levels and beyond. So the task of *building* union groups or reviving union activity is not straightforward; this may involve political groups, full-time officials and the self-consciousness of participants that comes from experience and practice. In sum, the question is how memberships develop and sustain a trade union consciousness and, more importantly, a practice in the current climate and conditions. The answer lies in an understanding of the complexity of social relations and not a one-sided emphasis on or neglect of any one factor, something that marks the limit of

Gall's (1998) otherwise important (and flattering) contribution to the renewal debate. In a comprehensive review of the debate, he underwrites the centrality of left political groups in providing the grist to a mature renewal, principally by maintaining their 'political independence' and thus laying claims to leadership roles and the critical conscience of union organization and struggle (Gall, 1998, pp. 154–5). The point is that unless such groups are both in and of the union form, their contribution is necessarily limited to that of the outsider. This proposition is not an advocacy of narrowly focused interactions and relationships or a celebration of spontaneous union and political activity. Rather, it is a recognition that the construction of active and participative unionism, within the framework of a wider trade union movement, is both inherently political and extremely difficult to accomplish, as illustrated above.

However, there is a prospect in these developments which should be considered before a final judgement is made about the significance of this emergent form of trade unionism. Given the thrust and scope of recent managerial concerns, particularly with respect to seeking the active support of workers as individuals for the changes that are taking place, it is possible that these new local leaderships could be seduced into supporting these proposals. There is the prospect that these union leaderships could come to see passive support as the price they must pay for their continued role as workers' representatives. Additionally, they may come to see that the only way they can begin to influence specific decisions is by acquiescing in the broad framework of relations that are being constructed in workplace after workplace. In these respects, these leaderships face the dangers of incorporation.

Union leaders may be persuaded in this direction by the problems they face in maintaining their presence as representatives in the workplace. Their vulnerability is underwritten by continued threats to facility time, particularly in the public services and utilities, although not exclusively so. More starkly, in situations of persistent uncertainty and rolling programmes of redundancies, there is always the prospect that the leadership will be *persuaded* to accept redundancy. In some areas, where managements have begun to break up their workforces into separate but related business units, cross-representation has been questioned, suggesting attempts by management to define the basis of representation of these new leaderships. For many union leaderships human resource management is a set of management policies which rest on a *de facto* restriction of union concerns, coupled with informal intimidation of these leaderships. Thus managerial policies of incorporation, whatever the form taken, have been underpinned by more coercive attempts to control working time and work organization and activity.

There is, thus, a possibility that union leaderships may be co-opted into relationships and positions that take them away from the membership. One possible counter to such threats is for unions to seek legal backing for this form of representation. While legislation, guaranteeing a role and place for local leaders, would confirm these leaderships in position, there are two problems with such policies. First, in seeking such remission unions tend to be deflected from the immediate day-to-day concerns they confront. The broader issues are put to one side as they wait for the election of a government that may reinforce their beleaguered position. Second, and more importantly, legislative support secures the basis for legally recognized leaders rather than leaderships who maintain their position through an active engagement with the memberships they represent and embody.

These developments raise the question of union democracy in a rather acute way. Clearly, one of the key features of democratic relations and forms of organization is the capacity for workers to organize at a local level and to play an active part in formulating and determining union policy and activity. Of course, such activism may be enhanced where workers have already developed a political consciousness and understanding of the political economy of trade unionism (Gall, 1998). This, however, is not the whole story. With the consolidation of local forms of organization or the reconstitution of the union form of organization at a local level, the opportunity for membership participation becomes more likely. In these circumstances it is likely that the self-organization of workers will be linked to the emergence of new leaders or leaderships who are able to recast their past practices so as to enable a broader based range of activity to be undertaken by union members. So this is not only a question of the structures and formal arrangements of local union organization, but also one of whether or not the membership is able and willing to act in ways that question and challenge current work and employment relationships.

The question of renewal

More generally, this study has wider implications for both the state sector and the private sector. It can be argued that in many industries, but particularly engineering, forms of participative unionism have long been in existence. This certainly is one of the points made by Darlington (1994) in his study of three manufacturing plants on Merseyside, in north-west England. There workplace union committees have maintained an active presence within their plants, despite the drastic effects of the restructuring that has taken place or the less than supportive stances of many full-time officials. This suggests that one of the key conditions for active and vibrant forms of workplace unionism is a work and employment circumstance that allows issues to be raised and settled at a local level. Where this is not the case it is very easy for solutions to be made outside the workplace, with national or full-time officials who do not work to the same imperatives as those in the workplace, a situation that has long characterized state sector trade unionism, including unions in the recently privatized utilities.

The difficulty for unions in capitalist societies is to bargain with and come to some accommodation with employers, while at the same time laying the foundation for opposing the relations that define work and employment in such societies (see Gorz, 1982). In general, as indicated above, unions enter into relations with employers (including the state) that reaffirm rather than challenge these relations. Even so, it remains possible that under particular circumstances unions might be able to pursue policies and practices which question key features of these relationships. For this to be achieved, it would be necessary for union memberships and their leaders to affirm the relative independence and autonomy of workplace unionism. Without this develop-ment, many union memberships are likely to remain relatively inactive and compliant, drawn into union activity on an occasional basis and unable to challenge the social relations of production in any fundamental way.

The issue for unions is how to realize the dual objectives of trade unionism, as both part of and in opposition to the labour–capital relation. This clearly is not a straightforward process, involving relations between unions and employ-ers as well as between unions and the state. This means looking beyond the way unions organize and addressing the political context of trade unionism (see Hyman, 1989, pp. 184–6). This would mean challenging the social democratic assumptions about trade unionism, in particular questioning the assumed partnership between unions and social democratic parties. That this is not mere speculation is apparent from the increasing formalization of relations between the unions and the British Labour Party during the 1980s, when there was a hollowing-out of this relation, a feature that has continued and, indeed, deepened during the 1990s.

Thus unions are at a watershed: can they meet the challenge of restructuring in unified, political and participative ways or are they destined for the by-ways of parochialism and marginalization? To date it would seem that the patterns of union development in these circumstances are varied and uneven, although there is the prospect that more participative and revived forms of trade unionism could emerge. To realize this promise, two issues must be con-fronted.

First, can previously centralized unions or those heavily dependent on full-time officer involvement reorganize so that workplace forms of trade unionism flourish? As indicated, it is not an easy or straightforward task to recast trade unionism. Over time unions acquire established and routine ways of addressing the issues they confront. More than this, the moves towards centralized forms of organization and activity in one period may be progressive and desirable, given the challenges of the time. The difficulty is not only to recognize when such forms of organization no longer suffice but to take the steps to transform unions in more positive ways. While there are some signs that this might be occurring, especially in the utilities and public services, any moves in this direction are still at a very embryonic stage and are likely to be contested in a variety of ways.

One particular difficulty that many unions may face is to create the circumstances whereby full-time officers and national union officials can begin to recast their activities so that the emphasis is on resourcing and support rather than leadership substitution at a local level. While many such officials have already moved in this direction, there is little sign that unions generally have underwritten this move (Kelly and Heery, 1994). There is a particular poignancy about some of the debates that have taken place in the context of proposed mergers between unions with very different traditions of organization, where the question for merged unions is whether to pursue forms of trade unionism based on membership involvement and lay officer control or full-time-officer-dependent forms of trade unionism. In part, the possibility of this debate indicates the unwillingness of many to recognize the tasks facing the union form of organization.

Second, can unions begin to lay the foundation for forms of organization which challenge the state and employers in broadly based ways, that move beyond the narrow preoccupations of a single workplace? One aspect of recent managerial initiatives has been to underwrite the particular and the specific issue, as the concern of strictly delimited workforces. This is a way of underwriting forms of sectionalism which managements deem as compatible with their own goals and concerns. The problem for unions is to address the immediate and particular while at the same time laying the foundation for a more general concern with the type of restructuring that is taking place. It is in this respect that questioning legislative initiatives becomes crucial, since it allows unions to link the obviously political with the day-to-day concerns of the workplace.

The union form of organization provides one of the few possibilities to question the form of state rule, although to pursue this may mean questioning traditional political relations. If unions do not raise these questions then the processes of marginalization are likely to result in a type of business unionism where the preoccupations of union memberships are likely to be narrowly sectional and economistic. Where unions have tentatively addressed some of these issues there is the prospect of laying the foundation for democratic and challenging forms of trade unionism. This, at least, is the promise, although not yet the reality.

The politics of renewal

The choice will be between a form of trade unionism that accommodates to government policies and restructuring and one that poses a more direct challenge to government policies and strategies, whatever party is in office. The first is likely to entail further sophistication in the development of centralized and accommodative forms of trade unionism; in the second case workplace-based unionism is likely to become more prominent, although organized and operating within broader union structures and organization.

The dilemma that advocates of centralized forms of trade unionism face is how to deal with the recognition that a union form of organization without an active and engaged workplace membership is a charade (see Heery and Kelly, 1994; Terry, 1996; Heery, 1998a). Given the importance of this point, these critics of arguments about union renewal have gone to considerable lengths to denounce the initial attempts to formulate an argument about union renewal, but at the same time defend the importance of workplace activism, provided it is within the broad structural and policy concerns of the union (McIlroy, 1995, 1997; Terry, 1996). Underlying these arguments is an assumption that the future of unions lies with an accommodation with sympathetic governments, in this case a Labour government. This in effect is the return to long-standing arguments about the virtues and benefits of social partnership between the two wings of the labour movement in achieving a just and equitable society, at least in relation to work and employment (Flanders, 1970).

The problem with this type of analysis is that it ignores the nature of such relationships. It has never been the case that unions have entered into such partnerships as equals in policy formulation, policy interpretation and policy implementation. At the end of the day, it is the Labour government, or its counterparts in office, which determines the parameters and content of governance in liberal democracies. Union leaderships and their representatives are the secondary partners in such arrangements, and it is well to recognize that this is the case. Indeed, there is a double burden for unions representing public sector workers, where they not only are the secondary partner in the relationship with government but are subordinate to the state as employer.

Instead, there is a case for unions seeking to establish their organizational independence and autonomy from all liberal democratic governments. The strength of the union form of organization is that it is the institutional expression of the collective worker in a capitalist society. As employees, workers combine together for the purposes of production and the provision of services. In this respect, the union form of organization represents the possibility of these workers expressing their common concerns and interests in such societies. It represents a moment of collective organization and interest that is unusual in such societies. It is for this reason that unions give attention to the basis of organization, in the workplace and at a local level.

None the less, this is not an argument for workplace autonomy and independence; rather, it is the recognition that the well-spring for the union form of organization goes well beyond an instrumental economism and is rooted in the experience of work, an expression of the social relations of production and service. It is an acknowledgement that workers in the public sector, the privatized utilities, manufacturing industry and elsewhere have common sets of interests. However, these interests are almost never expressed in identical ways and terms. The experiences and traditions of workplace groups, the particular location and place of workers in occupational hierarchies, the practices and policies of managements, the ideologies of trade unionism that are elaborated and developed over time – all give a particular twist to the way in which these interests are defined and elaborated. In many instances, this has resulted in exclusive politics, defending the privileges and prerogatives of one section of the workforce against another, or waged workers against non-waged workers. At other times, waged workers as union members have attempted to build inclusive union structures and develop appropriate policies and practices to realize such ambitions. The point is that these are approaches to trade unionism which are struggled over and contested.

But workplace activism and organization are only the first steps in realizing the union form of organization. One of the defining features of trade unionism historically has been the attempt in hesitant and uneven ways to lay the foundation to overcome fragmentation and sectionalism. One solution was to combine as unions, representing large sections of the workforce and organized so as to realize the unity of purpose that has characterized most unions at various times in their history. The difficulty is how to renew and redefine this unity of purpose in the circumstances of continued restructuring and re-evaluation of politics.

Too often commentary attempts to remove the basis of division and dissension within unions, between different levels of organization and between different sections of the workforce, as antithetical to unity (McIlroy, 1995, pp. 408–14, 417–21; 1997, pp. 121–2). The argument is then transformed into an account that decries the workplace, and downplays the importance of trade unionism at this level. In this respect, the question is: what are the conditions for securing those social partnerships which will achieve an egalitarian and equitable society? The answer is presented as one that achieves the election of sympathetic governments, who together with unions will implement the policies sought by both.

An alternative question is: how can workers combine with each other, and with other sections of the society, to defend and extend their common interests? Posing the question in this way directs attention to the social conditions for independent and inclusive forms of collective organization, based on the workplace but not confined to it. Such trade unionism will be both based in the workplace and organized so that there is the possibility both within industries and across industries, as well as beyond. It is in this respect that the debates about the organization and operation of trade unions are important. It is also in this context that the debate about union renewal acquires its importance. Clearly, there is unevenness and variation in workplace activity and practice within the different sectors and from one sector to another. The conditions for activity in one area and not another lie in a complex of factors, related to work and employment, managerial practice and the traditions and resources of trade unions in different areas. Whatever, the point is that without a workplace form of organization unions become hollow shells without any substantive base, as was the case of many unions, particularly in the public sector, for much of their history.

As indicated, there have been some moves by unions at a workplace level to affirm the relative autonomy of this form of trade unionism, although different patterns are evident in each sector. With the major restructuring of workplace practices, reinforced by government initiatives, managements have attempted to incorporate or by-pass unions. At the same time, there is evidence that some union memberships have responded to these developments through the encouragement of active and participative memberships prepared to push at the frontiers of control. These developments involve unions as national organizations. The analysis suggests that the preoccupations of national leaderships may run counter to the development of activist workplace unionism. It may mean that these trends will offset the moves towards the centralization of organizational practices and principles of unions at a national level. None the less, these are complicated relationships, and where national political and organizational concerns prevail, workplace-based union organizations may remain subordinated within the wider parameters of union concerns and objectives. This, however, is not predetermined, as action by national leaderships may stimulate active workplace unionism, as workplace members organize and act to deal with daily and immediate concerns of work.

Thus the union form of organization is both a promise and a falsehood. On the one hand, there is the possibility that unions will embark on a slow, uneven and uncertain process of reorganization and reconsideration of their trade unionism. This may result in the emergence of inclusive and independent forms of organization, whereby members can begin to represent and express their diverse concerns about their workplaces, the industries in which they work, the communities in which they live and the types of societies that they would like to emerge. On the other hand, unions are rooted in sets of relationships, pursuing particular and often exclusive objectives which set one group of workers against another, those in waged work against those who are not, those in one set of communities against those elsewhere. The question facing these memberships is what choice they will make. It is in this very specific sense that unions in the United Kingdom are at a crossroads. This is the end of the beginning.

Appendix: The Research Process

The research for the book was conducted over more than ten years. It builds on preliminary work done on selected workplaces in the late 1980s. At the time, I had just completed a large study of the then Society of Civil and Public Servants and was keen to explore the questions raised by this research in a focused way at a local level, examining the way that trade unionism was experienced in localities and in relation to the experiences of trade union members and their managers at this level. In this respect I was puzzled by an apparent divergence in the literature, where it was often argued that unions were in a state of decline, with the implication that the role and place of trade unions in both the economy and the polity were changing, to the detriment of unions as political and economic institutions. In my experience as a part-time trade union tutor and as a politically engaged academic, these accounts seemed unduly pessimistic and appeared to ignore the political and economic basis of collective worker mobilization. It was with these questions in mind that I embarked on this extensive research programme.

One of the key dimensions of the research was the access afforded me by many trade union groups in the West Midlands. This often derived from my involvement as a part-time tutor for the West Midlands Workers' Educational Association, as well as for individual unions, particularly NALGO/UNISON. These experiences and the people I met provided me with the opportunity not only to talk more widely and to meet trade union members and their leaders in the area but also to have my often crude and ill thought out ideas challenged and refined. It was this experience that enabled me not only to begin the research in the first instance, but to construct and develop a longitudinal and comparatively based project that continues to this day.

Project aims

The aim of the project was to examine theories and explanations of the relationship between management strategies and practices and local trade unionism, with specific reference to recent changes in labour and management relations, covering the public services, utilities and manufacturing. This allowed the interrogation and review of two key features of current debates: the continuities of forms of workplace representation; and the social processes of union renewal.

There were two stages to the research. In the first stage, from 1990 to 1993, twenty-four union groups drawn from the public services, utilities and manufacturing in the West Midlands region were studied. The material for the research was gathered by in-depth semi-structured interviews from key informants in each union group, complemented by observational material, questionnaire surveys and documentary research. In addition, so as to provide background contextual material, an annual survey of a selection of major employers and their union counterparts in the West Midlands was carried out. The second stage comprised a focused study in 1995 to 1996 of thirty-one union branches in the utilities and public services, following up issues raised in the first stage of the research. This phase of the research consisted of in-depth interviews with key union informants and their management counterparts.

Phase 1

The twenty-four workplace union committees in the West Midlands region were drawn from the public sector bodies, utilities and manufacturing enterprises in equal numbers. Where possible, I studied both the staff and the shopfloor committees in the same enterprise or government body. Complementing this, I conducted less detailed studies on another five union committees, following up particular themes that had come up in the core cases. I was also involved in leading ten union schools in the Midlands region which produced further information on workplace unionism. In each core case study I interviewed the leading representative(s) of each committee at least four times, twice in the first year and once in the two subsequent years, using semi-structured interview schedules. Where possible I also interviewed their managerial counterparts at annual intervals, altogether involving nine managers. The full-time officers for seven of the major unions in the region were also interviewed on an annual basis. These interviews were complemented by a questionnaire survey of the committee members each year. Where possible I attended union meetings (six) and visited workplaces (twenty-four). I also interviewed key commentators, from both employer and union groups in the region, such as the secretary of the regional TUC, thus providing an overview of union developments in the region. To further the comparative basis of the research, I carried out an annual postal survey of workplace unions in the three sectors, although the response rate was disappointingly low (overall 18.3 per cent) and uneven. Nevertheless, the information generated does provide confirmation of the trends and patterns seen in the core case studies.

Four sets of questions guided the research:

1. What changes are taking place in work and employment relations in the public services, utilities and manufacturing?
2. What is the impact of management proposals to change work and employment relations on local union organization and practice?
3. What is the importance of union organization and activity at a regional and national level in defining local union organization and practice?
4. What patterns of local trade unionism are developing in each of the above sectors of the economy?

These initial questions were supplemented by a further set of questions arising from more recent debates about trade unionism.

The debates about British trade unionism have pointed to the problems faced by trade unions, ranging from membership decline and the seeming acquiescence of unions to management initiatives, to marginalization and exclusion. First, Millward *et al.* (1992), who report on the third Workplace Industrial Relations Survey (WIRS), argue that unions are in a state of seemingly irreversible decline, as indicated by falling membership numbers, a narrowing of national union concerns and a massive reduction in official industrial action. Second, in an extensively documented article, Smith and Morton (1993) have presented a persuasive argument that unions, particularly in the state sector, are being by-passed and marginalized, with the result that they are increasingly confined to a relatively narrow remit of concerns and objectives. Third, other writers, focusing on the question of union power, have claimed that there are important differences between public and private sector unionism, particularly at a shopfloor level (Marsh, 1992, Chapters 8 and 9), with private sector unions acting more defensively than in the 1970s and the public sector unions adopting more adversarial approaches to industrial relations.

One of the questions that arises from these accounts is whether the form of unionism is changing and, if so, in what direction. This question has been alluded to in some of the most recent literature, where there has been a consideration of the way unions organize and operate, with suggestions that forms of managerial unionism (where the focus of union leaderships is on servicing perceived membership needs, with consequent reorganization and operation of union governance to further these aspirations) may be emerging

(Kelly and Heery, 1994). This research addresses these issues explicitly by examining two further questions:

1.   Is the form of unionism in each of these sectors undergoing change?
2.   If union form is undergoing change, then in what direction?

The starting point for the analysis is whether the predominant form of British trade unionism is in a state of crisis. This form of unionism has been characterized as centralized, hierarchical and reformist, at both national and local levels. It is a form of unionism which has rested on relatively limited degrees of membership participation and involvement, particularly at a workplace level. It is also a form of unionism, especially in the public sector, where the workplace has not been the prime focus of union concern, either organizationally or in terms of policy formulation and initiative. While this form of unionism prevailed during the 1960s and 1970s and seemed to make some gains in the social democratic context of the period, it is a form that no longer suffices. On the basis of this analysis, the arguments about the possibility and prospects of union renewal were addressed explicitly in this research (Fairbrother, 1996a).

It is in terms of these theoretical considerations that the research develops a distinctive approach in three related respects. First, unlike much of the research literature on local trade unionism, attention is given to the public sector (important exceptions are Terry, 1982, 1983; Kessler, 1986; the WIRS studies). Second, while there has been considerable comment and debate about the trends and patterns of workplace unionism, particularly in the private sector, this has not usually involved detailed case study research, a feature of this project (exceptions are Spencer, 1985; Cohen and Fosh, 1988; Fosh and Cohen, 1990). Third, this research has generated longitudinal data, thereby enabling a consideration of the way unions may be changing over time.

Representatives from each of the committees were interviewed as shown in Table A.1. The leading representatives of each committee (thirty-three in all) were interviewed (two hours plus) at least four times, twice in the first year and once in the two subsequent years, using semi-structured interview schedules.

The union committees covered in the research consisted of twenty-four principal committees (eight from each sector), with further interviews with union leaders from five union committees. The basis of selection was the level at which responsibility for representing members and negotiating on their behalf was at either branch level or the steward committee level. Unions were selected to cover public services, utilities and manufacturing on an equal basis,

Table A.1 Numbers of union representatives interviewed

Unions	1990/1	1991/2	1992/3	Total
Utilities	14	7	7	28
Public services	27	13	11	51
Manufacturing	12	9	8	29
Total	53	29	26	108

to allow the research to distinguish between different forms of ownership and the significance of restructuring. The case studies were paired by employer, with a CPSA and NUCPS branch from one Department of Social Security district, an MSF committee and AEU committee in one engineering plant and so on, permitting a measure of internal comparison and control across the region.

The interview research was complemented by a qualitative questionnaire survey of the committee members on selected committees each year, resulting in three sets of annual returns covering six principal union committees (Table A.2).

Table A.2 Committee member survey

Unions	1990/1	1991/2	1992/3	Total
Responses	48	38	30	116

The result was a rich database of qualitative material about the activity and position of stewards and branch executive committee members, complementing the other case study research.

In each case, material such as company reports, union agreements and other publications was collected and annotated. This was complemented by other publicly available material – for example, select committee reports in the case of the civil service – and use of the databases available at the University of Warwick. This resulted in an extensive corpus of research data, which is in the process of being analysed and incorporated into the reports on the project.

Where appropriate and possible, management staff were also interviewed, specifically the person responsible for negotiations with unions. This part of the research was complemented by interviews with eleven managers and senior employer representatives, on an annual basis. These interviews complement and add to the case study research. They have been complemented by the collection and analysis of public statements and addresses by management personnel: for example, the reports by chief executives in the civil service and their counterparts in the utilities and private sector.

During the course of the research ten union schools were attended, which produced further information about workplace unionism. The focus of these schools was local union organization in the context of restructuring. Detailed notes were taken and then incorporated as part of the overall database for the project. Although this work did not necessarily provide representative data, it provided indicative material about the trends and patterns of change and development involving unions in the three sectors.

Phase 2

The second phase of the research built on Phase 1, focusing on how local union groups were continuing to develop, as part of broader national union structures as well as in the workplace. In the course of Phase 1 it became clear that unions in the public services and utilities faced particular sets of problems arising from the comprehensive economic and political restructuring of the state sector that was taking place. One aspect of the debate focused on the questions of whether there was the beginning of change in more managerial and accommodative directions or whether there was a process of renewal and revival under way, particularly at the workplace level (Fairbrother, 1990a, 1996a; Heery and Kelly, 1994; Colling, 1995). On the basis of this varied research, it was not clear whether there was a consistent pattern of reorganization taking place in the public services and the utilities (Fairbrother, 1994b, 1996a; Colling, 1995).

Drawing on the implications of the first phase of the research, the second phase focused on the patterns of unionism that were emerging, both locally and nationally, among unions in the public services and the privatized utilities. This permitted a broadening of the scope of the earlier research, as well as a continued examination of the themes about local and workplace trade unionism. This research produced a range of data, which was then incorporated where appropriate in the analysis.

In statistical terms, research data for this stage of the project comprised 181 interviews, observations and extensive documentary material. Senior union branch officers were interviewed from thirty-one branches, a number of them at least five times. Respondents were drawn from four CWU branches, one STE branch, two UNISON gas branches, one UNISON water branch, three UNISON electricity branches, five UNISON health branches, eight UNISON local government branches, three UNISON higher education branches, two PTC branches and two CPSA branches in the Benefits Agency. National and regional officials were interviewed on the following basis: STE (two), CWU (two), UNISON (twenty) and eighteen managerial respondents.

The importance of the second phase of the research was that it permitted the themes identified in the first phase to be studied in detail. The reason for focusing on the public services and the utilities was that this was the most puzzling area of trade union development. It was here that the impact of economic and political restructuring was experienced in particularly acute forms, especially during the 1990s. It was also in these sectors that unions faced the consequences of a shift from national bargaining to more varied and in many cases more decentralized patterns of negotiation. In a number of cases, it became evident that the local union groups in these sectors were vulnerable to these changed relationships, in ways that were not as evident in manufacturing.

Nevertheless, an attempt was also made to follow up developments within the manufacturing sector. In the main, this took the form of brief follow-up interviews with key union respondents, tracking any major developments that took place after the first phase of the research. This enabled particular themes to be addressed and analysed, such as developments in union organization on occupational health and safety (Fairbrother, 1996b).

The presentation of the research material

The process of writing up the material went through three interrelated phases. First, the theories of trade unionism and the definition of issues were reviewed and revised as the research proceeded. Second, the field data were classified, analysed and organized around the themes of the book. Third, the data were moulded and remoulded as the analytic themes and issues were developed and refined. These three stages – theorizing, data capture and analysis – sometimes ran concurrently, sometimes successively. The important point is that writing was integral to the research work and that this book is the culmination of that process.

REFERENCES

Ackers, P., Smith, C. and Smith, P. (eds) (1996) *The New Workplace and Trade Unionism*, London: Routledge.

Atkinson, J. (1985) *Flexibility, Uncertainty and Manpower Movement*, Brighton: IMS Report, No. 89.

Bacon, N. and Storey, J. (1996) 'Individualism and collectivism and the changing role of trade unions', in P. Ackers, C. Smith and P. Smith (eds) *The New Workplace and Trade Unionism*, London: Routledge, pp. 41–76.

Baglioni, G. and Crouch, C. (1990) *European Industrial Relations: The Challenge of Flexibility*, London: Sage.

Bain, G. (1970) *The Growth of White-collar Unionism*, Oxford: Clarendon Press.

Bain, G. and Price, R. (1983) 'Union growth: dimensions, determinants and destiny', in G. Bain (ed.) *Industrial Relations in Britain*, Oxford: Blackwell, pp. 3–33.

Bassett, P. (1986) *Strike Free: New Industrial Relations in Britain*, Basingstoke: Macmillan.

Bassett, P. and Cave, A. (1993) *All for One: The Future of the Unions*, Fabian pamphlet no. 559, London: The Fabian Society.

Batstone, E. (1984) *Working Order: Workplace Industrial Relations over Two Decades*, Oxford: Blackwell.

Batstone, E. (1988) *The Reform of Workplace Industrial Relations: Theory, Myth and Evidence*, Oxford: Clarendon Paperbacks.

Batstone, E., Boraston, I. and Frenkel, S. (1977) *Shop Stewards in Action: The Organization of Workplace Conflict and Accommodation*, Oxford: Blackwell.

Batstone, E., Ferner, A., and Terry, M. (1984) *Consent and Efficiency: Labour Relations and Management Strategy in the State Enterprise*, Oxford: Blackwell.

Batstone, E. and Gourlay, S. (1986) *Unions, Unemployment and Inflation*, Oxford: Blackwell.

Bealey, F. (1976) *History of the POEU*, London: Blackman and Turner.

Bealey, F. (1977) 'The political system of the Post Office Engineering Union', *British Journal of Industrial Relations*, **15**(3), 374–95.

Belanger, J. and Evans, S. (1988) 'Shop controls and shop steward leadership among semiskilled engineering workers', in M. Terry and P.K. Edwards (eds) *Shopfloor Politics and Job Controls: The Post-war Engineering Industry,* Oxford: Blackwell, pp. 150–84.

Beynon, H. (1984) *Working for Ford,* London: Penguin.

Boston, B. (1987) *Women Workers and the Trade Unions,* 2nd edn, London: Lawrence and Wishart.

Boxall, P. and Haynes, P. (1997) 'Strategy and trade union effectiveness in a neo-liberal environment', *British Journal of Industrial Relations,* **35**(4), 567–91.

Boyer, R. and Drache, D. (eds) (1996) *States against Markets: The Limits of Globalization,* London: Routledge.

Braverman, H. (1974) *Labor and Monopoly Capital: The Degradation of Work in the Twentieth Century,* New York: Monthly Review Press.

Brighton Labour Process Group (1977) 'The capitalist labour process', *Capital and Class,* **1**, 3–26.

Briskin, L. and McDermott, P. (eds) (1993) *Women Challenging Unions: Feminism, Democracy and Militancy,* Toronto: University of Toronto Press.

Bronfenbrenner, K., Friedman, S., Hurd, R., Oswald, R. and Seeber, R. (eds) (1998) *Organizing to Win: New Research on Union Strategies,* Ithaca, NY, and London: ILR Press.

Brown, W. (1983) Britain's unions: new pressures and shifting loyalties, *Personnel Management,* October, pp. 48–58.

Carpenter, M. (1988) *Working for Health: The History of COHSE,* London: Lawrence and Wishart.

Carter, B. (1986) 'Trade unionism and the new middle class: the case of ASTMS', in P. Armstrong, R. Carter, C. Smith and T. Nichols (eds) *White Collar Workers, Trade Unions and Class,* London: Croom Helm, pp. 132–59.

Carter, B. (1991) 'Politics and process in the making of Manufacturing, Science and Finance', *Capital and Class,* **45**, 35–72.

Carter, B. (1995) 'A growing divide: Marxist class analysis and the labour process', *Capital and Class,* **55**, 33–72.

Carter, B. (1997) 'Adversity and opportunity: towards union renewal in MSF', *Capital and Class,* **61**, 8–18.

Carter, B. and Fairbrother, P. (1995) 'The remaking of the state middle class', in T. Cutler and M. Savage (eds) *The New Middle Class,* London: University College London Press, pp. 133–47.

Cavendish, R. (1982) *Women on the Line,* London: Routledge and Kegan Paul.

Central Intelligence Office (1998) *West Midlands Labour Market and Skill Trends,* Birmingham: Government Office of the West Midlands.

Chadwick, M. (1983) 'The recession and industrial relations', *Employee Relations*, **5**(5), 5–12.

Chartered Institute of Public Finance and Accountancy (1989) *Local Government Trends*, London: CIPFA.

Clegg, H. (1964) *General Union in a Changing Society*, Oxford: Blackwell.

Clegg, H. (1976) *Trade Unionism under Collective Bargaining*, Oxford: Blackwell.

Coates, D. (1989) *The Crisis of Labour: Industrial Relations and the State in Contemporary Britain*, London: Philip Allan.

Coates, D. (forthcoming) 'Models of Capitalism in the New World Order: the British case', *Political Studies*, **47**(4).

Coates, K. and Topham, T. (1986) *Trade Unions and Politics*, Oxford: Basil Blackwell.

Cockburn, C. (1977) *The Local State*, London: Pluto Press.

Cockburn, C. (1983) *Brothers: Male Dominance and Technological Change*, Basingstoke: Macmillan.

Cohen, S. and Fosh, P. (1988) *You Are the Union: Trade Union Workplace Democracy*, London: Workers' Educational Association.

Colling, T. (1991) 'Privatisation and the management of IR in electricity distribution', *Industrial Relations Journal*, **22**(2), 117–29.

Colling, T. (1995) 'Renewal or rigor mortis? Union responses to contracting in local government', *Industrial Relations Journal*, **26**(20), 134–45.

Colling, T. and Ferner, A. (1992) 'The limits of autonomy: devolution, line managers and industrial relations in privatized companies', *Journal of Management Studies*, **29**(2), 209–27.

Committee of Public Accounts (1989) *Twenty-fourth Report: Department of Social Security Operational Strategy*, HC 179, London: HMSO.

Cousins, C. (1988) 'The restructuring of welfare work: the introduction of general management and the contracting out of ancillary services in the NHS', *Work, Employment and Society*, **2**(2), 210–28.

Crouch, C. (1979) *State and Economy in Contemporary Capitalism*, London: Croom Helm.

Crouch, C. (1986) 'Conservative industrial relations policy: towards labour exclusion?', in O. Jaccobi, B. Jessop, H. Kastendiek and M. Regini (eds) *Economic Crisis, Trade Unions and the State*, London: Croom Helm, pp. 131–53.

Crouch, C. (1993) *Industrial Relations and European State Traditions*, Oxford: Oxford University Press.

Cully, M. and Woodland, S. (1998) 'Trade union membership and recognition 1996–97: an analysis of data from the Certification Officer and the LFS', *Labour Market Trends*, **106**(7), pp. 353–64.

Cunnison, S. and Stageman, J. (1993) *Feminising the Unions*, Aldershot: Avebury.

Cutler, T. and Waine, B. (1994) *Managing the Welfare State: The Politics of Public Sector Management*, Oxford: Berg.

Dahl, R. (1961) *Who Governs? Democracy and Power in an American City*, New Haven, CT: Yale University Press.

Dahl, R. (1985) *A Preface to an Economic Theory of Democracy*, London: Polity Press.

Daniel, W. (1986) *Workplace Industrial Relations and Technical Change*, Aldershot: Gower.

Daniel, W. and Millward, N. (1983) *Workplace Industrial Relations in Britain: The DE/PSI/SSRC Survey*, London: Heinemann Educational Books.

Darlington, R. (1994) *Dynamics of Workplace Unionism: Shop Steward Organisation in Three Merseyside Plants*, London: Mansell.

Department of Employment (1995) *West Midlands Labour Market and Skill Trends 1994/95*, London: Department of Employment.

Dicken, P. (1992) *Global Shift: The Internationalisation of Economic Activity*, London: Paul Chapman.

Doogan, K. (1997) 'The marketization of local services and the fragmentation of labour markets', *International Journal of Urban and Regional Research*, **21**(2), 286–302.

Dorfman, G. (1983) *British Trade Unionism against the TUC*, Basingstoke: Macmillan.

Drake, P., Fairbrother, P., Fryer, B., and Murphy, J. (1980) *Which Way Forward? An Interim Review of Issues for the Society of Civil and Public Servants*, Coventry: Department of Sociology, University of Warwick.

Drake, P., Fairbrother, P., Fryer, R. and Stratford, G. (1982) *A Programme for Union Democracy: The Review of the Organisation and Structure of the Society of Civil and Public Servants*, Coventry: Department of Sociology, University of Warwick.

Edwards, P. (1987) *Managing the Factory: A Survey of General Managers*, Oxford: Blackwell.

Efficiency Unit (1988) *Improving Management in Government: The Next Stage*, London: HMSO.

Elger, T. (1979) 'Valorisation and deskilling: a critique of Braverman', *Capital and Class*, **7**, 58–99.

Elger, T. (1990) 'Technical innovation and work reorganisation in British manufacturing in the 1980s: continuity, intensification or transformation?', *Work, Employment and Society*, Special Issue, May, 67–101.

Elger, T. (1991) 'Task flexibility and the intensification of labour in UK manufacturing in the 1980s', in A. Pollert (ed.) *Farewell to Flexibility? Questions on Restructuring of Work and Employment*, Oxford: Blackwell, pp. 46–66.

Elger, T. and Fairbrother, P. (1991) 'Inflexible flexibility: a case study of modularisation', in N. Gilbert, R. Burrows and A. Pollert (eds) *Fordism and Flexibility: Divisions and Change*, Basingstoke: Macmillan.

Elger, T. and Smith, C. (eds) (1994) *Global Japanisation: The Transnational Transformation of the Labour Process*, London: Routledge.

Elger, T. and Smith, C. (1998) 'Exit, voice and mandate: management strategies and labour practices in Japanese firms in Britain', *British Journal of Industrial Relations*, **36**(2), 185–207.

Fairbrother, P. (1987a) 'Public sector management, flexibility and trade union responses', *Trade Union Studies Journal*, **15** (Summer), 5–9.

Fairbrother, P. (1987b) 'Workplace industrial relations: restructuring and renewal', *Trade Union Studies Journal*, **16** (Winter), 14–16.

Fairbrother, P. (1988) *Flexibility at Work: The Challenge for Unions*. London: Workers' Educational Association.

Fairbrother, P. (1989a) 'State workers: class position and collective action', in G. Duncan (ed.) *Democracy and the Capitalist State*, Cambridge: Cambridge University Press, pp. 187–213.

Fairbrother, P. (1989b) *Workplace Unionism in the 1980s: A Process of Renewal?*, London: Workers' Educational Association.

Fairbrother, P. (1990a) 'The contours of local trade unionism in a period of restructuring', in P. Fosh and E. Heery (eds) *Trade Unions and Their Members: Studies in Union Democracy and Organization*, Basingstoke: Macmillan, pp. 147–76.

Fairbrother, P. (1990b) *Restructuring and Trade Unionism: Trends and Patterns in the Heartland*, London: Workers' Educational Association.

Fairbrother, P. (1991) 'In a state of change: flexibility in the civil service', in A. Pollert (ed.) *Farewell to Flexibility? Questions of Restructuring Work and Employment*, Oxford: Blackwell, pp. 69–83.

Fairbrother, P. (1994a) *Politics and the State as Employer*, London: Mansell.

Fairbrother, P. (1994b) 'Privatisation and local trade unionism', *Work, Employment and Society*, **8**(3), 339–56.

Fairbrother, P. (1996a) 'Workplace trade unionism in the state sector', in P. Ackers, P. Smith and C. Smith (eds) *The New Workplace and Trade Unionism*, London: Routledge, pp. 110–49.

Fairbrother, P. (1996b) 'Organize and survive: unions and health and safety', *Employee Relations*, **18**(2), 1–88.

Fairbrother, P., Moore, S. and Poynter, G. (1996) *UNISON Branch Organisation: Case Studies, Summary Reports and Recommendations*, mimeo.

Fairbrother, P. and Waddington, J. (1990) 'The politics of trade unionism: evidence, policy and theory', *Capital and Class*, **41**, 15–56.

Farnham, D. and Horton, S. (eds) (1993) *Managing the New Public Services*, Basingstoke: Macmillan.

Ferner, A. (1988) *Governments, Managers and Industrial Relations: Public Enterprises and Their Political Environment*, Oxford: Basil Blackwell.

Ferner, A. (1989) *Ten Years of Thatcherism: Changing Industrial Relations in British Public Enterprises*, Coventry: Warwick Papers in Industrial Relations No. 17, IRRU, University of Warwick.

Ferner, A. and Colling, T. (1991) 'Privatization, regulation and industrial relations', *British Journal of Industrial Relations*, **29**(3), 391–409.

Ferner, A. and Terry, M. (1997) 'United Kingdom', in H. Katz (ed.) *Telecommunications: Restructuring Work and Employment Relations Worldwide*, Ithaca, NY: ILR Press, pp. 89–121.

Fielding, S. (1995) *Labour Decline and Renewal*, Manchester: Baseline Books.

Fiorito, J., Jarley, P. and Delaney, J. (1995) 'National union effectiveness in organising: measures and influences', *Industrial and Labor Relations Review*, **48**(4), 613–35.

Flanders, A. (1970) *Management and Unions: The Theory and Reform of Industrial Relations*, 2nd edn, London: Faber and Faber.

Fletcher, R. (1973) 'Trade union democracy: a case of the AUEW rule book', in R. Barret-Brown and K. Coates (eds) *Trade Union Register 3*, Nottingham: Spokesman Books, pp. 125–49.

Flynn, N. and Taylor, A. (1986) 'Inside the rust belt: an analysis of the decline of the West Midlands economy. 1: International and national economic conditions', *Environment and Planning A*, **18**(7), 865–900.

Fosh, P. (1993) 'Membership participation in workplace unionism: the possibility of union renewal', *British Journal of Industrial Relations*, **31**(4), 577–92.

Fosh, P. and Cohen, S. (1990) 'Local trade unionists in action: patterns of union democracy', in P. Fosh and E. Heery (eds) *Trade Unions and Their Members: Studies in Union Democracy and Organization*, Basingstoke: Macmillan, pp. 107–46.

Foster, D. (1993) 'Industrial relations in local government: the impact of privatization', *Political Quarterly*, **64**(1), 49–59.

Foster, D. and Scott, P. (1998a) 'Conceptualising union responses to contracting out municipal services, 1979–97', *Industrial Relations Journal*, **29**(2), 137–50.

Foster, D. and Scott, P. (1998b) 'Competitive tendering of public services and industrial relations policy: the conservative agenda under Thatcher and Major, 1979–97', *Historical Studies in Industrial Relations*, **6**, 101–32.

Friedman, A. (1977) *Industry and Labour: Class Struggle at Work and Monopoly Capitalism*, London: Macmillan.

Frow, E. and Frow, R. (1982) *Democracy in the Engineering Union*, Nottingham: Institute of Workers' Control.

Fryer, R., Fairclough, A. and Manson, T. (1974) *Organisation and Change in the National Union of Public Employees*, Coventry: Department of Sociology, University of Warwick.

Fryer, R., Manson, T. and Fairclough, A. (1978) 'Employment and trade unionism in the public services: background notes to the struggles against the cuts', *Capital and Class*, **4**, 70–7.

Gall, G. (1998) 'The prospects for workplace trade unionism: evaluating Fairbrother's union renewal thesis', *Capital and Class*, **66**, 149–57.

Gallie, D., Penn, R. and Rose, M. (1996) *Trade Unions in Recession*, Oxford: Oxford University Press.

Garahan, P. and Stewart, P. (1992) *The Nissan Enigma: Flexibility at Work in a Local Economy*, London: Mansell.

Glyn, A. (1992) 'The "productivity" miracle, profits and investment', in J. Mitchie (ed.) *The Economic Legacy 1979–1992*, London: Academic Press, pp. 77–88.

Goldthorpe, J. (1984) 'The end of convergence: corporatist and dualist tendencies in modern Western societies', in J. Goldthorpe (ed.) *Order and Conflict in Contemporary Capitalism: Studies in the Political Economy of Western European Nations*, Oxford: Oxford University Press, pp. 315–43.

Goodrich, C. (1920) *The Frontier of Control: A Study in British Workshop Politics*, London: Pluto Press, 1975 edn.

Gorz, A. (1982) *Farewell to the Working Class*, London: Pluto.

Government Statistical Service (1996) *Civil Service Statistics, 1996*, London: HMSO.

Government Statistical Service (1997) 'Spotlight on the West Midlands', *Labour Market Trends*, September, 323–32.

Grainger, K. (1988) 'Management control and labour quiescence: shopfloor politics at Alfred Herbert's, 1945–1980', in M. Terry and P.K. Edwards (eds) *Shopfloor Politics and Job Controls: The Post-war Engineering Industry*, Oxford: Blackwell, pp. 84–115.

Guest, D. (1987) 'Human resource management and industrial relations', *Journal of Management Studies*, **24**(5), 503–21.

REFERENCES

Heery, E. (1998a) 'Campaigning for part-time workers', *Work, Employment and Society*, **12**(2), 351–66.

Heery, E. (1998b) 'The relaunch of the Trades Union Congress', *British Journal of Industrial Relations*, **36**(3), 339–60.

Heery, E. and Kelly, J. (1994) 'Professional, participative and managerial unionism: an interpretation of change in trade unions', *Work, Employment and Society*, **8**(1), 1–22.

Hirst, P. and Thompson, G. (1996) *Globalisation in Question*, Cambridge: Polity Press.

Hirst, P. and Zeitlin, J. (1989) Flexible specialisation and the competitive failure of UK manufacturing', *Political Quarterly*, **60**(2), 164–78.

Hoggett, B. (1991) 'A new management in the public sector?', *Policy and Politics*, **19**(4), 243–56.

Holloway, J. (1987) 'The red rose of Nissan', *Capital and Class*, **32**, 142–64.

House of Commons (1990) *Parliamentary Debates (Hansard), Session 1989–90*, Sixth Series, Volume 177, London: HMSO, 7–8w.

Humphreys, B. (1958) *Clerical Unions in the Civil Service*, Oxford: Blackwell and Mott.

Hunter, L., McGregor, A., MacInnes, J. and Sproull, A. (1993) 'The flexible firm: strategy and segmentation', *British Journal of Industrial Relations*, **31**(3), 383–407.

Hyman, R. (1971) *The Workers' Union*, Oxford: Clarendon Press.

Hyman, R. (1979) 'The politics of workplace trade unionism: recent tendencies and some problems for theory', *Capital and Class*, **8**, 54–68.

Hyman, R. (1989) *The Political Economy of Industrial Relations: Theory and Practice in a Cold Climate*, Basingstoke: Macmillan.

Hyman, R. (1991) 'European unions: towards 2000', *Work, Employment and Society*, **5**(4), 622–39.

Hyman, R. (1994) 'Changing trade union identities and strategy', in R. Hyman and A. Ferner (eds) *New Frontiers in European Industrial Relations*, Oxford: Blackwell, pp. 108–39.

Hyman, R. (1996) 'Changing union identities in Europe', in P. Leisink, J. Van Leemput and J. Vilrokx (eds) *The Challenges to Trade Unions in Europe: Innovation or Adaptation*, Cheltenham: Edward Elgar.

Hyman, R. and Price, R. (eds) (1983) *The New Working Class? White-collar Workers and Their Organizations*, Basingstoke: Macmillan.

Inland Revenue (1987) *Report of the Commissioner of Her Majesty's Inland Revenue for the Period 1 January 1986 to 31 March 1987, One Hundred and Twenty-Ninth Report*, Cm. 230, London: HMSO.

Inland Revenue (1988) *Report of the Commissioner of Her Majesty's Inland Revenue for the Year ending 31 March 1988, One Hundred and Thirtieth Report*, Cm. 529, London: HMSO.

Inland Revenue (1990) *Report of the Commissioner of Her Majesty's Inland Revenue for the Year ending 31 March 1990, One Hundred and Thirty-Second Report*, Cm. 1321, London: HMSO.

Inland Revenue (1991) *Report of the Commissioner of Her Majesty's Inland Revenue for the Year ending 31 March 1991, One Hundred and Thirty-Third Report*, Cm. 1767, London: HMSO.

Inland Revenue (1992) *Report of the Commissioner of Her Majesty's Inland Revenue for the Year ending 31 March 1992, One Hundred and Thirty-Fourth Report*, Cm. 2026, London: HMSO.

Inland Revenue (1996) *Report of the Commissioner of Her Majesty's Inland Revenue for the Year ending 31 March 1996, One Hundred and Thirty-Eighth Report*, Cm. 3446, London: HMSO.

Jefferys, S. (1988) 'The changing face of conflict: shopfloor organization at Longbridge, 1939–1980', in M. Terry and P.K. Edwards (eds) *Shopfloor Politics and Job Controls: The Post-war Engineering Industry*, Oxford: Blackwell, pp. 53–83.

Jenkins, K., Caines, K. and Jackson, A. (!988) *Improving Management in Government: The Next Steps* (Ibbs Report), London: HMSO.

Jessop, B. (1994) 'The transition to post-Fordism and the Schumpertarian workfare state', in R. Burrows and B. Loader (eds) *Towards a Post-Fordist Welfare State?*, London: Routledge, pp. 13–37.

Johnston, P. (1994) *Success while Others Fail: Social Movement Unionism and the Public Workplace*, Ithaca, NY: ILR Press.

Jones, B. and Rose, M. (1986) 'Re-dividing labour: factory politics and work reorganization in the current industrial transition', in K. Purcell, S. Wood, S. Waton and S. Allen (eds) *The Changing Experience of Employment: Restructuring and Recession*, Basingstoke: Macmillan, pp. 35–57.

Kelly, J. (1987) *Labour and the Unions*, London: Verso.

Kelly, J. (1988) *Trade Unions and Socialist Politics*, London: Verso.

Kelly, J. (1996) 'Union militancy and social partnership', in P. Ackers, C. Smith and P. Smith (eds) *The New Workplace and Trade Unionism*, London: Routledge, pp. 77–109.

Kelly, J. (1997) 'The future of trade unionism: injustice, identity and attributes', *Employee Relations*, **19**, 400–14.

Kelly, J. and Heery, E. (1994) *Working for the Union: British Trade Union Officers*, Cambridge: Cambridge University Press.

Kelly, M. (1980) *White-collar Proletariat: The Industrial Behaviour of British Civil Servants*, London: Routledge & Kegan Paul.

Kessler, I. (1986) 'Shop stewards in local government revisited', *British Journal of Industrial Relations*, **24**(3), 419–41.

Kessler, I. (1991) 'Workplace industrial relations', *Employee Relations*, **13**(2), 2–31.

Kessler, S. (1994) 'Incomes policy', *British Journal of Industrial Relations*, **32**(20), 181–200.

Laffin, M. (1989) *Managing under Pressure: Industrial Relations in Local Government*, Basingstoke: Macmillan.

Lane, T. (1974) *The Union Makes Us Strong: The British Working Class, Its Trade Unionism and Politics*, London: Arrow Books.

Lane, T. and Roberts, K. (1971) *Strike at Pilkingtons*, London: Fontana.

Lipset, S., Trow, M. and Coleman, J. (1956) *Union Democracy: The Inside Politics of the International Typographical Union*, New York: The Free Press.

McIlroy, J. (1995) *Trade Unions in Britain Today*, 2nd edn, Manchester: Manchester University Press.

McIlroy, J. (1997) 'Still under siege: British trade unions at the turn of the century', *Historical Studies in Industrial Relations*, **3** (March), 93–122.

MacInnes, J. (1987) *Thatcherism at Work: Industrial Relations and Economic Change*, Milton Keynes: Open University Press.

McIntosh, I. and Broderick, J. (1996) ' "Neither one thing nor the other": compulsory competitive tendering and SouthBurgh cleansing services', *Work, Employment and Society*, **10**(3), 413–30.

Maillie, R., Dimmock, S. and Sethi, A. (1989) *Industrial Relations in the Public Services*, London: Routledge & Kegan Paul.

Maksymiw, W. (ed. and comp.), with contributions from J. Eaton and C. Gill, (1990) *The British Trade Union Directory*, London: Longman.

Marginson, P., Edwards, P., Martin, R., Purcell, J. and Sisson, K. (1988) *Beyond the Workplace: Managing Industrial Relations in the Multi-establishment Enterprise*, Oxford: Blackwell.

Marsh, D. (1992) *The New Politics of British Trade Unionism: Union Power and the Thatcher Legacy*, Basingstoke: Macmillan.

Marshall, J., Hopkins, W. and Richardson, R. (1997) 'The civil service and the regions: geographical perspectives on civil service restructuring', *Regional Studies*, **31**(6), 607–30.

Martin, J. (1991) 'Devolution and decentralization', in J. Boston, J. Martin and P. Walsh (eds) *Reshaping the State: New Zealand's Bureaucratic Revolution*, Auckland: Oxford University Press, pp. 268–96.

Martin, R. (1968) 'Union democracy: an explanatory framework', *Sociology*, **2**(2), 205–20.

Martin, R., Sunley, P. and Wills, J. (1996) *Union Retreat and the Regions: The Shrinking Landscape of Organised Labour*, London: Jessica Kingsley.

Martin, S. and Parker, D. (1997) *The Impact of Privatisation: Ownership and Corporate Performance in the UK*, London: Routledge.

Martin, S. and Pearce, G. (1992) 'The internationalization of local authority economic development strategies: Birmingham in the 1980s', *Regional Studies*, **26**(5), 499–509.

Martinez Lucio, M. and Weston, S. (1992) 'Human resource management and trade union responses: bringing the politics of the workplace back into the debate', in P. Blyton and P. Turnbull (eds) *Reassessing Human Resource Management*, London: Sage, pp. 215–32.

Marx, K. (1976) *Capital: A Critique of Political Economy*, Vol. 1, Harmondsworth: Penguin.

Michels, R. (1962) *Political Parties: A Sociological Study of the Oligarchical Tendencies of Modern Democracy*, New York: Free Press.

Miliband, R. (1969) *The State in Capitalist Society*, London: Weidenfeld and Nicholson.

Miliband, R. (1982) *Capitalist Democracy in Britain*, Oxford: Oxford University Press.

Miller, C. (1996) *Public Service Unionism and Radical Politics*, Aldershot: Dartmouth.

Millward, N. and Stevens, M. (1986) *British Workplace Industrial Relations 1980–1984: The DE/ESRC/PSI/ACAS Surveys*, Aldershot: Gower.

Millward, N., Stevens, M., Smart, D. and Hawes, W. (1992) *Workplace Industrial Relations in Transition: The ED/ESRC/PSI/ACAS Surveys*, Aldershot: Dartmouth.

Minkin, L. (1991) *The Contentious Alliance: Trade Unions and the Labour Party*, Edinburgh: Edinburgh University Press.

Müller-Jentsch, W. (1988) 'Industrial relations theory and trade union strategy', *International Journal of Comparative Labour Law and Industrial Relations*, **4**(3), 177–90.

Nichols, T. and Beynon, H. (1977) *Living with Capitalism: Class Relations and the Modern Factory*, London: Routledge & Kegan Paul.

Nolan, P. and Walsh, J. (1995) 'The structure of the economy and labour markets', in P. Edwards (ed.) *Industrial Relations: Theory and Practice in Britain*, Oxford: Blackwell, pp. 50–86.

Ohmae, K. (1990) *The Borderless World: Power and Strategy in the Interlinked Economy*, London: HarperCollins.

REFERENCES

Ohmae, K. (1995) *The End of the Nation State: The Rise of Regional Economies*, New York: Free Press.

Osborne, D.E. and Gaebler, T. (1992) *Reinventing Government: How the Entrepreneurial Spirit Is Transforming the Public Sector*, New York: Plume.

Panitch, L. (1975) *Social Democracy and Industrial Militancy*, Cambridge: Cambridge University Press.

Pattison, I. (1973) *The New Scottish Local Authorities: Organisation and Management Structures*, Edinburgh: Scottish Development Department, Working Group on Scottish Local Government Management Structures.

Peetz, D. (1998) *Unions in a Contrary World: The Future of the Australian Trade Union Movement*, Cambridge: Cambridge University Press.

Pendleton, A. (1997) 'What impact has privatization had on pay and employment? A review of the British experience', *Relations Industrielles/Industrial Relations*, **52**(3), 554–79.

Piore, M. and Sabel, C. (1984) *The Second Industrial Divide: Prospects for Prosperity*, New York: Basic Books.

Pollert, A. (1981) *Girls, Wives, Factory Lives*, London: Macmillan.

Pollert, A. (ed.) (1991) *Farewell to Flexibility? Questions of Restructuring Work and Employment*, Oxford: Blackwell.

Pollert, A. (1996) 'Team work on the assembly line', in P. Ackers, P. Smith and C. Smith (eds) *The New Workplace and Trade Unionism*, London: Routledge, pp. 178–209.

Poynter, G. (1999) *Restructuring Services: Management Reform and Workplace Relations in the UK Service Sector*, London: Mansell.

Public Services Privatisation Research Unit (1996) *The Privatisation Network: The Multinationals Bid for Public Services*, London: PSPRU.

Purcell, J. (1993) 'The end of institutional industrial relations', *Political Quarterly*, **61**(1), 6–23.

Ramanadham, V. (ed.) (1988) *Privatisation in the UK*, London: Routledge.

Sabel, C.F. (1994) 'Flexible specialisation and the re-emergence of regional economies', in A. Amin (ed.) *Post-Fordism: A Reader*, Oxford: Basil Blackwell, pp. 101–56.

Severn Trent plc (1995) *Annual Report and Accounts 1994/5*, Birmingham: Severn Trent plc.

Severn Trent plc (1996) *Annual Report and Accounts 1996*, Birmingham: Severn Trent plc.

Sklair, L. (1995) *Sociology of the Global System*, 2nd edn, London: Prentice Hall.

Smith, C. (1987) *Technical Workers: Class, Labour and Trade Unionism*, Basingstoke: Macmillan Education.

Smith, P. and Morton, G. (1993) 'Union exclusion and the decollectivization of industrial relations in contemporary Britain', *British Journal of Industrial Relations*, **31**(1), 97–114.

Smith, P. and Morton, G. (1994) 'Union exclusion in Britain – next steps', *Industrial Relations Journal*, **25**(3), 222–33.

Social Security Committee (1991) *The Organisation and Administration of the Department of Social Security*, HC 550-I, London: HMSO.

Society of Civil and Public Servants (1983) *Future Organisation and Structure*, Conference Paper A, London: SCPS.

Spencer, B. (1985) *Workplace Trade Unionism: Making It Work*, London: Workers' Educational Association.

Spencer, B. (1989) *Remaking the Working Class? An Examination of Shop Stewards' Experiences*, Nottingham: Spokesman.

Spencer, K., Taylor, A., Smith, B., Mawson, J., Flynn, N. and Batley, R. (1986) *Crisis in the Industrial Heartland: A Study of the West Midlands*, Oxford: Clarendon Press.

Spoor, A. (1967) *White Collar Union: Sixty Years of NALGO*, London: Heinemann.

Study Group on Local Authority Management Structure. (1972) *The New Local Authorities, Management and Structure* (Bains Report), London: HMSO.

Tailby, S. and Whitson, C. (eds) (1989) *Manufacturing Change: Industrial Relations and Restructuring*, Oxford: Blackwell.

Taylor, R. (1978) *The Fifth Estate: Britain's Unions in the Seventies*, London: Routledge & Kegan Paul.

Taylor, R. (1995) *The Future of Trade Unions*, London: Andre Deutsch.

Terry, M. (1982) 'Organising a fragmented workforce: shop stewards in local government', *British Journal of Industrial Relations*, **20**(1), 1–19.

Terry, M. (1983) 'Shop stewards through expansion and recession', *Industrial Relations Journal*, **14**(3), 49–58.

Terry, M. (1988a) 'Introduction: historical analyses and contemporary issues', in M. Terry and P.K. Edwards (eds) *Shopfloor Politics and Job Controls: The Post-war Engineering Industry*, Oxford: Blackwell, pp. 1–23.

Terry, M. (1988b) 'The development of shop steward organization: Coventry Precision Tools, 1945–1972', in M. Terry and P.K. Edwards (eds) *Shopfloor Politics and Job Controls: The Post-war Engineering Industry*, Oxford: Blackwell, pp. 24–52.

Terry, M. (1989) 'Recontextualizing shopfloor industrial relations: some case study evidence', in S. Tailby and C. Whitson (eds) *Manufacturing Change: Industrial Relations and Restructuring*, Oxford: Blackwell, pp. 192–216.

Terry, M. (1995) 'Trade unions: shop stewards and the workplace', in P. Edwards (ed.) *Industrial Relations: Theory and Practice in Britain*, Oxford: Blackwell, pp. 203–28.

Terry, M. (1996) 'Negotiating the government of UNISON: union democracy in theory and practice', *British Journal of Industrial Relations*, **34**(1), 87–110.

Terry, M. and Edwards, P.K. (eds) (1988) *Shopfloor Politics and Job Controls: The Post-war Engineering Industry*, Oxford: Basil Blackwell.

Thornett, A. (1987) *From Militancy to Marxism: A Personal and Political Account of Organising Car Workers*, London: Left View Books.

Thornett, A. (1998) *Inside Cowley. Trade Union Struggle in the 1970s: Who Really Opened the Door to the Tory Onslaught*, London: Porcupine Press.

Trades Union Congress (1983) *Hands Up for Union Democracy*, London: TUC.

Trades Union Congress (1984) *TUC Strategy*, London: TUC.

Trades Union Congress (1988a) *Meeting the Challenge: First Report of the Special Review Body*, London: TUC.

Trades Union Congress (1988b) *Services for Union Members: Special Review Body Report on Services*, London: TUC.

Trades Union Congress (1989) *Organising for the 1990s: The Special Review Body's Second Report*, London: TUC.

Trades Union Congress (1991) *Towards 2000*, London: TUC.

Trades Union Congress (1994a) *Human Resource Management: A Trade Union Response*, London: TUC.

Trades Union Congress (1994b) *Employee Representation*, London: TUC.

Trades Union Congress (1997) *New Unionism Organising for Growth*, London: TUC.

Trades Union Congress (various) *TUC Annual Report*, London: TUC.

Treasury (1991) *Competing for Quality: Buying Better Public Services*, Cm. 1730, London: HMSO.

Tuckman, A. (1992) *'Out of the Crisis': Quality, TQM and the Labour Process*, Tenth Annual Conference on the Organisation and Control of the Labour Process.

Turnbull, P. (1988) 'The limits to "Japanisation" – just-in-time, labour relations and the UK automotive industry', *New Technology, Work and Employment*, **3**(1), 7–20.

Undy, R., Ellis, V., McCarthy, W. and Halmos, A. (1981) *Change in Trade Unions: The Development of UK Unions since the 1960s*, London: Hutchinson.

Undy, R., Fosh, P., Morris, H., Smith, P. and Martin, R. (1996) *Managing the Unions: The Impact of Legislation on Trade Unions' Behaviour*, Oxford: Clarendon Press.

Unofficial Reform Committee (1912) *The Miners' Next Step: Being a Suggested Scheme for the Reorganisation of the Federation*, London: Pluto, 1973 edition.

Waddington, J. (1992a) 'Trade union membership in Britain, 1980–1987: unemployment and restructuring', *British Journal of Industrial Relations*, **30**(2), 287–328.

Waddington, J. (1992b) 'Restructuring representation: trade union mergers 1980–1988', in D. Cox (ed.) *Facing the Future: Issues for Adult Education*, Nottingham: University of Nottingham, Department of Adult Education in association with The Society of Industrial Tutors.

Waddington, J. (forthcoming) 'Trade union membership and recruitment: struggling to meet new challenges', in E. Gabaglio and R. Hoffmann (eds) *European Trade Union Yearbook, 1998*, Brussels: ETUI.

Waddington, J. and Whitson, C. (1997) 'Why do people join unions in a period of membership decline?', *British Journal of Industrial Relations*, **35**(4), 515–46.

Westwood, S. (1984) *All Day, Every Day: Factory and Family in the Making of Women's Lives*, London: Pluto.

Whitfield, D. (1992) *The Welfare State: Privatisation, Deregulation, Commercialisation of the Public Services: Alternative Strategies for the 1990s*, London: Pluto Press.

Whitson, C. and Waddington, J. (1994) 'Why join a union?', *New Statesman and Society*, 18 November, pp. 36–8.

Williams, S. (1996) 'Meeting the needs of the individual: the nature and differences of recent trade union modernisation policies in the UK', unpublished PhD thesis, University of Sunderland.

Williams, S. (1997) 'The nature of some recent trade union modernization policies in the UK', *British Journal of Industrial Relations*, **35**(4), 495–514.

Willman, P., Morris, T. and Aston, B. (1993) *Union Business: Trade Union Organisation and Financial Reform in the Thatcher Years*, Cambridge: Cambridge University Press.

Wood, P. (1976) *The West Midlands* (with a contribution on the Potteries, coal and power by A. Moyes), Newton Abbot: David & Charles.

Young, H. (1990) *One of Us: A Biography of Margaret Thatcher*, London: Pan Books in association with Macmillan.

INDEX

（